Lotus Blossoms and Purple Clouds

Contemporary Buddhism

MARK M. ROWE, SERIES EDITOR

Recently published in the series

Guardians of the Buddha's Home: Domestic Religion in the Contemporary Jōdo Shinshū
Jessica Starling

Morality and Monastic Revival in Post-Mao Tibet
Jane E. Caple

Buddhist Tourism in Asia
Edited by Courtney Bruntz and Brooke Schedneck

Monastic Education in Korea: Teaching Monks about Buddhism in the Modern Age
Uri Kaplan

Buddhism and Business: Merit, Material Wealth, and Morality in the Global Market Economy
Edited by Trine Brox and Elizabeth Williams-Oerberg

Lotus Blossoms and Purple Clouds: Monastic Buddhism in Post-Mao China
Brian J. Nichols

Lotus Blossoms and Purple Clouds

Monastic Buddhism in Post-Mao China

Brian J. Nichols

UNIVERSITY OF HAWAI'I PRESS
HONOLULU

Paperback edition 2023

Printed in the United States of America

Library of Congress Cataloging-in-Publication Data

Names: Nichols, Brian J., author.
Title: Lotus blossoms and purple clouds : monastic Buddhism in post-Mao China / Brian J. Nichols.
Other titles: Contemporary Buddhism.
Description: Honolulu : University of Hawaiʻi Press, 2022. | Series: Contemporary Buddhism | Includes bibliographical references and index.
Identifiers: LCCN 2022033503 | ISBN 9780824889005 (hardback) | ISBN 9780824893477 (pdf) | ISBN 9780824893460 (epub) | ISBN 9780824893484 (kindle edition)
Subjects: LCSH: Kaiyuan si (Quanzhou Shi, China) | Monastic and religious life (Buddhism)—China—Quanzhou Shi. | Buddhism—China—History—1949–
Classification: LCC BQ6345.Q362 K35 2022 | DDC 294.30951/0904—dc23/eng/20220720
LC record available at https://lccn.loc.gov/2022033503

ISBN 9780824893491 (paperback)

Cover art: Monks lead lay Buddhists in serpentine buddha recitation (*nianfo*) of the main courtyard on lunar twenty-sixth, 2009. Photo by the author.

University of Hawaiʻi Press books are printed on acid-free paper and meet the guidelines for permanence and durability of the Council on Library Resources.

For the biosphere, under assault from greed, ignorance, and ill will. May humans wake up and embrace a living future for all sentient beings.

Contents

Series Editor's Preface

READING THIS CREATIVE AND GROUND-BREAKING STUDY, IT is easy to imagine sitting with Brian Nichols and enjoying a meal with an abbot and senior monks at their monastery while they discuss daily affairs, local gossip, and national news. After the meal, we follow Nichols into the dharma hall to experience a rich soundscape of *dhāranī*s, mantras, and sutras. Weekly, we walk along with a few hundred lay devotees in a serpentine circumambulation of the main hall, learning the correct mudras from well-meaning participants along the way. Throughout the book we run into monks, security guards, temple administrators, and thousands of temple faithful who visit monthly to eat noodles and chant homage to Amitabha Buddha. Some afternoons we watch a pirated movie in the temple office while drinking fragrant tea and discussing Irish Catholicism with one of the monks.

Nichols' long engagement and unlimited access to Quanzhou Kaiyuan Monastery in southeast China provides us a unique engagement with a local monastery that is an active religious institution, a symbol of history and culture, and a tourist site. The monastery operates on a continuum that gives material shape to the aspirations of "revivalists" and "curators."

Nichols offers invaluable insights into the post-Mao religious puzzle, one that brings together monastics of all sorts, devotees, tourists, and state actors—as well as nationalist ideologies and religious revival—into a complex montage that resists facile, reductive binaries of secular/religious or traditional/modern. Instead we are joyfully enmeshed in the messy complexities of a living institution with deep historical roots, intertwined interests, and a cast of fantastic characters with different aspirations and motivations.

Acknowledgments

ETHNOGRAPHICALLY BASED WORK IS THE FRUIT OF more help and more diverse kinds of assistance than a statement of acknowledgment can capture; I am sure to miss many who have contributed to this book over the many years of its gestation. Most acknowledgments start with academic or emotional assistance, I prefer to foreground the material basis of this book to bear witness to the voices not heard for lack of funding. I am both fortunate and thankful to have received six years of financial support from Rice University as a graduate student (2002–2007). I am heartily thankful for the generous grants received from the Fulbright Program for ten months of research and fieldwork (2009) and four months of intensive language study (2008) at the Inter-University Program for Chinese language studies at Tsinghua University in Beijing, which provided a critical boost to my Chinese. I am also grateful to the Asian Cultural Council for funding three months' of fieldwork in China (2007). My research benefited from two summers with Venerable Yifa's Woodenfish in China program (2009, 2012), which brought me to dozens of temples across China and meetings with many clerics. I also benefited from Chen Jinhua's Buddhism in China program, which included lectures by top scholars and visits to several key monasteries (2009). In the final stretch, Mount Royal University provided invaluable support through a generously funded sabbatical (2018–2019) that enabled me to complete the manuscript.

I have benefited from the critiques, guidance, and collaboration with many scholars over the years at conferences, workshops, and universities where I have worked or studied. The following individuals have provided feedback at conferences and workshops or collaborated on panels related to this project: Gareth Fisher, Thomas Borchert, Xiaofei Kang, Charles Jones, Mayfair Yang, Stefania Travagnin, Jason Clower, Douglass Gildow, Mark Rowe, Ji Zhe, and Adam Chau. While preparing the manuscript, I benefited from Matthew Orsborn's willingness to proofread a chapter and answer questions about monastic ritual. I thank Anne Klein for constantly responding to my questions in the early stages of the project at Rice University regarding

Buddhism with "it depends who you ask," which helped me understand the need to contextualize everything; Rich Smith for his generous sinological help, careful readings, and corrections; Jeff Kripal for encouraging me to take a second and third look at this or that data or source with a new angle; and Susan Huang for introducing me to the field of material religion, which became an essential component of this project. I benefited from the professionalism of the University of Hawai'i Press in the final stages of the project, including the careful reading and suggestions of anonymous peer reviewers and the meticulous eye of my copyeditor, Glenn Court, who helped clean up the manuscript.

In China, many helped advance this research. Noting all of them is impossible but I would like to first acknowledge Yang Hongwei and Zhang Huailin for facilitating my stay in China and introducing me to Vice Minister Yu Xianfeng 余险峰 of the Fujian Bureau of Religion, who first suggested that I visit Quanzhou to learn more about its diverse religious heritage. I also thank the monks at Kaiyuan for hosting me and, at times, my family, especially the abbot Daoyuan 道元, and Fayi 法一, Desheng 德昇, and Benzhi 本誌. My research in Quanzhou was advanced by the monks at Kaiyuan as well as many others associated with the monastery and in the city of Quanzhou. Deserving special mention are Huang Yushan 黄玉山 and Cai Qicheng 蔡其呈, two dedicated enthusiasts for all things Quanzhou Kaiyuan. I also thank layperson Dazhuo 大拙 in Beijing for his assistance in translating Kaiyuan's *Monastic Gazetteer*.

Last, and certainly not least, I am grateful for the love and support of my family—especially Jamie and our two boys, Charles and William, and my parents, Jim and Kay.

Note on Conventions and Orthography

CHINESE NAMES AND TERMS ARE RENDERED IN *hanyu pinyin;* the first letter of proper names (of people, books, buildings, etc.) is capitalized. Generally, Chinese characters are provided for precision when needed. Because this is a book on post-Mao China, the default orthography is simplified Chinese characters; this includes proper names from pre-1949 China that are commonly simplified on the mainland as well as all terms and names directly associated with my field site. So, for example, the tenth-century name of the western pagoda is written 无量寿, instead of 無量壽. However, when citing pre-1949 records and some contemporary Taiwanese authors and books, I used traditional Chinese to remain faithful to the original. Additionally, some of my informants wrote their names in traditional Chinese; in these cases, I used traditional characters. Those who read Chinese will thus encounter both simplified and traditional characters. I apologize in advance for any frustration or confusion this may cause.

Introduction

IN 1966, THE CULTURAL REVOLUTION WAS UNLEASHED in an effort to rid China of the vestiges of its imperial and feudal past. A principal target of these destructive campaigns was religion. Groups of Red Guards sprang up all over China and carried out violence against symbols of the feudal order. They gathered and entered Quanzhou Kaiyuan Monastery in southeast China just as they did at religious sites across the country, with the intention of vandalizing its many cultural artifacts, including two towering stone pagodas from the Song dynasty (thirteenth century). As they massed inside the monastery, local residents quickly alerted the city's mayor, Wang Jinsheng 王今生, of the danger to Quanzhou's most famous historic site. Wang lived in the neighborhood and came immediately. An early enthusiast of the Communist Party, he had fought in the Liberation Army. Respected as a revolutionary leader, he was made mayor of Quanzhou in 1958 (Lin, Ceng, and Lin 2006). Wang confronted the Red Guards and explained that Kaiyuan Temple was a protected site. Holding a copy of its 1961 designation as a Provincial Level Protected Site of National Heritage, Wang told the crowd that he could call Zhou Enlai if they didn't believe him. The pagodas and monastery, he explained, were cultural treasures of the city and must be protected. In the end, he was successful, turning the Red Guards away and sparing the monastery and its treasures from the violence that devastated so many other sites, including other temples throughout the city and region.

Why was this monastery protected when others in the same city were not? When I visited Mayor Wang in 2006, I was escorted by a layperson from Kaiyuan Monastery who helped jump-start the interview by pointedly asking his friend, "Why, as a member of the Communist Party, a mayor, and a nonbeliever, did you protect Kaiyuan Monastery? What was the reason? What was your motive [*dongji* 动机]?" The ninety-one-year-old took some time to reply, but when he did it was clear—what he sought to protect was culture, not religion:

> Kaiyuan Monastery doesn't only mean religion. Kaiyuan Monastery is [also] a cultural relic, a carrier of many kinds of culture, a carrier of so much culture, why shouldn't I protect it? The two pagodas are a Quanzhou landmark! You come to Kaiyuan Monastery and you can see the culture of Quanzhou. If there is no Kaiyuan Monastery, the culture of Quanzhou would not be what it is. Kaiyuan Monastery represents the profundity and depth [*houzhong*] of this culture.... This is not a political view.... It is part of our national culture. I am a member of the Communist Party, I am not religious [*bu xin zongjiao*]; it's not just a temple, it's part of the our nation. I don't believe these things; don't talk about religion.[1]

His words were in line with the political orthodoxy prevalent since the mid-1980s, which has emphasized culture over religion in the restoration of religious sites across China (Ji 2011, 35). Nonetheless, this interview highlighted the prominent role played not only by political elites, but also by cultural properties themselves in protecting this monastery. I began to wonder what else may have supported the monastery over time as well as the other roles material culture plays in the restoration of religious life at the site today.

Kaiyuan is the largest monastery in the region, occupying about nineteen acres (seventy-eight thousand square meters) and in 2009 supported a community of some ninety monks.[2] In addition, it has buildings and artifacts from every imperial dynasty since the Tang dynasty in the ninth century.[3] The Song dynasty stone pagodas were studied by Paul Demiéville and Gustav Ecke in the 1920s as well as the pioneering sinologist Edouard Chavannes before them (Ecke and Demiéville 1935). Other Chinese monasteries were left in ruins from a string of disasters stretching from the Taiping Rebellion of the mid-nineteenth century through the Cultural Revolution of the mid-twentieth. Quanzhou Kaiyuan Monastery, however, has survived remarkably well. Questions about survival, restoration, and change were themes I circled back to as I strove to understand the principal characteristics and orientations of the site. The results of my study of lived local religion in historic and contemporary context offers a reconceptualization of what Chinese Buddhist monasticism is in practice.

The Study of Chinese Buddhist Monasticism

Monasteries are the central pillar of Buddhism throughout Asia; for millennia they have served as the home of monastics, sites of education, libraries of scripture, preserves of artistic treasures, and as gathering places for lay Buddhists and worshippers. Buddhist monasteries, however, have received surprisingly little scholarly attention. As Yifa, who produced the first monograph in English on Chinese monastic regulation, notes, "In contrast to doctrine, which traditionally has been the main focus of Buddhist scholarship, Sangha regulations and monastic practices have rarely been investigated. From its inception, however, Chinese Buddhism grew out of a concern with not only spiritual doctrine, but also practical matters of everyday behavior" (2002, 8). Timothy Brook concurs: "Whatever it was that Buddhologists or sociologists of religion wanted to know, it was not usually how Buddhism was practiced and how it survived (or did not) through its institutions" (2005, 144). James Robson echoes these sentiments in his introduction to *Buddhist Monasticism in East Asia*:

> It would be difficult to overstate the significance of monasticism within Buddhism.... Indeed, it is a topic that some might argue has been distinctly understated given the central role that it has played throughout the historical development, and geographic spread, of the tradition.... If there is one thing that we can say for certain about Buddhist monasteries and monasticism it is that they warrant the sustained attention of scholars of Buddhist studies, since what goes on inside and outside of their imposing gates is of central concern to our understanding of Buddhism as it functioned as a living religious tradition. (2010a, 2)

Robson is introducing a collection of essays on medieval monasticism in China and Japan and thus writes "functioned as a living tradition" in the past tense rather than in the present. My research looks to medieval sources but focuses on the restored traditions, social realities, and material features of the monastery in the present. It answers this call to reveal the "occluded histories" of Buddhist monasteries and sheds light on institutional Buddhism as a living tradition (2010a, 16).

To my knowledge, four scholarly books on single sites provide exceptional ethnographic insight into Buddhist monasticism: Robert Buswell (1992) on Piney Expanse Monastery (Songwang-sa), a Zen training site in South Korea; Esther Bianchi (2001) on Iron Statue Monastery (Tiexiangsi), a Tibetan nunnery in China; Jørn Borup (2008) on Japan's largest Rinzai Zen Temple complex Myōshinji; and Caroline Humphrey and Hürelbaatar Ujeed (2013) on Mergen Monastery in Inner Mongolia. In addition to these are studies that are not restricted to a single site; the most relevant are George Dreyfus's (2003) study of Gelukba monastic training and, especially, Holmes Welch's (1967) of Chinese monastic Buddhism.[4] I reference each of these studies at various points, but Holmes Welch's I carried with me throughout my research. His *The Practice of Chinese Buddhism 1900–1950* (1967) and Johannes Prip-Møller's *Chinese Buddhist Monasteries* (1937) are the foundation for later scholarly studies of Chinese Buddhist monasticism. Taken together, these two texts provide an excellent overview of the monastic layout, monastic architecture, organization, duties and practices of monks, as well as much of the prominent statuary. Both, however, may be said to focus on what Welch refers to as the "elite" or model monks and monasteries, which accounted for less than 5 percent of the total monastic population (1967, 3–4).[5] In addition, Welch's work, based on interviews with exiled monks in the diaspora, was limited by his lack of access to mainland China (Nichols 2017).

When I began my research at Kaiyuan in 2006, one of the monks discouraged me from conducting research there, saying I should go to Mt. Taimu's Pingxing Monastery 太姥山平兴寺, home to around four hundred monks undergoing a strict training regime. Interestingly, when I spoke with the abbot of Xiamen's Nanputuo Monastery thirteen years later in 2019, he said the same thing: I should spend three months at Pingxing Monastery, he advised, to understand the true practice of monastic life. What both of these monks were encouraging me to do was to study a model monastery. What I told both of them was that I wanted to study a more "ordinary" (*putong* 普通) monastery, albeit one of regional importance, but a monastery with many tourists, in an urban setting without the exemplary features of model monasteries such as Pingxing.[6] It is important to understand such urban centers of devotional practice, which have become the public face of Buddhism throughout Asia.[7]

How, though, did I settle on this site? It was a characteristically hot and humid June in the ancient port city of Quanzhou on the southeast coast of China, and I was standing in front of the granite ordination platform at Kaiyuan. One of the monks, whom I had just met, was telling me that when ordinations had been held here a few years earlier they had had to build a platform to the side because the Ming dynasty statues on the platform were considered cultural relics that could not be moved. He laughed at the irony; it was a famous orthodox Nanshan Vinaya ordination platform that had survived wars and calamities but could no longer be used precisely because of that. Desheng, the abbot's assistant, did not laugh when he criticized nearby devotees placing a handful of incense sticks into the burner: "What do these people think? Do they want the Buddhas and bodhisattvas to be choked by smoke? I always tell them to just use one to three sticks." That night my wife and I and our nearly two-year-old son were treated to a sumptuous vegetarian feast at a nearby restaurant by Desheng and general manager Fayi. The restaurant, catering to

Buddhist vegetarians, was new, spotless, and tastefully decorated with plants and a fountain in the foyer. I was intrigued and anxious to learn more about these monks, rebuilding Buddhist traditions with the ardent support of the community and this site, rich in cultural heritage, as a window onto the survival and revival of religion in post-Mao China.

Focus and Theory

The ecology of the institution is front and center in this study. Holmes Welch examined institutional features of Buddhism but did not anchor his study on a single site, nor was he able to observe the life of monasteries firsthand (1967). Borup's study is based on a single site and its institutional features, but is fundamentally based on textual materials, primarily from the temple organization (2008). The texts and surveys used are only incidentally supplemented by observation from the field, whereas this study is based primarily on participant-observation and interviews. Similarly, James Flath's study of the Temple of Confucius is focused on a single site but not on the living traditions (2016). The best available study of a living East Asian monastic community is Buswell's (1992). It is anchored around his home monastery and explores experiential, historical, and sociological features of the tradition. The biggest difference between it and this study, apart from my nonmonastic positionality, is that he was at a traditional functioning Zen training center. None of these studies, then, is of a typical Chinese monastery with monastic schedules but no traditions of communal meditation or study. That is the first distinguishing feature of this study and one that promises to provide a more applicable understanding of Buddhist monasticism as it has been lived throughout Chinese history.

From the beginning, I committed to an inductive approach to avoid having my findings be overdetermined by theory, working assumptions, or normative ideas about what Buddhism is. Given such a large and complex site, I decided to focus first on the monastic community, as opposed to laity or officialdom; second, on institutional aspects rather than individual narratives; and, last, on features of the site and revived traditions that seemed most significant to the monastic community or were observed to be most significant. Such an approach—focusing on what stands out as significant for the community under investigation—has guided other important anthropological studies of Buddhism, including most recently the work of anthropologist Gareth Fisher, who in his study of lay Buddhist preacher circles in Beijing focused on recurring tropes used by his interlocutors (2014). Similarly, Stanley Tambiah's study of the veneration of living Buddhist saints, the popularity of lay meditation, and amulets in Thailand grew out of their salience in the lives of those he studied (2007). Whereas Fisher's and Tambiah's studies were more solidly emic (insider) in orientation, exploring the lifeworlds of their informants, this study combines emic categories and perspectives as well as etic or scholarly-theoretical perspectives. In my research, five aspects of life at Kaiyuan monastery continually asserted themselves, whether in interviews, other discursive presentations, or participant-observation: liturgical rites, material culture, founding myths, the temple administrative commission, and the trope "84,000 dharma gates." To make features of monastic life more legible, I use the etic terminology—such as liturgical rites, material culture, spatial analysis, and founding myths—rather than the myriad local terms used to indicate specific rituals, structures, or legends. Each feature or trope, having emerged as most salient over many months of fieldwork, serves as the anchor of one chapter.

In addition to the five chapters on prominent features or themes, two chapters provide critical historical context, an etic aspect of this study shared with Buswell and Borup. Emphasizing the importance of historical context to ethnography, John Lagerwey writes, "Everything the ethnographer sees is the product of history" (2010, 172). Together, the history and key features of the site offer a re-description of what Chinese Buddhist monasticism is as a living tradition. The value of such a re-description is evident in Timothy Brook's assessment: "Factoring the concrete sociality of religious life into the study of Buddhism opens the analytical possibility that what goes on is not incidental to Buddhism but constitutive of the historical practices to which we, and those who have done them, assign its name" (2005, 146). The concrete sociality revealed by this study places unexpected features like liturgy, *dhāraṇī,* architecture, and legends of preternatural correlative response (*ganying*) at the center of this re-description of Buddhist monasticism.

Related to emic and etic approaches to study is a point Diana Eck raises, that scholars of Asian religions must take a dialogical approach to overcome the Orientalist bias that silences the self-representation of the Other (2000). With respect to the study of Buddhist icons, Bernard Faure advises we examine them anthropologically in their cultic context to arrive at a phenomenology of the affect or power of icons in order to overcome Orientalist obsession with aesthetics and symbolic meaning (1998). Dialogue requires not only listening and (phenomenological) observation, but also clarity about researcher positionality and voice. Our "voice" is always situated; situatedness is fundamentally about relationships and recognizing that our voice shifts when our audience, interests, or questions shift. The most recognizable shifts are those in changes of relation corresponding to common shifts in identity: speaking as a parent, speaking as a child, speaking as a spouse, as a student, as a teacher. Then there is speaking to a pet, speaking to a judge or a police officer who has pulled you over. With each change of situation, with changes of relation, how we present ourselves, how we express ourselves, shifts. As academics, we often "wear many hats" and engage in various types of discourse. These are our multiple selves or voices that we inhabit to accomplish various tasks. Some of the voices I inhabit in this book that reflect methodological multidisciplinarity are the historical (interested in changes over time), anthropological and ethnographic (interested in the cultural practices and articulations), phenomenological (interested in the experiential components of the site), and—for lack of a better term—"buddhological" (contributing to understanding of the Buddhist tradition in the context of religious studies). The five key features of monastic life presented markedly different sets of issues not amenable to a single theory or line of inquiry. I was committed from early on to make this project multidisciplinary, convinced that such a complex phenomenon could only be understood integrating historical, ethnographic, and religious studies methods and approaches.

In the end, I found the most fruitful material for working with my data (interviews, field notes, videography, and texts) in the growing field of spatial studies that informs Brian Dott's (2005) study of pilgrimage to Mt. Tai and Flath's (2016) study of Kong Temple, but which Kim Knott (2005, 2008, 2010) has done more than anyone to develop into a method for the study of religion. The spatial turn is based on the understanding of space as dynamically produced through the imbrication of physical, mental, and social aspects first advanced by Henri Lefebvre in *The Production of Space* (2009) and Michel de Certeau in *The Practice of Everyday Life* (1988).[8] It is a critique of earlier Cartesian and Aristotelian notions of space as a blank, abstract, backdrop, tabula rasa, or container. In the study of Buddhist monasticism, this led earlier scholars such as Holmes Welch to treat monasteries as containers for religious adepts and their activities and a distinct lack of attention paid to other features noted in historical sources such as material culture, founding myths, and social and political relations (Robson 2010b). Spatial theory and its intersection with studies in material religion have been helpful in thinking about the interplay of the different elements constitutive of life at the monastery, including ritual practices, material culture, and history.

One may reasonably wonder why in a book focused on the contemporary period I should dedicate an entire and lengthy chapter to the imperial and modern history of the monastery. Both De Certeau and Lefebvre articulate the way history in its full richness is a constitutive part of any present space. Where de Certeau speaks of "stratification" understood as a "piling up of heterogeneous places," of a linking together of "totalities that have fallen into ruins" (1988, 200–201), Lefebvre speaks of a diachronic dimension to space, of the need for an "'etymology' of locations" (2009, 37).[9] These views justify my dive into the historical layers of the site to understand its present, which is (literally) built on the stratified ruins and survivals of previous generations of buildings and full of references to past events, legends, and personages. I map ancient traces (architectural, mythical, material, ritualistic) to their present manifestation, somewhat like one finds in Flath's study of Kong Temple (2016), but whereas Flath is more exclusively interested in materiality and architecture, this study includes the religious community and their communal traditions.

Susan Naquin's study of Beijing temples does a better job than any of elucidating many of the understudied aspects of monasteries (2000, 1998). As Robson points out, "Some of the *underrepresented* characteristics of monasteries found in contemporary local sources include a focus on setting (natural landscape), the structure (architectural elements), the contents (relics, statuary, paintings, powerful deities), and the history (eminent monks associated with the site, key political recognition) of those sites" (2010, 44, emphasis added). Naquin's study of temples and monasteries in sociohistorical context produces rich material and reaches many conclusions about the social roles of temples of all kinds in the imperial period that were witnessed as living phenomena at my field site in Quanzhou. What Naquin was not able to do was to ask her interlocutors questions and make eyewitness observations that go beyond any textual data; such is an advantage, as well as a challenge, of ethnographic work, which, at its best, uncovers diverse views, practices, voices, and situations unaccounted for in published documentary sources and canonical texts (Nichols 2019a). We might say that historical-textual (that is, conscious) scholarship like Naquin's interprets the *opus operatum* (the finished or conscious business, so to speak) of temples, whereas the ethnographic method, such as the research presented here, translates the modus operandi constituting the unconscious or inarticulate life of a social group, in this case a Buddhist monastery. This book builds on Naquin's historical work and joins the broader scholarly effort to develop a re-description of Chinese Buddhism by reaching beyond the canonical sources and master narratives to local texts, material culture, and oral testimony to decenter normative narratives (Z. Ng 2007, 18–19; Sharf 2002; Robson 2010b; Fisher 2014). This book examines lived religion at a Buddhist monastery in post-Mao China and reveals the ecological relationship between the monastery and the community that includes the dynamic production of religious and secular values that enables the site to serve various interests and ends as detailed in the chapters to follow. In shedding light on monastic Buddhism in contemporary China, this study contributes to a growing body of knowledge on the revival of religion in post-Mao China, none of which at the time of this writing provides a detailed account of the lived experience of Han Buddhist monasticism.[10]

The Post-Mao Revival of Religion

Quanzhou Kaiyuan's current revival began soon after the death of Chairman Mao in 1976. In December 1978, at the meeting of the Third Plenum of the

Eleventh Party Congress Central Committee, Deng Xiaoping initiated the economic reforms that soon led to the opening of cities and special economic zones along China's southeast coast. The first provinces opened were Fujian (across from Taiwan) and Guangzhou (across from Hong Kong).[11] Four cities in these provinces were designated special economic zones in 1980; these included Xiamen, which is a one-hour drive from Quanzhou. In tandem with these economic measures, the repressive measures directed against religion during the Cultural Revolution were repudiated and a form of religious freedom was revived.[12]

The new religion policy was formalized in 1982 with the issuance of *On the Basic Viewpoint and Policy on the Religious Question during Our Country's Socialist Period.* Commonly known as *Document 19,* this policy guaranteed the freedom to believe or not believe in religion and the freedom to practice religion at officially recognized religious activity sites (*zongjiao huodong changsuo* 宗教活动场所). The five officially recognized religions are Buddhism, Daoism, Islam, Protestantism, and Catholicism; each of these has an official mediating association between it and the state. In the case of Buddhism, this agency is the Buddhist Association of China, or BAC (*zhongguo fojiao xiehui* 中国佛教协会) which has a national office in Beijing and provincial and municipal branches all over China. The economic opening and the relaxing of controls against religious practice were a boon to temples across Fujian, which has come to have the largest number of Buddhist monasteries and temples in all of China (Ji 2004).[13] Quanzhou Kaiyuan, as the most prominent monastery in an important home of overseas Chinese with links to Taiwan and Southeast Asia, was quick to receive financial support from overseas Chinese to fund the earliest stages of revival.

Sources and Methods

My method moves from history to ethnography and is based on participant-observation, interviews, and analysis of documents and other materials arising from or directly related to my field site. I lived on site for extended periods totaling around seven months of more than twenty-six spent in China from 2005 to 2019. My longest stretches on site were in 2006, 2007, and 2009. One of the keys to conducting research of this kind is access. I was fortunate to gain access through personal connections (*guanxi*) with a well-positioned provincial authority who was an acquaintance of my in-laws as well as of the abbot. I lived in a room that lay between the abbot's quarters and the rooms of two senior monks. I ate with the abbot and the senior monks on a daily basis and observed comings and goings; I was present for the visitors who arrived, as travel plans were made and executed, as special rituals were held, or crises arose and were responded to. The full access I enjoyed at the monastery enabled me to develop an unusually complete picture of the textured life and functioning of the monastery in real time. Although I lived at the monastery and ate with the monks, I did not wear robes, shave my head, or otherwise pretend to be a monk. I was what may be called an observer as participant. My role as researcher was known; I had free access to the site; I observed the various liturgical services many times; and I began to participate in services toward the end of my research. Dialogue is related to the issues of voice and positionality mentioned. Early on I was accepted by the monks as an empathetic outsider, a scholar of Buddhism with the Chinese dharma name Chuankui 传魁, longtime vegetarian, experienced meditator, and half-Chinese given that I was married to a Chinese woman, speak Chinese, prefer to eat with chopsticks, like Chinese food, and am a connoisseur of Chinese teas. After a couple of years, I essentially became an insider, having developed long-term friendly relationships with several monks and nonmonastics, known to all the monks, and recognized by laity and other persons associated with the monastery. Nonetheless, my positionality should be contrasted with the insider status of both Buswell in South Korea and Dreyfus in Dharamsala, who each trained and practiced as the monks they wrote about.

In 2009, I was based in Xiamen and made frequent trips to Quanzhou, often spending the night on site. Much time was spent traveling, often with monks, to other temples in Quanzhou, other parts of Fujian, and elsewhere in China. For example, I traveled with some of the monks to the World Buddhist Forum in 2009 in Wuxi, Jiangsu. I also joined two programs, one in the summer of 2009 and another in 2012, that took me to dozens of famous temples in Xi'an, Suzhou, Zhejiang, Jiangsu, and Mt. Putuo.[14] On my own, I visited many other temples around Beijing and in Sichuan and Yunnan. These visits enabled me to speak to and observe monastic and lay Buddhists all over China, which in turn helped me refine questions and build a broader context for my study.

In addition to participant-observation, I also made extensive use of interviews. Over the course of my research, I have conducted semistructured and unstructured interviews with eighty-two people related to this project, among them monks, nuns, lay Buddhists, officials, worshippers, tourists, business owners, and temple employees. The most extensive were with Kaiyuan monks and include multisession interviews with ten of them and briefer conversations with the others. For comparative purposes, I had single conversations with more than twenty monastics not from Kaiyuan but instead from all over China on specific points about ritual traditions, practice, temple management, and tourism. In conducting these interviews and incorporating them into this study, I remain aware of the problematic nature of oral testimony. Interviewees have agendas; they self-censure; and memory is constructed. Despite these problems, oral testimony is sometimes all that we have and it can be accurate, and even when it is not fully accurate it remains meaningful. When memories and stories are not perfectly faithful they still reveal issues, concerns, and perspectives that are not only important to the self-understandings of individuals and communities, but also critical to understanding lived religion. Oral historian Alessandro Portelli makes a discerning point about oral testimony: "The oral sources used in this essay are not always fully reliable in point of fact. Rather than being a weakness, this is however, their strength: errors, inventions, and myths lead us through and beyond facts to their meanings" (1991, 2). Errors in testimony are a strength, because they lead us out of the forest of facts to meaning. Here it is useful to recall Wilhelm Dilthey's attempt to place the human sciences on distinct methodological footing from the natural sciences, with hermeneutics based on (empathetic) understanding (*verstehen*) of lived experience (1962). Alessandro Portelli goes further: "The importance of oral testimony may lie not in its adherence to fact, but rather in its departure from it, as imagination, symbolism, and desire emerge. Therefore, there are no 'false' oral sources... 'wrong' statements are still psychologically 'true,' and that this truth may be equally as important as factually reliable accounts" (1991, 51). If we are serious about understanding our informants and their priorities, their accounts of events are always meaningful. It is up to the researcher to identify the salient patterns within a community, which suggest shared meanings, issues of importance, and features of "cultural memory" (Assmann 1995).

Fewer than a dozen individuals, monastic and nonmonastic, who proved both knowledgeable and eager to talk, became my primary informants, and I consulted with them frequently. In addition to and sometimes during interviews, I often walked around inside and just outside the site with camera and notepad, accompanied and unaccompanied, gathering information on activities, exchanges, behaviors, social networks, and other phenomena. After several months of fieldwork, I had generated rich enough streams of data to isolate prominent issues, concerns, and patterns through analytic induction and triangulation between observations, interviews, and documentary sources. What topics or issues did informants constantly raise or emphasize? What were the most prominent forms of activity on site? What was the role of nonmonastics in the management of the site? How were decisions made and power shared? What kinds of religious cultivation were practiced? How do tourists and lay Buddhists engage with the site, with the monks, with the material culture? The issues, concerns, phenomena, or conceptions that emerged repeatedly in interviews or observations in 2006 became my initial points of interest (codes). These were noted and further inquiries made to define the depth and contours of these concerns or practices. Further inquiries included follow-up interviews and on-site observations that I used to check my understandings and interpretations with key informants in 2007 and 2009.[15] In 2012 and 2019, I made weeklong visits to my field site and the region for additional follow-up interviews and observations. In 2019, I also began to communicate with several informants using the Chinese social networking app WeChat (*weixin*), which facilitated clarifications as I finalized my manuscript.

The primary emic terms or in vivo codes that emerged through this arduous research process from the ground up, categorically grouped were cultural objects/culture (*wenwu/wenhua*), purple clouds/mulberry lotus dharma world/spiritual efficacy (*ziyun/sanglian fajie/ling*), tourist/worshipper (*youke/xiangke*), temple administrative commission/monks (*guanyuanhui/sengren*), Buddha recitation/prostration (*nianfo/baifo*), rituals for the dead/universal Buddhas (*chaodu/pufo*), morning and evening assemblies (*zaoke/wanke*), and 84,000 dharma gates/cultivation (*baiwan siqian famen/xiuxing*). These groups of words and phrases were in turn treated under the five rubrics mentioned: liturgical rites/communal practice (chapter 3), 84,000 dharma gates/monks (chapter 4), material culture/space (chapter 5), founding legends/preternatural events (chapter 6), and the temple administrative commission/curators (chapter 7).

From 2009, my research into ritual activity began to shift from mostly observing, photographing, and filming to direct participation in the daily and weekly liturgical programs. This enabled me to temporarily inhabit the worlds of monks and lay Buddhists through immersion in collective ritual action. This provided me with valuable and unexpected insight into how the liturgical program affected one's body and mind during the event, shortly after, and beyond. I incorporated this data with interviews and observations enabling me to offer a more rounded interpretation of the religious life of the site.

Related to embodied participatory dialogue is my choice to use language in this book meant to evoke the vibrant life of the site as well as the ardor, pride, faith, skepticism, doubt, and other emotions my informants expressed. What may read as romanticized descriptions are words and phrases drawn from informants meant to capture aspects of devotional activity or based on the testimony of many ardent supporters of the site. At other times, they may be an attempt to evoke the life and activities of this site from my own mindful observations in ways that would be meaningful to my informants and resident clergy. Certain readers may find my evocative descriptions and interpretations of some aspects of the site idealized, but I hold that such evocative language is an important way for ethnography to provide access to the living breathing presence of the site.[16]

The intensity of my laser focus on a single site to develop textured representations and understandings is in line with the method of "thick description" that Clifford Geertz advocated and bears affinity with microhistory understood as a focus on everyday features in the study of a single event, place, or person (1973). This study, like microhistories, subverts master narratives with their teleological presumptions by reducing the scale of observation in "acknowledgment of limitations of existence" (Ginzburg 2012, 197; Foot 2007). This study is reduced to a large, irregular city block in Quanzhou, its material features, and the people who dynamically intersect with that space and those features in the making of Kaiyuan Monastery. Each chapter is full of rich details intended to evoke the lived material and social life of the monastery.

For Imperial and Republican period history, I turned to archival materials, including epigraphy. The most important textual source for the imperial history of Kaiyuan is the seventeenth-century *Gazetteer of Quanzhou Kaiyuan Monastery* (*Quanzhou kaiyuansi zhi* 泉州开元寺志) by Yuanxian. I checked it against and supplemented it with Dagui's 大圭 *Biographies of Purple Cloud Bodhisattvas* (*Ziyun kaishi zhuan* 紫云开士传) from 1348. I also used Kenneth Dean and Zheng Zhenman's 郑振满 three-volume collection of epigraphic materials from Fujian. I consulted many other primary historical sources, including Huang Zhongzhao's 黄仲昭 (1435–1508) *Gazetteer of Fujian* (*Bamin tongzhi* 八闽通志) and the *Gazetteer of Jinjiang County* (*Jinjiangxian zhi* 晋江县志) from 1830.[17]

Chapter Summaries

The book is divided into three parts. Space extends through time diachronically and serves synchronically (simultaneously) as a meeting point of diverse social relations (Knott 2005, 23–25). Part 1 is the diachronic exploration of the history of the monastery. Chapter 1 provides a deep dive into the history of the site from the Tang dynasty (618–907) to the Maoist period (1949–1976), emphasizing elements and referents that remain accessible today and identifying patterns of patronage by elites, the regulatory and interventionist state, and continual modulations of material culture. The Song dynasty (960–1127) witnessed the development of 120 cloisters at Quanzhou Kaiyuan, making it a veritable university in a multiethnic international port city. From the late Ming (1368–1644) to the early Qing (1644–1911), Kaiyuan produced three patriarchs of the Obaku school of Zen in Japan. In the Republican period (1911–1949), Kaiyuan participated in the revival of Buddhism and hosted several eminent monks of the era. The history of the monastery continues with chapter 2, which provides a more compressed diachronic dive into the post-Mao period. The recent history of the monastery is divided into three phases of restoration that witness the return of religious practice, the renovation of the buildings, and the recovery of adjacent properties lost in earlier periods. The recent history provides necessary context to social relations and religious revival in the post-Mao period.

The remaining chapters are more synchronic in their approach in order to highlight essential features of the monastery in the contemporary period. Part 2 explores the religious life of the monastery. Chapter 3 examines the nature of communal religious activity tracing it through recurring daily, monthly, and annual schedules that establish heterogenous time against the tide of modernity. It identifies the central role of particular soundscapes and reveals a distinctively liturgical approach to Buddhism. The three primary strands of religious tradition running throughout the liturgical program provide a new sense of what religion entails at a Buddhist monastery: regular use of *dhāraṇī,* Pure Land Buddhism, and the veneration of ancestors. Chapter 4 uses a person-centered approach to identify forms of self-cultivation among individual clergy and relates the biographies of seven monks, comparing them with patterns found among the biographies of monks collected by Holmes Welch (1967).

Part 3 of the book examines the material dynamics in sociopolitical context. Chapter 5 examines the rich and unique material culture of the site and the different ways space is produced through engagement with concretized schemes of meaning and value represented by the statuary, pagodas, trees, buildings, and other material features. Three models of interaction between material culture and individuals are identified: a place of religion, a site of history and culture, and a park. The clergy are aware of these different values and skillfully promote them to various stakeholders.

Chapter 6 explores how founding legends of preternatural events are used to both brand and sanctify the site. Drawing on the three social identities identified in chapter 5, stories of sympathetic resonance are deployed and experienced in three ways: for the religionist, these stories enhance the monastery's reputation of spiritual efficacy; for the tourist, they mark Kaiyuan as a unique place of historical interest; and for those seeking recreation, they may be colorful distractions or just white noise. What is important is how the persistence of these legends continues to inspire others and bolster traditional cosmologies of sympathetic resonance in a bounded universe. I propose that the temporal heterogeneity in chapter 3, coupled with the spatial heterogeneity of chapters 5 and 6, serves to resist or disrupt projects of modernity and/or is revelatory of a failure of the totalizing discourse of secular modernity.

Chapter 7 analyzes the conflict and cooperation between two groups with managerial claim to the site, the monks, and the temple administrative commission. To get at their primary orientations, I frame the relationship as one between curators and revivalists. I argue that a spectrum exists in China from museumification of religious sites to the restoration of those dedicated to religious practice, with sites like Kaiyuan creating a hybrid identity as a tourist site and a place of religious practice.

Taken together, the chapters collectively examine the complex space of the monastery in terms of the Lefebvre/Knott triad: material features (chapter 5), ideology in terms of branding and sanctification (chapter 6), and sociopolitical dimensions (chapters 3, 4, and 7). The conclusion weaves together the several threads that emerge over the course of the book to assess what we have learned about Chinese Buddhist monasticism as an institution and as a community of practice and how it might face current challenges into the future. The conclusion also interrogates the nature of the religious and the secular in understanding Chinese religion and the role religion may play as a place of resistance to the monoculture of secular modernity.

Many books could be written about any one site. I have attempted to write one that takes advantage of both my positionality and my access to present a multidimensional portrait recognizable to the monks who have made it their home, the laity and worshippers who prostrate and make offerings, and tourists who admire the built environment. In addition, I place the five defining features of the site in conversation with scholarship on Buddhism and the *longue durée* of local history to ground and contextualize my findings. This study decenters normative notions to broaden our conception and deepen our understanding of what a Buddhist monastery is, what it does, how it does it, and why.

Part I

History

1

The Monastic Cycle

Patterns of History

KAIYUAN MONASTERY IS TODAY, AS IT HAS been since its founding, the largest Buddhist monastery in the city of Quanzhou: it occupies the most expansive grounds (seventy-eight thousand square meters), houses the largest number of monastics, and boasts the oldest and most valuable buildings and antiquities. Traces of this site's 1,300 years of history at the monastery are in the form of buildings, artifacts, trees, inscriptions, and stories told by tour guides and local lay and monastic Buddhists. To appreciate these features of the monastery, one must have some understanding of their history. This history, punctuated with preternatural tales, strewn with cultural properties, and dignified with eminent personages, is the source of the monastery's distinguishing features, which have been instrumental in securing its longevity and reputation. This chapter sketches the history of Kaiyuan Monastery from its founding in 686 through the end of imperial China to 1975, a span of more than 1,280 years, emphasizing aspects of history that remain part of the texture of the site today and identifying salient historical patterns that provide important context for understanding the post-Mao resurgence of Buddhism.[1]

The diachronic perspective used to relate history in this chapter reveals patterns of growth and periods of contraction, times of inspired leadership and times of neglect. Holmes Welch, in his pioneering surveys of modern Chinese Buddhism, terms such patterns of decline and renewal the "monastic cycle" (1968, 87–90). The nadir of the cycle is when a monastery's buildings have fallen into a state of disrepair and most of its monks have dispersed. Restoration (*chongxing* 重兴) typically begins with the emergence or appointment of a capable monk who leads the material and moral renewal of the monastery with lay and monastic support. Although cycles of decline and renewal are evident in the history of Kaiyuan Monastery, these cycles are far from even or regular. Apart from genuine large-scale restoration of a site is the need for regular upkeep to prevent a monastery from becoming dilapidated. Ming dynasty records speak of the need to frequently restore and repair monastic buildings every thirty to fifty years, otherwise they would have to be completely rebuilt (Brook 1993, 162–163). It is important to distinguish regular upkeep of a monastery, a sign of steady vitality, from full-scale restoration. Similarly it is important to distinguish maintaining the status quo from so-called decline (J. Wu 2008, 279–280). The patterns that emerge from this historical sketch provide important context for the current restoration.

Closely related to patterns of decline and renewal are the interrelated themes of elite patronage and state involvement, both supportive and regulatory. The Chinese state has always considered the regulation of religion to be one of its tasks (A. Yu 2005; Schlütter 2005). State policies and their implementation have variously promoted and expanded the monastery on the one hand and suppressed its growth or activities on the other. This chapter reveals the ways that patronage and neglect have always related to broader economic, social, and political conditions; as those external conditions change, the evolution of the monastery shifts correspondingly. This again provides important context for the modern and contemporary periods, which include similar patterns of patronage and regulation.

The Tang Dynasty

In lunar February of 686 (the second year of Chuigong) during the Tang dynasty, citizen Huang Shougong 黄守恭 had a dream while napping. A monk begged to have his land for a temple. Elder Huang said, "Should my trees bloom white lotuses, I shall concede." Pleased, the monk thanked him and suddenly disappeared. Two days passed and the mulberry trees bloomed white lotuses. The local authorities considered this an auspicious event and asked to build a place for practice (*daochang* 道场). The empress granted permission and named it Lotus Flower. The monk Kuanghu 匡护 was asked to serve as abbot.[2]

This well-known legend relates the story of how Kaiyuan Monastery was established when Elder Huang (629–712) donated his mulberry orchard to the monk Kuanghu after his mulberry trees miraculously bloomed white lotus blossoms.[3] One of the most revered objects at Kaiyuan Monastery today is an ancient mulberry tree said to be a direct descendant of the legendary ones. Although the legend includes preternatural elements, there is no reason to doubt the historical veracity of a land donation to establish a monastery in 686 CE.[4] It was at precisely this time that the conversion of private estates into monastic estates had become so widespread that Emperor Xuanzong, in 713, issued a decree to curtail the practice.[5] When the monastery was founded, it was located on what was then a sparsely inhabited frontier coastal plain between the Luoyang 洛阳 and Jin Rivers 晋江. The settlement was not yet called Quanzhou, nor was the monastery called Kaiyuan Monastery. When the local authorities petitioned Empress Wu Zetian 武则天 (r. 683/90–705), an ardent patron of Buddhism, to establish a monastery, she consented and named it the Lotus Flower Temple 莲花寺 to commemorate the lotus blossoming mulberry trees.

Kuanghu as founding abbot immediately set out to build a buddha hall. Tradition holds that as this main hall was being built a purple cloud was seen hovering over the area. Recognizing this as an auspicious sign, the hall was nicknamed the Purple Cloud Hall and the monastery itself the Purple Cloud. The main gate and monastic living quarters known as the Venerated Site Cloister (Zunsheng yuan 尊胜院) were built the following year, in 687.[6] Within two years, then, Kuanghu had established three structures that formed the initial nucleus of the monastery: the main gate, the main hall, and the Venerated Site Cloister.

In a move that would ultimately cause the name of this vibrant era to remain in circulation, Emperor Xuanzong ordered each prefecture to have a monastery named for the current period, that of Kaiyuan.[7] In 738, then, the monastery received the name by which it has been known since, Kaiyuan Monastery. As part of their responsibility to the emperor, Kaiyuan monasteries were to hold national ceremonies such as that marking the emperor's birthday.[8] Charged with responsibilities to honor the emperor, Kaiyuan Monastery was sent a buddha statue by Emperor Xuanzong himself. Although this statue has long disappeared, a stonc inscription hangs above the door of the main hall today that reads "Imperially bestowed statue of Buddha" (*Yuci foxiang* 御赐佛像).[9]

If Kaiyuan Monastery enjoyed a golden age, it was during the five hundred years between 850 and 1350. Its properties were spared in the infamous Huichang Persecution of Buddhism (842–845) because Kaiyuan, as the official state monastery in the prefecture of Quanzhou, was protected.[10] As Fujian absorbed Buddhist refugees from the north and more monasteries were established, cloisters were established at Kaiyuan to accommodate masters and their disciples. In 865, a wooden pagoda was built in the eastern part of the monastic grounds and named "country stabilizer" (*zhenguo* 镇国) by Emperor Yizong 懿宗. Although Kaiyuan Monastery's east pagoda would go through several transformations over the next four hundred years, it had been established and would retain the imperially bestowed name of *zhenguo*.

The first two centuries of Kaiyuan Monastery also witnessed the building of a sutra library and the mummification of master Zhiliang 智亮, the "bare-shouldered-monk" (*tanbo heshang* 袒膊和尚), thought to have been from India. What is claimed to be his mummified corpse remains at Kaiyuan today. Quanzhou's port was already involved with maritime exchanges with South India and the presence of Indians in Quanzhou is therefore plausible.

Although much of China suffered turmoil accompanying and following the dissolution of the Tang dynasty, Quanzhou and Kaiyuan Monastery in isolated Fujian thrived. The principal reason for Kaiyuan's success in the period between the Tang and Song dynasties was continual patronage by the Wang 王 family, which ruled the kingdom of Min (Fujian) (884 to 945) during the interregnum.[11] Wang Shengui 王审邽 had four Buddha statues made and added to the one donated by Emperor Xuanzong, bringing the number of Buddhas enshrined to its current number of five. Wang Shengui was succeeded in 904 by his son Wang Yanbin 王延彬, who was then about eighteen or nineteen years old. He had been born in one of Kaiyuan Monastery's halls two or three years after the arrival of the Wang clan in 884. Wang Yanbin was an enthusiastic supporter of Buddhism in Quanzhou and an unmatched patron of Kaiyuan Monastery: records suggest that he sponsored the building of more cloisters there than any other single individual. It is said that Yanbin "was a talented writer of poems and loved to discuss Buddhist theories—whenever poets or Chan masters visited, he would keep them as long as he could."[12] The *Compendium of the Five Lamps* (*Wudeng huiyan* 五燈全書) includes Wang Yanbin as a disciple of Chan master Huileng 慧稜, whom he had invited to Fujian in 870.[13] Lay Buddhist Yanbin is thus considered a fourteenth-generation Chan patriarch.[14]

In 916, during Yanbin's tenure as prefect, the Western pagoda was first constructed by Yanbin's uncle and king of Min, Wang Shenzhi; it was a wooden seven-story pagoda named the Pagoda of Amitāyus (infinite life, *wuliang shou* 无量寿). The patronage of Wang Yanbin and the Wang family demonstrates the connections between Kaiyuan Monastery, political elites, and the city of Quanzhou that remain a feature of the monastery's identity from that time forward.

By the onset of the Song dynasty (960–1279), Kaiyuan Monastery was a growing one that had dozens of cloisters (or subtemples) led by Chan masters, masters of the vinaya, and masters of Yogācāra. It would seem that a description of Quanzhou attributed to the great Confucian scholar Zhu Xi 朱熹 (1130–1200) must refer to this rich period of its history: "In days of old this was a Buddhist kingdom, the streets were full of sages."[15] This couplet, in the calligraphy of master Hongyi, today hangs outside the main hall as well as inside the main gate of Kaiyuan Monastery, bringing echoes of this glorious past into the present for those aware of its historical references.

Kaiyuan Monastery at this early period was already marked by three traits that would continue to shape its identity for centuries to come: it was made grand by cultural properties; its founding had been marked by auspicious events that set it apart from Quanzhou's other major monasteries; and it served as home to eminent monks that attracted patrons and preserved its reputation as a place of merit.

The Song Dynasty

Quanzhou had become a busy international port specializing in the transshipment of goods from the Indian Ocean and Southeast Asia to China's inland cities. The wealth generated by this trade would lead to the construction of magnificent stone bridges and pagodas throughout the region that have remained remarkably well preserved into the twenty-first century; monks played an instrumental role in the construction of both pagodas and bridges. Quanzhou's magnificent granite architecture is thought to represent a local tradition not found in other parts of China.[16] The two major developments to the physical plant of Kaiyuan Monastery during this period both involved monumental construction carried out under the careful guidance of Buddhist monks. The first was the establishment of Kaiyuan Monastery's ordination platform. The second was the conversion of the east and west pagodas from brick into stone toward the end of the Song dynasty from 1228 to 1250.

Although the current ordination platform dates from the Ming dynasty, Kaiyuan's first ordination platform was built during the Northern Song (960–1127) in 1019.[17] Tradition holds that its name is derived from a Tang dynasty well known as the Amrita Well (*ganlu jing* 甘露井) which sits below the platform.[18] Kaiyuan's pagodas were rebuilt by the monk Shouchun 守淳 as seven-story brick pagodas in the early thirteenth century of the Southern Song (1127–1279). Soon, however, the monk Zizheng 自证 set out to rebuild the pagodas in granite. The five-story west pagoda, completed in 1237, remains standing.[19] The conversion of the east pagoda from a seven-storied brick pagoda into a five-storied stone pagoda began in 1238 under the supervision of the monk Benhong 本洪. Benhong was only able to complete the first level, but the carvings in greenstone (*qing shi* 青石), which he oversaw along the base, are considered the finest at the monastery.[20] The panels are not only artistically masterful, they also exhibit a most impressive knowledge of Indian Buddhist literature.[21] A monk named Tianxi 天锡 completed the fifth story and the pinnacle in 1250.[22]

The reconstruction of the east and west pagodas in stone was the crowning event of a prosperous period of growth and consolidation during the Song dynasty. Although the early decades were a period of efflorescence for both Quanzhou and Kaiyuan Monastery, the closing decades became a time of consolidation that contrasted with the expansion and innovation of the interregnum and early Song. The early period included the official designation of Kaiyuan Monastery as a Chan monastery by order of a former cabinet secretary turned prefect of Qizhou 蕲州 named Qiao Langzhong 乔郎中 who invited Chan master Ziqi 子琦 (d. 1115) of Hui'an to serve as abbot.[23] This change brought the monastery into conformity with prevailing tendencies in the Song dynasty that made Chan the dominant form of monastic Buddhism, but which meant little change to the institution beyond having an abbot associated with a particular lineage of transmission, in this case the Huanglong 黄龙 (Yellow Dragon) lineage of Linji Chan.[24] By the end of the Song dynasty, Kaiyuan Monastery was a virtual university of one hundred and twenty cloisters housing well over a thousand monks, specializing in specific sutras or skills such as engineering.[25]

The Yuan Dynasty

Under the Yuan dynasty (1279–1368), Kaiyuan Monastery would lose its cloisters and its status as a Buddhist "university." In 1285, nine years into Mongol rule, the old monastery was abolished and in its place arose the Great Kaiyuan Everlasting Chan Monastery (Da kaiyuan wanshou chansi 大开元万寿禅寺). It was a big name for what was in reality a dramatically smaller, controllable, and cohesive monastery. In 1285, the scale of Kaiyuan was decimated as 117 of the 120 affiliated cloisters that clustered around the central axis were abolished by state directive.[26] The following year, the Chan master Miao'en 妙恩 (d. 1293) was invited to become the inaugural abbot of the newly configured monastery. Over the seven years he served as abbot, Miao'en led the monastery in a spate of building designed to refashion it as a distinctively Chan monastery. His building program included Kaiyuan's first Chan hall as well as its first Hall of Patriarchs (Zushi tang 祖师堂) and the Donor's Ancestral Shrine (Tanyue ci 檀越祠). The Chan hall has been lost, but the other two remain important and unique features of the monastery.

Miao'en was succeeded by Qizu 契祖 (1230–1319) and in 1319 Qizu was succeeded by Ruzhao 如炤 (d. 1331), who had served as Miao'en's close attendant for several years. Ruzhao made a practice of writing sutras in his own blood. He copied the *Lotus Sutra* in blood while at Fuzhou's Xuefeng Monastery and then wrote the *Flower Ornament Sutra* (*Huayan jing*) in blood after returning to Kaiyuan; this blood sutra remains in Kaiyuan's library.[27]

As the Yuan dynasty wore on, signs appear that Kaiyuan began to cultivate a role that would form part of its identity from that time forward: it became self-conscious as a site of religious, historic, and cultural value—in today's vernacular, a site of religious tourism. The first clear indication of this historical self-consciousness came in 1327, when two ornamental walls were erected outside the main gate known as the East and West Bounding

Walls (Dongxi erfang 东西二坊). On these walls were notices announcing the presence of Eight Auspicious Phenomena (Ba jixiang 八吉祥) and Six Unique Sites (Liu shusheng 六殊胜).[28] Such publicly displayed notices indicate a need the monastery felt to advertise its propitious features, features that pointed to the past greatness of Kaiyuan Monastery. It had reached a peak during the Song dynasty in terms of its size and its number of eminent residents; decline had set in from the Yuan onward. The self-reflexivity, the looking to the past for evidence of greatness and the need to self-promote that greatness through billboard-like inscriptions all point to a kind of decadence that had set in and still haunts Kaiyuan, as it does all great institutions that outlive a glorious past.

This historical self-reflexivity on the part of Kaiyuan's monks is further revealed by the composition of *Biographies of Purple Cloud Bodhisattvas*. Written by Kaiyuan's Mengguan Shi 梦观氏 at the end of the Yuan dynasty in 1348, it is a collection of biographies of Kaiyuan's monks from Kuanghu onward. The timing of Mengguan's writing suggests that he quite rightly sensed the impending disaster and sought to record for posterity what was known about the luminaries of Kaiyuan's illustrious past—a curatorial impulse. It was Mengguan's record that inspired Yuanxian to write the *Quanzhou Kaiyuan Monastic Gazetteer* at the end of the Ming dynasty and served as his primary source. Timothy Brook describes the role played by gazetteers that became very common in the seventeenth century: "A monastic gazetteer was a celebration of a particular institution; it was also an investment designed to protect it against the relentless enemies of embezzlement, encroachment, and physical decay" (2005, 147–148).

Just after Mengguan completed his *Biographies,* the departmental magistrate (*jianjun* 监郡) Xie Shiyu 偰世玉 wrote a name board for Kaiyuan Monastery's main gate reading, "The Buddha Land of Southern Quanzhou" (Quannan foguo 泉南佛国). This final gesture of exaltation came in 1350 and may be seen to mark the end of an era, not only for the monastery but also for the city of Quanzhou. Those examining Kaiyuan Monastery at the end of the Yuan dynasty saw its greatness in its past rather than in the present or the future. Perhaps they were prescient. For soon the city and the monastery would be devastated in the violence that accompanied the end of the Yuan; neither can be said to have ever recovered their pre-Ming greatness.[29]

In the middle of the fourteenth century, China and the city of Quanzhou were undergoing the birthing pains of what would become a new dynasty. Unrest, rebellion, and lawlessness were spreading out from points of intense suffering born of flood and famine. In 1357, Kaiyuan Monastery suffered wholesale destruction by fire; the only remains were stone: pavements, foundations, platforms, columns, stupas, inscriptions, and, most notably, the pagodas. The collapse of the Yuan dynasty sounded the death knell for

Quanzhou's international trade. Kaiyuan would rebuild, but it would never flourish as it had before. As the *Kaiyuan Gazetteer* relates, "The recurring famines and widespread pillaging and plundering at the end of the Yuan dynasty were disheartening to the temple. By 1397 (thirtieth year of *Hongwu*) the temple monks were nearly wiped out in the disaster" (Yuanxian 1643, I.2a).

The Ming Dynasty

The founding of the Ming dynasty (1368–1644) returned order to the city but it would be thirty years before the full restoration of Kaiyuan's monastic buildings and its sangha would never reach pre-Ming levels. Local officials reported the dire situation to the emperor, who sent the eminent monk-official Zhengying 正映, who was then serving as the Tripitika prefect (*dianzang* 典藏) at the leading monastery of the Ming capital, Nanjing's Tianjie Monastery 天界寺, to serve as Kaiyuan Monastery's abbot.[30] Kaiyuan's main hall had already been rebuilt when Zhengying became abbot in 1398, so he immediately set out to rebuild the dharma hall, the ordination platform, and the hall of patriarchs. His rebuilding, completed in 1400, is a classic case of a comprehensive restoration following a period of decline and destruction. It made Quanzhou Kaiyuan one of only a handful of large Buddhist monasteries in Fujian during the early Ming.

Five years after the death of the Hongwu emperor (Taizu), a great patron of Buddhism assumed the imperial mantle, the Yongle 永乐 emperor (Chengzu 成祖, r. 1403–1424).[31] During the Yongle period, Kaiyuan Monastery continued the renewal of its physical plant, which had begun at the end of the Hongwu period under the direction of the monk Zhichang 至昌. It was at this time that several small stupas arranged along the sides of the main courtyard were installed (these remain today). Although no record confirms this, it seems most plausible that it was during Zhichang's expansion of the main hall's platform that the seventy-two decorative sphinx carvings (figures with a human face and lion's body, known in Sanskrit as *vyala-vari*) were incorporated into the base of the platform. The temple from which these sculptures originated was destroyed in the violence that accompanied the collapse of the Yuan. These sculpted stones were thus available and their incorporation into the base of the platform may have simply been a matter of repurposing useful, aesthetically valuable materials. In support of this view is the incorporation of Yuan dynasty stone tombstones into the Ming dynasty city wall.

Whatever the merits of Zhengying and Zhichang and other monks of that period, an apparent lack of momentum may be attributed in part to insufficiently developed institutional mechanisms for the training of monks. Zhichang's series of largely aesthetic improvements to the monastery's physical plant continues the theme that emerged at the end of the Yuan dynasty, a shift in emphasis to accommodating nonmonastic visitors. I refer to such improvements as directed at "hardware" during the contemporary era, following such usage by my informants. Just as "improvements" made at the end of the Yuan in the form of the bounding walls suggested hints of decadence, so do the additions by Zhichang suggest a shift in focus away from monastic training and practice to the accommodation of visitors and lay Buddhists. All of Zhichang's additions can be seen to enhance the experience of visitors—covered walkways helped keep guests shaded and dry; the extended platform outside the main hall accommodated greater numbers of incense-burning worshippers; the ponds would have provided a place for visitors to earn merit by releasing fish into them and the rows of stupas in the main courtyard served to enhance the aesthetic and religious experience of visitors.[32] These developments would certainly have also enhanced the monastery for its monks, but it remains nonetheless true that they would contribute more to the experience of visitors and lay Buddhists than to the training of monastics.

Our Ming dynasty chronicler Yuanxian describes the moral and physical decline of the monastery: "Since the *Yongle* period [1403–1424] there has long been a void in leadership. The Chan ethos has gradually washed away [*min* 泯] and the venerable old monks have dispersed like clouds to the four directions" (1643, 19b). Not only had the long-lived Emperor Shizong issued orders leading to the destruction of monasteries and the laicization of monks, but the socioeconomic fabric of southern Fujian was also in disarray. Because of the weak government, much power lay with southern Fujian's lineage collectives, which fought to increase their land and power.[33] Kaiyuan Monastery suffered as its land and buildings became sold, mortgaged, or occupied by nonmonastics in rapid succession. By the end of the Ming dynasty, more than 85 percent of Kaiyuan's landholdings had been sold off or seized by others, falling from the Song dynasty high of more than 4,500 acres (273.5 *qing*) to just over two (36.5 *qing*) by the end of the Ming.[34]

Conditions began to improve from this low point during the reign of the great patron of Buddhism Emperor Shenzong 神宗 (1563–1620), who oversaw the Wanli period Buddhist restoration throughout China. Monasteries were built on a more lavish scale than had been seen in centuries and Buddhist scriptures were printed and distributed across the country.[35] It was during this period of Buddhist renewal under imperial support that Kaiyuan Monastery entered a period of restoration I call the Late Ming restoration that echoes the current era. Both periods may be seen as times of a dramatic rebuilding of monastic hardware after a period of devastating decline.

The first indication of a change in Kaiyuan's fortunes was the building of the Purple Cloud Screen or reflecting wall (*zhaoqiang* 照墙) across from the main gate by the vice mayor (*juncheng* 郡丞) Ding Yizhong 丁一中 in 1570 (it remains in situ).[36] This was a physical change, external to the monastery proper, that will mirror developments in the contemporary revival. True restoration of the monastery proper began in 1594 when the vice censor-in-chief, Huang Wenbin 黄文炳, a descendant of Elder Huang, reported the temple's dire situation to the emperor (Yuanxian 1643, I.2b).[37] With Shenzong's approval, intruders were expelled from monastic properties and repairs were undertaken with funding and leadership from laypersons.

In 1596, Huang Wenbin led the Purple Cloud Huang family in the rebuilding of the Donor's Ancestral Shrine, which continues to serve as a memorial hall for Elder Huang, Kaiyuan's founding donor.[38] The leading role played by the Huang clan in the late Ming rebuilding of Kaiyuan Monastery also reflects the growing power held by lineage collectives during this period.[39] In 1596, in the wake of the monastery's steps toward revival, Chen Zhizhi 陈止止 wrote the first monastic gazetteer for the temple.[40]

In 1604, a great earthquake struck Quanzhou, leveling buildings across the city. Impressively, Kaiyuan's east and west pagodas did not collapse. The Late Ming restoration continued under the powerful backing of Quanzhou native Zheng Zhilong 郑芝龙 (1604–1661)[41] who led the reconstruction of the main hall (*daxiong baodian* 大雄宝殿) in 1637 with Zeng Ying 曾樱. It is their hall that visitors see today. All of the wooden columns were replaced with ones of stone. At this time, two exquisite sixteen-sided columns from Quanzhou's long-defunct Hindu temple were transferred to Kaiyuan Monastery and incorporated into the back porch of the main hall.[42] Made of green limestone, each column has twelve carvings depicting Hindu deities (Shiva, Krishna, and others) and motifs. These columns are still at the back of the main hall and stand as a reminder of both the religious diversity and tolerance that once flourished in Quanzhou as well as the loss of that diversity that accompanied the collapse of the Yuan.[43]

Zheng Zhilong installed a large iron incense burner in front of the main hall and repaired the main gate.[44] It is this late Ming reconstruction that is the basis for the gate that stands today. The gate has been rebuilt or restored several times over the years, but its present style is not thought to have significantly diverged from that of the late Ming reconstruction. It is also thought that the stone columns used today date from the late Ming construction or earlier.[45]

The local gentry invited Yuanxian (1578–1657), a monk from Fuzhou's Mount Drum monastery, to give teachings at Kaiyuan Monastery in the winter of 1635. Yuanxian accepted their invitation and would go on to acquiesce to their requests that he write a gazetteer for Quanzhou Kaiyuan. Yuanxian completed the *Kaiyuan Gazetteer* in 1643. In it, he mused that the time seemed like one of renewal and hoped it would in fact blossom into a time of growth of the dharma at Kaiyuan Monastery. His thoughts on the Late Ming restoration provide insight into a congruent situation facing Kaiyuan today: "The Buddha Land of Quanzhou is truly full of old monasteries, but only one has stood more than a thousand years, Kaiyuan—'The great fruit has not been eaten.' Its reputation has not declined, and those nostalgic for things old can still hear about and experience it" (Yuanxian 1643, I.1a).

This passage hails the longevity and greatness of Quanzhou Kaiyuan. The enigmatic aphorism "The great fruit has not been eaten" (*shuoguo bu shi* 硕果不食) has been chosen by Yuanxian with care and warrants closer examination. The line is taken from the *Yijing* 易经 or *Book of Changes* and appears in the exegesis of the top and only *yang* (unbroken) line of hexagram twenty-three (*bo* 剥, peeling, stripping, splitting apart, or flaying) (Lynn 1994, 280–283). The scene painted by this hexagram is the end of autumn, when all things are turning brown and dying and a destructive storm blows in, tearing apart the trees of an orchard. Atop a lone damaged tree is a large fruit left uneaten that is destined to fall and bring forth a new tree and, ultimately, a restored orchard. That is the positive message of the top line referenced by Yuanxian.

When the scholarly monk Yuanxian visited Kaiyuan at the end of the Ming dynasty, it was emerging from a period of neglect, demise, and occupation. He artfully chose this image from the *Yijing* to suggest Kaiyuan's promise of revival after a century of disaster. The poetic metaphor suggests Kaiyuan Monastery reemerging from the seeds of its own fruit after a period of terrible neglect. Kaiyuan had suffered occupation and mistreatment during the sixteenth century and was at last beginning to see signs of recovery and new life. Yuanxian's image from the twenty-third hexagram was both poetic and apt. Yuanxian also exhorted Kaiyuan's late Ming dynasty monks to be less concerned about recovering lost properties and to focus instead on the cultivation of virtue and the practice of meditation. If monks will tend to their own discipline and cultivation, Yuanxian goes on to counsel, their virtue will give rise to benefits, such as the support of laypersons. In the end, it would seem that this restoration had enough momentum to endure the decades of instability in Fujian that preceded and followed the founding of the Qing dynasty (1644–1911), which would produce some of the monastery's most influential monks.

The Qing Dynasty

As Jiang Wu explains, the late Ming revival of Buddhism continued and peaked in the early Qing (2008). Not only were buildings repaired and rebuilt during the decades of instability but monks were also trained in the Chan and Pure Land traditions with such consistency that a streak of noteworthy masters were produced over the first century of the Qing dynasty. These masters added several chapels and shrines to Kaiyuan Monastery that, like the pre-Yuan cloisters, served as residences and places of practice for adepts and their disciples. I propose that the instability of the times actually contributed to the vitality of Buddhism at Kaiyuan, and in Fujian more generally, by creating a hostile environment from which literati and other men of talent left for the tranquil and contemplative setting of the monastery. According to Jiang Wu, significant numbers of Ming officials and literati refused to join the Manchu government and joined Buddhist communities instead, contributing to a gentrification of Buddhism (2015, 26–27; 2008, 269).[46] The trend began during the middle Ming after the literati opening to Buddhism represented by Neo-Confucian Wang Yangming (1472–1529).[47] The turmoil of the times also created conditions in which Buddhist masters from Fujian undertook the perilous journey to Japan; in their so doing, a new school of Zen was created in Japan, the Obaku or Huangbo 黄檗 school.[48] Three Kaiyuan masters of the Qing dynasty traveled to Japan to lead the Obaku school of Zen; others left their mark on Buddhism in Fujian.

It was during this period that Chan master Ruhuan Chaohong 如幻超宏 (b. 1604) founded the Duqin chapel 度亲庵 at Kaiyuan, which he built with the support of two members of the Huang family.[49] During his tenure as leader of the chapel, Ruhuan engaged in Pure Land practice and the release of life with his colleague Chan master Weishen 惟深. Weishen had the ambition to build a temple to Cundī Bodhisattva (Zhunti pusa 准提菩萨) out of faith in the power of reciting the *Cundīdevī-dhāraṇī* (大准提陀羅尼經), the *dhāraṇī* of Cundī Bodhisattva, one of six incarnations of Guanyin in the esoteric tradition.[50] Construction began in 1662 with the assistance of the layman Daochong 道冲 and was completed in 1664. The finished temple was in fact a scaled-down replica of Kaiyuan Monastery's principal buildings—the main hall, ordination hall, dharma hall, and corridors—and enshrined a statue of Cundī Bodhisattva.[51] The Cundī Chan Temple was repaired in 1861 and has been rebuilt over the centuries, including quite recently; today it is commonly referred to as Small Kaiyuan Temple (小开元寺) and used as a museum. Ruhuan, the most eminent Chan master of Fujian at that time, served as abbot of the Cundī Chan forest for a time.

In 1666, at about the same time as the construction of the Cundī Temple was under way, the rebuilding of the ordination hall was initiated and completed.[52] Although it has been renovated at various times over the centuries, the structure stands today. In 1688, seven relics were brought from Mt. Drum's Yongquan Monastery to the ordination hall; they were stored in a small relic stupa and remain in the hall.

Another eminent monk of seventeenth-century Fujian is Chan master Muan 木庵 (J. Mokuan, 1611–1684) who was a disciple and dharma heir of Yinyuan Longqi 隐元隆琦 (J. Ingen Ryuki, 1592–1673). Yiyuan was himself a disciple of Huangbo Zhudasha, who was thus the grand master of both Muan and Ruhuan. Yinyuan, in fleeing the turmoil that followed the collapse of the

Ming in Fujian, traveled to Japan, where he founded the Obaku school of Zen. The Obaku (Ch. Huangbo) school became the third largest school of Zen in Japan, after Rinzai and Soto, on which it exerted significant influence, and today has some 460 branch temples in Japan.[53]

Muan became a novice at Kaiyuan Monastery when he was sixteen and took the tonsure at nineteen.[54] He traveled for a short period and returned to Kaiyuan at the age of twenty-two and founded the Amitabha Chapel (Mituo an 弥陀庵) there. He became fully ordained at twenty-four and dedicated himself to the pursuit of Chan. He was elected Kaiyuan's general manager (*jianyuan*) at the age of twenty-five but soon left to study with several Chan masters in Zhejiang. In 1642, he again returned, writing poems commemorating the Eight Auspicious Phenomena and the Six Unique Sites.[55] In 1644, he became Yinyuan's disciple and received dharma transmission from him in 1651, thus becoming the thirty-third patriarch of the Linji Chan lineage. In 1655, Muan traveled to Japan, a year after Yinyuan had made the journey. In 1664, he became the abbot of the Wanfu Monastery 万福寺 (J. Mampuku-ji), the headquarters of the Obaku school in Japan that Yinyuan had founded in 1659 on land bestowed by the emperor of Japan and located in Uji 宇治, outside Kyoto.[56] In receiving dharma transmission from Yinyuan (first patriarch of the Obaku school) and succeeding Yinyuan as abbot of the head Obaku monastery, Muan become the second patriarch of the Obaku school in Japan in addition to being the thirty-third patriarch of the Linji lineage. Muan, along with Yinyuan and Jifei 即非, was a renowned calligrapher; together they are known as the Three Brushes of the Obaku school. Of the three, however, only Muan is noted for his poetry as well as his painting.[57]

Two other monks from Kaiyuan traveled to Japan and became abbots of Mampuku-ji and patriarchs of the Obaku school: Shengchui Fangbing 圣垂方炳 (1656–1725) and Dapeng Zhengkun 大鹏正鲲 (1691–1774). Fangbing was a native of Anxi, located in the mountains outside Quanzhou city. He first went to Japan in 1693, where he served as the abbot of Fuji Monastery 福济寺 (Quanzhou Temple), which had been founded at the end of the Ming dynasty in 1628 by master Juehai 觉海, a monk from Quanzhou, and had been led by several monks from Quanzhou since then. He later served as the eleventh abbot of Uji's Mampuku-ji, from 1719 to 1725, and was a noted calligrapher. Zhengkun was a native of Quanzhou's district of Jinjiang and first went to Japan in 1722. After serving as abbot of Fuji Monastery, he became the fifteenth abbot of Mampuku-ji (1745 to 1748) and later the eighteenth abbot (1758 to 1765). He was especially noted for his painting of bamboo and his seal carving (Shen 1990, 84–86). Kaiyuan Monastery thus produced three patriarchs of Japan's Obaku or Huangbo school of Zen from the middle of the seventeenth century to the middle of the eighteenth century. This impressive accomplishment during this period in Chinese Buddhist history demonstrates a lingering vitality in both Quanzhou and Kaiyuan's ability to nurture eminent monks during the seventeenth and eighteenth centuries of the final imperial dynasty.

Contributing to the success of Kaiyuan Monastery during the first part of the Qing dynasty was the generally favorable attitude of Qing emperors to Buddhism and the ongoing support of the local gentry. The eighteenth century witnessed the regular maintenance of Kaiyuan.[58] In 1727, some forty years after its last rebuilding, the Donor's Ancestral Shrine was again in need of repair; repairs were carried out by members of the Nan'an Huang family.[59]

The early Qing vitality did not last. Kaiyuan's decline began in tandem with the social chaos that had begun to engulf South China as pirate raids grew increasingly more frequent and devastating from 1795 to 1810. Bai Yude 白玉德, the commander general (*zongdu* 总督) of Fujian and Zhejiang Provinces, was dispatched to Quanzhou in pursuit of pirates (Western bandits, *yangfei* 洋匪). On top of social and economic troubles, Quanzhou was then suffering a drought and the people were desperate for rain. It is recorded that Yude earnestly prayed for rain at Kaiyuan Monastery and that very night rain began to pour down, continuing the following day and ending a potentially devastating drought. Crops were rescued and the good harvest that followed saved the lives and livelihoods of thousands. Yude, having noticed that Kaiyuan's main hall was damaged and that many walls were crumbling, was moved to donate his own salary toward repairs and solicited others to contribute to the renovation project. Quanzhou's prefect and the people of Quanzhou contributed according to their means; full restoration of all the halls began in the spring of 1805 and were complete by the end of the summer. Yude made an inscription to commemorate this comprehensive restoration of Kaiyuan's buildings in 1805.[60]

As conditions throughout the Qing empire worsened, confrontations with European powers resulted in two Opium Wars (1839–1842 and 1856–1860) and discontent in South China exploded in the Taiping Rebellion (1851–1865). The Taiping Rebellion led by Hong Xiuquan 洪秀全 (1823–1901) has been described by Frederic Wakeman as "the world's most disastrous civil war," claiming between ten and twenty million lives (1966, 3). The turmoil wrought untold destruction on Buddhist monasteries and their libraries and cultural treasures. Devastation of monasteries was particularly widespread in South China, which had long been a stronghold of Buddhism.

Kaiyuan's monks like other male residents of Quanzhou are reported to have joined the anti-Qing-restore-Ming forces (*fanqing fuming duiwu*).[61] It was at this time that a female disciple of the monks named Miaoxiang 妙香 (c. 1803–1888) became abbot (*zhuchi*). She is reported to have been a local vegetarian auntie (*caigu*) who became a nun. Her name appears in an inscription on the name board above the entrance to the Hall of Ordination Platform.

The inscription states that she, serving as abbot, and her disciple Huilian 慧莲 completed restorations in 1870. It was under her leadership during this unstable period (c. 1851 to 1888) that the monastery was not only preserved but also renovated.[62]

Beyond the destructiveness of the Taiping Rebellion, Holmes Welch described the end of the Qing dynasty as marking the "end of an epoch for Chinese Buddhism" (1968, 11). Welch was referring to the seizure of Buddhist monasteries for use as schools carried out with limited enforcement after the 1898 edict of Emperor Guangxu 光绪 and reiterated by a 1904 government order to use available temple properties for the establishment of schools (Goossaert and Palmer 2011, 44–50; Welch 1968, 296–297). This was a shift from the general Qing policy of offering Buddhist monasteries protection; by the end of the Qing, the emperors had finally come under the influence of the literati, who had been calling for such re-outfitting since the early Qing, some two hundred and fifty years earlier.[63]

In the final decade of the Qing dynasty, one development was attested by local tradition, namely, the presence of two local schools of opera on site. Monks were involved with one of the groups and my informant said that some if not most of the monks involved in opera were "incense and flower" monks (*xianghua heshang*).[64] Such monks shave their heads and wear robes, but marry and have families. Regardless of the precise status of its inhabitants at this time, the monastery had ceased to train monks and was ripe for reform.

The Twentieth Century: From Promise to Chaos

By the early twentieth century, although Kaiyuan remained standing, its halls were empty and quiet. Reflecting on the state of the monastery during the late Qing, the Republican period (1911–1949) preface to the *Kaiyuan Gazetteer* laments,

> It is regrettable that since the time of Qianlong and Jiaqing 嘉庆 [1735–1820], sages and worthies [*shengxian* 圣贤] have not appeared and the monastic rules have loosened every day. Up to the current Republican period things have severely deteriorated [*boluo* 剥落] but an opportunity has arrived for the dharma to be revived.[65]

Kaiyuan's structures had survived the destructive force of the Taiping Rebellion, but the monastery fell into a state of neglect that left it effectively deserted at the beginning of the twentieth century. The desolate scene at Kaiyuan at the beginning of the twentieth century was repeated at monasteries throughout the region. After the dust of the Taiping Rebellion had settled, however, a generation of leaders emerged to rebuild monasteries and restock Buddhist libraries. The efforts of these leaders were largely focused in southeast China (Birnbaum 2003, 124–125).[66] At Kaiyuan, the restoration was led by two prominent monks of the era, Yuanying 圆瑛 (1878–1953) and Zhuandao 转道 (1872–1943). The dharma hall, which had last been repaired during the Ming dynasty and was in need of replacement, was rebuilt as a concrete two-story building with a second-floor sutra library (*zangjing ge* 藏经阁). The hall of merit (*gongde tang* 功德堂) was built at the same time as the dharma hall to which it practically adjoins. It was built to house the spirit tablets of the temple's past masters and lay patrons. Amid all of this activity in 1925, Kaiyuan's ancient mulberry tree was struck by lightning and split into three. A rock was placed under one section to support it; on this rock was carved "This tree bloomed lotus blossoms in the second year of Chuigong (686); this support, allied with the will of heaven, prevents damage."[67] These buildings and additions all remain part of the monastery today.

The most import development was the establishment of a school and orphanage under the leadership of Yuanying. Yuanying was from Fujian and served as abbot of several famous monasteries. He was an important reformer who responded to early twentieth-century threats to take over monasteries and convert them to schools by forming the Buddhist Association of China (Zhonghua fojiao hui 中華佛教會) with Taixu and others, a national organization that could represent Buddhist interests. Elected as its first president, he served seven terms in that role between 1929 and 1949 (Welch 1968, 41). Yuanying also established two Buddhist orphanages as a way to make Buddhism more responsive to the modern context. The first was the Ningbo Buddhist Orphanage in 1918; the second was at Kaiyuan Monastery in his home province of Fujian.[68] At both, students were taught literary and practical arts to prepare them to be educated and productive members of society. In the fall of 1924, Yuanying, Zhuandao, and Zhuanwu met in Quanzhou to make preparations for the orphanage.[69] Tradition holds that, three days after these monks had arrived at the monastery in lunar September of 1924, Kaiyuan's peach trees bloomed red lotus blossoms.[70] This legend has been memorialized by four large characters that now appear on the wall to the west of the main gate: "Lotus-Blooming Peach Tree Reflects the Auspicious" (Taolian yingrui 桃蓮映瑞). Offices and dormitories were constructed and the opening ceremony of the Kaiyuan school and orphanage was held on the day of the Mid-Autumn Festival, August 15 of the lunar calendar, in 1925. The charity was established out of a wish to benefit less fortunate children and was called the Compassion for Children School (Cieryuan 慈兒院).

With the construction of the school, the dharma hall, and the hall of merit, as well as the renovation of the two pagodas, Kaiyuan Monastery was officially restored and again one of the premier Buddhist monasteries in

Fujian, Yuanying serving as abbot. To mark this restoration, the Huang family, which had generously contributed to the effort, donated additional funds for recarving woodblocks of the Ming dynasty *Record of Quanzhou Kaiyuan Monastery*. In 1933, Zhuandao and Zhuanwu 转物 (fl. 1920–1940) invited Nanputuo 南普陀寺 abbot Zhuanfeng 转峰 (1879–1952) to serve as Kaiyuan's abbot. Zhuanfeng, who had established the Minnan Buddhist Seminary at Nanputuo in Xiamen where he then served as principal, accepted the offer.

Zhuanfeng led large ordination ceremonies at both Kaiyuan and Chengtian Monasteries in 1931 and 1936 (L. Yu 2005, 197).[71] The vitality expressed in these developments (holding ordinations, supporting a school and orphanage, renovating the complex, restoring monastic life) helped put Kaiyuan back on the map as a place of Buddhist practice in the south. In the 1930s, it attracted master Hongyi (弘一; 1880–1942), one of the most prominent Buddhist monks of the twentieth century. Known as a veritable renaissance man turned master of vinaya, he spent the last fourteen years of his life in southern Fujian between Xiamen, where he landed in 1928, and Quanzhou, where he passed away in 1942.[72] He found the warmer climate suited his health and the local population's enthusiasm for Buddhism created a receptive audience for his teaching (He 2005, 372–373).

Master Hongyi was invited to Kaiyuan Monastery by Zhuanwu in 1933 (L. Yu 2005, 310). This initial two-month visit was the first of many by master Hongyi. He would have been pleased to find Kaiyuan's Nanshan Vinaya ordination platform in an excellent state of repair. Perhaps it was this that inspired him to establish the School of the Nanshan Vinaya (Nanshanlu xueyuan 南山律学苑) at Kaiyuan in May of 1933 (He 2000, 11). The school was established in the rooms of the Venerated Site Cloister, where Hongyi stayed while at Kaiyuan (Chen and Su 2015). Hongyi gathered students and scholars and organized seminars on the Nanshan Vinaya using copies of the vinaya he had brought from Japan (H. Wang 2001a). These studies were published by Hongyi, a prolific writer of texts elucidating Buddhist teachings. Hongyi's focus on the Nanshan Vinaya and the establishment of this study institute at Kaiyuan were remarkable developments in Chinese Buddhism, which had not seen such sustained interest in the vinaya for centuries.[73]

From Quanzhou, Hongyi returned to Xiamen Nanputuo, where he gave lectures and in 1934 opened the Minnan Cultivating Buddhist Standards Academy 闽南佛教养正院, which served as a kind of sister academy of basic studies for monks not attending the more academically oriented Minnan Buddhist Academy 闽南佛学院, also located at Nanputuo (He 2005, 377–378).[74] At Kaiyuan in 1935, Hongyi helped with Buddhist education in the Compassion for Children School (Chen and Su 2015). In demand and always on the move, giving teachings all over the region, Hongyi returned to Quanzhou in 1937, accompanied by venerable Miaolian 妙莲 (1913–1999), a native of Shanghai, who traveled with Hongyi as his personal attendant and never left his side.[75] In Quanzhou, Hongyi divided much of his time between Kaiyuan and Chengtian Monasteries. His time in Quanzhou has left its mark on Fujian Buddhism and a powerful impression on those who met him. Miaolian became his close friend and confidant and at the end of his life Hongyi would entrust him with his affairs: "At the time of my death and afterwards my person and effects, I leave in the hands of Miaolian. No one else is to interfere."[76] On lunar September 1 in 1942, three days before his death, Hongyi wrote his final four characters, "sorrow and joy mixed" (*beixin jiaoji* 悲欣交集), and handed them to Miaolian. Hongyi passed away at the age of sixty-three at the Quanzhou Wenling Old Folks Home 泉州温陵养老院 on September 4, 1942. His remains were cremated at Chengtian Monastery and distributed between two major relic stupas in Quanzhou.[77] Miaolian remained at Kaiyuan, where he eventually became abbot and established a Master Hongyi Memorial Hall to display Hongyi's personal effects, calligraphy, memorabilia, and photographs. Hongyi's calligraphy of lines attributed to Zhuxi, describing southern Fujian as a "Buddhist kingdom" (*foguo*) hang in Kaiyuan's main gate and main hall. The collection of Hongyi's belongings remains on display in the Hongyi Memorial Hall in the east of the monastery grounds.

The Disruptions of War

Had the times been different, perhaps a dramatic revival of Kaiyuan Monastery may have developed under the influence of the charismatic renaissance man and Buddhist master Hongyi or the inspired leadership of masters Yuanying, Zhuandao, Zhuanwu, and Zhuanfeng. As it was, however, decades of turmoil lay ahead and any lasting revival would be postponed indefinitely. My sources indicate that about thirty monks were at Kaiyuan during the war with Japan. Three bombs were apparently dropped on the monastery at the time but only one exploded, spreading shrapnel that caused one of the columns of the dharma hall to shift from its base and left several pockmarks on three of the columns. Whatever damage sustained was repaired in the early 1950s and does not appear to have been particularly serious.[78] Graffiti inside the west pagoda attests to the presence of soldiers at Kaiyuan at the time. Life at the monastery was disturbed, but it was never abandoned.[79]

Venerable Guangjing 广净 (d. 1998) was a native of Xianyou in Fujian and spent time at Xuefeng Monastery in the 1930s.[80] After the war with Japan, he served as the general manager (*jianyuan*) of Kaiyuan from 1950 to 1954. Guangyi 广义 served as Kaiyuan's general manager for eight years. After the Communist victory, Guangjing and Guangyi fled to Southeast Asia, according to an unverifiable local tradition, after being advised to do so by Chan master Xuyun (虚云 1840–1959). The two dharma brothers fled to

Hong Kong and then to Singapore.[81] One of their dharma brothers from Nan'an Xuefeng Monastery, Guang'an 广安 (1923–1996) remained at Kaiyuan throughout the Maoist period.

The Maoist Period

With the Communist victory and the establishment of the People's Republic of China (PRC) in 1949, atheism became the state-sponsored ideology and policies were implemented to restrict religious practice and religious propagation. In 1951, the Religious Affairs Bureau, or RAB (Zongjiao shiwu ju 宗教事务局) was established in Beijing. Its purview was to enforce state religious policy, which effectively meant monitoring and controlling religious groups: no religious group could be formed, no religious text published, no religious figure appointed to office without its permission.[82] The Buddhist Association of China, or BAC (Zhongguo fojiao xiehui 中国佛教协会) was established in 1953 to serve as an intermediary between the Religious Affairs Bureau and Buddhists and assist in the implementation of state religious policy. This association was different in purpose from the early ones established during the Republican period by monks to protect the interests of monks and monasteries. The Communist period BAC, on the other hand, was established by the state to promote the state's socialist agenda (Goossaert and Palmer 2011, 153–160).[83] The same year the BAC was formed in Beijing, a branch office was established at Kaiyuan Monastery, the Jinjiang Buddhist Association (Jinjiang fojiao xiehui).[84]

The effect of the new policies on religion during the 1950s was nothing short of the decimation of the Chinese sangha.[85] The major sources of income for monasteries had been income from the properties they owned, donations from the wealthy, and income from rituals. By 1960, all of these sources of income had effectively disappeared in the wake of state-orchestrated action. The Land Reform Act of 1950 called for the confiscation of lands held by Buddhist monasteries as well as Daoist and Confucian temples to be redistributed (Welch 1961, 2; Goossaert and Palmer 2011, 160).[86] The government took over the farms and their associated houses—which Yuanying, Zhuandao, and Zhuanwu had purchased and were being used to fund the operation of Kaiyuan's orphanage and school. Kaiyuan's monks met with a set of pressures that caused their already small numbers to fall, as did the number of monks across the country. The monk population declined, but Kaiyuan was never fully abandoned and Miaolian was named abbot in 1953 (Zhou 1999, 43).[87] During the 1950s and early 1960s, crops were grown in small plots around the monastery. Perhaps as many as twenty to thirty monks tended the monastic plots, which were separate from the plots of the school and orphanage.[88] Apart from tending their own plots, monks were also sent to work outside the monastery:

Guang'an was sent to feed pigs at Chengtian Monastery; others collected firewood or went to the coast to collect and dry salt.[89]

The Curatorial Turn

Although Kaiyuan Monastery's identity as a home of monks and a place of religious practice and devotion was radically undermined by Communist policies in the 1950s and early 1960s, another identity was systematically encouraged, that of a site of historical and cultural relics. I call this the Maoist period curatorial turn, which has continued in the post-Mao period. Traditional sources of monastic income were severely restricted or eliminated by Communist policy, but the state-sponsored preservation and restoration of monasteries, pagodas, and Buddhist caves of historic and cultural value was undertaken with a zeal not seen for generations (Goossaert and Palmer 2011, 159). Between 1951 and 1958, dozens of monasteries and pagodas, including Kaiyuan, were repaired with state funds.[90] "In all over a hundred odd monasteries and pagodas in China were repaired," Welch reports, "mostly between 1951 and 1958" (1972, 150). The temples restored included the Lama Temple (Yonghe gong 雍和宫) in Beijing, Lingyin Temple in Hangzhou (restored for $200,000), Xuanzhong Temple in Shanxi (home of Japanese Pure Land, restored for $110,000 from 1954 to 1956), Xuanzang's Dayan pagoda in Xi'an (restored for $20,000) and Mount Wutai temples ($400,000 spent between 1951 and 1959).[91] These monasteries and others, such as Xiyuan Temple 西园寺 in Suzhou, were allowed to retain a small population of monks who had been politically educated and were well informed about state religious policy; in addition, they typically housed branch offices of the BAC, such as at Kaiyuan.

Why did the government take such an interest in Buddhist historical monuments and allow some of them to retain small groups of monks? Reports of the day described the protection and restoration of Buddhist sites as an effort to protect the "people's art" (D. Yu 1971, 55). Created by human toil, they deserved preservation as a display of national and cultural pride and evidence of the feudal past through which China had passed on its way to the enlightened future.[92] In the 1950s, this development may be seen as part of a movement to create museums to memorialize artifacts and events of national pride and document the progress of the revolution. It was part of the project of nation-building that included circumscribing religion in a particular way, namely, as a phenomenon of the past. Another important role in preservation of model monasteries tended by monks or nuns was to use them as a showcase to foreign visitors, especially those from Buddhist cultures (Goossaert and Palmer 2011, 159; Keily 2016, 241).

Kaiyuan Monastery is a typical example of the forced curatorial turn in Maoist-era Chinese Buddhism. In 1952, it received ¥30,000 of state funds for restoration and preservation work; Xiamen's Nanputuo Monastery, by comparison, received ¥1,000 the same year (Welch 1972, 425). Kaiyuan had suffered neglect during war with Japan and its major halls were restored with this money. Some of these funds were used to carry out minor repairs on the east and west pagodas and the building of low stone fencing around them.[93] The receipt of these funds, the restoration work managed by the state rather than the monastery, and the establishment of the Quanzhou Heritage Management Committee (Wenwu guanli weiyuan hui 文物管理委员会) in the early 1950s officially marked Kaiyuan Monastery's curatorial turn.[94] The Heritage Management Committee was charged with the study and protection of Kaiyuan's cultural relics. Members of the institute produced minor studies and reports on the temple's history in their effort to catalog its historical relics. Between 1958 and 1960, the heritage management committee oversaw a number of what would now be called visitor experience improvements, such as the painting of the main hall and main gate, the rebuilding of Kaiyuan's worshipping pavilion (*baiting*) adjoining the main gate, repairing the corridors stretching along the main courtyard, and improved landscaping around the pagodas.[95]

In 1961, Quanzhou Kaiyuan was designated a Provincial Level Protected Heritage Site (Shengji wenwu baohu danwei 省级文物保护单位) by the Fujian provincial government. This designation was made in response to a directive issued by the State Council in 1961 titled "On Working to Strengthen Cultural Heritage Protection Management" 关于进一步加强文物保护管理工作. It was this provincial designation that Mayor Wang used to protect Kaiyuan from Red Guards five years later. As late as 1962, local bureaucracies and cultural agencies were funded and functioning. The Quanzhou Heritage Management Committee published a detailed report on the temple's many properties of cultural heritage titled *Fujian's Quanzhou Kaiyuan Temple* (福建泉州开元寺), reflecting research undertaken by the Fujian Provincial Cultural Management Association Work Group (Fujiansheng wenguanhui gongzuo zu 福建省文管会工作组) and supported by the Quanzhou Heritage Management Committee, the Jinjiang Special Commission Bureau of Culture (Jinjiang zhuanshu wenhua ju 晋江专署文化局) and the Quanzhou Maritime Museum (Haijiao guan 海交馆).[96] The book functioned as a report on the history and cultural artifacts of the monastery but included no material about the living religious traditions, reflecting the state's interest in cultural preservation and material history.

It was during this period that Kaiyuan Monastery took on a new role as a preserve of not only its own cultural properties, but also the cultural heritage of the city of Quanzhou. In 1953, a *dhāraṇi* pillar dating from 854 was moved to Kaiyuan, where it had been found under the drawbridge of Quanzhou's old western gate (Lin Zhao 1959, 45). This is the first known modern instance of an off-site relic being moved to Kaiyuan to protect it, display it, and at the same time enhance the property of the monastery as a preserve of cultural heritage. These instances would continue and multiply as the years passed and Kaiyuan became established as a trove of historic artifacts from the city of Quanzhou. The Quanzhou Heritage Management Committee, located on the premises of the monastery, had jurisdiction over such items and facilitated their transfer to the monastic grounds, where they could protect and study them. Many cultural properties from other temples in Quanzhou were moved to Kaiyuan during this period.[97] Historical artifacts continued to be moved into the early 1970s, including a huge Song dynasty boat and a decorative screen from the temple of the city god.

Concentrating the cultural properties of the city in this one location was a way to centralize management of what began to be valued as items of cultural heritage. Large temples, whether Buddhist, Confucian, or otherwise, were centers of such cultural properties and were naturally selected as the venues to collect, study, and display China's imperial heritage. The old Confucian temple of Xi'an, for example, had begun to collect stone stele inscriptions during the Song dynasty and today has added buildings for the display of statuary and other antiquities so that it is now one of the important museums in Xi'an and is known as the forest of steles (*beilin* 碑林). Another that began to accumulate treasures from the surrounding city during the Maoist period is Shijiazhuang's 石家庄 Longxing Temple 隆兴寺 in Hebei.[98] Dozens of stone and metal statues and dozens of stone steles are now on display for visitors.

The development of temples as cultural showcases was an early part of Communist China's diplomatic strategy. As Welch notes, "By 1958 there was at least one monastic showplace in every major city on the tourist route; and monasteries elsewhere were repaired if they had significance abroad" (1972, 147). Quanzhou was not on the standard tourist route but had a remarkable pair of stone pagodas and was connected to foreign communities in Southeast Asia (through the Republican period efforts of Zhuandao and Yuanying), Japan (through the Obaku school), and even South India (through the Hindu sculptures incorporated into the back of the main hall). Just as it had survived previous campaigns to limit, restrict, or scale back the Sangha, it survived the early years of the People's Republic that devastated countless monasteries across the country. Chengtian, Quanzhou's next most prominent monastery, by contrast, became a huge pigsty: more than five hundred pigs were raised there from 1961 to 1964.[99] The support that Kaiyuan received during the first decade of the Maoist period was directly connected to its value as a site of historic and cultural treasures.

Although it received state funds to restore, catalog, and study its cultural properties, it also remained the home of a handful of Buddhist monks who served in the office of the municipal branch of the BAC and tended the halls. Among the monks who remained at Kaiyuan during the Maoist period were Guang'an and master Hongyi's attendant, Miaolian. In 1955, Guang'an planted two bodhi trees behind the main hall.[100] These trees remain today and are yet another feature for visitors to admire.[101]

In 1963, venerable Yuanzhou 圆拙 (1909–1997), who split his time between Putian's Guanghua Monastery, Chengtian Monastery, and Kaiyuan, was invited to assist Miaolian with the organizing of the Master Hongyi Memorial Hall.[102] Under the Maoist period curatorial turn, Kaiyuan was not allowed to develop its potential as a training ground for monks, but was allowed to improve the grounds and buildings, open a museum to display artifacts associated with master Hongyi, and serve as a showpiece for the history of southern Fujian. This is a role that Kaiyuan has maintained and was a status that helped it to survive the Cultural Revolution.

At the end of the 1950s, observers of China had begun to question the future viability of Buddhism. Arthur Wright writes in *Buddhism in Chinese History,* "We are seeing, I believe, the last twilight of Chinese Buddhism as an organized religion. The dispersed fragments of its cults and beliefs are beings systematically extirpated throughout the whole of society. . . . If, in the years to come, we look for the legacy of Buddhism in China, we shall perhaps find it still in literature and language, in drama and the arts" (1959, 122). When the Cultural Revolution was launched, Wright's predictions seemed prescient.

The Cultural Revolution

With launching of the Cultural Revolution in August of 1966, outward displays and practice of religion were forbidden and attacked in an effort to cleanse society of backward traditions. Most of Quanzhou's monasteries were severely damaged or destroyed during the Cultural Revolution; Kaiyuan was the only major one to have survived with its physical structures relatively unscathed.[103] In local literature and popular opinion, Kaiyuan, Chengtian, and Chongfu are Quanzhou's three most important Buddhist monasteries (*san da fosi* 三大佛寺). Of these three, only Kaiyuan retains a full array of monastic buildings. As related in the introduction, Kaiyuan, like other places of worship in Fujian and throughout China, was threatened by a mob of Red Guards as the Cultural Revolution swept across China in the fall of 1966. Miaolian barred the doors to Kaiyuan's dharma hall and sutra library, which held innumerable cultural treasures. When Red Guards approached the hall concerned residents in the neighborhood alerted Quanzhou's Mayor Wang Jinsheng.

In a story known throughout Quanzhou, Mayor Wang rushed to the scene and confronted the growing mob of Red Guards, explaining the 1961 provincial designation of Kaiyuan as a site of protected cultural heritage and offering to telephone Zhou Enlai.[104] This was the legal appeal. He also reached out to the civic pride of the youths, declaring, "Without the east and west pagodas, there is no Quanzhou."[105] Wang so succeeded in convincing the mob to abandon their destructive plans that several Red Guards who had heard his plea turned to other youths as they arrived and explained Kaiyuan's protected status to them. In the end, the mob turned away and Kaiyuan's many historic properties were left unharmed.

The monastery, then, was largely spared physical vandalism, though gold is said to have been removed from the gilded statues. The pagodas, statues, and major buildings remained unharmed. It was during the "Ten Year Disaster" (from 1966 to 1976), however, that Kaiyuan ceased to exist as a functioning monastery. Chongfu Monastery was made into a medicine factory and Chengtian Monastery into a cloth factory. As for Kaiyuan, religious activities were prohibited, monks laicized, statues covered, and the monastery was renamed the People's Market (Renmin shangchang 人民商场). It was the busiest place in the city—devotional activity ceased and commercial exchanges ensued. Food, clothes, and all necessities were on sale throughout the grounds, corridors, and halls. The ways of the monk were replaced by the ways of the butcher, the tailor, the barber, and the vegetable hawker. The pagodas, halls, and images may have remained but none of them were allowed to function as they had. Incense was supplanted by cigarette smoke. Prostrations, chanting, prayers were replaced with the banter of buying and selling. Instead of the ritual release of life was the butchering of life.[106]

Most of the people old enough to remember the Cultural Revolution are not eager to talk about Kaiyuan during that period. Those who identify themselves as Buddhists look back at the period as one of heartbreak. A prominent vegetarian auntie (*caigu* 菜姑) who was a disciple of Hongyi said she refused to visit the monastery when it was a market; she could not bear to see it desecrated much less contribute to its desecration.[107] Some who were less emotional or guarded described their visits during the Cultural Revolution: "I went there to shop, eat, get my hair cut, and buy clothes and shoes. There were many shops. You were given a small slip of paper and paid for goods or services at a central office."[108] Informants recalled that the statues in the main hall were covered with large drapes and that shoes, clothing, and fabrics were for sale where worshippers now chant and circumambulate. Along the two corridors that flank the main courtyard and main hall one could purchase farming implements, dried foods, prepared foods such as noodles and dumplings or get a haircut.

A Coterie of Monks

Although the monastery had ceased to function as such, its physical plant remained largely intact and its abbot, Miaolian, remained living on the grounds along with a coterie of nine other "laicized" monks. Miaolian, like other monks in China, was forced to renounce monastic life, grow out his hair, and take a wife. Together with a laicized nun, Yuanying 元英, he lived in the sutra library, which is completely surrounded by a large balcony, where he is said to have raised chickens to keep from starving.[109] Ten or eleven other monastics also remained living discreetly at Kaiyuan Monastery throughout the Cultural Revolution.[110] In addition to master Guang'an and the nun Yuanying, were Yuanzhuo 圆拙 (d. 1997), Shanjie 善戒 (d. 2007), Chuanxi 传锡 (d. 2005), Daoyang 道养 (d. 1983?), Daojing 道敬 (d. 2008), Miaodian 妙典 (d. 1984), Chuanzhong 传种 (d. 1989), and Shanyuan 善源 (d. 1983).[111]

A layperson named Wen Meng 文孟 is said to have assisted the monks by preparing meals and helping generally when needed, bringing the number of religiously oriented residents to twelve or thirteen. I have gathered twelve names, but thirteen is the number in the 2003 memoirs of Chuanxi. It is also quite possible that Chuanxi is referring to thirteen monastics and not counting layperson Wen Meng, which would bring the total to fourteen residents.

These monks were partially supported during this period by funds from Singaporean laypersons deposited in China during the Republican period to serve as "ten thousand years of food to support the way" (*wannian daoliang* 万年道粮).[112] Chuanxi writes that they grew winter melon, sweet potatoes, longan 龙眼, bananas, and other fruits and vegetables all year-round, enough to sell some in order to purchase rice (2004). Lin Hanzong notes that pumpkin and kongxin (a vegetable) 空心菜 were grown (2004). Chen recalled in an interview that kongxin and papaya were the best foods available from the Kaiyuan market at the time. He added that the monks would make the vegetables extra salty and pickled so no one would eat much.

Whereas Miaolian and his wife lived in the sutra library, the other clergy and Wen Bing lived in the five rooms of the Venerated Site Cloister and in the six rooms of the old guest hall (*lao ketang* 老客堂).[113] The Venerated Site Cloister had been maintained in one form or another since the founding of the temple in the Tang dynasty, when it served as the living quarters for founding abbot Kuanghu. There was something befitting and promising that in the darkest hours of the Cultural Revolution, when some were surmising the end of Chinese religion, monks inhabited Kaiyuan's Venerated Site Cloister, waiting for the chaos to end.

One of my informants, a Quanzhou local and devout lay Buddhist, said that Quanzhou Buddhists continued to worship in secret during the Cultural Revolution. "Could you find incense?" I asked. "Yes," I was told in response to this and similar questions about worship, such as the presentation of offerings or the making of prostrations. As I doggedly pursued this line of questioning, it emerged that, at least in Quanzhou, a tradition of religious devotion had survived, in secret, not only in the hearts but also in the day-to-day lives of at least a few devout individuals and families throughout the Maoist era, including monks remaining on the grounds of Kaiyuan Monastery.

I later determined that Holmes Welch had also learned of Kaiyuan's band of monks from an overseas informant in 1969. That year, Welch carefully wrote that

> In one large city on the south-east coast a famous old monastery continues to operate. There are 14 monks left (compared to 19 before the Cultural Revolution). They wear lay clothes and work on a nearby commune, but they eat vegetarian food. The great shrine-hall is locked and no one can enter to burn incense, but the other buildings are open. The monastery as a community of monks is still in being. (1969, 135)

This "famous old monastery" is none other than Quanzhou Kaiyuan. This identification can be affirmed by cross-referencing an appendix in Welch's 1972 account of Buddhism under Mao, which lists the names of thirty-one temples and their population of monks over time. After the start of the Cultural Revolution, only one temple with any monastics listed remains, and that is Quanzhou Kaiyuan with fourteen monks in 1969; the fourteen must be the same as those he mentioned in his 1969 article. The appendix further suggests that Kaiyuan was the sole exception to the rule among famous urban monasteries. The appendix lists the names of temples, cities, and holy mountains along with the number of monastics said to have been in residence in a given year from the 1930s onward. Of all the temples (thirty-one in number), mountains, and cities listed, only one records a monastic population of any size after 1965, and that is Quanzhou Kaiyuan's fourteen.[114] Despite the slight discrepancy between the twelve or thirteen monastics and one layperson of my research and the fourteen monastics provided by Welch's informants, a plausible solution is to read Chuanxi as recording thirteen monastics and add to this the layperson Wen Meng, bringing the number of residents to fourteen. In either case, both accounts agree that between thirteen to fourteen self-identifying Buddhists remained in residence three years into the Cultural Revolution. More fieldwork is needed to determine how many monastics persisted to maintain a discrete monastic identity during the period, but my research, supported by Welch, has determined this to be the case at Kaiyuan.[115]

Life for Kaiyuan's small band of determined monks was not without added hardships. During the Cultural Revolution, monks were not only not allowed to wear their robes, shave their heads, chant, burn incense, or prostrate, but also were regularly taken out and forced to kneel in public wearing humiliating placards or paraded around wearing pointed dunce caps. They were required to work during the day and to study, in the presence of a cadre, Chairman Mao's thought in the evening. Although they did not call one another by their full dharma names, according to Chuanxi, they used their monastic names disguised as secular names using the prefix "Old" as in "old Xi" for Chuanxi or "old An" for Guang'an (2004). Guang'an was forced to tend pigs kept at the site of Chengtian Monastery, which had been destroyed. Other monks collected sea salt or firewood in addition to tending the fields planted with fruits and vegetables around Kaiyuan. These monks maintained a religiously defined existence in the face of immense pressures, threats, and humiliation. Guang'an, who had studied at various Buddhist seminaries, remained a respected interlocutor among the educated of the neighborhood throughout the Cultural Revolution (Daoyuan and Chuanmin 2004). History has not yet recorded their collective courage and commitment—this account is a first step toward rescuing the narrative of Chinese Buddhist history during the Maoist period.

I have received both a detailed account about Guang'an from one of his personal acquaintances and a memorial booklet. Relating this material will provide more texture to this account of life under Mao. Guang'an was from a small village outside Quanzhou and was abducted at a young age by soldiers to fight in the civil war. Because he was the only boy in his family, his parents sold his sister in order to buy him back. He went on to become a monk and remained a dedicated monk committed to Buddhism for the remainder of his life. When his dharma brothers left for Southeast Asia, he remained behind at Kaiyuan and became a victim of the Cultural Revolution. He was labeled a bad element (*huai fenzi* 坏分子) and a rightist (*youpai* 右派) and occasionally paraded around by Red Guards wearing a dunce cap on his head or a humiliating placard around his neck.[116] He was required to stay at Kaiyuan, where he made a living by raising goats for milk and small birds, including parrots, which he could exchange or sell for necessities. When the Cultural Revolution ended, he "took off his [dunce] cap" and was put to work in a shop selling tea.[117] His story spans several periods and the denouement awaits our account of the post-Mao revival Kaiyuan, which follows.

In 1974, the same year that the Song dynasty boat was transferred to Kaiyuan, two other large historic objects were also moved from other parts of the city. The first was an elaborately decorated wall built in 1795 known as the Qilin Wall 麒麟壁, featuring the Qilin 麒麟 or Kylin (J. *Kirin*), a mythological being sometime referred to as a Chinese unicorn; it was moved from its place in front of the old City God Temple to Kaiyuan by the Heritage Management Committee.[118] The other object was a gate known as the *ling* star gate (*lingxing men* 棂星门) from Quanzhou's Confucian temple (*wenmiao* 文庙), which was transferred to the front of Small Kaiyuan Temple along with four dragon columns from the Xuanmiao Daoist temple 玄妙观.

Eight cannon from the Ming and Qing dynasties were placed outside Kaiyuan's front gate, among them one from 1624 (Ming) and another from 1842 (Qing).[119] Perhaps the most unusual item transferred to the monastery during the Maoist period was an unusual stone, originally located at Chengtian Monastery, featuring an image strongly resembling a Chinese style painting of a branch of plum blossoms. During the Cultural Revolution, it was broken into two pieces in an attempt to reveal that the auspicious image was merely a dye fabrication; the strange coloration, however, was found to exist into the depths of the stone. Devotees brought the broken stone to Kaiyuan and, putting it back together, placed it below the ancient mulberry tree for protection.[120]

During the Cultural Revolution, Kaiyuan was more than a market. The municipal Heritage Management Association remained operational, maintaining offices and dorms on the grounds of Kaiyuan and continuing to collect and oversee the protection of the monastery and the other properties brought there from locations around Quanzhou. The Kaiyuan shop sold rubbings made from the many steles collected.[121] Like Hebei's Longxing Temple, which similarly collected all the steles, statues, and other artifacts that had escaped the first waves of destruction, Kaiyuan became a site where any historic items might be placed for protection. The curatorial turn, then, for Kaiyuan Monastery was a consistent Maoist period development spanning the early years of the People's Republic and continuing through the death of Mao and beyond.

Most accounts of twentieth-century Chinese Buddhism cover the promising developments of the early twentieth century then decry the intrusions by the state in the 1950s, leading to the decimation of the sangha and destruction of temples during the Cultural Revolution. If this is not the end of the story in those accounts, the story is continued in overseas Chinese communities, Taiwan, or Hong Kong, where many mainland monks fled after the Communist victory.[122] When I began to discover that temples and clerics and traditions had not only been revived in mainland China but also survived into the 1990s and beyond, I was surprised. The research presented in this chapter and the next reveals a continuous narrative in the life of Kaiyuan from the Republican period onward. Although Kaiyuan's activities were upended during the Cultural Revolution, the dozen or so monastics who remained on site protected property and maintained a monastic presence. Meanwhile, other monks, such as Guangjing, remained active abroad and would come to Kaiyuan's aid in the late 1980s using the funding networks established in the 1920s and 1930s. The story of the tenacity of these monks is continued in chapter 2.

The Overview: Historic Patterns in Review

This chapter has taken us through more than twelve hundred years of Kaiyuan Monastery's long and distinguished history from its founding in the Tang dynasty to its survival under Mao. We have surveyed the stream of eminent monks who have graced its halls. We have witnessed an energetic building program that has continually maintained the core buildings of the monastery and has added stronger and taller structures over the centuries. We have noted the expansion of the monastery to a sprawling campus of 120 neighboring cloisters and the contraction of the monastery to its central axis and a handful of other structures. We have seen the monastery destroyed by fire, occupied by commoners, and abandoned by monks. But destruction, occupation, or abandonment never lasted; Kaiyuan has always recovered, rebuilt, and restored a measure of its past greatness. Such longevity is common enough in China, but it is not the norm. Many monasteries, especially smaller temples, have perished at one historical juncture or another, never to recover as a living place of religious practice. The fifteenth-century *Annals of Fujian* (*Bamin tongzhi*) enumerates more than five thousand temples, monasteries, cloisters, convents, and shrines across Fujian. Among these sites are 1,928 Buddhist monasteries (*si* 寺).[123] Today only a fraction of this number remain, but they include the most famous monasteries.

Examining the contours of Kaiyuan's history, we note patterns of rise and fall in which the state and elites play an important role. More specifically we may note three interrelated patterns that operate throughout Kaiyuan's history: patronage by elites, the regulatory and interventionist state, and modulations in material culture. These patterns provide a helpful index to the fate of monastic institutions in Chinese history as well as insight into the nature of institutional religion.

Just as the state and political elites could be a source of support and patronage of Kaiyuan, they also could restrict, control, and even dismantle the sangha and its monastic properties. A look at Chinese history suggests that state regulation of and interference in religious matters has been a constant characteristic of church-state relations in China (A. Yu 2005).[124] Certainly, state involvement in the affairs of Kaiyuan has remained a constant since its founding in 686.[125] We have reviewed the state's supportive role as a patron, but the pendulum swings both ways. The state has also been, at times, a force of discipline, contraction, and suppression. History has demonstrated, however, that Kaiyuan as Quanzhou's largest and most prominent monastery has been spared during the most severe periods of state-orchestrated suppression, such as the Tang Huichang Persecution of 845, the prohibitions of the Ming dynasty, and even the Cultural Revolution. Kaiyuan experienced its first severe state-orchestrated contraction under the Yuan dynasty with the abolition of 117 cloisters. Ming policies led to two periods of restoration, but between these periods Kaiyuan declined to a miserable condition in which it lost most of its income-producing lands (most of which were never recovered), and its population of monks teetered on the verge of collapse. This mid-Ming dynasty collapse offers parallels to the situation of Kaiyuan during the Republican and Maoist periods in terms of loss of lands, widespread laicization, and occupation of monastic property.

André Laliberté and Stefania Travagnin identify the question of the revival and decline of Buddhism in modern China as a key topic of recent scholarship in China and abroad (2019). In particular, they raise a question around the accuracy of the binary decline (*shuailuo* 衰落) and revival (*fuxing* 复兴). In his study of the rise and fall of Chan Buddhism in the seventeenth century, Jiang Wu describes a cyclical pattern of growth and decline, but argues that using such terms tends to be distorting and fosters attention on "revival" at the expense of "decline" (2008). He also argues that the terms are used to designate "two different modes of existence," one a temporary movement, the other a more enduring state-sponsored local institution (279). With respect to the early twentieth century, the late Ming, and the early Qing, these were indeed temporary movements deserving the title "revival," understood as a period in line with sociocultural and political currents that lead to revitalization. The Song dynasty, however, was a time of steady growth and proliferation of cloisters that indicates flourishing conditions, which inspired the couplet referring to a Buddhist kingdom full of sages. The productivity of the cloisters in training, scholars, engineers, fundraisers, and contemplatives was a peak unlikely to be recaptured. The current post-Mao situation, however, is no such flourishing or revitalization, at least not yet. Instead it is much the same as Kaiyuan's early Ming and late Qing periods of restoration, namely, restoring, rebuilding, and renovating (*xiufu* 修复/*chongxiu* 重修).

The material examined here also agrees with Jiang Wu's study of seventeenth-century Chan revival material on a related point, namely that the key impetus for revival or decline is from external factors (2008, 281–285). I find that the biggest factors contributing to growth and decline are external factors in society (gentry, literati elites) and politics (government support or suppression), but that internal factors under direct control of monastics such as talent or ambition also play a role, sometimes directly attracting support or protection. Throughout its history, Kaiyuan has relied on funding and patronage from the social and political elite; it was their offering of support or withdrawal of support that led to periods of growth, maintenance, or decline.[126] This chapter thus provides support for what Timothy Brook (1997) and Holmes Welch document and what Welch terms "the unending contradiction between the desires to suppress and to support" (1968, 134). The two documented periods of gentry or state suppression of Chinese Buddhism are the 1380s (Brook 2005, 150; 1997) and 1950s (Welch 1972). Both were periods of loss of support at Kaiyuan, supporting the view that external factors are most important in the rise and fall of monastic fortunes.

This historical overview provides crucial contextualization for both the Cultural Revolution and the present restoration. In short, neither are unprecedented in China's history and recognizing the type of church-state relationships that have operated throughout Kaiyuan's history and throughout Chinese history is important to bear in mind. The PRC has consistently reaffirmed its commitment to state regulation of religious affairs. Such commitment is directly at odds with the liberal principle of separation between church and state, which despite its being a pillar of modern secular states is simply not embraced by China and various other states. If we are to understand religion in China, or anywhere, we must abandon or bracket a whole host of presuppositions, first among which is the assumption that religions [ever] operate without state interference. Letting go of this will enable us to see how relationships between actors are built, modified, resisted, and subverted and, consequently, how power is [always] shared. How this applies to Kaiyuan's revival and current status is the subject of both chapter 2 and chapter 7, respectively.

The material culture of Kaiyuan Monastery has evolved over time, reflecting periods of expansion and contraction, doctrinal priorities, and political shifts. Good examples of such material shifts are the two stages in Kaiyuan's evolution as a Chan monastery. During the first, which began at the end of the eleventh century, several cloisters became affiliated with the Chan school. After the Yuan consolidation is the second stage, the ascension of Miao'en and the construction of the two most telltale structures of a functioning Chan monastery. These structures are a Chan hall and a hall of patriarchs, which express in material culture what are arguably the two most salient features of the Chan school—meditation and lineage.

Other elements of material culture manifest historical trends, such as building the revolving sutra cabinet during the Song dynasty when such items became popular merit-making machines, a feature that suggests a desire to attract more devotees. The rebuilding of the ordination platform according to the specifications of the Nanshan Vinaya in the twelfth century evinces a trend within the vinaya school at that time as well as a concern with getting ordinations right to ensure their efficacy. These examples suggest the potential value of tending to material culture as a key conveyer and enabler of religious meaning, significance, and trends. A multipronged analysis of these material dimensions of religious space is the subject of part three of this book. Readers most interested in the dynamic production of space through spatio-material relations with religious and political actors may turn directly to part 3. All other readers should continue reading to gain insight into the path of post-Mao recovery and the nature of religious practice.

In addition to tracing the diachronic development of material culture, which manifests the agency of monks in shaping new frameworks for religious practice, this chapter has identified broad patterns of decline and renewal in Kaiyuan Monastery's history and the key role played by elites and the state as external factors. The following chapter continues Kaiyuan's story by examining the post-Mao restoration.

2

The Post-Mao Revival

Stages of Recovery

KAIYUAN'S POST-MAO RECOVERY PROVIDES A WINDOW ON the first three decades of the unprecedented revival of Buddhism in post-Mao China. It is a narrative that has only begun to be revealed in book chapters and articles, none of which reconstruct the chronology of revival with the kind of ethnographic detail provided here. The restoration, which began soon after the death of Mao in 1976, received its initial spark from a small coterie of monks who had remained at the monastery throughout the Cultural Revolution. Further restoration was facilitated by contact with Fujian monks who had migrated to Southeast Asia before the Cultural Revolution along paths blazed by monks such as Zhuandao.

Kaiyuan's post-Mao recovery is examined in three stages: 1976 to 1988 (laying the groundwork), 1989 to 1999 (full renovation), and 2000 to 2019 (the Daoyuan era). The first stage saw the return of monastic leadership and public worship at the monastery after a decade-long hiatus and an important visit by Zhao Puchu, president of the Buddhist Association of China (BAC), who helped lay the groundwork for Kaiyuan's recovery. The second stage saw the full-scale renovation of Kaiyuan's buildings with Singapore funds capped by a visit from then President Jiang Zemin, which unequivocally affirmed Kaiyuan's revival as a site of nationally recognized cultural heritage and religious practice. The third stage spans the first two decades of Daoyuan's tenure as abbot, increasing prosperity, the recovery of property, and continual physical enhancements. During the first two stages, from 1976 to 1999, the revival of transnational networks linking Quanzhou and southern

Fujian with Southeast Asia and funding by overseas Chinese was an important factor. The data presented here support similar observations made by scholars regarding the funding of the religious revival in southeast China (see, for example, Dean 2010, 1998; Ashiwa and Wank 2006), and taken with that provided by Yoshiko Ashiwa (2000) provides a fuller picture of the transnational clerical networks in Minnan supporting the restoration of Buddhism in contemporary China.[1]

My research suggests, furthermore, that since the mid-2000s funding from overseas sources has become increasingly insignificant as the local community has grown more prosperous. This growing prosperity has enabled the current abbot Daoyuan to not only reclaim monastic property from other entities and engage in continual restoration, rebuilding, and new enhancements to the property, but also regularly make large donations to charitable causes. In general, Kaiyuan's recovery has focused more on developing the "hardware" required to pursue the monastic enterprise (the physical plant, number of monks, steady sources of income, recovery of ritual forms) at the expense of cultivating the "software" (which includes study, monastic discipline, and regimes of self-cultivation, that is, meditation). Although study, discipline, and meditation are normative for the project of Buddhism and Yuanxian describes them as the three legs of the tripod of old Kaiyuan (Yuanxian 1643, 1a), they are less fundamental to a Buddhist monastery as a brick and mortar institution serving a community with other needs. What kind of an institution this monastery is, what kind of community it serves, and what their priorities are will become more clear in the chapters that follow. This chapter traces Kaiyuan's trajectory of revival to highlight the processes that have shaped and led to Kaiyuan's current state of restoration. The revival of religious activities is the focus of chapters 3 and 4, allowing this chapter to focus on institutional developments, which have dominated executive decisions throughout all three stages of recovery.

Chairman Mao died in September of 1976 and the arrest of the Gang of Four the following month marked the end of the Cultural Revolution.[2] No new direction in policy, religious, economic, or otherwise, was formalized until the Third Plenum of the Eleventh Party Congress in December of 1978, when Deng Xiaoping set out on a course now referred to as reform and opening (*gaige kaifang* 改革开放). The reforms set in motion became articulated as policy in the constitution adopted in 1982 that guaranteed freedom to believe or not believe in religion and engage in "normal religious activities" (*zhengchang de zongjiao huodong* 正常的宗教活动) (Pas 1989, 6–7). Since then, the officially recognized five religions—Buddhism, Islam, Daoism, Christianity, and Catholicism—have officially been on a path of recovery, each with their own trajectories. Kaiyuan began to recover in stages soon after the death of Mao. The following account of the early stages of the monastery's recovery is based on oral accounts from individuals who resided at Kaiyuan during the 1980s and 1990s and from local residents and officials with particular knowledge about the site. Getting this story has not been as easy as it might seem: most people are not interested in Kaiyuan's stages of recovery and often do not have a clear memory of how it proceeded. What I outline is a reliable account gleaned from hours of interviews with dozens of individuals with firsthand knowledge of the events related as well as reports or notices of relevance.

One principal source for the earliest years of Kaiyuan's restoration is the local monk Daoxing 道兴. Daoxing became a novice at Zhangzhou's Nanshan Monastery 南山寺 in 1980, although he did not receive full ordination until 1988 at Guangdong's Nanhua Temple 南华寺. From 1980 to 1984, he served as Kaiyuan's guest prefect and was an eyewitness to Kaiyuan's earliest years of recovery.[3] Under normal circumstances, a novice would never be allowed to fill that role or hold any other rank. But given the lack of able-bodied monks early on, many young monks and novices were allowed to take positions traditionally reserved for more senior monastics. Daoxing returned to Kaiyuan after three years in Guangdong and again lived at Kaiyuan from 1987 to 1999, during which time he held various clerical positions. He and his friend Chuanjian 传建 of Xiamen's Puguang Temple 普光寺 provided much of the framework and content of Kaiyuan's developments during the 1980s and 1990s.[4]

The Beginnings of Recovery

Quanzhou residents have said that people began to burn incense and bow to Buddhas at Kaiyuan as early as 1976. In 1978, Miaolian was reinstalled as abbot and remained in that position until his death in 1998. He had lived in the sutra library during the Cultural Revolution and survived to oversee the earliest period of restoration of religious traditions at Kaiyuan. The minor stirrings of devotional Buddhism reached a crescendo on April 4, 1980, which marks the official recovery of religious practice at Quanzhou Kaiyuan Monastery. The date corresponds to the Qingming Festival (Clear and Bright) sometimes called Tomb-Sweeping Day because it is traditionally marked by cleaning the graves of ancestors and making offerings to them. In 1980, however, this festival was still not publicly permitted except as a kind of memorial day celebration of revolutionary heroes. To get around this prohibition, a memorial celebration to mark the one-hundredth birthday anniversary of former abbot Zhuanfeng (*zhuanfeng heshang yibai zhounian jinian* 转峰和尚一百周年纪念) was held at Kaiyuan and included seven days of Buddha recitation (*nianfo*). It was a way for Quanzhou citizens to celebrate under the guise of a temple-specific ceremony that also provided ritual benefit to ancestors. This service is said to have attracted some ten thousand people and was the first time crowds of such size had been seen at a religious function in the city for more than two decades; it signaled in a very concrete manner that open religious expression was again permissible. Earlier any sign of devotional activity at Kaiyuan had been rare, but afterward the monastery began a slow and steady recovery. With increased public interest came a need to provide a facelift to the neglected buildings and grounds, which remained occupied by several different nonmonastic work units (*danwei*).

At the head of fundraising efforts in the first years of recovery was the monk Guang'an, who was finally able to follow his dharma brothers to Southeast Asia after ten years of humiliation and "struggle" as a "bad element." Under the new policy under Deng Xiaoping, travel restrictions were lifted and Guang'an was able to travel to the Philippines in 1983 and Singapore in 1986. Following the example of Kaiyuan's Republican period monks, Guang'an looked to overseas Chinese communities in Southeast Asia for financial support. He succeeded in collecting several thousand renminbi, which he brought back to Quanzhou to be used toward Kaiyuan's recovery. He served as the general manager of Kaiyuan for a short period before passing away at the age of seventy-three in 1996, highly regarded by those who knew him (Zhuanfa 2004).[5]

In March of 1982, Kaiyuan was recognized in the second batch of important national heritage protected sites (国家级第二批重点文物保护单位) by the State Council; the following year, it was named an important national Han Buddhist temple (全国汉族地区佛教重点寺院) (Huang 2005, 18–19).[6] Quanzhou Kaiyuan's relatively complete set of buildings from the Ming and Qing dynasties and two exceptional monumental pagodas from the Song dynasty were instrumental in attracting recognition at these national levels. Being so designated is critical to any site hoping to attract tourists at a national or international level. The designations are part of the state's effort not only to promote economic development but also to influence, frame, and ultimately control sites of religious activity or significance. Mechanisms of control come in various forms, but the most localized form of influence is the temple administrative commission, an entity explored in chapter 7. These designations reflect the power of the state and the continued working out of the statist enterprise informed by a project of modernity (Asad 2010; Ashiwa and Wank 2009). As part of China's national heritage, the monastery falls under the jurisdiction of the Bureau of Culture; as a site of "normal religious activities," it falls under the jurisdiction of the Religious Affairs Bureau at the provincial level and the State Administration for Religious Affairs at the national level; as a Buddhist monastery, it falls under the jurisdiction of the Buddhist Association of China, which has branches at national, prefectural, and municipal levels. The monks and their monastery are not now nor have ever been fully autonomous; their relationship with the state is filtered through two ideological constructs, "normal religion" and "cultural heritage." Kaiyuan's monks have been required to master these two discursive fields to work with state officials and pursue the restoration of Buddhist monastic traditions.

Whereas 1980 marked the beginning of recovery and the resumption of openly held religious ceremonies, 1983 to 1984 saw a series of material signs of achievement that marked the recovery as one that was more than a phantom. Physical recovery proceeded with the regilding (*tiejin* 贴金) of Kaiyuan's major statues using 2.5 kilograms of gold at a cost of ¥160,000 ($61,000), ¥32,000 of which reportedly came from Singapore.[7] As Kaiyuan began to return to life as a cultural attraction that also welcomed religious devotees, it began to receive a stream of high-level visits that, on the one hand, pushed municipal authorities to ensure that it was well maintained and, on the other, let the public know that the temple was once again "open for business."

Zhao Puchu at Kaiyuan

One of the first and most important high-level visits was by the president of the Chinese Buddhist Association, Zhao Puchu 赵朴初 (1907–2000), in 1983 to celebrate the Yuanxiao festival, which traditionally marks the end of Chinese New Year celebrations and occurs on the fifteenth day of the first lunar month. Zhao Puchu was without peer as a Buddhist leader in mainland China during the 1980s and 1990s.[8] His position enabled him to perceive and resolve at least three problems that helped set Kaiyuan on the path to monastic revival and greater autonomy: management, income, and communal meals.

At the time of Zhao Puchu's visit, Kaiyuan's main hall and ordination hall were both still under the management of the heritage management committee and, according to monks there at the time, not fully open for worship, but more museum like. Members of the Heritage Management Committee staffed tables inside halls and even slept in the halls. This was done, as the committee saw it, to ensure the protection of the valuable properties inside the halls, which remained under their jurisdiction. The monks and lay Buddhists resented the encroachment on spaces they considered places of worship. This undesirable situation was corrected through the influence of Zhao Puchu, who arranged for oversight of monastic halls to be transferred to Kaiyuan's monks.[9] The Heritage Management Committee maintained offices on the grounds of Kaiyuan, but they would not last.

The second issue Zhao Puchu is credited with resolving concerned the livelihood of the monks. Since the end of the Cultural Revolution, Kaiyuan's monks had supported themselves by selling souvenirs and other goods in small shops. This was not only undesirable from the monks' point of view but also a poor way to fundraise. Zhao Puchu was able to help the monks negotiate their way out of working in shops and support themselves by donations. To encourage donations, a local tradition commonly referred to as Buddha recitation time (*nianfo qi* 念佛期) was revived. It was decided that the monks would institute a Buddha recitation day on the twenty-sixth lunar day of every month to encourage visitors and attract donations. At first, few attended these gatherings, which included communal recitation in the hall of the ordination platform. In the mid-1980s, as many as five hundred people came. By 1994, the numbers had increased enough that the recitation was moved to the main hall to accommodate the crowd.[10]

An additional situation Zhao Puchu is credited with reforming is the sharing of rice. Before his visit, Kaiyuan's monks maintained their own supplies of rice, which they would individually provide to layperson Wen Meng, who would then prepare the meal in one large pot to be shared by all the monks. If someone contributed less, problems could arise. After Zhao Puchu's visit, this system was reformed and all of the rice was combined to form a common store from which meals were prepared. This change may seem trivial but was an important step in developing the kind of communal atmosphere essential for a monastery to function.

As income was generated from increasing donations and more monks were ordained, Kaiyuan built a large dining hall (*wuguan tang*) between 1986 and 1987 that could accommodate more than two hundred people. The population of residents at Kaiyuan, including active and retired monks and novices, had increased from around two dozen in the early 1980s to as many as five dozen at the end of the 1980s.[11] The construction of the dining hall marks the end of Kaiyuan's first stage of recovery, which witnessed steady progress toward the reestablishment of a self-sufficient sangha exercising authority over the halls, supported by a growing body of lay devotees attending monthly *nianfo* days. The dining hall was not only a milestone in Kaiyuan's recovery, it was also an investment in the future of the monastery as a place for the cultivation of a religious community engaged in forms of communal practice. Zhao Puchu was instrumental in setting Kaiyuan on this particular trajectory, one that offered monastics a future.

After assisting Quanzhou Kaiyuan, Zhao Puchu went to Nan'an Xuefeng Monastery to help the monks there negotiate their path to revival.[12] Zhao Puchu was an instrumental figure in helping Buddhism transition into forms acceptable to the Communist Party. His brief visit at this early period was a crucial step in Kaiyuan's return to functioning as a home of monastics. At the time of his visit only one other Buddhist monastery had been revived in the city of Quanzhou, Chongfu. It had been rebuilt and discussions were under way to rebuild Quanzhou's other important monastery, Chengtian, but its restoration would not be complete until 1990.[13] Kaiyuan had been the first to revive and paved the way for other temples, both large and small, to follow its lead.

In addition to developing into a site for the sangha, Kaiyuan continued to develop as a site for tourists as it had during the early years of the

Maoist period. In 1983, Kaiyuan Monastery was visited by the former king of Cambodia, Norodom Sihanouk (1922–2012), and his wife. In preparation for this high-level visitor, the west pagoda was washed. A local resident recalled that it was after this visit by an international political figure that people began to return to worship in greater numbers and more regularly. The visit is commemorated today by a photograph on display in Kaiyuan's Museum of Buddhist History.

Kaiyuan also began to receive visits by international delegations of Buddhists. From 1979 to 1989, five delegations of clerics from Japan's Obaku school of Zen visited Quanzhou Kaiyuan. One came bearing a statue of Kaiyuan's master Mu'an, who is venerated in Japan as one of the early and most talented patriarchs of the Obaku school. The small statue was once enshrined in Kaiyuan's hall of patriarchs.[14] Early visits to Buddhist temples in China by Japanese delegations from 1979 to 1989 helped restart forms of devotional religious practice at Quanzhou Kaiyuan, Shaolin Temple, and Bailin Temple (Ji 2013, 46). A final elite visitor during this first stage of recovery was the Chinese-designated Panchen Lama, who visited Kaiyuan in 1986. Each high-profile visit legitimated Kaiyuan as a cultural and religious institution and encouraged other Chinese, both local and nonlocal, to visit as tourists and in worship.

In 1984, the central name board in the center of the main gate that reads "Great Kaiyuan Everlasting Chan Temple," the title given by Kublai Khan during the Yuan dynasty, was repaired and its characters gilded.[15] With this addition and a growing reputation as a place of history, culture, and beauty, Kaiyuan was voted one of the ten most scenic spots in Fujian Province in 1986 (Huang 2005, 18–19). It was well on its way to developing as a home for monks and site of cultural heritage that welcomed visitors and worshippers.

Restoration of Kaiyuan's Central Axis

Kaiyuan's Buddhas and Bodhisattvas were once again gilded and worshipped, but the large wooden halls showed the wear of time, the elements, and termites. A second stage of recovery was inaugurated in the summer of 1989, when a group of monks from southern Fujian (Minnan) who had settled in Southeast Asia before the Cultural Revolution returned to Kaiyuan and determined to have its buildings restored. These monks were Hongchuan 宏船, Guangqia 广洽, Guangjing, Guangchun 广纯, and Qinghui 晴晖. Hongchuan, Guangchun, and Qinghui were all associated with Singapore's Putuo Temple, which had been founded by Zhuandao; Guangjing and Guangqia were disciples of Kaiyuan's former abbot Zhuanfeng.[16] They received government approval and had the former mayor, Wang Jinsheng, serve as the chairman of the restoration committee (泉州开元寺修建委员会). Work began in July of

1989 and was completed five years later, in the summer of 1993. The main hall, the main gate, the hall of the ordination platform, and the sutra library were all restored with new tiles and new paint. A stele was erected in the main courtyard of the monastery in 1993 to commemorate this most recent of Kaiyuan's many restorations. As detailed on the stele, Singapore's Putuo Temple funded work on the main hall, ordination hall, Hongyi museum, and sutra hall, and Singapore's Longshan Temple 龙山寺 helped fund the restoration of the main gate.[17] Wu Songbai also reports that Singapore's Pujue Temple, which had been founded by Zhuandao, contributed ¥5,500,000 ($1 million) in funds for Kaiyuan's 1993 restoration.

This work was officially declared complete during the celebration of Chinese New Year in 1993, well in time for a visit by President Jiang Zemin on June 24, 1994. Jiang was guided by Zhang Zhenhao 张真好, the head guide of the guest reception branch of the Temple Administrative Commission. This visit was trumpeted throughout the city and region and photographs of the president touring Kaiyuan are displayed in the Kaiyuan Buddhist museum. His expression of interest and approval sealed Kaiyuan as an officially recognized place of cultural value and, in the eyes of the Buddhist community, as an officially sanctioned place for religious practice. Although international visitors had begun to arrive as early as 1983, throughout the 1980s Kaiyuan's recovery was steady but modest; it was the full restoration of the early 1990s and the visit by Jiang Zemin that made it clear that Kaiyuan had "arrived." It was a place of cultural value, a sight to see, a place to be.

Visits by Zhao Puchu and Jiang Zemin have both been an important boost to Kaiyuan's recovery efforts and calligraphy by each of them is kept by the monastery commemorating their visits. This calligraphy was printed in the monastery's 2005 commemorative volume and photos taken during their visits hang in the museum of Buddhist history. Photographs of visits by local and national political leaders are found in monasteries throughout China and are clearly a way of establishing legitimacy if not talismanic-like protection. These visits functioned as a form of political patronage, offering recognition and legitimation, critical elements of political capital.

Support from overseas Chinese in Singapore and the Philippines was an important ingredient in Kaiyuan's first decade of recovery. Since the end of the 1990s, however, formal contact between Kaiyuan and the overseas Chinese communities in Southeast Asia has declined. One informant, who had participated in fundraising activities in Southeast Asia, claimed that a contributing factor is a Singaporean policy regulating such activities.[18] Although this may indeed be one factor, the most important reason for the decline is the growing prosperity of mainland China in general and in Fujian in particular, which has been increasingly evident since the 1990s. Kaiyuan's monks simply had no compelling reason to go abroad in search of funds when so much wealth was being generated within their community. This is the situation that has prevailed since 2005.

Miaolian, master Hongyi's former attendant, served as abbot and oversaw the first two decades of Kaiyuan's post-Mao recovery. Miaolian was in poor and declining health throughout the 1980s and 1990s and passed away at the monastery at the age of eighty-seven on November 5, 1999. His funeral was held at Kaiyuan on November 11 and attended by more than two thousand people, including government leaders, clerics from other temples, and disciples.[19] Miaolian provided a tenuous link between Kaiyuan's current restoration and the revival of the 1930s. The collection of Hongyi's artifacts is part of Miaolian's legacy at Kaiyuan; the collection would come to be displayed in a new hall built by the succeeding abbot, Daoyuan.

The Daoyuan Era

At the time of Miaolian's death, Daoyuan, then in his sixties, was general manager of Kaiyuan and vice president of the Fujian BAC. Daoyuan was installed as the new abbot on July 20, 2000. He had become a monk late in life and circumstances seemed to have favored him in his rise to power at Kaiyuan. Whereas Miaolian had been quiet, passive, and contemplative, Daoyuan is bold, aggressive, and worldly. His tenure at Kaiyuan has been marked by three major themes: the recovery of monastic property, physical enhancements to the monastery, and strengthening of clerical leadership over the site. His actions most clearly demonstrate the overriding concern with hardware and administration.

Daoyuan was born in the small village of Chidian 池店 outside the city of Quanzhou in 1935; he was the second child in a family of seven, five boys and two girls. In 1969, during the Cultural Revolution, he was sent down (*chadui* 插队) to the rural Qingniu county 青牛县 (Blue-Green Cow) and lived there until he became a monk in 1986 at a temple in Shishi 石狮 (Stone Lion).[20] He took refuge under Chuanjing 传净 (1917–2017), an older monk at Kaiyuan, and thus considers himself a monk from Kaiyuan even though he did not live there until 1992.[21] In 1994, he was chosen by officials in the BAC, with agreement from the Fujian Provincial Bureau of Religion, to go to Brazil to serve as the head monk (*zhuchi*) at Guanyin Temple in Sao Paulo, where an older monk speaking the local Minnan dialect was needed.[22] After two years in Brazil, which Daoyuan recalls with great fondness, he returned to Kaiyuan, citing that his services were needed there.

The Recovery on Properties

When he returned to Quanzhou in February of 1996, the former abbot, Miaolian, was ill, and Daoyuan, who had served in a leadership position at

Guanyin Temple in Sao Paolo, took over management of Kaiyuan's affairs, first serving as the head guest prefect (*da zhike*) and then, in July of 1996, as general manager. Daoyuan's first task was the recovery of properties immediately bounding the central axis of the monastery that had come to be occupied by nonmonastic residents and organizations. The loss of some of these properties can be traced to the end of the Qing dynasty; others had become occupied over the past thirty years. What Daoyuan accomplished over the next ten years was no small feat and one that has won greater autonomy for the monastery. He was able to accomplish what he did using funds generated from the restoration of devotional life at the monastery, which is detailed in chapter 3.

His first task was to reclaim the property known as small Kaiyuan Temple, the scaled-down replica of Kaiyuan's main buildings first built during the Qing dynasty in the northeast corner of the monastery. In July 1997, he successfully negotiated with the individuals living there to move out, offering a total of one million renminbi to compensate them. Although officially recognized religions are allowed to reclaim property that belonged to them before 1949, in practice, it is clear that they must provide financial compensation to those evicted.[23] In the northwest corner was a department of landscape and gardening (*yuanlin guanli chu* 园林管理处) that had become established over the previous several decades. In 1998, Daoyuan succeeded in negotiating their removal.[24] In 2002, Daoyuan succeeding in clearing away private homes and a bank that had encroached on the main entrance. Just behind the guest hall is the old Land and Water Temple, which during the Maoist period had been occupied by a troupe of puppeteers (*muer tuan*). This group was evicted and the temple returned to use as a shrine hall. In 2004, property in the far northeastern part of the temple that had been lost at the end of the Ming and early Qing dynasties was recovered. A newly constructed two-story building served as the residence of the abbot, two high-ranking monks, two helper monks, and a monk who works in the office of the Quanzhou BAC on the grounds of the monastery. After spending millions of renminbi to compensate the affected stakeholders, Daoyuan enjoyed remarkable success in clearing the property of nonmonastic entities.

Enhancements to Kaiyuan's Physical Plant and Restoration of Traditions

In 1997, when Daoyuan served as Kaiyuan's general manager, a renovation committee was established, former mayor Wang Jinsheng serving as director and Daoyuan as vice director. A total of ¥6 million ($750,000) was spent on renovations including a regilding of the statues for ¥1,200,000 and ¥1,000,000 ($125,000) to organize and repair scriptures in the sutra library with the help of professional provincial archivists.[25] This was a curatorial move carried out to enhance Kaiyuan's position as a trove of cultural treasures. It was not, that is, part of any plan to revive scholarship, but instead part of a project of cultural preservation that also fit into the discourse of cultural heritage necessary to gain a broader base of favor among local officials.

In 2000, Daoyuan established the Anyang Cloister (Anyang yuan 安养院) at a cost of ¥9 million ($1,125,000). The centerpiece of this cloister is an underground columbarium for the ashes of patrons who have purchased plots. Special sections are set aside for the remains of overseas Chinese, who make up a significant portion of the community served; overseas disciples are provided an opportunity to return home for their final resting place; as they say in Chinese, "falling leaves return to the roots" (*luoye guigen* 落叶归根). The columbarium generates approximately ¥4 or ¥5 million (about $700,000) per year and when it is full will have generated approximately ¥100 million (more than $14 million). The cost of interring the ashes of one person and a spirit tablet is ¥4,200 ($600). Ashes are kept in individual vaults and spirit tablets are housed in a large hall aboveground that came to displace the old hall of merit (*gongde tang*) where spirit tablets were previously housed. This development of the mausoleum was explained by the monks as a valuable service to the public as well as a way of generating income.

Daoyuan's first major act as abbot was the hosting of a great three platform ordination ceremony in January 2001. It had been more than seventy years since the last one, held in 1925, and, according to some reports, the third time since the founding of Kaiyuan 1,300 years earlier (Daoyuan et al. 2005, 72). It was a grand affair during which 320 monks from all over China as well as ethnic Chinese from Southeast Asia were ordained. This was the ceremony that Desheng felt was comical because a platform had to be constructed for use next to the ordination hall because the actual ordination platform is covered with Ming dynasty statues designated cultural treasures that therefore could not be moved.

The second major act for Daoyuan as abbot was the opening of the Quanzhou Museum of Buddhism at small Kaiyuan Temple on April 22, 2001. The project had begun in 1999 when Daoyuan convened the Quanzhou Buddhism Museum Preparation Committee, chaired by himself with Chen Pengpeng from the Quanzhou Heritage Management Association (Wenwu guanli hui 文物管理会) serving as advisor. Zhao Puchu participated in the grand opening and wrote the name board for the museum. The renovated small Kaiyuan Temple was transformed into a museum of 3,200 square meters, consisting of five halls connected by corridors, landscaped with flowers and plants. The antiquities on display span 1,400 years of Buddhism in Quanzhou and panels summarize developments in Quanzhou Buddhism throughout the imperial and Republican periods. The complex includes halls of stone sculptures, temple bells, metal objects, and sculptures taken from Kaiyuan and other sites in the Quanzhou region. Among the more notable items are three stone sculptures from the Tang dynasty, including a mustached Guanyin once set in a niche of the pagodas, a purple sandalwood sculpture of Dizang bodhisattva from the Ming, an excellent stone sculpture of Bodhidharma also from the Ming, gilded bronze statues from the Ming and Qing, a large steel tripod cast by Zheng Zhilong in 1637 (one of five), large bronze bells from 1132 (Southern Song) and 1325 (Yuan), as well as bronze and iron bells from the Ming and Qing dynasties.

This museum included items from all over the region that had been collected at Kaiyuan from 1950 onward under the supervision of the Heritage Management Association. The museum was a way of displaying the artifacts to the public; it was in the interest of the Heritage Management Association and was approved by Daoyuan to enhance the property of the monastery. Establishing such enhancements is, next to recovering property occupied by nonmonastics, the most important theme of Daoyuan's tenure of leadership.

Some ¥2 million was spent in planning, designing, and expanding the Hongyi Memorial Hall and garden in the northeast part of the monastic grounds. The hall displays a priceless collection of artifacts and photographs bequeathed to Miaolian, Hongyi's attendant. On display are twenty-two photographs of Hongyi, including eleven from the early twentieth century, calligraphy, paintings, and seal carvings by Hongyi, sheet music he composed, and copies of sutras he collected in Japan. A courtyard garden was created before the Hall of the Buddha's Life (Bensheng yuan 本生院), outlining this courtyard and surrounding the small Kaiyuan Temple are more than four hundred new granite sculptures, each costing ¥7,600. The sculptures are based on a book of paintings by Hongyi's disciple Feng Zikai 丰子恺 (1898–1975) accompanied by the calligraphy of Hongyi. Called *Paintings to Protect Life* (*Husheng huaji*), the book was first published in 1929. The paintings depict the content of classical poems and Buddhist tales dealing with the protection of all forms of life from insects to cows; Hongyi wrote verses to accompany the illustrations (Tarocco 2008, 32, 71–73).[26] They are expressions of art as well as expression of a Buddhist moral injunction to protect life. Daoyuan says he was drawn to this project because of both the Hongyi connection and the environmentalist (*huanbao* 环保) theme.

The abbot Daoyuan has consistently expressed an interest in developing both environmental awareness and more sustainable practices. Concern about the environmental impact of burning so much paper led the monastery to install a filter in the 2010s to remove ash and particulates from the smoke by passing it through water and releasing steam. Practices promoted in the 2010s include encouraging devotees to use fewer sticks of incense and replacing devotional candles with LED lights that look like candles. Although the impact of such efforts is modest, they perhaps lay the groundwork for additional efforts by future leadership. The most recent initiatives include leading an effort to reduce incense burned at temples and require the use of environmentally friendly incense (*huanbao xiang* 环保香).

Daoyuan had a new two-story building constructed next to and in the same style as the building at the back of small Kaiyuan that then served as the Hongyi Memorial Hall. The new building is called the Hall of the Buddha's Life (Bensheng yuan) and was completed in 2007; it enshrines two gilded statues of Sakyamuni Buddha portraying his birth and his performance of austerities as well as fifty-eight granite sculptures depicting scenes from the life of the Buddha Sakyamuni. The sculptures in this hall were created at an expense of more than ¥400,000.[27]

In 2002, along the sides of the main gate, Daoyuan erected two large bounding walls reading "Dharma World of the Lotus-Blooming Mulberry Tree" and "Auspicious Lotus-Blooming Peach Tree" referencing auspicious stories associated with the monastery. The new walls are a deployment of cultural symbols to indicate the return of Kaiyuan as a sacred space, as a spiritually efficacious place with an auspicious past; such branding is examined more closely in chapter 6.

Daoyuan has not been particularly concerned with preservation in the mode of the Maoist-era Heritage Management Association. His recovery, renovation, and building has been directed at infrastructural improvements or institution building rather than cultural preservation. This orientation may be expressed as revivalist (interest in renewing) rather than curatorial. He has expressed this orientation by not hesitating to replace rather than restore damaged cultural properties. He had the eight *vajra* protectors on the ordination platform replaced in 2006, for example, after one of them was damaged. He also had the dharma hall and sutra library demolished and reconstructed in 2008 (the contents and other salvageable ornaments were all preserved in storage), for reported structural weakness associated with damage from the Sino-Japanese War. In 2009, he ordered the replacement of all five Buddhas in the main hall when one head fell off because of termite damage. I am not privy to all the details of these decisions, but observers have debated the necessity of some of them.[28]

The Fate of the Orphanage under Daoyuan

As Kaiyuan's recovery continued through the 1980s and 1990s, the orphanage and school remained on the eastern edge of the monastic complex. After the death of Mao, the school was reconstituted and classes resumed, but no monks were involved in its operation or administration. Under Chinese law, religious institutes are not allowed to operate schools for general education. Thus what had been a school and orphanage established by Yuanying and the Republican period trio of monks became a school operated by the state. I was informed that in 2003 a Hong Kong business person wanted to replace the school with a large building and make it a center for charity in Quanzhou. When Daoyuan heard this he was angry, promptly rushing back from a meeting he was attending in Shanghai. The temple had just gotten a computer and one of Kaiyuan's monks was asked to compose a letter to local officials in response. The monk typed for four hours to report to the government why the proposed construction should not be approved, why a tall building should not be built so close to the monastery. The city officials joked that if Daoyuan cared so much that he should buy the property back. In response, Daoyuan asked how much it would cost. The official said that he might be able to help him deal with the situation for ¥10,000 to ¥20,000; Daoyuan immediately offered ¥2 million, which was more than enough. This anecdote reveals something about Daoyuan that has enabled him to fight on behalf of the monastery to recover properties and remove entities encroaching on the monastery. It is how the abbot has made his mark.

The students were immediately moved to a special school (特殊學校); the buildings that had been used as classrooms and offices became converted to other, somewhat peripheral, uses; still others were demolished. The Hubao Building 虎豹楼, for example, is a two-story structure once used by teachers that includes offices and possibly living quarters; in the 2000s, it held the offices of the Quanzhou Buddhist Association; in the 2010s, these were moved to the Venerated Site Cloister. The school auditorium (*litang*), a large room with many chairs and a large television, is now used by a group of lay Buddhists who regularly hold *nianfo* meetings there.[29] Just west of this building is a two-story structure that in the 1980s served as an art school. The art school personnel were evicted and the building is now used as a guest reception area or guest hall (*ketang*); it also had apartments on the second floor for a few higher-ranking monks. In front of the guest hall is now a landscaped area that includes the western gate. Thus the elementary school and orphanage has been wiped away from the landscape of Kaiyuan. The charity established by Yuanying and Zhuandao had survived war with Japan, civil war, and the Cultural Revolution, but ironically was unable to survive the revival under way in contemporary China.[30]

Since becoming a monk in 1986, Daoyuan has become a politically well-connected leader of one of the largest and most important monasteries in the region. Given the nature of government oversight of religious groups, it is important if not imperative to cultivate good relationships with relevant officials. As well as being a trustee in the National BAC, the vice president of the Fujian BAC, and the president of the Quanzhou BAC, Daoyuan is also a member of the ninth Fujian Political Harmony Consultation Committee (Zhengxie 政协) and a permanent member of the Quanzhou People's Congress. Daoyuan reads the *People's Daily* every afternoon and watches news programs and Chinese operas on television at night, sometimes after 11 p.m. When I first met him, in 2006, he had an image of Chairman Mao on the screen of his cell phone and expressed admiration of him; he maintains good relations with Party members. By 2009, he had upgraded to an iPhone and had lost the Chairman Mao image. He is required to regularly attend political meetings, as are other high-ranking monks, to remain briefed on the state's views and policy regarding religion and the management of religious sites. He is responsible for managing Kaiyuan's income and deciding how to invest and donate large amounts of monastic funds as well as what improvements to make at the monastery. One of Kaiyuan's monks said that this responsibility and the related pressure are considerable and that most monks would find them onerous and bewildering; it seems to be a job made for Daoyuan, who appears to relish the challenge of dealing with such entities and managing finances.

Daoyuan described himself in an interview as being "self-enlightened through karmic causes" (自悟因缘成就) as a young man. When asked about the greatest challenges of being abbot, he said there were none and that he "meets any challenge with faith and willpower."[31] When asked what was most difficult about Buddhist practice, he implied that he was able to deal with any difficulties that may arise because he "uses stable faith to subdue unskillful states."[32] When asked about managing the temple, he identified two parts, management of hardware (*yingjian* 硬件) and of software, or personnel, (*ruanjian* 软件). He explained that hardware includes buildings, cultural heritage, and environment and that software includes the organization (*jigou* 机构), system (*zhidu* 制度), and talent (*rencai* 人才). His management of the hardware has centered on Kaiyuan's status as a protected national heritage site and restoring the basic architectural form of the monastery in accordance with laws governing protected relics with the support of the Heritage Management Committee. The management of people is focused on finding young and promising monks to serve in monastic offices. Daoyuan is proud that the monastic office personnel have remained relatively steady over the years. He believes that his greatest accomplishments are restoring the monastery and helping the needy and those in distress (*jikun fuwei* 济困扶危). When asked about the practice he recommends for the monks, he said, "Propagate the dharma as your household duty; benefiting living beings is your profession."[33] He also spoke of being an abbot as work in human resources.[34] These suggestions that being a monk is a kind of profession (*shiye*), his being an abbot involved in human resources management, and his references to monks as personnel (*renyuan* 人员) indicate why many at Kaiyuan consider being a monk a job at a service corporation rather than a vocation or life project.

Daoyuan may neither be a scholarly expounder of Buddhist doctrine nor a soft-spoken and gentle monk, but he has arguably been the right person to fight to recover authority over the temple and its lost properties. In the 1980s, the monastery was occupied, not only by the two management committees, but also by more than eighty units (*danwei*) that included private homes, an elementary school, an art school, a puppet troupe, and a landscaping and gardening work group. The new abbot set about recovering full control of all of these properties by asserting his right as abbot to properties that previously belonged to the monastery. The prosperity of the times enabled the abbot to financially compensate those who were required to move, thus facilitating his recovery of monastic properties and relocation of dozens of individuals—he spent millions of renminbi this way. In 2006, Daoyuan stated that work on the temple since he began to manage affairs had cost more than ¥40 million (about $5 million).[35] Small Buddhist temples in urban areas are often surrounded by buildings; many of them occupy land formerly held by the temple; unlike Daoyuan, however, they have no way of recovering that property. Daoyuan possessed the right combination of personality, energy, connections, and access to money that enabled him to reclaim Kaiyuan's property for the sangha.

Over ten years, Daoyuan had recovered all the properties within the monastery's walls and, in some cases, had properties cleared or recovered adjoining the walls. He has not only refurbished Kaiyuan's halls but also built new walls and buildings (such as the Hall of the Buddha's Life and the abbot's quarters) and organized two museums (one for Quanzhou Buddhism, the other for master Hongyi). In addition to maintaining good relations with the various state agencies that have some level of jurisdiction over Kaiyuan, Daoyuan's focus has been on the recovery, restoration, maintenance, and enhancement of Kaiyuan's physical plant, in short, the hardware of the monastery. This is a theme at religious sites across China, of course, but in addition are examples, close to home for Kaiyuan, of leadership that has successfully invested in educating and training the sangha along with rebuilding. Xiamen's Nanputuo Monastery, for instance, reestablished the Minnan Buddhist Seminary in 1984 and has become one of the most important training grounds for monks in all China, with hundreds of clerics in residence.[36] This happened not because of the state, the BAC, or lay activists (although their support was important); what was instrumental was the leadership of the abbot Miaozhan 妙湛 (1910–1995), who perceived the importance and value of training clergy (Ashiwa and Wank 2006, 342–343). Daoyuan's leadership influenced the present character of Kaiyuan. His successor will influence its future—just what that future will be remains unknown.

Income and Charity under Daoyuan

Over the tenure of Daoyuan, Kaiyuan has grown into a center, not for meditation, study, or discipline, but for Buddhist ritual and devotional life. His efforts in clearing the property of other tenants and gaining more monastic control over the property has helped develop both the tourist potential and the devotional appeal of Fujian's largest urban monastery. The establishment of the underground mausoleum has been successful, not only financially, but also in expanding the connections between the monastery and the community. In 2009 Kaiyuan's annual income was approximately ¥28 million ($4.1 million). This figure is based on approximately ¥6 million per year in Buddha recitation day donations, another ¥6 million from 50 percent of gate ticket sales, ¥4 million from postmortem services, and the remaining ¥12 million from daily donations. Chapter 3 details the ritual and liturgical features of the monastery.

On the expense column are the stipends or wages for monks. The schedule of monthly pay in 2006 was ¥1,800 for the abbot, ¥1,600 for the general manager, ¥1,400 for the assistant manager (*fusi*) and the abbot's attendant (*yibo*), ¥1,200 for other positions, and ¥900 for monks without positions. Other expenses are maintenance, repairs, and renovations, substantial for any monastery but especially for one as large as Kaiyuan. Some of these expenses can be gleaned from the enumerated renovations. Other expenses are the various supplies required, from food for the monks and for the lunar twenty-sixth day, to all the kitchen equipment and utilities. The salaries and benefits of the temple administrative commission are also covered by the monastery from entry fees.

In addition to many personnel, operating, and upkeep expenses Kaiyuan has donated from ¥1 to ¥5 million per year (some $130,000 to $650,000) since 2000, up to 15 percent or more of income in some years. Over the first few years of Daoyuan's abbacy, he estimated donating around ¥1 million per year. This amount has increased over the years along with Kaiyuan's income. The earliest act of charitable giving I know of in Kaiyuan's post-Mao period was a donation of ¥280,000 ($33,650) for flood relief in Fujian from 1997 to 1998. The following year, in 1999, Kaiyuan funded the building of the Fuqing Longtian Seaside Elementary School 福清市龙田镇海滨小学 south of Fuzhou for ¥200,000 and Daoyuan presided over the ribbon-cutting ceremony that February. The following year, 2000, Kaiyuan donated ¥270,000 to support development far away in Xinjinag, Northwest China.[37] More recently, in 2017, Kaiyuan donated ¥10 million (about $1.5 million) to fund the Quanzhou No. 1 Hospital. According to a monk in the abbot's office, ¥20 million (more than $3.5 million) was donated to charity in 2018. Every indication suggests increasing affluence for the monastery, leading to more sizable charitable donations. In addition to schools, hospitals, and disaster relief, funds have also been sent to help villages develop and other development projects, all of which suggest an interest in maintaining good relations with government officials, if not also responses to government requests. Regardless of the precise arrangements, charitable munificence is an important way of giving back to the community and state that is in line with Buddhist values of compassion and generosity. It is also a way of maintaining a positive reputation as a contributor to social development in the community and in the nation. Such reputation is attested to in plaques and banners of commendation from provincial, town, city, and neighborhood agencies. In short, it is a good way of keeping in everyone's good graces: the laity, general public, and officials alike. It is also a helpful way to diffuse any scrutiny or concern about the wealth generated by successful temples such as Kaiyuan.[38]

"Branch" Temples

As the largest monastery in the region, the earliest to revive, the one with the most impressive cultural treasures, and the one with the largest gatherings of worshippers, Kaiyuan has been a base for ambitious monks to collect funds for building or rebuilding smaller temples in the region.[39] Monks engaged in these activities of restoring temples are enhancing their status, to be sure, but they are also acting in accordance with a venerable and highly meritorious Buddhist tradition of spreading the dharma (*hongfa*) by building temples. This phenomenon can be traced back as far as the ninth century at Kaiyuan, when private cloisters for masters began to be built by the dozens. During the Republican period (1930s), the practice reappeared as Kaiyuan monks collected funds from Southeast Asia that enabled them to establish small temples in Quanzhou, such as Same-Lotus Temple (Tonglian si 同莲寺) and Múxi Temple 幕西寺, which, according to Daoyuan, was originally founded by Zhuanfeng for his vegetarian auntie (*caigu*) disciples in the 1930s or 1940s.

The Republican period phenomenon has reemerged over the past fifteen years.[40] More than fifty small temples have been rebuilt by monks associated with Kaiyuan since the mid-1990s; in each case, they have installed themselves as the head monk (*zhuchi* 住持) or abbot of these temples.[41] To date, the most energetic rebuilder of temples in southern Fujian is Guangjing, the former general manager of Kaiyuan, who, having become a respected monk in Singapore, returned to Quanzhou with funds to restore Kaiyuan and dozens of other temples. He is credited with helping rebuild forty-eight or forty-nine temples, the largest project being Nanshan Xuefeng. He rebuilt Muxi Temple with funds from Singapore's Longshan Temple.[42] He had Same-Lotus Temple rebuilt and enlarged as a home for vegetarian aunties. When he died in 1998, leadership of this temple passed to his disciple Chuanjian, who had served as Kaiyuan's guest prefect (*zhike*). Chuanjian now lives in Xiamen where he serves as abbot of Puguang Temple 普光寺, a temple he rebuilt. As for the current abbot, Daoyuan, he has raised funds and established himself as the abbot of Qingjing Temple 清净寺, which is said to have about eight resident monks. Kaiyuan's general manager in 2009, Fayi has funded the rebuilding of two small temples where he now serves as head monk, Stone Pavilion Temple 石亭寺 in Quanzhou and Lotus Lake Temple 莲湖寺 near his birthplace in Hui'an. Stone Pavilion Temple is named for an old stone hall at the center of the small mountain temple. The restoration of the monumental stone gate leading to the site cost ¥8 million and was complete in 2019. Daoxing found patrons to fund the restoration of two small temples on Mt. Qingyuan, which he now leads, Ci'en (Compassion-Kindness) Temple 慈恩寺 and Amitabha Temple. Administrative monk Desheng as of 2019 was still developing his own mountain temple, Guangji Temple 广济寺, a short drive from Kaiyuan. If not for the prestige and visibility of being at a venerable monastery, it is unlikely that Kaiyuan's monks and former monks would have enjoyed the success they have had in collecting alms for such ambitious projects. Monks from smaller temples do not have the same ability, unless they happen to have extraordinary charisma or connections, to attract such donations. Head monks at smaller temples typically attract enough patronage to maintain their small temple and the handful of monks or novices that live there, but nothing near the kind of funds necessary to build or rebuild a temple.

With the early restoration of Kaiyuan and its ability to attract funding from lay Buddhists abroad and at home, it became a conduit for restoring temples across the region. In 1978, fewer than half a dozen temples were active. In 2009, there were more than 500 active temples, 420 registered and as many as one hundred unregistered.[43] Quanzhou Kaiyuan, the great fruit, has helped replant the seeds of dharma in post-Mao China.

The Restoration of Outer Forms and Corporate Structure

This chapter has traced the three phases of history leading to the reestablishment of a functioning Buddhist monastery after the death of Mao. The overriding focus has been restoring the physical structures of the monastery, clearing the grounds of nonmonastic work units, and restoring monastic management and local worship. In addition, Daoyuan has focused on organizing and opening the museum of local Buddhist history, reorganizing and reopening the Master Hongyi Memorial Hall, and establishing the Anyang Cloister columbarium. Rising standards of living in the region have led to increasing income for the monastery, which Daoyuan has used to help build schools, hospitals, and other developmental and relief projects. The monastic organization has been revived and a group of younger monks has been chosen to assist the abbot. The chapters that follow turn to a more synchronic approach to the site in order to uncover the nature of religious life and the dynamics that go into creating a place of religion, culture, and history.

Part II

Religious Life

3

Communal Religious Life

Liturgical Rites

THOUSANDS OF DEVOTEES REPEATEDLY INTONING *NAMO AMITUOFO* (Homage to Amitabha Buddha) step in rhythm with one another as they wind around the main courtyard shaded by towering banyan trees hundreds of years old in the hot and humid spring. This scene is repeated religiously on the appointed day every month. On festival days, even more people crowd into the temple, but none exhibit this collective act of devotion so powerfully. Where does this scene fit into the religious life of the monastery? Monks lead the circumambulators and the chanting, but they are not the primary beneficiaries of this exercise. What are the key forms of monastic life exhibited at this site? To help develop a sense of the fundamental features of communal religious life at Kaiyuan Monastery, this chapter examines the governing elements of the daily, weekly, monthly, and annual calendars and how they fit together to establish the contours of life at an urban Buddhist monastery.

Monastic life is a fundamentally regimented existence that requires following a prescribed regime; the clearest window into that regulated life is an examination of the schedules and calendars followed. This chapter argues for the fundamentally liturgical basis of practice at mainstream Chinese Buddhist monasteries. The chanting of sutras, *dhāraṇīs,* and the names of buddhas and bodhisattvas is far from the Buddhism emphasized in introductory books and books written for general readerships that focus on a heroic quest for individual enlightenment and insight into the nature of things using philosophical analysis and the technology of meditation. Nonetheless, devotional and liturgical practices are the core of religious practice at Chinese Buddhist monasteries.[1] They are not unique to Chinese Buddhism, however. In his study of Myōshinji, the head temple of the most significant branch of Japanese Zen, Jørn Borup examines the range of Buddhist practices at the site and notes the centrality of worship: "Although not always recognized as such, Buddhism in very much a religion of worship. This is also true of Japanese Zen Buddhism, both as part of the daily rituals of the monasteries and of the periodical rituals of the lay devotees" (2008, 186). In the 1980s, Griffith Foulk remarked about Zen in Japan that "if we are to judge from observable behavior, no mode of religious expression is of greater concern to Zen Buddhists than rituals in which offerings are made to ancestral spirits" (1988, 177). Offerings made to ancestral spirits play a central role at Kaiyuan as well, but more is involved.

This chapter surveys the ritually punctuated schedules and calendars followed at Kaiyuan, which are the only regular communal activities of the sangha, as a window onto communal religious life. The three ethnographically based accounts of Buddhist monastic schedules of which I am aware do not go much beyond listing holidays (Welch 1967; Buswell 1992; Foulk 1988). Residing on site and observing and participating in the day-to-day, week-to-week, and month-to-month rituals, I came to realize that these rituals served as the fundamental form of communal monastic practice and therefore warranted closer examination. To convey the nature of this religious practice, I provide a thick description of the structures and communal features of regularly scheduled ritual practices (daily, weekly, monthly, and yearly) before considering the fundamentally liturgical nature of Chinese monastic Buddhism.

Daily Services

In 2006, a monk's day officially began at 4:00 a.m. The basics of the daily schedule were as follows:[2]

Morning

3:30–4:00	Wake up, temple block (*ban*)
4:00–4:15	Bell (*zhong*)
4:15–4:30	Drum (*gu*)
4:30–5:40	**Morning service** (*zaoke*)[3]
6:15–7:30	**Breakfast**
7:30–10:40	Free time (cleaning, chores, study, resting, visiting)
10:40–Noon	**Lunch**
Noon–4:00	Free time

Evening

3:50	Temple block to announce evening service
4:00–4:30	**Evening service** (*wanke*)[4]

5:00–6:00	**Dinner**
7:00–7:15	Evening bell
7:15–7:30	Evening drum
7:30–8:00	Evening board
9:00	Lights out

Two things are clear from this outline: first is that morning and evening services along with the three daily meals are the only form of communal practice, second is the centrality of dharma instruments (*faqi* 法器) in organizing the day. The centrality of these five assemblies is captured by the Chinese phrase "the five daily liturgies" (*wutang gongke* 五堂功课). In addition to the "morning bell and evening drum" (*chenzhong mugu* 晨钟暮鼓), a phrase synonymous with monastic life, dharma instruments carry forward the daily services and all the liturgical rituals. The social tapestry of the temple and the communal religious fabric of the monastery are woven to no small extent with the sounds of bells, drums, chimes, blocks, boards, and wooden fish.

Morning at the Monastery

At 3:00 a.m., the monastery is dark and quiet, even the streets that are normally busy to the south and west of the monastery are quiet. The grounds are still and the shadowy silhouettes of the pagodas evoke the medieval world of old Quanzhou. Just as one begins to feel all alone in an abandoned temple, the silence is broken by the sharp sound of wood striking wood. It is very much like the sound of the bamboo knocker fountains found in Japanese gardens, or perhaps the sound of a tile or small pebble striking hollow bamboo that aroused the mind of Zen master Xiangyan 香嚴 (ninth century) to awaken (Ferguson 2000, 172–173). The striking of this wooden temple block is the duty of one monk, the striker, who must arise before all the others, around 3:00 a.m. and wake them up; traditionally, abbots would assign a habitually tardy monk to this task. The striker, who at Kaiyuan is heavy set, seems to waddle as he makes his rounds, striking the wooden block with a small wooden mallet from 3:30 to 4:00 a.m.[5]

The next individual to emerge is the monk who opens the hall of the ordination platform where the large bell and drum are located. I have never seen him enter the hall but have seen the lights of the hall flicker on. Suddenly the bell sounds, or if one is close enough to the hall, first the melodious chanting of the striker before he swings the long wooden beam to strike the bell. When the large bell first sounds, it is taking over from the temple block; the two acknowledge the handoff by a brief series of call and response: bell, block, bell, block, bell. In Chinese these handoffs are called joinings or connections (*jie* 接), but I prefer to think of this form of instrument interaction as a handshake or call and response. These continue from the time of the temple block through the end of the morning service.[6] The striker continues chanting and striking until he has struck the bell 108 times using three sets of eighteen fast and eighteen slow rings, said to represent the ringing away the 108 defilements (*kleśa*).[7] As the bell sounds, the monks will begin to stir and get ready for the day and a third and fourth monk appear known as the incense and lamp attendants (*xiangdeng* 香灯). One enters the dharma hall to light the candles, the other the ordination hall to get ready to sound the drum. After approximately fifteen minutes of the bell, the drum comes in. After a brief handshake, the drummer takes off with the energetic and rhythmic hammering of the large drum just across from the large bell in the ordination hall. These sounds emanate from the slats in the hall of the ordination platform. The sounds seem to be amplified by the hall itself. The contrast between the bell and drum is quite striking. The one is sharp, piercing, ringing; the other, dull, droning, and booming. These monks seem to be calling the day into being, raising *yang,* using surprisingly lively *qi* on the bell and drum. The block, the bell, and the drum start the day. Profane homogenous time of modernity is subverted. The intention, agency, precision insist on this—bell, block, bell, block, bell. It is akin to a key entering a lock, opening a door of time, a new day of dharma.

As the drum begins, monks in their robes begin to emerge from their cells; the drum is hammered with three sets of eighteen fast, eighteen slow for a total of 108 strikes to the beat of the Great Compassion mantra (*dabei zhou* 大悲咒). Monks make their way toward the dharma hall, adjusting their robes as they enter the hall between 4:00 and 4:30 a.m. They take their places on the right or left of the hall standing between cushions, then face forward and

FIG. 3.1 Monks at a morning service in the dharma hall, 2006. Photo by the author.

prostrate toward the front of the hall. After prostrating, they stand and turn to face the middle aisle between the rows of cushions. The drummer, sweating in his undershirt, concludes around 4:30 a.m., making a handshake with the large bell in the dharma hall, which signals the start of the morning service.

The Morning Service

The monks assembled are usually joined by three or four laywomen dressed in black gowns. They stand on the right side at the end of the last two rows. The number of monks regularly attending the morning service from 2006 to 2019 ranged from twenty-five to thirty-five. This communal service repeated daily in the early morning and early evening is the defining communal religious practice of modern Chinese monastics. It is called simply the morning and evening service (*zaowan ke* 早晚课) and is based on the *Zhaomu kesong* included in the *Various Sutras for Daily Recitation* (*Zhujing risong*) first edited and assembled by the important Ming dynasty scholar-practitioner monk Zhuhong in 1600. Pi-yen Chen describes the centrality of these services:

> They [morning and evening services] denote the two periods of solemn liturgical practice held during early morning and evening, the practice of which is the primary duty of all monks and nuns in Chinese Buddhism. The daily service is the most important daily function in contemporary Buddhist monasteries. As the first and the last daily communal religious activities, morning and evening service has been designed for purifying the mind and promoting the religious sentiment of the sangha. (2002, 229)

This importance has been reiterated by monks I have spoken to throughout southern Fujian.[8] As I doggedly asked the abbot of Nanputo about forms of practice revived at monasteries in China, I also asked about his view of morning and evening assemblies as a form of cultivation. His answer is worth quoting in full.

> Well, *zaowan ke* is generally not considered a form of cultivation. *Zaowan ke* is something every temple has, something absolutely necessary [*bibukeshao* 必不可少]. It is a small part of cultivation. It will help improve your practice [*cujin zuoyong*], but *zaowan ke* can't represent practice on its own. Still, it is still necessary; like drinking water. People must drink every day, but it won't fill you up.[9]

His view that it is an obligation of all monks was shared by other monks I have asked about it, but his analogy of its being water, not food, seems to illustrate the shared view best. Although morning and evening services are an obligation, they are not considered a form of cultivation on par with meditation or study. This suggests a problem if monks are not participating in the daily assemblies. The ethnographic fact that at Kaiyuan generally fewer than half of the monks regularly attend morning and evening service would then seem to be a failing. Monks with positions and other duties are excused from attending. Young monks at Kaiyuan are expected to memorize these daily liturgies as soon as possible, if they have not already done so as preparation for their ordination. Welch's principal informant about monastic life reported that his first task as a monk during the Republican period was to memorize the morning and evening liturgies (1967, 351). The daily recitation helps, but generally younger monks in the back rows mumble along with the others or keep silent because they have yet to memorize the mostly obscure passages. Perhaps the laywomen who have memorized the service serve as an encouragement for those monks who have yet to do so.

The daily services are held at 4:30 a.m. and around 4:00 p.m., before the evening meal.[10] The daily services are the first thing monks do after rising and getting dressed and the last thing they are supposed to do before settling down for the evening; thus it is meant to orient their lives toward communal religious cultivation. Chen Pi-Yen has carefully studied Chinese Buddhist liturgical music and the morning and evening service and describes its significance: "It is the core liturgy of Chinese Buddhism, and it occupies the preeminent position among monastic activities" (2010, 8).[11] The morning service liturgy is centered around a concern with purifying the mind, thus establishing conditions for a day of meritorious living. The evening service turns thoughts to the Pure Land of Amitabha, as one prepares to retire for the day.

As mentioned, monks with other duties and titles are exempt from participating in morning and evening services because it is thought to interfere with their other obligations. The result of this exemption on religious cultivation is profound. Fewer than half of Kaiyuan's monks attend daily services with any regularity. The number generally is about thirty, but can increase to between forty and forty-six on the first and fifteenth of the lunar month. Put differently, about half of the monastic population does not fulfill a basic obligation recognized as a fundamental form of communal religious cultivation throughout the Chinese Buddhist world. Exempting these monks from daily services would be more understandable if their other duties provided an opportunity for daily communal practice other than mealtimes, but such formal opportunities are not currently available at this site.

It seems disadvantageous that more monks do not participate in the daily liturgical services but may be comparable to the tradition of having an elite core of meditators who are supported by the rest of the monks. Robert Buswell describes such an arrangement in the *Zen Monastic Experience*

Table 1 Components of the Daily Services

Morning	Evening
Offering of Incense	*Amitābha Sūtra*
Śuraṅgama Dhāraṇī (*lengyan zhou*)	Mengshan's Rite for Feeding Hungry Ghosts
Great Compassion Dhāraṇī (*dabei zhou*) added (lunar first and fifteenth)	*Gāthās* of Merit Transfer
Ten short *dhāraṇīs* (added lunar first and fifteenth)	*Gāthās* praising the Buddha
Heart Sutra	Circumambulating Buddha recitation
Gāthās of Merit Transfer	Three Refuges
Gāthās praising the Buddha	*Great Compassion Dhāraṇī*
Circumambulating Buddha recitation	Praise for Qielan
Ten Great Vows of Samantabhadra Bodhisattva (added lunar first and fifteenth)	
Three Refuges	
Praise for Weituo	

(1992). The difference, which is no small affair, is that at the monastery where Buswell practiced all monks were required to attend morning and evening services *except* the meditating monks. Thus all save a select number of administrative monks were engaged in regular communal practice, either meditation or the daily liturgies. The morning service Buswell describes, however, is less burdensome on the monk—about fifteen minutes long, versus the thirty minutes to more than an hour at Kaiyuan (1992, 38–39).[12]

An exceptionally graceful and controlled monk is tasked with the lead role for preparing and making offerings to the Buddha with highly stylized gestures and movements as part of the service. This monk uses the center aisle and all others are arrayed along the sides. The offerings presented include incense and a bowl of freshly steamed rice, which lay volunteers begin making early in the morning. An assistant monk stands just outside the hall to assist the leader, in particular by running to get the rice offering when it is ready. In addition to the lead chanting monk who stands in the top left row, nearest the Buddha statue, monks play a drum and bell set (*bao zhong gu*), a large chime (*qingbo* 磬钵), the hand chime (*shouqing* 手磬), and large and small wooden fish (*muyu* 木鱼). These dharma instruments take over from the large bell inside the dharma hall with a series of handshakes between the bell, the large chime, and large wooden fish. The dharma instruments keep rhythm and provide a musical quality to the morning and evening services which assists in memorization and concentration.[13] The importance of keeping a steady rhythm is emphasized by the contemporary monk Chen-hua: "The community's spiritual work depends upon a measured rhythm for chanting. This is a matter of utmost significance. The loudness and tempo of the bell and wooden fish should be moderate. Never be careless" (1992, 150). The service is manifest through sound and rhythm.

As much as 80 percent of the morning service involves the recitation of *dhāraṇīs* and mantras (*tuoluoni* 陀罗尼, *zhou* 咒); the principal one being the *Śuraṇgama Dhāraṇī,* which tradition has it was taught by the Buddha to Ānanda to remove lustful thoughts from his mind; thus it is an important part of the traditional monk's training—lustful thoughts being a common distraction to the spiritual progress of monastics, young and old. It is considered a good way to begin the day. The *dhāraṇī* may be said to have some meaning, namely, as a mnemonic device or condensed summary for Indian Buddhist sutras, but for all the monks of this study and Chinese monks in general *dhāraṇī* have no articulate meaning, just sound.[14] Although they experientially lack articulate semantic value, they are understood by the monks in line with Mahayana teachings to have power (and thus sometimes are translated as "spell") and to be an important part of a bodhisattva's training.[15] Apart from any esoteric power *dhāraṇī* may have, that they are Chinese transcriptions of Sanskrit and function as combinations of syllables means that they can clear the minds of those reciting them much better than recognizable strings of words, which inevitably trigger additional associations and thoughts. Asked about their experience with morning and evening services, monks have all mentioned the ability to clear their minds of distractions and concerns and make them more relaxed. When asked about his views of *dhāraṇī* and whether they benefited his practice, one of the more articulate and enthusiastic monks replied,

> It can preserve all virtuous dharmas [*shanfa*] so that they are not lost and prevent all evil dharmas from arising. This is its essence/best feature [*jinghua*]. It is the secret dharma gate of buddhas and bodhisattvas. All buddhas and bodhisattvas spoke the *dhāraṇīs,* all of this I completely and firmly believe [*jianxin*], also after reciting I feel very peaceful and comfortable, because [the *dhāraṇī*] is full of the compassion and wisdom of Buddhas and bodhisattvas. . . the *Great Compassion dhāraṇī,* the *Rebirth* [*wangsheng*] *dhāraṇī,* the *Ten Short dhāraṇī,* and the *Śuraṇgama dhāraṇī* are ones we must recite every day. As long as one chants them from the heart, they will cast out delusions and bring peace to our hearts. I have very clear personal experience practicing these so I have great faith in *dhāraṇī!*

This monk has greater facility in discussing Buddhist ritual than most, but his enthusiastic embrace of *dhāraṇīs* as an efficacious and experientially verifiable path to virtue and wisdom is in line with recent studies of the place of *dhāraṇīs* in Chinese monastic training. In particular, Richard McBride examined the overlooked place of *dhāraṇī* on the Mahayana bodhisattva path and in mainstream Chinese monastic training in the medieval period (2005). He writes,

> I have emphasized hitherto ignored evidence from Buddhist literature that strongly suggests that Buddhist intellectuals and eminent monks conceptualized *dhāraṇī* and spells as integral components of mainstream Sinitic Buddhism. . . . *Dhāraṇī* have a firmly established position in the Mahayana doctrine of the bodhisattva path. They were perceived to be part of an ordinary monk's religious cultivation and a by-product of meditation. In this respect they are closely associated with an advanced monk or bodhisattva's acquisition of the spiritual penetrations, supernormal powers and the ability to work miracles. (2005, 113)

Scholars have generally overlooked the importance of *dhāraṇī* in monastic life, dismissing them as a proto-Tantric relic (McBride 2005). Beyond the medieval period to the early modern, we find the famous Ming dynasty Chan master Zibo (1543–1604), dubbed the last great Zen master of China by J. C. Cleary, similarly praising and recommending the recitation of *dhāraṇī* (1989, 136–138). What the contemporary sangha shows us is that this remains an essential part of being a member of a monastic community in China and a respected form of practice leading to the highest goals of the tradition for many monks, institutionalized for centuries through the daily service.

The chanting, driven forward by the rhythmic accompaniment of the bronze chime and wooden fish and punctuated by the hand chime and small hand cymbals, is meant to focus and purify the mind. Over the course of the service, monks will stand alternately facing forward and facing those across the aisle and perform prostrations. Toward the end of the service, the monks begin to chant a simple mantra as they are led out into the central aisle, around the back of the Buddha statue, and then zigzag through the rows of cushions on both sides of the aisle. This mantra changes according to the annual and monthly ritual calendars. At Kaiyuan, the most common mantra used in the morning is "Homage to Bodhisattva Guanyin." Others are "Homage to Buddha Amitabha" and "Homage to Śākyamuni Buddha." Three circuits around the hall are made before returning to their original cushions. Known as *raofo* 绕佛 (circumambulating Buddha), it might be better translated as serpentine Buddha recitation. It is a kind of walking meditation combined with variations of the fundamental practice of Mahayana and Hindu traditions, chanting mantras.

The logic of beginning the day at 4:30 in the morning with these *dhāraṇīs,* praises, and recitations is to purify the mind, body, and speech, the three sources of karma (*sanye* 三业) before beginning to engage with others and with the torrent of distracting thoughts and interactions that may come throughout the day. The voice chants Buddha teachings, the body is engaged only in the service, and the mind is meant to rest or focus on the recitation; in this way body, speech, and mind are able to be purified through participation in the morning and evening services and other forms of recitation.[16] As a mindful participant in these assemblies, I can attest that body and mind are immersed in a buddhicized environment in which all senses are engaged: one sees monks and laypersons in robes, a buddha statue, smoke rising from incense; one hears chanting and dharma instruments; one smells fragrant incense; one feels (out) the air vibrating with dharma instruments and chanting and feels (in) the body prostrating and circumambulating; and there is nothing to taste but one's saliva. The morning and evening services are a full body-speech-mind immersion, a purifactory bath. I would not have known this from observing or interviewing alone; this is where the value of embodied participation and mindful phenomenological observation and description come into play. We are just beginning to understand the extent to which things are known, not by the head, but by the body (Menakem 2017). Katherine Hayles terms the knowledge that our bodies generate moment to moment, especially our stomachs and hearts, "nonconscious cognition" (2017). Patricia Campbell makes this point in her exploration of the role of ritualized learning in Buddhist practice in North America: "Ritualizing can generate a kind of knowing that is located in blood, bone, and muscle, and in an embodied, gestural entity that we call the mind" (2011, 208). The morning and evening services are fundamentally about this kind of embodied learning.

Meals in the Dining Hall

After morning service, the monks exit the hall single file and process to the dining hall, some stepping away to return to their dorms. When I asked about monks not taking their meals in the dining hall, they said that some like to order food, including nonvegetarian food, to be delivered to their rooms. For those who do eat in the dining hall, doing so is an important part of communal practice because the hall is where almost all the monks take their meals on a daily basis, ceremoniously and in silence, some using their own traditional begging bowls. Meals are called by striking the wooden board in the shape of a fish hanging outside the refectory. Once the monks have gathered in the dining hall, recitations are uttered and a monk makes a ritual offering of rice to hungry ghosts on a pedestal just outside the main entrance.

After feeding the hungry ghosts, the meal may begin. Monastic discipline is more on display during meals than at other times. The long narrow tables found in monastic dining halls are an outstanding material feature that contrasts with Chinese society at large, where the typical table for groups is round, so that everyone faces one another, supporting a communicative if not convivial atmosphere. Such tables allow space for monks to sit side by side as if at a long bar save that no one faces them. This material feature institutionalizes the solitary nature of individual cultivation. Another critical and exemplary embodied feature is silence. The meal is taken in silence, again a noteworthy departure from the Chinese norm, as anyone who has been in a restaurant with Chinese diners can attest. Having experienced meals in monastery refectories on several occasions, I can report that the meal, particularly when one keeps in mind the five contemplations, is a powerful vehicle of cultivation. Monastic dining halls are called the hall of five contemplations (*wuguan tang* 五观堂). These contemplations are the five thoughts to keep in mind at mealtimes (*shi cun wuguan* 食存五观) and are meant to keep one's mind focused in a proper way. They are to, first, remember how much work was expended to provide this food; second, ponder whether one's virtue is sufficient to receive this offering; third, guard one's mind from fleeing and being seized by greed-lust (*rāga*) or other hindrances (*kleśas*);[17] fourth, properly take [this food] as good medicine for your withering body; and, fifth, eat only to sustain the body to practice the dharma.[18]

The five contemplations present ideas found throughout Buddhist scripture, such as that eating is to support the body to have strength to put the path into practice and that one should guard against impure thoughts. In addition, they include ideas particular to the vocation of a monastic. For example, one is reminded that the monastery food is provided by others expressly in support of the Buddhist vocation and that one should prove one's worthiness by practicing virtue. The first contemplation is directed outward, toward the many people who labored to grow, harvest, prepare, and serve the food that sits in one's bowl. Among the feelings generated is gratitude, which leads directly to the second contemplation, "Do I deserve such generosity?" This contemplation is part of a monastics' expected self-reflection, which includes regular self-confession (*chanhui* 忏悔). The feelings generated by these thoughts include shame over shortcomings and commitment to strive for improvement. This leads directly to the third contemplation, which offers a way to immediately cultivate the path and make one's mind worthy at least now while consuming the offering by practicing mindfulness to clear the heart-mind (*xin* 心) of errant thoughts and feelings. The fourth contemplation supports this effort by training the mind not to approach the food as we may be wont to do, judging it as well seasoned or not, as a good temperature or not, as nicely presented or not, but rather to see the food simply as medicine to keep our body fit. The final contemplation completes this meditation by reminding us that this food provides us with energy to practice the dharma and that we should keep this in mind as we eat, as we leave the hall, and as we continue our day.

Although monks can be expected to be distracted by other thoughts while eating and are not always successful in carrying out the five contemplations with care, the dining hall nevertheless imposes the conditions that facilitate self-reflection, namely, narrow tables and silence. In 2006, the proctor monitored the dining hall to ensure that order was maintained; he impressed me as one of if not the most stern of the monks at Kaiyuan. The required silence removes social demands other than sitting and eating. When sitting sit, when eating eat. Can one practice this Chan teaching in a typical social meal with family, friends, or even strangers? Not easily. But the material features of the dining hall and the monastic regulations governing its use cooperate to facilitate an embodied session of cultivation.

An unusual feature of meals in the dining hall at Kaiyuan is the absence of the abbot; it is unusual because this is traditionally one of the duties of the abbot and is followed at other monasteries in China.[19] The abbot has a personal chef who prepares meals for him and his small staff of clerics. As a guest of the abbot, I too generally dined with the abbot and members of his staff. The abbot's chefs (he had three from 2006 to 2009) are not professional and the food produced in his kitchen is not necessarily much better than that in the dining hall. The abbot's kitchen, however, did serve eggs, which were not served in the dining hall.[20] At his evening meal, the abbot typically has a simple bowl of rice porridge or congee (*zhou*)—a Chinese comfort food par excellence, but nothing fancy. The problem, apart from the unusual use of eggs in the abbot's kitchen, is the lack of communal solidarity that comes from not eating with the other members of the sangha; it weakens the ties between common and elite monks. The latter frequently have the opportunity to take their meals elsewhere, with lay patrons, at banquets or meetings. The abbot and the three or four monks who live in his quarters almost never took meals in the dining hall in the middle and late 2000s. Meals with the abbot are typically times to discuss matters of monastic business, news, or other mundane affairs and thus one less opportunity for contemplation, which monks dining silently in the hall of five observances are afforded three times a day.

Meals are not prepared by monks, but by lay volunteers.[21] Upholding the tradition in Chinese Buddhism, all meals are vegetarian. The food is simple, typically includes rice and three dishes, one of which is often Chinese cabbage, others tofu or vegetables or soup. Breakfast includes warm soy milk, vegetables, and rice porridge (*zhou*). On special occasions, they will have Chinese stuffed steamed buns (*baozi*)—a crowd pleaser. The evening meal is referred to at Kaiyuan as "dinner of hidden [from ghosts] food" (偷食晚餐) or "medicine and stone [needles]" (*yaoshi* 药石), that is, medicine. These euphemisms are to deflect from the violation of the monastic rule to not eat after noon, which some monks at Kaiyuan intermittently observe; the East Asian sangha has long considered an evening meal a type of medicine (which was not prohibited by the Buddha). Apart from the rule of silence and ritualized dimension of the meals, the regular and communal nature is a powerful regulatory force in the lives of the monks. It provides a kind of regularity that promotes, in some sense, personal discipline, and sets them up for success if they are motivated to practice forms of self-cultivation.

I found the regularity of meals as well as the lack of choice regarding food to be liberating as one less thing to have to think about or plan for. Monks are freed of the daily cognitive load required to make decisions about meals; one just has to show up, but to show up on time. There is no choice about when to eat, though there is in terms of what to take of the three or four dishes and how much to get, but one is free from worrying what to cook, order, or buy. This is not the same as begging in the earliest strata of Buddhist monasticism, though it is similar in the lack of choice. One eats what is provided and should practice gratitude. This element also inspires one to do one's best as though to earn such provisions.

Between lunch and dinner, the evening service is held in the dharma hall. In the evening, the emphasis is on directing the mind to the Pure Land, as well as penance for misdeeds and self-admonishment to strive to practice. Apart from the prevalence of esoteric *dhāraṇīs,* another marked feature of the morning and evening service is the institutionalization of Pure Land Buddhism in a number of ways, including buddha recitation (*nianfo*), reciting the vow to be reborn in the Pure Land, and most especially in the evening service through reciting the *Smaller Pure Land Scripture* (Skt. *Sukhāvatyamrtavūha Sūtra,* Ch. *Amituo jing*). The *Smaller Pure Land Sutra* introduces Amitabha's Pure Land, praises Amitabha, and exhorts all to chant the Buddha's name to be reborn in the Western Pure Land. These services have been the core practice of all schools of Chinese Buddhist monasticism for at least four hundred years: "Chan on the outside, Pure Land on the inside."

The goal of the evening service is said to lead participants to the Pure Land through practicing the five gates of *nianfo:* worship (*libai* 礼拜), praise (*zantan* 赞叹), the vow [to be reborn in the Pure Land] (*zuoyuan* 作愿), contemplation of the virtues of the Pure Land and Amitabha (*guancha* 观察), and merit transfer (*huixiang* 回向).[22] Amitabha is the Buddha who vowed to bring those who call him into his Pure Land. The practice began to be promoted in sixth-century China as an appropriate form of practice for the age of degenerate dharma.[23] Practitioners believe that it is important to often *nianfo* so that it will become second nature and therefore easier to do at the moment of death when it is thought to be most important to make contact with the saving grace of Amitabha. *Nianfo* is also used as a form of meditation; chanting the name of Amitabha is thought to be an effective way of stopping the flow of thoughts and entering a state of *samādhi* (*sanmei*), or meditative absorption.[24] Amitabha's Pure Land is described in the Pure Land sutras as a land of trees and ponds of precious jewels, stones, and metals that is "pure and serene, resplendent and blissful."[25] Once born there, one is destined to achieve liberation in the following birth. Birth in Amitabha's Pure Land has become the central goal of the average Chinese Buddhist. The goal is achieved by *nianfo,* but also by generating merit and raising the mind of compassion and enlightenment (*bodhicitta*).

The end of the day is marked from 7:00 to 7:30 in the evening by the sounds of the bell ringing from the hall of the ordination platform, followed by the booming of the drum. The day begins with the block and bell and ends with the drum and block. Several times as I walked out after dinner, I encountered two monks walking together, circumambulating the hall of the ordination platform as the bell and drum were being sounded. It seemed to be part exercise, part socializing, and part religious cultivation. Circumambulating statues, texts, relics, and the like has long been considered a meritorious practice in Buddhism. Doing so as the bell and drum are being sounded allows a sonic accompaniment to walking and breathing that helps clear and focus the mind.

Evenings are quiet. The gates have been closed and locked and the visitors and tourists have left. Thus concludes our sketch of the communal features of a typical day, framed by the block, bell, and drum. The dharma instruments produce a distinct soundscape that divides the day and breaks up time, producing intentionally heterogeneous time in contrast to the ideal of homogenous time of modernity.[26] The theme of heterogeneity of space returns in chapters 5 and 6. How individual monks spend their days is returned to in chapter 4. Now we turn to activities held on a weekly basis.

The Weekly Calendar

The larger Buddhist monasteries in Quanzhou all have weekly public *nianfo* or Buddha recitation sessions. At Kaiyuan, these are held every Tuesday and Friday. The *nianfo* sessions are held in the main hall, which is the site of all of Kaiyuan's major public ritual services, such as the release of burning mouths (*fang yankou*) and various rituals to eliminate disasters and bring benefits. Most significantly, however, it is the site of the well-attended twice-weekly Buddha recitation sessions and the monthly Buddha recitation (discussed later). These regular gatherings of laypersons (weekly and monthly) are significant because they are unusually large and attest to the relative vitality of Buddhist traditions in southern Fujian.[27]

Two to three hundred lay devotees donning the dark brown or black robes of a layperson regularly attend the twice-weekly *nianfo* meetings, whereas the monthly lunar twenty-sixth meetings are attended by more than two thousand devotees, including more than three hundred who wear layperson robes. The robes are simply worn over street clothes; typically, laypeople unceremoniously change into and out of these robes in front of the main hall. Approximately 95 percent of those wearing robes and regularly attending the twice-weekly services are older retired women with short hair. Two men regularly join the women, and always a few middle-aged women do. Monks lead the laypersons in chanting the *Amitabha Sutra,* which culminates in the recitation of "Homage to Amitabha Buddha" as all participants circumambulate the main hall in a serpentine way. These services begin about 2:30 in the afternoon and last an hour. The *nianfo* service is thus longer than the typical morning and evening liturgical service and is thus more of an investment by the laywomen, almost all of whom are older than sixty-five and on their feet practically the entire time.

I was welcomed when I joined them. I found that most women had memorized the liturgy. Only some followed along in small red scripture books. The first half of the service is chanted while standing and occasionally bowing toward the buddhas; the second half is the circumambulation. Most participants remained focused on the service the entire time. Only a few chatted with friends at the beginning and during the brief pause preceding the circumambulation. Monks played dharma instruments and led the stylized chanting using microphones and amplification. Laywomen orchestrated the circumambulation by signaling to each row that should file out and guiding the participants, such as myself, who were not in robes. We were directed to file in at the end of the line following the laity in gowns. Fewer than 10 percent of participants were not in gowns.

The first time I joined them, I followed their lead and began with my hands together, at my chest, prayer-like, as in the *añjali mudrā*. I did not notice that as we turned the first corner the women placed their hands in the meditation mudra with the right hand on top of the left with the thumbs touching. I was quickly corrected; as soon as we began walking next to the line of lay Buddhists facing us (serpentine circumambulating) a woman excitedly waved her hands and signaled how I should hold my own. I quickly complied. What it told me was the seriousness of the practice in the eyes of the regulars, or—better—the invariability of certain ritual elements. Roy Rappaport, an important ritual theorist, emphasizes invariability as a critical and meaningful dimension of liturgy: "To *perform* a liturgical order, which is by definition a more or less invariant sequence of formal acts and utterances *encoded by someone other than the performer* himself, is *necessarily to conform to it*" (1999, 118, emphasis in the original). That I was corrected in how to hold my hands and was able to walk in serpentine formation in unison with more than two hundred others points to conformity with a set of encoded sequences. In what ways is conforming to a preordained order significant? Rappaport continues, "Participants enliven the order that they are performing with the energy of their own bodies, and their own voices make it articulate. They thereby establish the existence of that order in this world of matter and energy; they *substantiate* the order as it *informs* them" (1999, 125, emphasis in the original). Participation in the codified liturgy is an acceptance of what it represents and legitimizes it. The importance of such liturgical assemblies in the early days cannot be overstated as vehicles for reinscribing space with religious meaning, by instantiating and enlivening ancient traditions of Pure Land practice in post-Mao China. Through the enactment of formal *nianfo* assemblies, Amitabha Buddha and his vow to bring the faithful into his Pure Land is reestablished as a social fact. As Rappaport notes, "As far as present day society is concerned, Jupiter, Woden, En-Lil and Marduk are no longer anything more than figments of ancient imaginings, for no one continues to establish or re-establish their being by calling their names in ritual" (1999, 279). It is through active conformity with liturgical precedents, in this case chanting Amitabha's name within a collective body, that create a living tradition of social facts.

The woman correcting the position of my hands also alerted me to a dimension of the practice I had failed to notice when observing from afar, the use of the meditation mudra. I had read that *nianfo* practice could be a form of contemplative or meditative practice, and now I saw that they even used the meditation mudra while circumambulating and kept their heads down, trained on the floor. Experiencing the rhythmic and embodied nature of the chanting and walking in unison with more than two hundred others made it clear how this practice was very much a form of contemplative practice that with time and commitment could serve as a vehicle of deeper cultivation.[28]

One element that especially impressed me was passing and seeing every other person in the hall during the circumambulation. This generates a strong sense of being together, being one in the task at hand. A task of, from my point of view, glorifying the Buddha, praising his name. As with morning and evening assemblies, communal *nianfo* practice intentionally facilitates complete engagement of body, speech, and mind (Ch. *sanye*; Skt. *trini-karmani*) —body through standing and walking, speech through chanting, mind through concentration on the task at hand. All of this combines for a powerful, and with the final mantra, focused experience. That it is an hour long suggests comparison with Catholic mass. One major difference is the relative taxing nature of *nianfo*. One is always standing or walking and always vocalizing; it seems like a greater commitment; one does not simply sit in a pew for most of it. My voice was tired shortly after *nianfo*. As I recorded in my field notes, "There is a collective, communal energy that gets produced in the session and I can see it being very satisfying. Possibly a bit of a rush for people, something to look forward to and keep them coming back. And presumably doing this week after week it goes deeper."

These gatherings and the energy generated can be understood as offering a meaningful respite from day to day obligations of life, work, and family. They may also be seen as an example of Durkheim's collective effervescence or Victor Turner's communitas.[29] Both Durkheim and Turner understood ritualized assemblies as encouraging those assembled to conform to norms, values, and behaviors represented by the symbols deployed (Olaveson 2001, 98). As Robert Sharf writes, "Participation in a living ritual tradition reaches beyond the vagaries of the intellect to one's somatic being; ritual habituation indelibly inscribes the self with a set of perceptual orientations, affective dispositions, and autonomic responses that are, in effect, precognitive" (2005, 249). For the Pure Land devotee, the extended nature of this collective chanting sears the chant into one's heart-mind (*xin*), to use the Chinese term. How does that manifest? One way is like a song that gets stuck in one's head, except rather than catchy lyrics or a pop song tune, the melody and words are of salvific significance, words believers hope to have baked into their hearts and minds. Days after the *nianfo* session, I woke up with the tune in my head. Other lay Buddhists cheerfully agreed that this happened to them too.

When the session is complete, the monks quickly file out of the hall and back to their dorms to change from their ceremonial robes of bright yellow to their regular robes of dull yellow or rust color. The laywomen gather in small groups to chat as they remove their dark brown robes and fold them into their bags before leaving the temple. These sessions thus also serve a social function; women get together and visit before and after and many come and go in small groups. A religious ritual is probably never just about religion. The twice-weekly *nianfo* sessions are among the most vibrantly religious events that take place and yet they also serve a distinct social function for the typical lay Buddhist. Such rituals are also an important way of world-making and identity construction. By holding the sessions, Kaiyuan and other large monasteries in the area provide an opportunity for older women and anyone else who wishes to join to engage in this traditional form of Buddhist practice that Chinese Buddhist tradition considers a gate to higher stages of realization with others engaged in collective pursuit.

The Monthly Calendar

In Theravada countries—Sri Lanka, Thailand, Myanmar, Laos, and Cambodia—the most important regular communal activity of the sangha is the fortnightly recitation of the *prātimokṣa* vows known as *uposatha* (*busa* 布薩) on the first and fifteenth of the lunar month, the new and full moon days (Gombrich 1988, 106–110). This is a tradition that has not been important in China in modern times. Welch reports that he only knew of one monastery where vows were recited (1967, 110). Kaiyuan and other Quanzhou temples do not have a tradition of reciting the *prātimokṣa,* but they do expand the liturgy used in the morning and evening recitations and more monks join the service at this time.[30] On these days, the liturgical chant is "Homage to Śākyamuni Buddha." At the end of the service, monks file out of the dharma hall and proceed to the hall of patriarchs (*zutang*), where they burn incense and prostrate to their Chan ancestors from India and China, past abbots, the temple founder, eminent monks associated with the temple (including Yuanying, Zhuandao, and Zhuanwu), parents, virtuous monks of the Sangha, and the current abbot. Laypersons and worshippers will also visit the temple in much greater than average numbers, make donations, and burn gold paper on these days, considered days of greater auspiciousness.[31] Thomas Dubois reports that temples in rural North China were typically locked up every day except the first and fifteenth (2005, 58). As ethnographer John Lagerwey points out, elderly women in Southeast China aim to worship at several temples on the first and fifteenth of each lunar month based on a belief that Buddhas descend to inspect the world on these days (2010, 151).[32] With the increase in devotional activity comes an increase in donations, which makes these days an important source of income for temples throughout Fujian.

Lunar Twenty-Sixth Nianfo *Day*

The biggest day, however, at Buddhist temples throughout southern Fujian is the day designated to serve free noodles to devotees. At Kaiyuan, this day is the twenty-sixth day of the lunar month. On it, the monastery is crowded with thousands of worshippers and lay Buddhists who come to burn incense, offer fruit and flowers, make donations, eat bowls of noodles, burn gold paper, and chant Buddha's name. Monks estimate from twenty to thirty thousand worshippers each month and at least double or triple that for the first and last months of the year, with up to one hundred thousand during the first month of the lunar year. Locals say that the tradition was initiated by Yuanying, Zhuandao, and Zhuanwu during the War against Japanese Aggression in the 1930s to alleviate the suffering of the locals. Records attest to offerings of porridge disaster relief dharma assemblies (施粥救灾法会) in 1936 as part of flood relief that year (Zhuanfa 2004).[33] At that time, noodles were offered as needed. Now, however, they are prepared once a month, on the twenty-sixth lunar day. Regardless of its precise origins, the tradition of offering free noodles once a month has been institutionalized at Buddhist temples across the city of Quanzhou; each temple holds their day on different days of the lunar month. I visited a very small temple restored by one of Kaiyuan's monks in

FIG. 3.2 Crowds with offerings and incense in front of the main hall on a *nianfo* day (lunar twenty-sixth), 2006. Photo by the author.

the mountains outside Quanzhou, home to only two resident monks, but they had two huge woks and a gas burner set up expressly to make large batches of noodles each month.

Preparation of noodles begins in the days leading up to the twenty-sixth. Noodles are handmade by lay volunteers and dried in the open air by laying them on plastic tarps strewn about the shrine to Elder Huang (Tanyueci), the hall of patriarchs, and elsewhere. Preparation begins the evening before the big day. Volunteers work all night preparing vast amounts of cabbage, bok choy, and bean sprouts along with the soup stock, eventually boiling noodles as dawn breaks. The noodles are prepared and cooked in a crude yet adequate kitchen area at the back of the monastery. The front gate of the monastery, including the central doors that are normally closed, are opened at 4:00 a.m. By 8:00 a.m., the monastery is crowded and buzzing with visitors, inside and out bearing offerings of flowers, fruit, vegetables, noodles, snacks, candy, incense, candles, and gold paper. The scene outside the front gate is lively, colorful, and evocative of a market scene with dozens of vendors set up with temporary stalls selling fruits, gold paper, flowers, and incense.

Four long tables are set up in two rows on the large platform that stretches before the main hall. Visitors crowd these table with red tote bags of offerings as worshippers fill the spaces around the main hall. In 2006 and 2009, in addition to opening the monastery to worshippers, vendors were also allowed to enter and spread out their wares on mats or directly on the concrete courtyard or corridors. The vendors sold anything from kitchenware to antiques. The day essentially becomes an open market and provides insight into how religiously based gatherings contribute to neighborhood economies. The scene is crowded, lively, and festive. A handful of uniformed security officers are hired by the monastery to keep an eye on the distribution of noodles and crowds in general. When I attempted to film visitors with bowls of noodles, I was stopped from doing so. The concern was that foreigners had filmed such crowds in the past and used the images to show China was poor; the officer did not want it to happen again.[34]

In addition to consuming a bowl of noodles, visitors also make offerings of various kinds. Almost everyone offers incense. Visitors light sticks of incense using candles set out and lit by monks in trays in the main courtyard in anticipation of the visitors. They generally bow toward the main hall and toward the front gate before placing their sticks of incense in the burner in the main courtyard. The burner rapidly fills up and gloved laypersons and monks are on duty to remove and extinguish sticks continually to make room for more. Some visitors hold their incense at their chest or foreheads, kneel on the stone pavement facing south, then north, absorbed in prayer. Parents and grandparents can be seen instructing young children how to hold incense, bow, and, sometimes, kneel, socializing the next generation to these traditional forms of worship. Although offering incense may seem disconnected from the heart of Buddhism from a modernist point of view, it is mentioned in the earliest Indian sutras and vinayas, where the Buddha states that offering incense may be understood as a "messenger summoning the Buddha" (Yifa 2002, 10). For most worshippers and lay Buddhists, offering incense and prostration is connected to making a vow (*fayuan* 发愿) or request (*xuyuan* 许愿) or repaying a fulfilled wish (*huanyuan* 还愿).[35]

Essentially all visitors on this day will offer incense at the front (five Buddhas) and back (Guanyin and Lohans/Arhats) of the main hall and in front of the hall of the ordination platform (Vairocana 卢舍那大佛, Weituo 韦驮, and so on). Some will continue to the dharma hall, but practically none make it all the way back to the hall of patriarchs.[36] Space in front of the ordination hall is not especially wide and becomes extremely crowded on these days. After offering incense and bowing to Vairocana and the other figures in the ordination hall, many visitors then burn gold paper in the furnace, which lies immediately to the east of the ordination platform. Worshippers will make cash donations at each of the halls and at special tables set up to the east of the main hall, where their names and amount donated will be recorded. In 2006, four or five large laundry bags were placed at each table for collecting donations. Donations at these special tables are associated with the noodle soup offered and considered auspicious; it is thought that one must donate according to one's means to benefit from eating the noodles. Visitors generally make donations well in excess of the cost of the noodles. The day is a critical source of funds for the monastery. The donations collected on lunar twenty-six *nianfo* days are enough to meet most of the temple's regular expenses, including stipends for the resident monastics. In addition to supporting the monastery, the donations, from a Buddhist point of view, are a way of enabling patrons to cultivate the important Buddhist virtue of generosity. *Dāna* (charity) is the first of the six "perfections" a Buddhist should strive to cultivate. Although all forms of moral behavior are understood to garner merit, making donations to the sangha is the most commonly practiced action for lay Buddhists.[37] By donating to the sangha, they are planting a seed in a "field of merit" thought to enable them to reap great merit in return.

According to my informants, the tremendous amount of money that flows into the temple on lunar twenty-sixth days made up about 20 percent of the monastery's income in 2006, a total of approximately ¥500,000 each month, ¥6 million per year (about $750,000). Given such funds, I was inclined to see this as a method of generating income; and indeed it must be seen as such. But it is also more than that. Even within the orbit of cash donations, it is more than that. In addition to the general sense of merit generated for donors is the more immediate effect of cultivating generosity as an antidote to greed and selfishness. Seen in such a light, the transfer of ¥6 million per year from individuals to the monastery represents a significant (and quantifiable) reduction of avarice and egoism.

The noodle soup is prepared in huge pots that are then transported by cart from the kitchen area to a largely open area between the main hall and the east pagoda. Ceramic bowls are provided, washed, and reused; people may also bring their own bowls and many do. People stand in line waiting to be served the soup, which they generally take away to east of the central axis to find a place to eat among hundreds of individuals spread out, sitting here and there, under trees, on steps and so on, happily consuming bowls of auspicious noodles. The energy in the air is palpable, as one enthusiastic woman exclaimed: "This temple is a place of bodhisattvas, these bodhisattvas have been feeding people here for a long time!"

At 10:30 a.m., a Pure Land recitation ceremony, like the one held every Tuesday and Friday, is held in the main hall. The only difference is that the number of participants increases from about two hundred to some two or three thousand. That many people cannot fit inside the main hall, but three hundred can. When they begin to circumambulate, they wind through and around the hall and then out the front doors. As they leave the hall, they fall into two lines toward the east and the west pagodas, respectively, before meeting back in the front part of the main courtyard. The rest of the worshippers follow suit in turn. In this way any number of visitors can join the assembly led by monks in reciting "Homage to Amitabha Buddha." The participants zigzag around the courtyard three or four times before meeting in the middle and returning to the main hall, chanting all the while. Monks playing the wooden fish and large chime (*qingbo*) remain in the main hall chanting, the sounds being broadcast over loudspeakers, but monks will carry and use dharma instruments like the hand chime (*shouqing*) at the head of the lines. The more than two thousand individuals chanting in unison as they fill the monastery's massive courtyard is a tremendous sight of living faith and devotion in a country that had only recently determined to allow such expressions to take place. The abbot typically surveys the scene as he walks through the crowds with his hands behind his back, holding his cell phone.

The festive day usually begins at 4:00 a.m. on the twenty-sixth but in the lunar months of January and March, the central doors of the main gate are opened at 11:00 or 11:30 the previous evening, the lunar twenty-fifth. Hundreds of visitors crowd around the entrance and hundreds more gather in the streets out front, a scene of festive anticipation. When the doors are opened, the guests stream in. It is considered especially auspicious to be among the first to visit and make offerings on these days.[38] The scene on the street in front of the monastery and throughout the central axis is carnival-like. Crowds of worshippers stretch up and down the length of the street to the south of the monastery. More vendors than ever are set up outside the main gate and along the street beyond the entrance. Just inside the gate, vendors at

FIG. 3.3 Lay Buddhists, led by monks, circumambulate the main courtyard in front of the main hall chanting "Homage to Amitabha Buddha" on a *nianfo* day (lunar twenty-sixth), 2006. Photo by the author.

two tables sell bags of traditional Minnan offerings known as five fruits, six vegetarian offerings (*wuguo liuzhai* 五果六斋). The fruits can be any five fruits except guava (*fanshiliu* 番石榴) and the vegetarian offerings can be any five plus shitake mushrooms (which must be included). People continue to pour in from the main gate from 11 p.m. until about 4 a.m., then, after a lull, begin to enter in large numbers from about 6 a.m. onward. The routine is the same as any lunar twenty-sixth at Kaiyuan, just longer, more people, more noodles, more volunteers, more donations, more offerings, more everything.

The level of energy on these nights, as well as on the morning of the first day of the lunar new year, is high inside and outside the monastery. I have been told that Quanzhou people like excitement and crowds (*renao* or, in Minnan, *lau-jiat*) and I have witnessed the Quanzhou fever for such boisterous crowds at several festivals and lunar twenty-sixth events at Kaiyuan and during the 2009 Lantern Festival (*yuanxiao jie*) in the city. Near the Confucian Temple (*wenmiao*) in Quanzhou where a parade took place, crushing crowds reminded me of Mardi Gras in New Orleans. Paul Sangren identifies this love for excitement and crowds as a feature of Minnan religiosity associated with the goddess Mazu in Taiwan, affirming the living spiritual power of Mazu (2000; see also Lagerwey 2010, 170). The passion for excitement is also identified as one of the central features of popular religious life in North China. In Shaanbei dialect, they say *honghuo* 红火, which can be translated as "red-hot sociality" (Chau 2006). Adam Chau identifies this quality as a fundamental mark of success in a religious festival, wedding, or funeral, yes, red-hot social funerals (again reminding me of New Orleans jazz funerals). Not only does it mark an event as successful, generating face and prestige for the host, it also contributes to the success of the event by forming an important component of the affective experience. Ian Reader also identifies noise, excitement, and crowds as key to a successful pilgrimage site (2014, 127).

What these scholars have found with respect to the workings of popular religion and pilgrimage bears on the power and success of lunar twenty-sixth events at Kaiyuan. Worshippers come because they seek blessings; the monastery has a reputation as a place of spiritual efficacy and that efficacy is thought to be enhanced on these days. A visitor with this mindset who arrives at an empty courtyard would naturally question the efficacy of the enshrined deities, buddhas, and bodhisattvas; in matters of *ling* 灵 as in secular matters, people vote with their feet. If the same visitor finds a courtyard bustling with people jostling for positions in front of Vairocana or Guanyin, then the efficacy of those beings is instantly manifest—why else would so many people crowd around them?

The monthly buddha recitation day is an important and unique institution in Quanzhou. It is the major source of income for monasteries and the major platform of interaction between temples and their communities.

Kaiyuan's lunar twenty-sixth *nianfo* day regularly brings from ten thousand to thirty thousand visitors and remains a cornerstone of the monastery's economic self-sufficiency, bringing in some ¥6 million annually.[39] Unlike the Japanese pilgrimage market, which is marked by competition for pilgrims and rivalry between sites (Reader 2014), Quanzhou temples demonstrate a cooperative approach. Each Buddhist temple in Quanzhou, small or large, has its own designated buddha recitation day, held on a different day of the lunar calendar—the third for Chengtian, the ninth for Southern Shaolin Monastery, the seventeenth for Same-Lotus (*tonglian*), the eighteenth for Chongfu, and so on. Given the number of temples, I am confident that a zealous and resourceful layperson can attend these auspicious *nianfo* days on most if not all days of the year in southern Fujian. Similarly, Susan Naquin believes that in Qing dynasty Beijing one could shop at different temple markets every day of the year (2008, 86). Rather than holding monthly markets, however, southern Fujian holds buddha recitation and noodle days.

The Annual Calendar

The year is punctuated with four large festivals and several smaller ones. The most important days follow the lunar-solar calendar, which begins on the second new moon after the winter solstice (Chinese New Year). The four major events provide a carnival-like atmosphere attended by thousands of worshippers. The first is the celebration of the Spring Festival (Chinese New Year, lunar January 1–15), which is not especially Buddhist but is nonetheless brought into the Buddhist ritual context with two weeks of large dharma assemblies, the longest festival of the year. Midsummer is marked by the ever-popular Ghost Festival (*moulian jie,* lunar July 12–16), rightly recognized as the second most important festival of the year after Spring Festival (Orzech 1989, 1995). The remaining important festivals celebrate the most popular Buddhist figure in the Chinese pantheon, the bodhisattva of compassion, Avalokiteśvara or Guanyin. Guanyin's passing is marked in the early summer (lunar June 18–20) and Guanyin's ordination is commemorated in the fall (lunar September 18–20). All of these festivals are marked with additional sutra recitations that typically span multiple days and liberation of life (*fangsheng*) ceremonies. Devotees may register to have their names placed in the main hall on paper tablets during each of these festivals to receive the merit said to be generated by the laborious recitations. In 2006 and 2009, all festivals also included a release of burning mouths ritual on the evening of the final day of the festival. By 2019, however, the release of burning mouths was held only during New Years and the Ghost Festival. The birthday of the Buddha (lunar April 8) is also marked by the bathing of a small Buddha statue, but it is not a particularly large event at Kaiyuan. Guanyin's birth (lunar

February 19) is also marked, but is not as big an event as the others. Another busy set of days mark the Qingming Festival (traditional tomb-sweeping day, solar calendar April 4–5). Holmes Welch's informants mentioned the same annual events with the exception of the Qingming festival (1967, 108–109). A thick description of the communal religious life at this site must also include the characteristics of the major festival days, beginning with the Chinese New Year.

Chinese New Year

Months before the New Year, signs are prominently posted inside the main gate announcing the upcoming dharma assemblies (*fahui*) and the tremendous merit and benefits to gain from participating, sponsoring, or otherwise donating at these times. Chinese New Year is marked with a ten thousand Buddha penance framed as the Spring Festival 10,000 Buddha Great Dharma Assembly to Plant Good Fortune and Eliminate Disasters, which involves chanting ten thousand names of the Buddha over the first fifteen days of the lunar new year (for example, February 18 to March 4 in 2007, and the first two weeks of February in 2009) using the *Wanfo hongming baochan* 万佛洪名宝忏 (the first chapter of the *Sutra of Buddha Names* 佛说佛名经 T.14, no. 440). Monasteries traditionally use ten days for this recitation, which is also known as the Dharma Assembly Worship of Ten Thousand Buddhas (*bai wanfo fahui* 拜万佛法会), but Kaiyuan stretches it to fifteen. Buddhas, bodhisattvas, and dharma protectors are invited to come and the chanting takes place in the main hall. More than a dozen monks in bright yellow robes officiate, surrounded by two hundred to three hundred lay Buddhists in black and brown gowns behind them who follow with small red liturgy books. In 2009, three sessions of chanting were held in the morning and two sessions in the afternoon. The chanting is broadcast over loudspeakers mounted on the main hall and carries throughout much of the monastic complex, spreading a sonorous blessing of "buddhaness."

The ceremony is performed with the intention of bringing lasting peace and happiness to all beings. Lay Buddhists and worshippers are invited to make donations in order to be recognized as official patrons of this grand ceremony and thereby share in the tremendous merit generated by the ritual activity. Those donating at the appropriate level will have their names and petitions (for example, peace for the whole family) written on red slips of paper known as tablets (*luwei* 禄位 or *paiwei* 牌位) placed in the main hall. An informational sign is posted at the gates and outside the main hall encouraging this form of patronage. The signs explain that the tablets will entitle sponsors to share in the "difficult to measure" merit of the Ten Thousand Buddha Dharma Assembly held to bring good fortune and eliminate misfortune (*zhifu xioazai*). The signs detail benefits that will come to those who participate, most of which are worldly in nature (long life, health, wealth, success in career) as well as wisdom and world peace. Preceding the listing of these benefits is a statement of reasons more specifically Buddhist and religious, such as engaging in devout worship to open the Buddha gate, renew the power of the dharma, and benefit all. Patrons are invited to participate at different levels. In 2007 and 2009, a family could secure a paper tablet with their name on it for ¥100. Patrons with more means were invited to sponsor the event as a master of merit (*gongde zhu* 功德主) for ¥10,000, as an assistant master for ¥5,000, or as a charitable deeds sponsor (*suixi huishou* 随喜会首) for ¥2,000. Other levels of sponsorship include a great offering ceremony (*shang dagong pufo*) ¥3,000, a special morning service ceremony (*sui zaoke pufo*) ¥1,000, an ascending the hall great feast or assembly (*shang tang dazhai*) ¥10,000, an arhat feast or assembly (*luohan zhai*) ¥1,000, and a ruyi feast or assembly (*ruyi zhai*) ¥500. Monks sit at a table just outside or inside the main hall where patrons may register their names and make their donations. This process begins about two months before the event takes place to enable patrons plenty of time to earn a place in the main hall to accrue the benefits associated with the grand ten thousand Buddha ceremony. On average, about twenty families sponsor at the ¥10,0000 level, ten families for ¥5,000, and as many as eight thousand for ¥100. These figures amount to more than ¥1 million from Spring Festival rites, notably, the vast majority of which comes from those donating ¥100 (totaling ¥800,000).

With so many levels of sponsorship or participation available, the implication and a popular understanding is that the more one donates, the greater the benefit. One monk complained that the logic of gaining more merit by donating more money was ludicrous:

> This is a Chinese tradition based on economic considerations. It is not based on Buddhist doctrine. You cannot buy merit! Think about it. If you could, people with more money would be able to have the most merit, this is ludicrous! It's just a way for the temple to make money. Otherwise it would be difficult to bring in funds. . . . This is very far from Śākyamuni's thought.[40]

Although this monk criticized the practice of linking merit to amounts of money, what Gareth Fisher calls the "cash-merit relationship," he recognizes that the monastery itself promoted such a view by advertising different levels of support based simply on cash amounts (2008). As Kim Gutschow in her study of Tibetan nuns in North India points out, a gap separates the way merit is supposed to work and the way it is popularly understood to work (2004). She writes,

> A wealthy donor is considered to earn more merit by giving up all his possessions than the pauper who has little to offer. In theory, the merit accrued is supposed to be proportional with the donor's ability to give. In practice, however, most people act as if the absolute size of the gift alone determines the amount of merit earned. (2004, 87)

Fisher, in his study of a Buddhist temple community in Beijing, similarly argues that although "Both monks and lay people agreed that, as a theological point, the investment of more money does not necessarily lead to corresponding gains in merit." In practice, a working assumption is "reinforced in a number of different ways" that "the more money one gives to a member of the clergy or to the temple, the more merit one will receive" (2008, 150–151). The research here supports what other scholars have found concerning the ways that practice and conception diverge from orthodoxy with respect to the cash-merit relationship.

From a phenomenological perspective, what impressed me most about these days of chanting in the main hall, was the explicitly religious atmosphere of the monks, surrounded by hundreds of laypersons, all participating in the ceremony and broadcasting the blessings out into the courtyard and surroundings by loudspeaker. Holistically, what this reveals is the comfortable alliance between economic needs of monks and the religious needs of lay Buddhists and worshippers. By religious needs, I mean personal needs addressed by participation in public rituals based on symbols of ultimate value (buddha) tied to cosmological conceptions (karma and rebirth). These dimensions are manifest visually, audibly, and olfactorily. An important point is that money is collected and deposited in the monastery's coffers, not used to enrich investors, officials, or nonclerical employees, as is the case at some sites in China.[41] Thousands of these red slips of paper each bore the petitions of families or individuals in the hall when I was on-site in 2009. At the bottom of the informational sign was written "Quanzhou Great Kaiyuan Monastery" along with the contact names of two monks. This contrasts with temples under nonclerical management, where ritualistic activities may be organized and money collected by nonmonastics; such is not the case at Kaiyuan. This comparative issue is addressed in chapter 7.[42]

Incorporated into this festival on the lunar ninth is a celebration of the birthday of Śakra, Lord of Heaven (*shiti huanyin* 释提桓因), a Buddhist version of Indra, also referred to at this site as the Jade Emperor (*yuhuang dadi* 玉皇大帝). An important feast day in Daoism, the ninth day of the first lunar month is also celebrated at Buddhist monasteries in Minnan. On this day, a vegetarian offering ceremony (*gongtianzhai yi* 供天斋仪) is held at 7:00 a.m. in the main hall. Also called the "vegetarian offering pray for blessings dharma assembly" (*zhaitian qifu fahui* 斋天祈福法会), all beings in heaven are invited to share in the offerings, after which they are distributed to those present. In 2009, large bowls of candy and peanuts were thrown into the crowd of lay Buddhists and worshippers. It again reminded me of Mardi Gras celebrations in the United States, where crowds compete to get beads, trinkets, and candy thrown during parades. I picked up some peanuts in shells. The monks led around four hundred attendees out of the hall to circurcumambulate around the main courtyard before reentering the main hall to end the ceremony.

Shortly afterward, at 9:00 a.m., is a liberation of life ceremony. Those I have witnessed have all involved the release of birds, most often small birds in long rectangular cages, but one full of doves in 2006 that subsequently came to nest under the eaves of several buildings, had become a permanent part of the temple by 2009 and were still present in 2019. The liberation of life ceremony is conducted with eleven monks, five standing at each side of a small square table set in the main courtyard and the lead monk standing at its head, leading the liturgy. One monk plays a hand drum while others play the wooden fish and cymbals. Monks wear yellow robes and chant; some follow along in small liturgy books. On the square table sits a small statue of Guanyin with flower offerings and a vase containing pure water and a willow branch. Behind the table is the cage of birds. All the monks chant common chants such as the Great Compassion mantra and the *Heart Sutra* as the lead monk sprinkles water on the animals using the willow branch, bestows the dharma upon them and the triple refugee. One laywoman excitedly explained the value of this ceremony: "The animals are part of the six paths of sentient life, the monks are able to offer them refuge and bestow the dharma upon them so that they can be reborn in higher states, relieving so much suffering!" At the conclusion of the ceremony, the cages are opened and the animals released. The first liberation of life ceremony I watched did not turn out well for some of the birds. The ladies in brown robes scrambled to tear open the cages in order to earn merit from being the one to release the animals. In their zeal, however, several birds were injured, some seriously. A chorus of criticism has sprung up surrounding the practice in China, which includes over-commercialization and environmentally harmful practices such as releasing animals into inhospitable habitats (McCarthy 2019, 92–95). One of my informants said that it can be wasteful and has advised lay Buddhists to donate money to an animal protection society, to protect, for example, panda bears, as a more meritorious practice.

On the fifteenth day, the tablets are removed from the main hall in preparation for the "perfectly auspicious release of burning mouths ceremony" (*yuanman jixiang yankou* 圆满吉祥焰口), which is held on the evening of the final day from 6:00 to 10:30 p.m. The release of burning mouths

FIG. 3.4 A liberation of life ceremony conducted by monks, surrounded by lay Buddhists, in the main courtyard in 2006. Note the "treasure box" stone stupa (1145 CE) to the right. Birds to be released are in cages in front of the portable altar, mostly off screen. Photo by the author.

(*fang yankou*) ceremonies begin at sundown and are the most theatrical and striking of all. The leader of the ceremony sits in the middle of the hall, high above the other monks, wearing the ceremonial five-pointed Vairocana hat. Based on the *Burning Mouths Yoga* (*yujia yankou*), all the monks chant the sutras, mantras, and *dhāraṇīs* throughout the ceremony. Along with the leader is an assistant with whom he chants dialogues, a further theatrical flair. The melody, I was told, was based on Jiangsu opera. The leader also accents his chanting by forming mudras, sounding the *vajra*-topped bell and wielding the *vajra* (*jin'gang* 金刚, Tib. *dorje*) and other instruments.[43] By way of example, the leader uses the vajra-fist mudra and chants the hell-smashing spell and other mantras to open the gates of hell so that he as Guanyin may descend to save the hungry ghosts. The leader also picks up a grain of rice and recites a mantra to turn it into a mountain of rice to feed the hungry ghosts. The rite is thoroughly tantric and its prominence in contemporary Chinese monasticism is one of the ways esoteric Buddhist ritual has become part of the fabric of Chinese Buddhism.

Below the lead monk is a large table at which sit six or ten monks, three or five on each side, facing one another. Each participant has a copy of the ceremony book they use to follow along. Several monks ring *vajra*-tipped bells in unison. Another sits off to the side playing a drum and bell set. Laypersons kneel in attendance and offer incense when instructed to do so by the hall monitor monk. An additional monk is on hand to provide hot drinking water. The ceremony requires an odd number of monks. The instances of the ceremony I witnessed have had one leader, six or ten accompanying reciters, one drummer, one hall monk, and one assistant—a total of ten to fourteen monks. In 2006, a ceremony could be commissioned for ¥3,000 ($375), most of which goes into the temple's general coffers.

During the ceremony, two altars are erected outside: one is set with offerings of fruit, incense, and flowers for Guanyin; the other is set with offerings of food, oil, incense, and bags of paper money with gold leaf offered to a spirit tablet. The ceremony, held under the cover of dark, marked by melodious chanting, punctuated by bells and drums, is an atmospheric feast for the senses. This ritual was introduced during the Tang dynasty and has remained an important feature of monasteries, in part for its ability to generate funds and in part by the demand for a ceremony which could benefit the deceased. As one of Kaiyuan's more informed monks explained, the lead monk, following classical Tantric ritual, embodies Guanyin bodhisattva and then descends to the realm of hungry ghosts, using mantras opens their mouths, and offers them food, drink, and instruction in the dharma so that they may be released from their suffering. Dizang bodhisattva also plays an important role after Guanyin opens that gates of hell (Yü 2001, 325–328). Thus the rite is called the "release [from suffering] of [hungry ghosts with] burning mouths" who can neither quench their thirst nor satisfy their hunger. It is thought to generate tremendous merit that those commissioning the rite typically transmit to benefit departed family members in general or those specifically sponsoring a performance.

Qingming Festival

Following Spring Festival, the true beginning of spring may be thought to arrive with the Qingming Festival, celebrated on April 4 or 5 of the solar (Gregorian) calendar. Over the three days of this holiday in Quanzhou, most people visit ancestral graves to clean them up and make offerings, hence the occasion is often referred to as the tomb-sweeping festival. Graveyards in the hills outside of town become busy with families on outings; firecrackers add to the festive nature of these early spring gatherings. Nowadays car alarms join the cacophonous chorus, set off by the fireworks. Qingming Festival has become a series of pronouncedly busy days at Kaiyuan because of the building of the Anyang Cloister columbarium and enlarged hall of ancestor tablets. Over the course of the festival, thousands of families stream into the temple, primarily from the back entrance, which is closest to the Anyang Cloister. Several tables have begun to be set up in front of the entrance to provide a place for individuals to set their bags of offerings. Families burn incense and offer fruits and flowers to their ancestors. The amount of paper money burned on these days overwhelms the furnace. In 2019, the large furnace, used for paper houses, was used as temporary storage for gold paper to be burned later, while the smaller furnace was kept at capacity. Families typically arrived with one or more bags to burn just as they would traditionally burn at the gravesite of ancestors. The traditional belief is that ancestors are able to receive such burnt offerings, but many today, encouraged by the state, see such traditions as symbolic gestures of regard that direct emotions in a positive way.

Kaiyuan has two furnaces for paper offerings located next to one another just east of the ordination platform. One, the most common, is for gold paper (*jinzhi* 金纸), offered on a daily basis by the public and in great quantities during the Qingming Festival, lunar 26, and other special days. The other is a large rectangular sheet metal building, used to burn paper houses and larger paper items offered to the dead. The furnace for gold paper is a tall hexagonal brick structure and almost always emits smoke, which is why it was eventually fitted with a filtering system. At the bottom of the furnace is a metal grating that allows the melted gold leaf to fall into a well below the furnace that is accessible by a somewhat hidden set of stairs. The gold is regularly collected and sold, making it another regular source of income.

The monks do not hold special dharma ceremonies for Qingming other than helping manage the continual flow of worshippers, incense, and paper offerings. Many people do stop by the main hall to make an offering, usually ¥100 or to light a Buddha light (*dian mingguang*); the fee for more than ten years to light a small Buddha statue for a year has remained ¥200 (about $40).[44] A monk explained the significance of lighting the light as destroying darkness, removing obstacles, afflictions and troubles, creating peace, health, and happiness for the sponsoring family (almost always a family). Kaiyuan has long been a place for worshippers to visit during the Qingming Festival. They began coming in large numbers from the start of the revival in the 1980s, but the abbot has significantly enhanced the importance of this festival at Kaiyuan by building the large facility to inter the ashes of loved ones, which then becomes the site for veneration during the Qingming Festival.

Buddha's Birthday

Buddha's birthday (*fodanri* 佛诞日) is marked on the eighth day of lunar April (in 2019 this was May 12) and is celebrated in the traditional way by "bathing" a statue of the standing infant Buddha. Monks participate by chanting sutras, invoking the names of the sage 称圣号, praising the Buddha, circumambulating the Buddha, and finally ritually bathing the Buddha. The monks dedicate the merit earned through these devotional acts to all beings with the wish that hearts are cleansed of impurities so that their natural purity may shine forth. Devotees in attendance are then allowed to take turns "bathing" the baby

Buddha themselves, using a ladle dipped in water surrounding the statue. As they do, they are invited to speak their own intentions, preferably about washing away impurities and reaching the purity of the Buddhas. Kaiyuan, however, imposes no particular requirements. Each person pours one ladle of water and moves on. At temples outside China devotees may be instructed in what intentions to state and may pour three ladles. Such rituals are characteristically looser at Kaiyuan: in 2019 it took about two hours for around a thousand people to participate. When I asked why fewer people came to this festival than to others, I was told that every temple held its own ceremonies so people went to their local temples. Celebrated throughout the Buddhist world, the Buddha's birthday is seen as an important and universal celebration. At Kaiyuan, however, it is not singled out or highlighted with the kind of enthusiasm and crowds seen for other festival days as it is, for example, in parts of Southeast Asia.

Guanyin's Ordination and Passing

The days marking the ordination and passing of Guanyin are celebrated over three days with a grand Three Thousand Buddha Penance that involves, predictably, chanting three thousand names of the buddhas using the *Sanqianfo gongming boachan* 三千佛洪名宝忏. A liberation of life ceremony is also held. In 2006 and 2009, a release of burning mouths ceremony was held on the evening of the final day, but by 2019 this had been discontinued. Guanyin's ordination is celebrated from the eighteenth day of lunar September (November 4 through 6 in 2009) and her passing is commemorated from lunar June 18 through 20 (August 8 through 10 in 2009). In 2009, worshippers were invited to sponsor this ceremony at levels of ¥5,000 or ¥2,000 ($700 to $300) or participate at the basic ¥50 ($7) level. Individuals may register their names with monks in the main hall from about five weeks before the ceremony. By 2019, no fees were charged for registering names and paper tablets. Any loss of income is more than offset by the many who make offerings in the merit boxes on festival days. The names of those registering are posted in the hall and they are said to gain immeasurable merit from the Three Thousand Buddha Penance.

The Ghost Festival

The Ghost Festival or Ullambana Festival (*yulanpen* 盂兰盆) commemorates the yogic efforts of the Buddha's disciple Maudgalyāyana (Mulian 目连) to save his mother from suffering as a hungry ghost as related in the *Yulanpen Sutra* and the *Sutra on Offering Bowl to Repay Kindness,* which first appeared in China in the sixth century.[45] These sutras relate how Mulian, unable to help his mother, seeks Buddha's advice. Buddha explains how the assembly of monks on lunar July 15 should gather en masse to receive offerings from the laity and perform *chaodu* (超度) to relieve the suffering of seven generations of ancestors. Stephen Teiser details how the Chinese sangha adapted the Indian tradition to Chinese notions of renewal, which coincided with the end of the traditional summer retreat (1988, 26–35). The first recorded celebration in China dates to 561 and is celebrated once again at temples like Kaiyuan over five days, from lunar July 12 through 16. Traditionally, the whole lunar month of July is thought to be a time when the ghosts of departed relations return to visit the living. The *chaodu* is realized, as I understand it, in reciting the Emperor Liang's Precious Penance (*lianghuang baochan*) and making offerings. Monks gather in the main hall from 8:00 to 11:00 a.m., with two short breaks, and again from 2:00 to 4:00 p.m., with one short break, for a full twenty-four hours of chanting over five days. The penance (*chan*) is associated with averting disasters, removing hindrances, and promoting happiness and used for *chaudu* (to release souls from suffering); the merit generated is dedicated to those named on lotus seats (*lianwei* 莲位) in the main hall after each session. More than eight thousand families register, slips of paper with the name of the deceased and the name of the patron to be pasted on boards in the main hall during the *chaodu*. A release of burning mouths ceremony is held in the evening of lunar July 15. Thousands of worshippers and devotees offer incense and burn paper offerings every day of the Ghost Festival celebration. Like the other major festivals, it is a time of *renao* religiosity, which again demonstrates compatibility between the needs of devotees with fulfilling perceived obligations to ancestors and the economic needs of running a monastery.

One monk explained that the benefits of *chaodu* are not only for the deceased. This, he pointed out, was a common misconception. Instead, it benefits the dead and the living (*mingyang liang liyi* 冥阳两利益) of the six realms. *Chaodu* can be performed anytime at Kaiyuan for a fee of ¥20,000 ($4,000), which usually involves several families pooling their resources to hold a ceremony for their ancestors. The ceremony during the ghost festival only requires a ¥50 contribution to participate, which brings in around $100,000. A hundred years ago, the Ghost Festival would have been celebrated in a grand way throughout the city, but now the celebration is more subdued. The largest communal gatherings are at Quanzhou's larger Buddhist temples, such as Kaiyuan (Heise 2012). This shift would seem to be a sign of success for the religion policy, which seeks to restrict communal religious activity to registered religious sites such as Buddhist temples.

Holding these multiday ceremonies are said to generate tremendous (even limitless *wuliang*) merit, which the monks are thought to be able to transfer to those individuals sponsoring these rituals. As with other religious clerics, Buddhist monks in ritual roles act as intermediaries between lay patrons and cosmic powers, transforming luck into destiny, improving future outcomes, conceptualized as merit and the benevolence of (cosmic) bodhisattvas.[46] This merit can only be generated with a combination of ritual know-how and clerical manpower—Kaiyuan, unlike most smaller temples, has plenty of both and is therefore able to stage these ceremonies and bring in greater amounts of income while generating a lively calendar of religious events which convince the local public that Kaiyuan is a place of spiritual efficacy (*ling*).

This ritual know-how, in addition to supporting the operations of the monastery, also translates into an opportunity to generate personal income for the monks involved in performing the rituals—monks receive modest amounts of money for their participation. Monks at Kaiyuan are all aware that ritual know-how is a profitable skill that one may learn there. This is one of the reasons monks are attracted to this monastery; it is also the reason that other monks who prefer to cultivate knowledge or other forms of practice are not attracted to Kaiyuan, which is rightly seen as not providing a systematically supportive base for such pursuits. I know of one young monk who sincerely wished to deepen his knowledge of Buddhism and meditation, was frustrated to find that such opportunities were lacking at Kaiyuan, and therefore left. It has also been suggested that monks with less education and from rural backgrounds are generally more eager to learn and participate in ritual services and that more educated or urban monks try to rise up through the clerical hierarchy. The path of those pursuing administrative positions is taken up in chapter 4.

Conclusion: A Fundamentally Liturgical Form of Religion

This investigation concludes that daily, weekly, monthly, and annual liturgies are the basis of communal religious practice at Kaiyuan and most Chinese Buddhist monasteries. Within these liturgies and the contexts of their deployment, we can isolate four primary strands of religious tradition: use of *dhāraṇī,* Pure Land Buddhism, esoteric Buddhism, and veneration of ancestors. *Dhāraṇī* dominate the morning service and play an important role in the evening service. The most obvious esoteric elements are the taking of refuge in the Vajra guru during the evening service and the elaborate *fang yankou* ritual replete with elements of Vajrayāna deity yoga, and the material culture of the temple (H. Wang 2001b). Pure Land Buddhism is most clearly institutionalized in the evening service and in the weekly and monthly *nianfo* sessions. The Chinese tradition of veneration of ancestors is present in the communal liturgical calendar most visibly in the three-day celebration of the ghost festival, during Qingming Festival, and in the fortnightly worship in the hall of patriarchs (*zutang*). Ancestor veneration is even more emphasized in the postmortem rituals commissioned by families throughout the year and in regular offerings of gold paper in the furnaces to the east of the ordination platform.

In short, although Chinese Buddhism is recognized as having been dominated by Pure Land and Chan schools since the Song dynasty (for more than a thousand years), the Pure Land tradition has come to dominate monastic practice, with veneration of ancestors a thematic concern and esoteric elements playing an unappreciated role. The feature of communal religious life of most importance to the Chinese sangha is the rhetorical obligation of morning and evening services. Monks who attend regularly have the opportunity to grow within the practice, but the majority of Kaiyuan monks do not attend regularly. From 2006 to 2019, the most influential and consistent aspect of communal religious life at Quanzhou Kaiyuan has been twice-weekly *nianfo* sessions consistently attended by some two hundred to two hundred and fifty lay Buddhists, the lunar twenty-sixth free noodles and *nianfo* day regularly attended by more than ten thousand with two to three thousand circumambulating the temple grounds and performing *nianfo,* and the annual festivals each attended by ten to fifty thousand or more. Of these, the most regular events are the *nianfo* sessions on Tuesdays and Fridays and lunar twenty-sixth. These *nianfo* events, held eight or nine times each month, are led by seven or eight monks chanting and playing dharma instruments. Among the several unexpected conclusions from my research into communal religious practice is that more lay Buddhists benefit from the activities organized at Kaiyuan than monks. The monastery serves the public as a place of devotion, filial piety, and *nianfo* practice. Monks are likely to advance in their practice only if they have a mind to take advantage of the opportunities for self-cultivation afforded by their status as monastics. The interruption of monastic traditions in mainland China for at least half of the twentieth century has left contemporary monastics without a rich pool of qualified mentors to guide monks in any form of communal cultivation beyond the morning and evening services.

In addition to revealing the nature of communal religious practice at Kaiyuan, this chapter has also provided insight into the ritual economy associated with the monthly and yearly calendars. The communal ritual activities which attract the local community reveal the nature of monastic and lay relationships and key mechanisms of ministry and support.

The crowds ranging from ten to thirty thousand that regularly fill the temple monthly on lunar twenty-sixth and may swell to even larger crowds on festival days over the year have continued to form and even increase between 2006 and 2019. In addition, the ritual programs for these special days has remained relatively stable over these years. Among the conclusions to be drawn is the very comfortable alliance between the (financial) needs of the monastery and the (moral and social) needs of the local population. The translation of economic prosperity in the community to material prosperity at the monastery has been noted since the founding of the monastery in the Tang dynasty. The people of southern Fujian, as former Mayor Wang Jinsheng noted, have warm feelings for the Kaiyuan Monastery. The mayor spoke about the history and material culture of the site, but what this chapter reveals is the crucial role played by a monastic community able to organize and maintain an active ritual calendar to bring the site to life and satisfy the expectations of worshippers and lay Buddhists. We continue to explore the nature of religious life in the following chapter by focusing on paths taken by individual monks.

4

Monks

84,000 Dharma Gates

I WAS IN FAWEN'S OFFICE; A COMPUTER and a monitor sat on a desk nearby where we recently watched a pirated version of *Slum Dog Millionaire*. He had asked whether India was really like that (poor and dirty); parts of it were, I said. He could not believe that the home of Buddhism could be so chaotic (*luan*). We had known each other four years and sat at a small table on which was a tea tray with tea cups, tea pot, and electric kettle. As always, we drank tea as we chatted. The tea was Iron Guanyin (*tieguanyin*), Fujian's famous fragrant oolong tea; the temple gets high-quality tea from well-to-do patrons; we drank it all day long. They say it is possible to get drunk if you drink too much. Maybe we had because when Fawen answered his cell phone and Deru asked what he was doing, he responded, "drinking alcohol (*hejiu*) with Stone Dragon" (my Chinese name); he quickly corrected himself, "drinking tea" (*hecha*), "drinking tea." We both laughed. I had never seen Fawen drink nor had I any reason to believe he does. We discussed the influence of tourism on the monastery and the conversation turned to the state of practice at the monastery. We talked about morning and evening services; he said that they were "the most basic level of practice." He did not seem to have a very high opinion of them. We talked about keeping the precepts and came to the conclusion that the current situation was not ideal. I asked when it ever was ideal. He responded, "The ideal situation is we continuously work toward our own perfection." He went on to say that "Chinese Buddhism has suffered a period of interruption [*zhongguo fojiao shoudao yiduan shijian de zhongduan*]; an interruption from liberation [1949] to

1980, about thirty years. At the time of the implementation of the new policy on religion [*huifu zongjiao zhengce yihou*], there were no monks. Because there were no monks, standards were lowered [*jiangdi biaojun*]."

At this point, Fawen switched gears to make a comparative point, "Eh! I recently read some news about Catholicism that expressed a similar situation . . . the US Catholic church child-molestation scandal [*chouwen* 丑闻]—big news, turned out that after one case was exposed there were more than one hundred others that came out . . . big scandal . . . harmed all these boys . . . this was big news." What Fawen wanted to talk about was what he had read about the Catholic clergy in Ireland traditionally being drawn from the best and brightest:

> Long ago, the best and the brightest of the family would join the Church and this was considered a high position and honor, but with social changes the Church has become a less desirable option and no longer attracts the best qualified. In fact, no one wanted to be priests so they had to lower standards, and accept less qualified clergy. This resulted in a low quality clergy with shallow belief which has led to this huge scandal. Now in Chinese Buddhism we have a similar situation. After 1980, there were no qualified people to become monks. A good number of people ordained as monks did not have firm belief in Buddhism, it's easy to break precepts and easy to make mistakes [*rongyi fanjie, rongyi fan cuowu*].

I suggested that historically monks also broke precepts and that today there may be some temples where precepts were kept. "Very few," Fawen replied. "Before most were good, a few bad, now most are bad and a minority are good. The problem lies in the quality of our monks being low." There was much talk about quality (*zhiliang*) in Fujian at the time, good and bad quality products as well as good and bad quality people. The conversation turned to married clergy in Catholicism and Buddhism and Fawen claimed that many monks in China are married, including at Kaiyuan. In Shanghai, he suggested, they were quite open about it. When I asked about disciplining such monks, Fawen suggested that the only recourse would be the abbot. It turned out that Chinese Buddhism had its own scandal. Although married clergy have been an accepted part of Japanese Buddhism since the nineteenth century (Jaffe 2011) and Korean Buddhism had struggled with married clergy factions since the 1920s (Buswell 1992), married clergy were not officially recognized within Chinese Buddhism.

That was in 2009. Ten years later, I was back at Kaiyuan and Fawen and Deru and several others were still there, but almost half of the monks were gone. Over the previous five years, the abbot had (finally) purged the monastery of all legally married monks. One would hope the quality of the remaining monks would be better. This is not necessarily the case, however. No matter how seriously the married monks took their roles as clergy, they were ejected, leaving behind unmarried clergy who had mixed levels of understanding and commitment. What then is the nature of practice found among Kaiyuan's monks? What kinds of cultivation does one find among this first generation of ordained monks in the post-Mao period?

When it comes to discussing forms of practice a phrase often heard throughout Minnan, if not other parts of China, is "84,000 dharma gates." The implication is that the ways individuals may approach and practice the dharma are innumerable and vary by individual disposition, proclivities, and circumstances. When I spoke to the abbot of Nanputuo Monastery in 2019, he mentioned the Chan tropes chopping wood, carrying water, and boiling rice as well as meditation, *nianfo,* worship, and sutra recitation as possible gates of dharma. When "84,000 dharma gates" was mentioned in conversation with Kaiyuan monks the same year, I asked what particular dharma gates were promoted at the monastery. The head monk emphasized the freedom all monks have to pursue their individual paths. Another pushed back: "What higher forms of practice and training are available for monks?" Answering himself, he said, "None." The head monk replied that he should not say "none" but agreed that it takes time to develop such deep understandings or levels of practice. It took decades, he emphasized, a lifetime even, to reach a high level of understanding of Buddhism. The other monk lamented the lack of a spiritual guide (*jingshen de yingling*) to lead group practice. The head monk replied that it was impossible to have such group practice given the individual differences among monks. The only option was individual self-guided practice. The other monk said he hoped that institutional guidance for practice would exist some day.

This conversation sealed my view regarding the nature of higher religious cultivation at Kaiyuan over the course of its post-Mao restoration. As discussed in chapter 3, communal practice exemplifies a liturgical tradition with roots stretching back to the earliest traditions of monastic Buddhism in China. Morning and evening services are described by monks at Kaiyuan and elsewhere as the most basic form of practice. The abbot of Nanputuo, like Fawen before, suggested that it was so basic that it was not even practice, just a *part* of one's practice that could aid one to deepen their ("real") practice. This chapter explores the nature of individual practice in the absence of the kind of spiritual guide or abbot that Chan monastic texts describe as an enlightened authority. According to medieval Chan monastery guidelines, the authority of such abbots was such that the buddha hall was to be replaced by the dharma hall, where the abbot would preside. Neither the abbot of Kaiyuan, nor the abbots of most monasteries, are known to give dharma talks in the dharma hall. When asked about such deficits, monks generally refer to the interruption of Buddhist education and practice in China for thirty to fifty years preceding reform and opening, which has left the sangha with very few qualified teachers. Alas, monks are left to work out their practice "as islands unto themselves" as the Buddha commended in the *Dīgha and Saṃyutta Nikāyas* (Walsh 2012, 245; Bodhi 2012; 2003, 882). Before turning to these individual paths, this chapter considers a few preliminary concerns regarding problems with belief as a window into either religious identity or practice leading to the need for a more person-centered, practice-centered approach.

Scholars engaged in the study of lived religion in China are generally confronted with a perplexing array of behaviors and beliefs that defy simple classification in terms of doctrinal or religious affiliation. To understand the lived religion of Buddhist monasteries, it is necessary to go beyond doctrinal labels such as Chan or Pure Land, which mask more than they reveal when it comes to understanding how religiosity is expressed by varied actors at these sites. One way to do this is to approach religiosity as a diverse and person-centered phenomenon. This approach enables us to identify individuals and groups of actors according to their modes of religious behaviors rather than by how well they conform to some canonical ideal.

The Problem with Belief

Because beliefs and notions of religious identity tend to be more fluid and less committal in China, a focus on practice is a more reliable gauge of religiosity. A groundbreaking survey of religious experience in contemporary China conducted by Xinzhong Yao and Paul Badham from 2004 to 2006 found a striking disconnect between statements about religious identity (which we normally think of in terms of beliefs) and the behaviors and attitudes of interviewees. Regarding Buddhism their survey found that

> Only 4.4 percent identify themselves as Buddhist and only 5.3 percent say "yes" when asked bluntly whether they believe in reincarnation. Yet 27.4 percent pray to Buddhas or Bodhisattvas and over half think that their families and friends are the result of what they had done in a previous life. Even more surprising 77.9 percent tend to affirm the Buddhist concept of causal retribution and the doctrine of *karma*. (Yao and Badham 2007, 9)[1]

Similar results were found for Christianity, folk religion, and Confucianism—low rates of religious identification and high rates of behavioral and other forms of affirmation. Although decades of antireligious campaigns and propaganda must account for much of this reluctance to identify oneself as a believer in a particular faith, it is also the case that popular Chinese religiosity is not as susceptible to neat categorization in terms of doctrinally based faiths and very similar trends have been found in Japan (Heine 2012).

Both Adam Chau in his study of popular religion in China (2006) and Robert Buswell in his account of Zen monasticism in Korea (1992) explicitly raise the problem of belief in their studies of lived religion in East Asia; but they do so in different registers. Chau raises the problem of the language of belief, whereas Buswell focuses on the importance of recognizing what he calls the context of belief. Chau points out that the language of "belief," so important to Christian religiosity, is simply absent from the discourse of the people in his study; they simply did not explicitly speak of "belief in deities" (2006, 60). I generally encountered the use of the nominal form beliefs in conversations with more educated monks and lay Buddhists, but especially with officials, speaking about folk beliefs (*minjian xinyang*) or freedom of religious belief (*zongjiao xinyang ziyou*). This is the kind of language that Stig Thøgersen refers to as Ganbunese (the language of *ganbu* or cadres), which he contrasts with Baixingese (the language of *laobaixing*, common people) in order to highlight its politically constructed status (2006, 112).[2] This way of talking about beliefs is the official and modern way of speaking about religion so that it may be categorized and thereby regulated. It thus belongs to the modern nation-state building enterprise of the Chinese Communist Party, not to the ordinary people, who do not regularly use those terms because it is not how they conceptualize the world. They have generally not brought critical distance between themselves and what "we" would call their beliefs.

In his discussion of the context of belief, Buswell points out that Zen beliefs cannot be adequately understood by reading canonical Zen literature such as the lamp anthologies (*jingde chuandenglu*). Hagiographies and other teaching materials offer idealized portraits of Zen experience, Buswell argues, they expressly do not "provide an accurate account of how Zen monks of the premodern era pursued their religious vocations" (1992, 5). Buswell maintains that noncanonical sources such as gazetteers and epigraphic sources are important for correcting the idealized views of Zen masters derived from Zen teaching stories and hagiographies, but insists that "much of the import of Zen beliefs and training may never be known, or at least may be prone to misinterpretation" without taking into account the lived experience of Zen monastics. Buswell frames his concern by citing I. M. Lewis's 1986 *Religion in Context*:

> As I. M. Lewis has convincingly argued, religious beliefs are "functions of situations and circumstances," and describing those beliefs is "meaningless unless accompanied by a minutely detailed

> exposition of their deployment in actual situations. . . . The detachment of beliefs from their ambient circumstances produces gross distortion and misunderstanding." (Buswell 1992, 5)[3]

Buswell and Lewis suggest that we must focus on the living context in which religious beliefs are deployed rather than on idealized accounts in the literature of a tradition. Regarding the problem of belief, first, one must remain circumspect when treating the lived religiosity of Chinese people; it should not be expected to fully conform to expectations based on normative accounts portrayed in elite corpora of texts. One should not expect the monks and their patrons to exhibit the roles portrayed in the vinaya, Buddhist sutras and treatises, tales of eminent monks, or Chan genealogies. They may sometimes think and behave in ways recognizable in Buddhist literature, but very often they do not. We may, for example, look at an account of the monastic rule forbidding eating after the noon meal. In the early twentieth century, Heinrich Hackmann, taking normative oral accounts about Baohua Shan 宝华山 at face value, wrote in his *Buddhism as a Religion* that "the evening meal is forbidden . . . [the monks] are only allowed tea to drink."[4] Johannes Prip-Møller was able to clear up this confusion by spending several weeks at Baohua Shan and discovering that "drink tea" in this context was an euphemism for having a evening meal (1937, 221). This is now well known, but what a difference the corrected understanding makes for assessing the level of ascetic commitment of monastics. What else, we should ask, do monastics do or not do? In 2013, for example, it was reported that Bhutanese health officials have begun to provide condoms to monks in Bhutan to prevent the spread of sexually transmitted diseases, which have been found among the monastic community (Arora 2013). Reports like this do not warrant jumping to conclusions but certainly remind us that any monastic precept may have found an unexpected cultural interpretation. In this case, scholarship suggests a tradition among Himalayan branches of Buddhism that has turned a blind eye to nonpenetrative "thigh sex."[5]

The second point to recall is that most Chinese do not express their religious identity in the neat and clear ways suggested by the labels Buddhist, Daoist, or Confucian. Religious professionals may be meaningfully identified as Daoist priests, Buddhist monks, or spirit mediums, but even then understanding the nature of their beliefs and practices is another question. A person-centered approach is what can reveal what Buddhist monks think and do.

Scholars have used person-centered approaches, which focus on understanding the religiosity of individuals, to shed light on religious phenomena in China and India (Roberts, Chiao, and Pandey 1975) and in Taiwan (Harrell 1974). Other scholars have taken a person-centered approach to understanding sacred places (Roberts, Morita, and Brown 1986). This chapter uses a person-centered approach to explore the roles and approaches to practice taken by monks. Monks (*chujia ren*) are one of four general groups of people directly associated with Kaiyuan. The others are lay Buddhists (*jushi*), worshippers (*xiangke*), and employees of Kaiyuan and the temple administrative commission. Because I discuss worshippers, laity, and the management commission elsewhere, the focus here is on the clergy—that is, monks.[6]

The Monastics

First among the actors at any monastery are the monastics, a category that includes both novice (*shami* 沙弥) and fully ordained monastics, both male (*sengren* 僧人) and female (*nigu* 尼姑).[7] In what does the monastic vocation entail? From the first centuries of Buddhism in China, monks have written about the monastic vocation and the monastic institution; the first was Daoan (312–385), an important early Buddhist leader who cataloged and corrected Buddhist sutras in China and is credited with devising a set of three rules to guide the functioning of Chinese Buddhist monasteries.[8] As related in Huijiao's (497–554) *Biographies of Eminent Monks* (*Gaoseng zhuan*), Daoan's supplemental rules dealt with three areas of concern: offering incense and ascending the platform to give a dharma talk; daily devotional practices including prostration and circumambulation (*xingdao*), including rituals accompanying food and drink; and procedures for a repentance ceremony during the fortnightly *uposatha* 布萨 (*busa,* the communal recitation of the *prātimokṣa* or *jieben* rules).[9] Two hundred years after Daoan, the Tiantai patriarch Zhiyi (538–597) wrote about the monastic institution in *Establishing Regulations* (*Lizhifa* 立制法). As Mario Poceski describes it, "The text presents a picture of a contemplative community with a regimented daily routine that encompasses three broad areas of religious life: communal rites and meditation (*zuochan* 坐禅), solitary periods of cultic practice devoted to repentance rituals (*bie-chang chanhui* 别场忏悔), and participation in the daily work of running the monastery (*zhi sengshi* 知僧事)" (2003, 50). Zhiyi also divided monks into three general categories: those focused on performance of penance rituals, those training in seated meditation, and those engaged in practical business of the monastery (Yifa 2002, 20). A similar threefold division exists from the eleventh century in a set of ten guidelines composed by the Tiantai monk Zunshi (964–1037) for his public monastery: those who study, those who chant and meditate, and those who help run the monastery (Yifa 2002, 35–37). The earliest complete code for the Chan school was the *Rules of Purity for the Chan Monastery* (*Chanyuan qinggui*) by Chanlu Zongze in 1103. In addition to detailing the duties and authorities of monastic officers, it provides guides for a host of mundane activities with notes on the importance of deportment in various ritual settings.[10] Together, these codes present a multifaceted picture of what monastic life can consist of, including self-cultivation, practical management of the monastery, and regular ritual activity including penance. In broad stokes, monastic life in China today remains recognizable as regulated life with options to focus on self-cultivation, ritual performance, or the practical running of the monastery. In addition, the late Song summaries of the no longer extant but famous *Baizhang Pure Rules* (*Qingqui*) stipulate the need to remove pretend monks to ensure the purity of the sangha (Yifa 2002, 29). Monks have long, if not always, run the gamut from sincere devotee to boorish dilettante, from ritual master to meditative adept, from business manager to fake monk (*jia heshang* 假和尚). The monks at this site are a similarly diverse sample.

Every monastery has institutional concerns, which is to say that each is concerned with surviving within given economic and political realities. These institutional concerns are met by an administrative hierarchy that has been a hallmark of Buddhist monasticism since the imperial period. Scholarship has begun to draw attention to the importance of institutional features of Buddhist monasticism. Jonathan Silk has written a monograph on the role of service or administration (*vaiyāpṛtya*) in Indian monastic Buddhism (2008). His book helps draw attention to the importance of administrative aspects of the monastic vocation, which a close study of the sources reveals was recognized as an important dimension of the monastic enterprise alongside the careers of study and preaching (*adhyayana*) and meditation (*dhyāna*).

In 2006, an assignment board was posted detailing assignments for twenty-seven posts at Kaiyuan. Almost half were custodial positions, such as watching or caring for various halls, caring for the grounds, and watching the gates. The remainder were task specific, based on traditional monastic positions. Monasteries are headed by an abbot (*fangzhang* 方丈) or head monastic (*dangjia* 当家), below whom are personal assistants to the abbot (*yibo* 衣钵), general managers (*jianyuan* 监院), and their assistants (*fusi* 副寺). These figures constitute the executive; although power is concentrated at the top in the abbot, day-to-day tasks are handled by relevant officers as needed for such things as procurement, financial records, communications, and so on. The guest prefect (*zhike* 知客) heads the office responsible for processing and accommodating visiting monks as well as handling public relations more generally. In regard to practice, officers oversee the entire assembly (*dujian* 都监), see that order is maintained during ceremonies and in the halls (*sengzhi* 僧祇), and oversee decorum and lead the morning and evening service (*weina* 维那).[11] These monastics not only fulfill their assigned roles but also engage in practices that vary considerably from individual to individual.

Rank-and-file monastics show a broad range of interests and degrees of dedication; they also differ, along with all monastics, in the forms of personal cultivation they choose. Some choose to chant sutras, some copy sutras,

FIG. 4.1 The abbot and two head monks reading newspapers outside the abbot's quarters, thirty or forty feet from the door of the author's room in 2006. Photo by the author.

others meditate or practice *nianfo*. Some monastics are more literate than others; some participate in rituals, others do not; some meditate, most do not. The eminent Ming dynasty monk Zhuhong (1535–1613) was involved with religious practice as well as institution building and warned others of the difficulty in maintaining practice when managing the business of a monastery (Brook 2005, 151–152). Those with positions are indeed often busy with monastic duties and are often left with little time for forms of cultivation. Among clerics at any monastery, a considerable degree of diversity in behavior, abilities, disposition, motivations, and knowledge is only to be expected.

As chapter 3 suggests, monks without administrative positions have considerable free time, which they use in a great variety of ways. Many engage in mundane pursuits (reading the newspaper, browsing the internet, playing computer games, visiting, drinking tea). Others may be engaged in providing house calls, that is, performing rituals away from the monastery. Monks who do this can earn as much as ¥4,000 a month, a high monthly salary in 2006 when average (unskilled) full-time work in Quanzhou is in the ¥2,000 range. Others are engaged in forms of personal enrichment (music, calligraphy) or study. Most monks have personal phones and, like their nonmonastic peers, social media accounts. Some, especially those in the administration, will promote and report on special events and festival days at the monastery to their social media followers. This is also a way of communicating with lay followers.

In regard to Buddhist sutras, several monks intermittently engaged in reading (*dujing* 读经) and studying (*xuejing* 学经) various sutras, but most interaction with scripture is in the liturgical practices of chanting (*nianjing* 念经) or reciting sutras (*songjing* 诵经). The only place this might be different is at a Buddhist seminary, where monastics typically engage in the academic appreciation of Buddhist scripture, thus emphasizing discursive engagement. Some monks can be heard reciting sutras in their rooms in the morning and accompanying themselves with the wooden fish and hand chime. Monks reported reciting the *Diamond Sutra* (*Jingang jing* 金刚经) and the *Dizang Sutra* (*Dizang jing* 地藏经). Such monks have generally been in higher positions and did not regularly join morning and evening services. The sutras monks most commonly reported reading were the *Lotus Sutra,* the *Flower Ornament Sutra* (*Huayan jing* 华严经), the *Laṅkāvatāra Sūtra* (*Lengyan jing* 楞严经), and the *Platform Sutra* (*Liuzu tan jing* 六祖坛经). Individual monks mentioned reading the *Āgamas* (*A'han jing* 阿含经), *Brahma Net Sutra* (*Fan'gang jing* 梵纲经), the *Medicine Buddha Sutra* (*Yaoshi jing* 药师经), and the *Dharmaguptaka Vinaya* (*Sifen jieben* 四分戒本). These texts collectively represent a wide sampling of Chinese Buddhist teaching and the monks mentioning them were able to discuss Buddhist topics in an informed manner with one another or lay Buddhists. No opportunities for formal study or dharma teachings led by monks for fellow monks or laity were available, however. Advancing one's understanding was entirely self-directed.

When it comes to meditation, Kaiyuan Monastery has no organized periods like those at other monasteries, such as seven- or ten-day retreats. Neither is any hall suitably appointed for seated meditation; the kneeling cushions found in the main hall and dharma hall are not appropriate for seated meditation. If monks choose to practice meditation, they do so in their own rooms. A handful have practiced in their rooms either regularly or intermittently over the years. A more visibly verifiable form of contemplative cultivation is circumambulation around the monastery grounds during off-peak hours in the early morning or evening. In addition is the monk focused and disciplined in regularly circumambulating the eastern courtyards of the monastery.

The most common form of personal cultivation among monks, lay Buddhists, and worshippers is prostration to buddhas and bodhisattvas (*baifo* 拜佛) and offering incense (*xingxiang* 行香). These practices are both incorporated into all communal liturgical ceremonies and constitute a basic level of practice for monks throughout the Buddhist world. The abbot of Nanputuo explained the value of all forms of practice as enabling the individual to cultivate mental tranquility and sensitivity to stray thoughts (*wangxiang* 妄想). If one does not engage in contemplative practices from prostration to meditation, one will be swept away by stray thoughts and fantasies without noticing when they arise. Prostration and offerings, as the basic elements of worship, are meant to diminish egoism and enhance generosity.

In sum, the forms of personal cultivation exhibited at this site are carried out independently and for the most part inconsistently. They include from most to least common: prostration and offering incense; chanting or reciting sutras; reading and studying sutras, monastic codes, Buddhist teachings, blogs, and online content; contemplative circumambulation; and seated meditation. Based on historical precedent and textual references, what forms of self-cultivation are missing from this list?

Missing Forms of Practice

Chapter 3 mentions that the fortnightly recitation of the *prātimokṣa* (*busa*) has not been a common practice at Buddhist monasteries in China in modern times. The tradition of reciting the rules of discipline, common throughout Southeast Asia, is traced back to the Buddha, who is said to have called for "full and frequent assemblies" of monks to be held for the reciting of the rules of discipline (Gombrich 1988, 109). It is also a time for confessing one's violations of them and vowing to do a better job of upholding them. It is thus the traditional mechanism in Buddhist monasteries to reinforce rules of virtue and decorum through recitation and confession. Noting the fundamental role of monastic vows and the place of the *prātimokṣa,* Donald Lopez writes, "It was the maintenance of these vows by monks and nuns that was said to justify the alms they received from the laity. Hence, perhaps *the most important of monastic ceremonies* was the *upoṣadha* ceremony, in which the monks of a given monastery or area gathered together to recite their vows" (Lopez 1995, 503, emphasis added). Although Lopez is writing an essay for the volume titled *Buddhism in Practice,* he is basing his views on Buddhist texts rather than ethnography and is writing in past tense. Although it appears to have not been emphasized in China over the past hundred years at least, this statement provides a doctrinally based argument for the importance of the ritual. The absence of regular recitation of the rules and vows may be assumed to contribute to a lack of basic knowledge regarding the rules expected of ordained monastics. The absence of a tradition of organized self-reflection on these rules must also be seen to contribute to a difficulty in maintaining discipline within the monastic community as well as a manifest lack of emphasis on such discipline. In short, this is a significant tradition that has been largely missing from Chinese monasticism for more than a century.

Another feature of a functioning Chan monastery is a schedule for meditation in a Chan hall. "Meditation (*zazen*) is at the core of Zen. For centuries, this Zen meditative quest has been pursued within the framework of a distinctive monastic life, regulated in every detail to maximize the practice of meditation," Martin Collcutt writes about medieval Japan (1981, 133–134). Accounts of monastic life in modern times provided by Buswell (in Korea) and

Welch (in Republican period China) both emphasize the importance of meditation. Welch writes, "The heart of Buddhism is enlightenment. The heart of the monastery was the meditation hall where enlightenment was sought" (1967, 47). In the Chinese tradition, Welch notes, meditation is most commonly associated with a specialized Chan hall. In contemporary China, several monasteries have revived Chan halls. I have visited and meditated in dedicated Chan halls at Hebei's Bailin and Jiangsu's Gaomin Monastery 高旻寺 (site of Xuyun's enlightenment) in China. Both are among the most respected Chan halls in contemporary China, along with Jiangxi Mt. Yunju Zhenru Chan Monastery 云居真如禅寺 (an important Caodong monastery), Wutai Puhua Monastery 普化寺, and Guangdong Yunmen Monastery 云门寺 (home of the Yunmen school of Chan).[12] Chan halls have also been revived in Fujian at Gushan in Fuzhou and Xiamen Nanputuo, though practice seems to be limited to intermittent retreats. From these monasteries and others in contemporary China, we know that traditions of meditation training exist today as they have in the past, simply not at Quanzhou Kaiyuan and the vast majority of monasteries in China. Why not? The short answer is that not enough teachers are qualified and meditation is not a priority of the leadership.

Although these general observations provide a helpful overview, we can only get a sense of the trajectory of the monastic career by examining individual monks. Brief profiles of seven monks at Kaiyuan, four high-ranking and three low-ranking, will give a sense of the range of motivations and backgrounds among monastics in contemporary China. This will introduce the individuals behind the robes who, to an outsider, are too often a homogenous mass. Names have been modified in the interest of maintaining a measure of confidentiality, though no one requested such anonymity. The following sections present portraits of monks largely in their own words.

Dali

Dali was born in the mid-1970s in Fujian and visited Kaiyuan as a youth; he became a monk in 1996. His mother was a Buddhist nun, but during the Cultural Revolution she was forced into lay life and had a family. Following the implementation of the new policy on religion, she returned to life as a nun with her own small temple. Dali's sister became a Buddhist vegetarian auntie (*caigu*); in short, Dali's entire family has come to dedicate themselves in one way or another to Buddhism.

Since childhood, Dali has had poor health, limiting his livelihood options to some extent. He tried his hand at business by opening a small retail store but it was not successful. It was after this failure that he decided to try life as a monk. He originally thought he would try it for two or three years, but found that he enjoyed the life and has remained a monk since. Dali has risen within Kaiyuan's hierarchy to a high position. He is comparatively young to be of high rank and not particularly educated in Buddhist doctrine or history, but is considered handsome by others, thoughtful, and good with people, as well as a disciple (*tudi*) of the abbot. These qualities, along with his business experience, suit specialization in administrative and financial affairs. His general outlook seems to be informed by his responsibilities; and he typically speaks about the monastery much as one might speak about running a business, exhibiting easy fluency in discussing revenue and expenditures and the like, but less comfortable discussing higher Buddhist teachings. He is so busy with administrative affairs that he has practically no time for advanced cultivation or study; his health has also seen ups and downs over the years. One activity he has set out to improve is his calligraphy, which is an important skill for high-ranking monks and abbots. In 2019, he spoke of recently having spent time reading and struggling with Buddhist sutras. His conclusion was that it could take decades to reach a deep understanding of such material.

Farong

Farong was born around 1970, is from Southwest China, and does not speak the local dialect. After graduating from college, he became a teacher of Chinese at a middle school in his home province. He did not especially like it, however, feeling that it did not suit his introverted personality. He likes to travel independently and every school holiday did so on his own. In China, tourist and travel destinations inevitably include many temples; on visiting temples as a tourist, he developed an interest in Buddhism.

He decided to become a monk somewhat abruptly during a Chinese New Year holiday at the end of the 1990s. At the time he was not happy with his work and he did not enjoy the Chinese New Year celebrations; he always felt they were crowded and noisy. He went to travel in the mountains of Hunan. While staying in a hostel, a roommate announced that he wanted to become a monk. This person told him a lot about how good life as a monk is, especially not needing to worry about things such as food, money, or clothes. His reasons were not about Buddhism in particular but about the lifestyle. Farong decided to become a monk as well. The two of them visited many large temples, but none would accept them. It is more difficult to gain entry to large temples; they ask for proof of singleness, parent's permission, and so on, Farong explained. It is much easier to become a monk at a small temple that has few monks, but they tried to go to big temples because his friend knew that life was easier at larger temples; smaller temples require more physical labor. One temple let them stay for a few days; it was there that Farong met a monk whose precept master was from his same province and suggested this master might accept him as a disciple. Farong traveled two hours to meet this master who did accept him as a disciple.

Before Farong became a monk, he knew little about Buddhism, and had only superficial impressions from having witnessed ritual performances. His master was older, conservative, and strict. He instructed Farong in which texts to read. At his ordination, he was the only monk ordained. Before ordination, he had to take a test that required him to memorize large sections of the morning and evening service book; he passed the test after one week of study. His tonsure master was a Caodong Chan master with more than a hundred disciples. He is the only son in his family (he has a younger sister) and his parents did not at first support his decision but have come to accept it because he is happy.

Farong found it easy to master Buddhist rituals and became known for his easy demeanor and sonorous chanting voice. Although he was a respected ritualist, he felt that rituals were not the true path and feared they were a waste of resources. Thus he has given them up to pursue personal cultivation, including sutra chanting as a form of meditation. He chants the *Heart Sutra* (*Xinjing* 心经), *Diamond Sutra* (*Jingang jing*), and the *Earth Treasury [Bodhisattva] Sutra* because they are shorter and has read other sutras like the *Platform Sutra*. He states that the teachings most influential on him are from the *Āgamas*. Farong is one of the few monks with a university education, which gives him greater ease with administrative and secretarial arts leading him to rise through the monastic hierarchy. It has also influenced his efforts at starting a blog related to exploring Buddhist traditions and critically evaluating particular folk traditions (Nichols 2016). He feels that keeping the precepts is the most challenging part of being a monk but that he has been able to quickly improve without a wife. Two things he feels are different since becoming a monk are his way of thinking and mental state (*sixiang he xinjing* 思想和心境). He is well respected by laypersons and monks alike.

Deru

Deru was born in Fujian in the early 1960s. In the 1980s, he had a job in which he earned ¥75 ($9) per week, then switched to a job at a frozen meat factory where he could earn ¥1,500 ($200) per month. Although he could earn much more money in this job, he did not like working with dead animals. One day a friend took him to a temple, where he was introduced to Buddhism. He found that he liked it. In particular, he was attracted by the feeling of tranquility. He was also having difficulties with his girlfriend: he felt she did not understand him and he had doubts about the prospect of marriage. He had a friend who had gotten married and was not happy. He feared that balancing the needs and desires of a wife with those of one's parents and in-laws was an impossible task.

He became a lay Buddhist and two years later quit his job to become a monk. People did not understand why he was unhappy or why he would give up a good job. But, he said, they have come to understand the unreliability of work in a changing economy. He recalled the day his head was shaved as one of momentous change. As the shaving was under way, his mind went blank. He could not see or hear what the other monks were saying, a state that lasted around two hours. His tonsure master, a member of the Caodong Chan lineage, said this was because he was taking such a dramatic step in his life. He was thirty years old and though he had had several girlfriends he was still single. He was ordained in 1990 with more than eight hundred others at Shanghai Longhua Temple 上海龙华寺, which he described as the first Buddhist Association of China organized ordination in the post-Mao period. He spent time at two monasteries in Fujian before landing at Kaiyuan.

Ten years later, he had risen to a high position in the Kaiyuan hierarchy. Deru is loud and energetic and receives many visitors. When I first met him, he lived in his own room, which included a private bathroom. Like other monks of rank, he has his own washing machine and furnishings that he has acquired, which include a wooden "arhat" bed and matching tea table, made at a cost of ¥5,000 ($625), which was more than two months of the average salary in Fujian at that time. On the small low table was a hot plate for boiling water for tea, which included a side for sterilizing cups. He had a computer with a high-speed internet connection that sat on a simple desk. In 2006 and 2009, his speakers continually played the sounds of instant messages being received on his QQ account, which arrive to the sound of sets of three sharp raps on a wooden door.[13] The Amitabha mantra also played continually over a small *nianfo* machine that looped a recording of monks chanting to the rhythm of wooden fish and bells. This device sat on a shelf that was part of Deru's personal shrine, which included a golden Buddha, a photo of his tonsure master, and an intricate white porcelain sculpture. Most monks at Kaiyuan live in relatively spartan conditions. I mention these more luxurious ones because they are shared to some degree by most of the higher-ranking monks at large monasteries. At Kaiyuan, fewer than a dozen have this stature.

Given his previous experience of secular life, I asked him about being a monk and eliminating desires. His answer points to one of the great difficulties of realizing the ideals of the tradition:

> Once born you don't need to be taught [desire]. It's the same as eating; as soon as you're born you know to look for something to eat. Once a certain age, you just have it. It seems that if you see a pretty girl on the street you want to keep looking. Everyone is the

> same, so it is just human nature [*renxing ziran*] to have it. Getting rid of lust [*quchu qingyu*] is against human nature [*weikang renxing*], so becoming Buddha is extremely difficult [*suoyi chengfo tainan*].[14]

Deru never performed rituals because he did not consider them a proper form of practice: "My master told me, 'Money is easy to make; but the debt hard to repay' [*jinqian haozheng*; *jinzhai nanhuan*]. So I don't want to perform ceremonies. The sutras are from Sakyamuni Buddha, it's using other person's work to make money, which is why I don't do it." Deru's preferred form of cultivation is chanting scripture while accompanying himself with two or three dharma instruments at the same time.

Anlu

Anlu is from Anhui 安徽 and was a sickly child; he said nurses could not find a place to give him a shot in his rear or put an IV in his arm that had not already been poked. His principal complaint was a hardened part of his neck. The medicine prescribed for him cost ¥100 ($12) per month, which was more than his family could afford. It was also said that for a person in his condition the best treatment would be to live as a monk in a temple, so he became a novice at the age of fifteen. He continued the medicine for one month then stopped taking it because his health improved and the hard area on his neck had cleared up. At the age of twenty, he became fully ordained along with 350 others at Guangzhou Guangxiao Monastery 光孝寺 (a famous monastery associated with Hui'neng). His master belonged to the Pure Land school.

He came to Kaiyuan because he hoped to learn more than he was at the small temple in the south, which was how to play dharma instruments in ceremonies but not much else. He had practiced meditation for three months at another monastery and wished to continue his practice but found the conditions unsuitable at Kaiyuan. He had also spent one and half years in a Buddhist seminary but had left for undisclosed reasons. He was disappointed with the lack of opportunities for study and meditation at Kaiyuan and passed time practicing calligraphy before leaving for another temple after a year and a half. When I met him, he proudly showed me a set of vinaya books he worked to put into practice and wrote for me a list of books he felt were most important for his study of Buddhism. Some he had read, others he had not. These included all of the Buddhist sutras mentioned in this chapter as well as two books on history, *The History of Buddhist Religion* 佛教宗教史 and *The History of Chinese Buddhism* 中国佛教史. He impressed me as a young, earnest monk who wanted to practice and study Buddhism but was still seeking the best conditions to do so; in accord with tradition of the "homeless life," he continues his search.

Bulin

Bulin is the only son in his family and at the age of ten decided he wanted to learn martial arts. His parents could not stop him from going to Shaolin Temple to study. He planned to stay half a year; it was harder than he expected, though, and he thought about running away. Some older students had run away; he thought it was because they knew how to run away; at ten he was too young to figure out how to escape. He could have asked his parents to get him out, but it would have been a loss of face. The first thing he did when he went home was to take a bath. When his father saw his legs bruised and his back with red marks all over it, he could not conceal his tears. His mother, sisters, aunt, and everyone in the family who saw the bruises cried and tried to stop him from returning to Shaolin Temple. But, feeling that after half a year he was just getting started, he did not want to waste the pain he had endured; he also missed the friends he had made; so he went back.

He first studied and mastered the basics of elementary kung fu (*tongzi gong* 童子功); at fourteen, he began to study the use of weapons. Over the years, he has traveled and performed all over China and Southeast Asia. When he turned seventeen, he became a kung fu instructor but did not like the pressure, the workload, or his boss, who was tough on him and blamed him if anything went wrong. Some monks began to joke with him that his head was already shaved, why didn't he become a real monk where life was much easier? Bulin confessed, "To be honest that is the only reason I wanted to become a monk. I didn't know anything about Buddhism. I saw with my own eyes that a monk could receive a red envelope [*hongbao*] containing ¥2,000 ($250) just for burning a tall stick of incense for someone!" He could not believe it; the life of a monk was so easy, he thought, he would become a novice.

After a few years, life was so easy that he was bored. He wanted to travel, try another place; a friend introduced him to Kaiyuan. In 2006, he, like other regular monks, was paid a stipend of a little over ¥900 ($115) per month. He has no regrets about becoming a novice but feels that his life has been so easy and comfortable that he would not be able to handle secular life.

Chuanfa

Chuanfa was born in northern China in the early 1970s. Living with other students in his college dorm, he was struck with fear of ghosts in the middle of the night, especially when walking out to the restroom. He felt that the

Diamond Sutra might be helpful so he went to the local bookstore to buy a copy. The closest thing available, however, was a summary of the *Diamond Sutra*'s central teachings, *What Does the Diamond Sutra Say?* 金刚经说什么 by the popular Taiwanese author of such introductory books to Buddhism, Nan Huaijin 南怀瑾. This book expanded Chuanfa's knowledge of Buddhism; he even adopted a vegetarian diet for a time. After graduation, he began part-time employment at a bank in his hometown but found it unfulfilling. At this time, he read *The Amitabha Sutra Explained* 阿弥陀经解 by Jinkong, likely the most well-known and popular Buddhist monk in the Chinese Buddhist world.[15] This book emphasized the efficacy of *nianfo*. Chuanfa set out to try this approach. He began practicing at a local temple, where he caught the eye of the abbot, who encouraged him to become a monk. This encouragement was the only push he needed. He was ordained at the age of twenty-five.

Chuanfa grew disillusioned with the claims of *nianfo* to produce awakening, rejected the approach, and continued to study on his own, first reading introductions to Buddhist teachings by Taiwanese monastic authors, in particular the monks Yanghui 养慧 and Huijian 慧律 and the nun Fazun 法遵. The most influential was the introduction to the tradition of Southern Buddhism (*nanchuan*) by Fazun, which introduced the teaching and practice of mindfulness, which Fachuan continued to study and practice for three years at a small temple in Fujian before traveling to Myanmar to study and practice there for fourteen months. Returning to Fujian, he was invited by the general manager to serve as director of the office of the Compassion Association, and later by the abbot to serve as the assembly prefect (*zhizhong* 知众) with responsibility to manage the lower-ranking monks for eight years, eventually returning to Burma to practice meditation for another eight months. He remains at Kaiyuan in an administrative position.

Chuanfa is a fan of Jack Kornfield, having read some of his books on meditation (translated into Chinese). It is likely that such reading has encouraged him to be critical not only of Pure Land Buddhism, a criticism shared with other educated monks at Kaiyuan, but also of Mahayana Buddhism more broadly as having been influenced by and mixed with too many folk traditions and beliefs unrelated to original Buddhism (*yuanshi fojiao*). His study and practice of Theravada traditions have convinced him that it is the path for him, though he complains of struggling to clear his mind during meditation on the breath. Anecdotal evidence—namely, monks in Suzhou and Daci Monastery 大慈寺 in Chengdu (Gildow 2014, 77)—suggests that Theravada has a future in China.

Fuhui

Fuhui's family fell into debt because of medical expenses associated with his mother's illness. At the age of fifteen, he was forced to drop out of school and work. He worked a string of jobs from auto repair to food service, from windows and doors to making chopsticks, from working at a clothing factory to farming. When I remarked that it sounded like hard work, he responded that such work was easier than practice and that mental afflictions (*neixin de fannao* 内心的烦恼) were far more complex. During these years, he was not attracted to eating and drinking and social life in general. At the time, a few monks lived in his home village and his cousin introduced him to the local temple. He was curious about the temple and wondered whether Buddhism might offer a new world (*xinde shijie* 新的世界). "I had no idea how rich the content of Buddhism was. That the Buddha and a few earnest practitioners are so great that they could conquer their egos and benefit others! For these reasons I have continued to choose to be a monk, this path. Nevertheless, one must also have appropriate karmic preconditions." The cousin who introduced Fahui to the temple also became a monk, but returned to secular life three months later. His younger brother also became a monk and disrobed six months later. He believes that he has been able to remain a monk because of his past karmic connection with the tradition, openness to the teaching, and an ability to accept the shortcomings of others.

He arrived at Kaiyuan in 2005. After a few years among the rank-and-file monks, he was posted in the main hall, where he keeps an eye on visitors to make sure they do not bring in incense or otherwise disturb the cultural relics. He is also there to answer questions from lay Buddhists and worshippers, accept donations, write receipts, and assist patrons with lighting Buddha lights. He explained that by lighting these lights one is symbolically eliminating the darkness (ignorance, misfortune, and so on) in one's family. He also advises lay Buddhists on practice and teachings. When I visited him in 2019, he was reading the *Flower Ornament Sutra* and expressed enthusiasm for its content. He impressed me with a facility and quiet passion for Buddhist traditions and their symbolic meanings and, from his point of view, genuine efficacy. He also enjoyed comparing Buddhism with other religions and discussing philosophical points of Buddhism, such as the two truths and nonduality. One of his preoccupations is clearing up confusions about Buddhism, Buddhist rituals, and Buddhist traditions that visitors express or exhibit. In this capacity, he had by 2019 likely become the most active informal dharma teacher on site.[16]

Patterns among Monastic Biographies

Although the seven profiles presented are a tiny sample, together they present several patterns worth noting. Only one of the seven became a monk after having studied and practiced Buddhism on his own. Only three had any experience with Buddhism before becoming a monk; the others knew very little about the religion apart from superficial impressions. Two were sickly children; one of these become a monk because of his condition and the prohibitive cost of treatment. Six were dissatisfied with their occupations immediately before becoming a monk—one's business failed, the others were unhappy for various reasons. Four were partially influenced in their decisions to become monks by visiting Buddhist temples, a fifth by living at a temple when he was studying martial arts. Four were influenced by casual remarks. Four indicate a discomfort with aspects of the secular social world and its ways. Two admit to being attracted by the promise of a life of ease. This last motivation is, I suspect, one that enters into the minds of many of Kaiyuan's monks and monks across China.

Welch gathered biographical information on thirty-nine Chinese monks from the first half of the twentieth century, twenty-eight from interviews and eleven from documentary sources (1967, 258–269). Of these cases, thirteen had some failure or disappointment and sought to escape the secular world, six had been ill as children, six had been orphaned, six liked monks and the atmosphere of monasteries, four were interested in Buddhist study and practice, two were persuaded by relatives who were monks, one wanted supernormal powers, and one felt hated by his parents. The reasons provided are comparable to those of the small sample from Kaiyuan at the beginning of the twenty-first century. The most common reason in both groups was disappointment in the secular world and a wish to escape it. Two of Kaiyuan's monks had been ill; four were partially influenced by enjoying the atmosphere of monasteries; two were influenced by family members in the sangha; and one (only one) demonstrated a prior interest in Buddhist study and practice. The only reason not recorded by Welch was a desire for an easy life. This reason is superficially similar to the desire to escape the secular world but remains more solidly of the world—an easy material life as opposed to one of freedom from secular cares. The other reasons suggest a good deal of consonance between early twentieth century and early twenty-first century motivations for joining the sangha.

Georges Dreyfus, who studied for fifteen years as a monk among the Tibetan community in Dharamsala, India, notes that "scholars [*dpe cha ba*] followed a strict schedule throughout their scholarly training," whereas "most monks [*grwa mang*] lead a relatively easy life" (2003, 65).[17] Thus the Tibetan Gelukba tradition incorporates a split between the scholar-monk core and the rest of the monastic body. A similar split existed in pre-1950s Tibet as well. Melvyn Goldstein describes two broad divisions among monks at Tibet's largest monastery, Drepung: those engaged in formal study of Buddhism, the "scholar monks," and those not engaged. The former accounted for about 10 percent of the monastic population (1998, 21). Similarly, Jørn Borup's study of the home temple of Rinzai Zen in Japan, Myōshinji, found that only

8 percent of the priests there meditated, a figure similar across Japanese schools of Zen (2008, 2010; Reader 1986, 14). At Kaiyuan in 2006 and 2009, this would mean that eight or nine of the monks would be part of such an elite group and in 2019, only four or five. Goldstein relates that the other monks were often illiterate and apart from some work obligations were "free to do what they liked" (1998, 21). This entailed earning a living because Drepung provided neither communal meals nor a sufficient stipend.

The split is analogous to that in the Korean Zen tradition Buswell describes, in which the meditators were separated from the rest of the monastic body to focus on meditation (1992). Dreyfus provides a detailed account of the training of the scholar-monk but almost no information about the lives of "most monks" (2003). One thing common to monks in the Tibetan tradition is a trial period designed to instill self-discipline; Dreyfus describes the trial period as a kind of "boot camp," which could last several years. No monks I spoke with in China mentioned anything about a rigorous trial period; some were required to memorize most of the daily service but that was to become ordained. Kaiyuan's monks generally fit into the category of "most monks" described by Dreyfus as leading "an easy life." What Kaiyuan and most other monasteries in China, are missing, however, is a core of monks receiving rigorous training. This lack is related to a lack of qualified, able-bodied, and ambitious leaders, especially in the early years of recovery.

Who are Kaiyuan's monks? Several have an earnest interest in studying the dharma, but most do not; some are quite knowledgeable about Buddhism, but most have relatively rudimentary knowledge; many specialize in rituals, others in administrative tasks; some paint, write calligraphy, or play the Chinese zither (*guqin* 古琴), others have no special abilities. The different profiles of monk reflect both the needs of monasteries and the vagaries of human ability and circumstance. A monastery must have administrative types and those who may serve in that capacity are often neither scholars nor contemplatives. If the monastery is to maintain a good reputation, it must also have monks who are, or who present themselves as, pious. If it is to meet the needs of a community that demands rituals, it must also have monks with the ritual expertise and the willingness to serve them; such monks often have little or no time for self-cultivation even if they have interest in doing so. These few comments, applicable to any time or place, have already begun to bring monks down to a less idealized plane of existence.

What about imposter monks, a concern of critiques in Chinese Buddhism for centuries? These are those judged by other monks and lay Buddhists as using the monastic identity for personal gain rather than religious cultivation. What can we learn about such monks from a site like Kaiyuan? I have been told by more than one monk that most at Kaiyuan consider being a monk a job rather than a spiritual vocation, not a quest to leave samsara but a pragmatic means to an economic end. Among such monks were married monks, who could be considered imposters, but these had been kicked out by 2019.

Although evidence suggests that Chinese Buddhism has long contended with imposter monks, the common narrative provided by more articulate monks and lay Buddhists draws attention to special challenges for post-Mao Buddhism. The narrative is that Chinese temples are being rebuilt at a pace that exceeds China's ability to train qualified monks to staff them. When restrictions against religious practice were eased and temples began to be recovered for religious use, too few qualified monastics were available to tend them; as a result, standards were lowered and many uneducated and unsuitable individuals became ordained monks and moved into temples; many even assumed positions of leadership. A good number of those ordained did not have a firm belief in Buddhism or understanding of its principles, making it easier for them to break precepts.

Multiple sources claim that many monks break the most basic precepts in such scandalous ways as drinking, having sex and families, and eating meat. Apart from seeing one monk looking, acting, and smelling drunk one evening, I have no eyewitness confirmation beyond certain reliable testimony. Across from the main entrance to the monastery was a sex shop. A few stores down was a place that sold homemade alcohol. I asked both stores whether the monks buy much; in each case the answer was not much (*buduo*). This obviously does not mean that most monks do such things, but does suggest that some do drink and carnally experiment. Such lax observance of monastic discipline is reported by the monk Chen-hua as a feature of smaller temples during the twentieth century (1992, 5). Regardless of what some monks may do in their free time, several monks at Kaiyuan have impressed me as being quite diligent, upright, and sincere.

Why, one may wonder, would someone ignorant of Buddhism want to shave their head and enter the order? Some of the questionable reasons for entering a monastery include fleeing a marriage that has soured or a business that has failed. Others may be attracted to what they see as an easy life or even a path of socioeconomic advancement, a path that confers more status or income than other options. These have been presented and are assumed to be poor motivations for a religious life. I maintain, however, that they are not in themselves damning. They are primarily so to an idealized view of monks. A natural counter might be, are not monks supposed to conform to an ideal type? To such a concern, I would reply, yes, and add that in some minimal sense Kaiyuan's monks outwardly conform to a monastic identity. They shave their heads, wear robes and monastic slippers, and appear to live apart from home and family in a devotional environment that rubs off on many of them to varying degrees. The problems with monastic discipline are not flagrant or in public view. Monks conform to some measure of what is expected of monks and in doing so they differentiate themselves from nonmonastics. For those who perceive their role as a kind of job and view Kaiyuan as a service provider, as a purveyor of merit and spiritual efficacy, such monks remain employed in a fundamentally religious role. It is not the expected or idolized vocation of canonical sources, but it is a career that has helped restore a vibrant devotional site and provides for the religious needs of the community.

I would be remiss to leave this assessment of unqualified monks on this sanguine note because some decry the lack of quality of many monks throughout China and at Kaiyuan specifically. After noticing that many monks seemed to skip meals in the dining hall, I asked one in attendance why many were absent. I was told that they ordered food to be delivered to their rooms and that some monks (younger ones in particular) were not satisfied on a vegetarian diet. Similarly, when I mentioned that it was common for monks to marry in Japan, I was told that some in China and at Kaiyuan also do, that some are married when they become monks and some even have children, that in some cases wives have gone to temples to look for their husbands. In the end, as many as forty monks of the population of ninety were expelled, by order of the abbot, sometime between 2012 and 2018 for having wives and children. The purge, though, failed to significantly improve discipline. Many of the remaining monks are said to have girlfriends, to change into street clothes, and to go out on the town at night. It seems that a choice was made to reject married monks but to tolerate those tactfully living out of wedlock. Could such a choice be justified in the context of Buddhist history?

Could it be that the claim repeated over and over again in scholarship on Buddhism from textbooks to studies of Buddhism and sexuality that sex unequivocally ends a monk's career is not the full story? According to Clarke Shayne (2009), it generally is not. Shayne finds that though sex is forbidden, all sets of monastic rules except the Pāli Vinaya include provisions for a monk who has committed sex to remain part of the sangha, albeit demoted to the level of novice and stripped of any status or authority. All vinayas outside the Pāli Vinaya include a story of Nandika who commits *pārājika* (breaks the code forbidding sex), subsequently feels remorse, reports to the Buddha, and because he is not concealing his breaking of the code is not expelled, but instead demoted to a novice status known as *śikṣādattaka* after completing a related penance. Further, Shayne points out, anthropological studies of Theravada Buddhist communities indicate provisions within monastic communities to keep *pārājika* monks in the community as penitential novices, indicating a discrepancy between the Pāli Vinaya and practices on the ground (Shayne 2009; see also Spiro 1982; Southwold 1983; Carrithers 1983).

Although Kaiyuan does not have any formal way of absolving or otherwise dealing with such infractions, at least the premodern Buddhist world has a precedent for tolerating monks having sex more than for monks getting married. Nonetheless, if such disregard for the most basic monastic precepts were widely known, it would be expected to negatively affect the success of such a monastery. Maintenance of monastic discipline, in other words, keeping the precepts or at least the appearance of keeping the precepts, has long been the most important factor in maintaining the public's support of the monastic order. In her study of Ming dynasty Buddhism, Yü Chün-fang notes that "it was the monks' failure to keep discipline that always evoked the ire of the public, while their lack of doctrinal originality or intellectual brilliance was apparently a matter worthy of little comment" (1981, 143–144). I concur that monastic discipline easily trumps doctrinal knowledge or meditational accomplishment in the eyes of the public, but I would go even further and suggest that an old temple, especially one with cultural relics and venerable historical reputation, may even be seen to attract throngs of worshippers and even lay devotees with the help of competent ritualists in the guise of monks. Such shaven-headed and robed figures or incense and flower monks (*xianghua heshang* 香花和尚) are able to religiously activate a sacred space in Fujian for all but the most critical and demanding. Lay Buddhists at Kaiyuan accept the presence of married incense and flower monks among the celibate precept upholding monks. Such monks apparently do a brisk business in funeral rituals known as incense and flower Buddhist rites (*xianghua foshi*) conducted off-site.[18]

When I first learned of incense and flower monks, I considered them imposters. But what does it mean if the average local lay Buddhists and worshippers accept these monks as having ritual power? My research into incense and flower monks, as well as that of Yik Fai Tam in Meizhou 梅州 in Guangdong (2012), finds that the common people (*laobaixing*) accepted incense and flower monks as legitimate and qualified Buddhist ritual masters, a status disputed by ordained clerics. For these communities, incense and flower monks must be accepted as an alternative type of Buddhist cleric. Their origin is thought to be in the early Ming dynasty. The founder of the dynasty, Emperor Taizu, had been a monk and established administrative reforms regarding the Buddhist tradition. One of these was to establish a threefold administrative typology of monks: meditation specialists (*chan* 禅), lecturing scholar-monks (*jiang* 讲), and ritual-esoteric masters (*jiao* 教). Then as now, the vast majority of monks fell into the third category, *jiao,* which does not (as one might expect) refer to teaching, but instead to *yujiajiao* 瑜伽教 (yoga–esoteric tradition teaching) understood as ritual specialist (242). From that time onward evidence indicates that incense and flower funeral rites were conducted by Buddhist ritual specialists, who evolved into today's incense and flower monks (240).

Regardless of such vernacular historical pedigree, my principal monastic informants as well as certain critical lay Buddhists in Quanzhou reject such monks as following the true path of Buddhism. The most critical local voice was a lay Buddhist who claimed that one could no longer find true Buddhism at Buddhist temples in China because so many had become focused on amassing wealth rather than training monks and teaching the dharma. His view of the fundamental problem with Chinese Buddhism was, nonetheless, shared by the more critical monks at Kaiyuan, namely, the common folk belief that Buddha is a god who can grant favors and blessings. This layperson and these monks decry such a view as far from the teaching of original Buddhism, which is to see Buddha as a great man (*weida ren* 韦大人) leading others on a heroic path to liberation. The only difference between these critical monks and lay Buddhists is that the monks participate in the institutional system that encourages such a view as expressed in festival celebrations (discussed in chapter 3), whereas critical lay Buddhists reject institutional Buddhism and pursue their own paths outside temples.[19]

We should accept that the average Buddhist monastery is a home for variously qualified and variously dedicated monks. The key to establishing standards of discipline or traditions of training is an abbot driven to cultivate such things. The leadership of the highest ranking figure is critical. As the abbot of Nanputuo pointed out, "If the top beam is skewed, the bottom will be crooked" (上梁不正下梁歪). For whatever egalitarianism that may exist in the Buddhist tradition, Chinese monasticism is fundamentally hierarchical. Responses to questions about enforcement of discipline inevitably point to the abbot; only the abbot has such power. As suggested in chapter 2, however, his priorities have been tending to Kaiyuan's physical plant, raising money, maintaining good relations with state officials, and developing the monastic management system—the institutional side of Kaiyuan. Thus the abbot, it may be argued, has a skill set that seems tailored to the early post-Mao restoration of institutional monastic traditions. This includes good relations with government officials, a strong and aggressive personality that has been able to clear the property of various occupants, and, last, a good sense of what traditions will most appeal to the masses and support the recovery of the monastery (rituals to eliminate troubles and bring blessings and the columbarium).

Concluding Thoughts

Going beyond labels and assumptions about Chan, Pure Land, Buddhism, or monasticism and using a person-centered and practice-centered approach, we encounter monks doing what they do and being who they are. For the administrative monks, who have the highest status and reputations, we should think balance sheets, meetings, business travel, hobnobbing with patrons, business deals, and contracts. These monks have little time and energy for any kind of self-cultivation, but they are essential for the material functioning of the monastery.[20] Most other monks, lacking expert guidance and instruction, stray from closely following the vinaya and have little idea of how to improve their practice beyond their instincts, associates, reading, or internet research. Although administrative monks will face the same situation indefinitely, other monks can be expected to face a variable situation tied to changes in leadership at the highest level. Consider, for example, youth basketball. One team has an easygoing father who lets the players run wild; another has a drill sergeant coach who demands discipline. If placed on the team with the drill sergeant, the so-called wild kids become models of discipline. The same is true of monks at a monastery.

In addition to leadership is the question of the broader social environment, an issue raised by monks and lay Buddhists alike. Apart from social pressures that value material acquisitions and wealth as signs of success is also, apparently, a local tradition of accepting incense and flower monks as religiously qualified to conduct Buddhist rituals for the community. These monks are said to be most common in areas near Nanjing and Shanghai, but present in other areas such as Guangdong and Fujian.[21] As for the economic pressure, one monk explained it simply: "We are like trees, money is like water. Trees can't live without water, we can't live without money." These two social facts combine to make monastic discipline a difficult, though not impossible, ideal to advance at Kaiyuan and other monasteries. On a more positive note, the social environment also includes greater access to printed materials and online information, which was a key factor in developing interest in and understanding of Buddhism by the monks who were so inclined, opening other paths of practice and cultivation among the proverbial 84,000 gates. In the next chapter, we turn to the part of the monastery that is more stable and arguably more universally honored than the monks, the built environment of the monastery itself.

Part III

Material Dynamics

5

Material Culture

Iron Temple, Water Monks

In the hall was a golden statue of the Buddha eighteen Chinese feet high, along with ten medium-sized images—three of sewn pearls, five of woven golden threads, and two of jade. The superb artistry was matchless, unparalleled in its day. ... The monastery had over one thousand cloisters for monks ... decorated with carved beams and painted walls ... the beauty of the cloisters was beyond description.

—*Yang Xuanzhi* 楊衒之 *(547 CE)*

Grass for a bed,
Blue sky for a quilt,
A stone for a pillow,
The world crumbles and changes.

—*Hanshan* 寒山 *(Tang dynasty)*

Along the base [of Kaiyuan's east pagoda] are carved greenstones (*qingshi* 青石). Their magnificent beauty is effortless and sublime (*huajing* 化境), fine and vigorous. It is supernatural work of divine chisels (*guigong shenfu* 鬼工神斧) that cannot be accomplished through human power.

—*Yuanxian (1643)*

BUDDHISM TEACHES THE IMPERMANENCE OF ALL COMPOUNDED things, the inevitability of suffering that arises associated with attachment to such impermanent things, and a path of homelessness and nonattachment leading to liberation from craving and suffering. In China, those treading this path in the most typical sense are individuals who have left home and family to pursue these lofty ideals in monastic settings. But monastic settings are often not what one might expect from individuals seeking liberation from worldly attachments. With its two Song dynasty stone pagodas that soar above the surrounding neighborhood and a grand Ming dynasty hall with five larger-than-life gilded Buddhas, Quanzhou Kaiyuan has an unusual share of both pomp and endurance. The grandeur of the painted and carved beams and the splendor of gilded statues at Kaiyuan and countless other Chinese monasteries make a not-too-subtle contrast with Buddhist ideals of simplicity and teachings on impermanence. The imposing structures and relative opulence of Buddhist monasteries in China has attracted critics since the fifth century who have pointed out the incongruity between the accumulation of material wealth and the Buddhist path of renunciation.[1] The *Guang hongming ji* 廣弘明集, for example, includes a critique of Xun Ji 荀濟 (d. 547), who called for monks to beg according to the Buddha's instruction rather than erect elaborate monasteries and store up wealth (*Guang hongming ji* 7.128c–131b, in Chen 1964, 187). In addition to critiques on moral grounds were those on socioeconomic grounds. A memorial by Governor Xiao Muzhi of Danyang 丹陽 in 435 complained of the economic stress caused by the inordinate number of stupas, monasteries, paintings, and statues (*Guang hongming ji* 6.127b, in Gernet 1995, 15, 321n75).

If we take the forest monk or mountain ascetic as ideal monastics, then ornate Chinese monasteries suggest decadence. Similarly, if we approach the gilded images and the lofty pagodas covered with icons from a Protestant-informed bias against externals, we too will reject them as spiritually inconsequential and unworthy of attention.[2] This chapter joins the growing body of scholarship on religion and material culture by seeking to appreciate the place of Kaiyuan's material culture in the religious and institutional life of the monastery.[3] My approach to material culture is through the lens of spatial studies (Knott 2010), understanding space to be created through dynamic relations, in contrast to place, which is simply a fixed location. My understanding of space and place follows Michel de Certeau's building on Maurice Merleau-Ponty (2012). Merleau-Ponty spoke of geometric space and anthropological space, which are analogous to de Certeau's distinction between fixed place and dynamic space, which is "actuated by the ensemble of movements deployed within it." As de Certeau continues, "Space occurs as the effect produced by the operations that orient it, situate it, temporalize it, and make it function" (1988, 117).[4]

To advance the study of religion and space and get into the mechanisms of spatial production, I adopt the idea of "cultural memory" developed by Jan Assmann (1995), who formulated it to account for what happens when we move from everyday private communicative memory to "objectivised culture," which includes the range of material culture from texts, artifacts, and images to the built and natural environments. This theory suggests that material culture represents a "concretion of identity" through which individuals *reconstruct* a social identity through dynamic relations that connect memory, culture, and a social group (Assmann 1995). By concretion of identity, I understand the sedimentation of values and meanings that point back to the systems and practices operative at the time of their creation. Historians attempt to retrieve the past, a study of the production of material culture. James Flath, for example, uncovers the conflicting interpretations of ritual and ritual priorities revealed in the rebuilding of Kong Temple over the centuries (2016). What nonhistorians do is recreate meaning with respect to their life histories, social and religious habitus, and, critically, present dispositions. This actualization of space is effected through the dynamic interrelationships between memory, culture, and social group. The concretion of identity within cultural memory is aided in a number of ways, including institutional support of some kind, an associated system of values, and a body of collective knowledge (Assmann 1995). The task of the ethnographer is to sort out salient patterns of meaning construction and behavior from the unscripted, unmediated, chaotic field. With respect to Kaiyuan, cultural memory is concretized in cultural artifacts such as scriptures, statuary, buildings, pagodas, stupas, and even trees. The cultural memory represented by Kaiyuan's body of material culture is primarily given form and values communicated through the monastic institution, Buddhist history, and the temple administrative commission. My long-term study of the site has revealed distinct patterns marking different groups of people who access the space and come away with different experiences. Different groups reconstruct different social identities in dialogue with Kaiyuan's material culture and the cultural memory it represents. I propose a tripartite model to capture the ways cultural memory is approached and activated through material culture in the making of space at Kaiyuan monastery.

Before turning to Kaiyuan, I review the relevant historical and institutional background to Buddhist monastic material culture. The evidence suggests that monasteries from an early period have exhibited material opulence and splendor and that this serves both the institutional and the religious purposes of the monastery in complex ways. Institutional needs include financial and political support; the religious purpose includes providing monastics and laypersons with a place for devotional practice, self-cultivation, and study.

The Artistically Embellished Buddhist Monastery

The use of cultural properties to beautify Buddhist monasteries and attract visitors and patronage may be as old as the institution of the Buddhist monastery. Tradition holds that the Jetavana Monastery, near Savatthi in India, is the first Buddhist monastery established.[5] The historical Buddha is said to have retreated there during the rainy season and sutras designate it as the location of many of his sermons. It served as the model for other monasteries and is, in short, the iconic Buddhist monastery.[6] Ancient texts speak not of austerity, however, but of its beauty, both natural as well as humanly wrought. The *Mūlasarvāstivāda Vinaya* (*MS Vinaya*) attributes at least a part of the Jetavana beautification plans to the Buddha himself.[7] The text tells how the Buddha authorized Anāthapiṇḍada, the donor of the monastery, to have paintings made to beautify Jetavana and suggests how the artwork should be arranged. The text concludes the construction of this iconic Buddhist monastery with these observations:

> Crowds of people who lived in Ṣrāvastī heard how the householder Anāthapiṇḍada had finished the Jetavana both inside and out with various sorts of colors and paintings and had made it remarkably fine, and many hundreds of thousands of people came then to see the Jetavana. (*Kşundrakavastu,* Derge Tha 262b.4 of the *MS Vinaya,* in Schopen 2004, 35)

This passage, celebrating the completion of the Jetavana Monastery, does not laud the construction of halls for meditation (*samādhi*), spartan cells for monks to keep their precepts (*śīla*), or didactic features to promote the dharma (*prajñā*). Instead it focuses on the "various sorts of colors and paintings" that made the monastery "remarkably fine" thus attracting "hundreds of thousands of people" who came to admire this new marvel. What the *MS Vinaya* indicates and what archeological discoveries in India have confirmed is that very early within the Buddhist tradition permanent monasteries were established and artistically embellished. Reflecting on the archeological record of northern India, Gregory Schopen asks,

> How is it that groups of ascetics, celibate men who were supposed to have renounced all wealth and social ties, left such largesse in the archeological record; how is it that they, and sometimes they alone, lived in permanent, architecturally sophisticated quarters, that they, and they alone, lived in intimate association with what we call art? Something is clearly wrong with this picture, and there is a good chance that we have not yet understood the people in North India who handled the coins we study or the pots we classify. (2004, 19)

Schopen notes the wealth, durability, and artistic sophistication of Indian Buddhist monasteries to which the archeological record attests and asks why. Indeed, what is going on here? What is behind this will to permanence and beauty? Buddhist monasteries in China and all over Asia offer a provocative parallel. Much of the most impressive material artifacts valued as works of art in China and throughout Asia are found at Buddhist sites. Among the most celebrated finds are the sculptures of the Mogao Caves 莫高窟 of Dunhuang 敦煌 (from the fourth to the fourteenth centuries), the Yungang Grottoes 云冈石窟 in Shanxi 山西 (from the fifth century), and the Longmen Grottoes 龙门石窟 in Henan 河南 (fifth to seventh centuries). Among the most impressive and important remains of the Tang dynasty are the clay sculptures found at Nanchan Monastery 南禅寺 and Foguang Monastery 佛光寺 in Shanxi, the Leshan Big Buddha 乐山大佛 in Sichuan 四川 (seventh century), and the trove of exquisite ninth-century treasures found at Xi'an's Famen Monastery 法门寺 in the 1980s. Examples may be multiplied throughout Asia: Borobudur in Indonesia, the Angkor complex in Cambodia, Heinsa Temple in South Korea, temples and gardens in Kyoto and Nara, the temples of Pagan in Myanmar, and temples in Bangkok, Ayutthaya, and elsewhere in Thailand. For ascetics who preach that all things are impermanent, in other words, Buddhist monasteries not only have an impressive ability to survive, but also exhibit a tremendous will to beautify.[8] Not only were Chinese monasteries aesthetically embellished, but monks also became connoisseurs and collectors of art (Weidner 2010).

The opulence of Buddhist monasteries in China was underscored by Yang Xuanzhi, the author of the sixth-century record of Luoyang's monasteries:

> Princes, dukes, and ranking officials donated such valuable things as elephants and horses, as generously as if they were slipping shoes from their feet. The people and wealthy families parted with their treasures as easily as with forgotten rubbish. As a result, Buddhist temples were built side by side, and stūpas rose up in row after row. People competed among themselves in making or copying the Buddha's portraits. Golden stūpas matched the imperial observatory in height, and Buddhist lecture halls were as magnificent as the [ostentatiously wasteful] E-pang 阿房 [palaces of the Qin dynasty (221–207 BCE)]. (Yang Xuanzhi, *Luoyang qielan ji* 洛阳伽蓝记, in Yang and Wang 1984, 5–6)

Although archeology provides evidence of elaborate monasteries, the *MS Vinaya* suggests the functions such ornate structures may have had beyond any religious role they may have served. Passage after passage relates how the embellishment of monasteries allowed them to attract visitors and inspire donations. The *MS Vinaya* does not explicitly state this as the main reason for beautification, but it seems that an association between accounts of captivatingly beautiful monasteries and the attraction of donors is regular enough that such a message would not have been lost on the monks who learned this text.[9] The passage cited earlier regarding the Jetavana demonstrates how beautiful monasteries could attract visitors. Schopen has collected several other references to the beautification of monasteries that include examples of the attendant riches such beautification could attract. In one passage, traveling merchants passed by monasteries and marveled at their "high arched gateways ... latticed windows, and railings" that were "like stairways to heaven" (*Vibhaṅga, Derge* 156b.4 in Schopen 2004, 32). These merchants were "deeply moved" (*dad par 'gyur te*) and made an "offering feast" (*mchod ston*) for the sangha. In another passage, merchants are similarly impressed with the beauty of an abandoned monastery and promptly set about endowing it with alms for sixty monks for three months with a promise to return and endow it for one hundred monks (*Vibhaṅga, Derge* 184a.1 in Schopen 2004, 31–32). Citing these instances and alluding to others in the *MS Vinaya,* Schopen writes, "Our Code refers to beautiful monasteries in beautiful settings, to paintings on monastery walls and on cloth. ... But in virtually every case these references refer as well—in one way or another—to the gifts and donations that such things generate" (31). Schopen's conclusion is that art and all things that beautify a monastery also serve, in the eyes of the *MS Vinaya,* as a means to generate donations (36–37).

Although Schopen's conclusions about Buddhist material culture focus on economic gains, other scholars have proposed a connection between the survival or longevity of religious sites in China and their material culture. Susan Naquin in her study of Tanzhe Monastery 潭柘寺, a large monastery outside Beijing, focuses on the role of material culture in securing survival. She notes that it survived the iconoclastic fury of the Cultural Revolution (1966–1976) and asks, "What were the secrets of Tanzhesi's success?" In answer she writes, "We should look at the interconnected dynamics of antiquity, sanctity, and scenery, all of which played their part in shaping the physical structure, visual and written record, and personal memories of Tanzhesi" (Naquin 1998, 205). In particular, she points out that representations of the monastery in literature from the Qing dynasty (1644–1911) onward focus on the physical and historic features of the temple such as its buildings, scenery, and trees. Similarly, Tracy Miller credits the survival of the Jin Memorial Shrine (*Jinci*) to the presence of the Northern Song dynasty Sage Mother Hall (constructed 1038–1102), which was recognized as an important heritage site in 1961 (2007, 103).

Quanzhou Kaiyuan Monastery

Like Tanzhe Monastery and others, Kaiyuan has been promoted as a place of history and culture since the end of the Ming dynasty (1368–1644). In 1961, it was designated a Provincial Level Protected Heritage Site by the Fujian provincial government. It was this identity that enabled its survival during the Cultural Revolution when it was protected from vandalism at the hands of Red Guards by Mayor Wang Jinsheng.[10]

Kaiyuan's material culture contributes to the beauty as well as to the historic and cultural value of the monastery, which, in turn, attracts tens of thousands of visitors per year who support the monastery through donations and entry fees. When asked about important or special features of the monastery, interviewees inevitably included Kaiyuan's pair of towering thirteenth-century stone pagodas, Ming and Qing dynasty halls, and centuries-old trees among the monastery's distinguishing features. Kaiyuan's material culture, not its traditions or revived practices, were foremost in the minds of many interviewees when asked about the site. Apart from inspiring economic and political patronage, what other roles might material culture have? Specifically, what kinds of response are activated by the cultural memory of Kaiyuan's material culture?

Earlier studies have been limited to the study of the archeological record, inscriptions, and manuscripts. I have been able to investigate additional roles played by material culture by taking into account the lived present. Over the course of seven months in residence at the monastery, I made careful observations and interviewed monks, laypersons, visitors, officials, and other members of the community. These interviews and observations provided insight into the rhythms of the monastery, the roles played by material culture, and how various residents and visitors relate to, understand, and interact with the material features of the site to dynamically activate and construct cultural memory and social identities. The phenomenological description that follows introduces the experience of entering the site and a brief tour highlighting features along the central axis and the two pagodas.[11]

Spatial Characteristics

Nicole Boivin criticizes the overemphasis on linguistically derived analyses of material culture in which "Material culture often became reduced to a mere sign, little different from a linguistic sign, its physical properties devoid of all but highly abstracted meaning" (2009, 271–272). She emphasizes the nonlinguistic nature of material culture as one of its important features (283). I maintain that a person's encounter with the collective material presence of most larger monasteries affects a nonlinguistic somatic response that can be analyzed using a combination of fieldwork consisting of interviews and participant-observation that includes phenomenological observation. Nonlinguistic or prereflective embodied knowing must ultimately be transformed into articulate cognitive content to provide communicable content of service to scholarship. Describing experience is something a participant observer trained with mindfulness is especially well suited to provide. Disciplined moment to moment experiential awareness directed out to the environment and in to personal feelings is a way to gather impressions while maintaining *epoché* with respect to judgments and conceptual frameworks and awareness of lapses of *epoché*. Such an approach offers the potential for improved phenomenological description through enhanced focus, clarity, sensitivity, and stability of observations. This can be seen as an application of mindfulness as (phenomenological) method first advocated by Francisco Varela, Evan Thompson, and Eleanor Rosch (1991).[12]

The main gate is an imposing wooden and stone structure holding two large guardian figures. The stone columns and red-painted beams of the Qing dynasty gate as well as its pair of towering guardian figures in brown, red, and gold lacquer with cryptic expressions are all part of a first impression. Inside the light is noticeably dimmer than the world outside. The dimness seems heightened by dust suspended in the air. Heavy-set guardian figures face the visitor. Three yellow cushions marked with impressions from

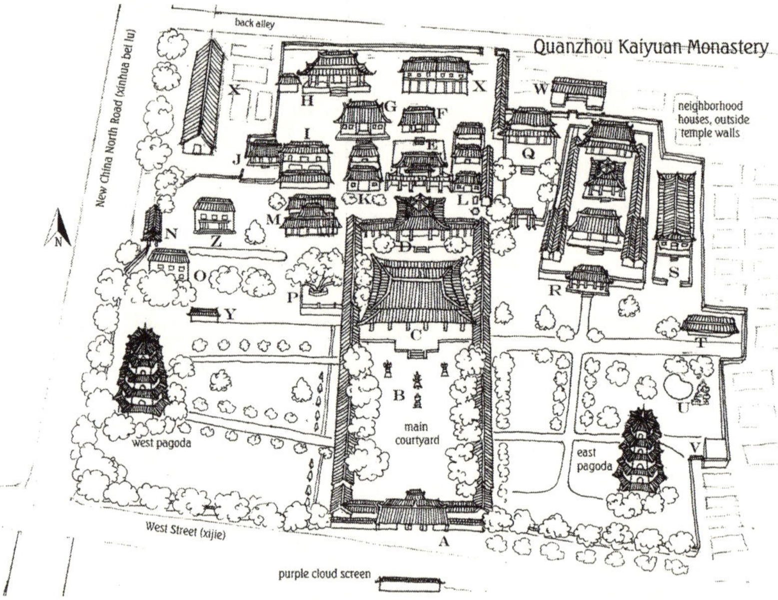

FIG. 5.1 Hand-drawn map of Quanzhou Kaiyuan Monastery. A. main gate and bounding walls, B. Song dynasty stupas, Ming dynasty silk furnace, incense burner in main courtyard, C. main hall with five Buddhas, D. ordination platform, E. dharma hall and sutra library, F. hall of patriarchs, G. dining hall, H. Anyang Cloister and underground columbarium, I. Venerated Site Cloister/ offices, J. Land and Water Temple, K. old hall of merit / offices, L. Donor's Ancestral Shrine, M. Buddhist goods shop and tour office, N. west gate, O. Office of Quanzhou BAC, P. ancient mulberry tree, Q. hall of Buddha's life / Buddhist Museum of Quanzhou, R. small Kaiyuan / Hongyi Memorial Museum, S. Ancient Boat Museum, T. post office, U. pond and rockery garden, V. public restroom, W. abbot's quarters, X. monastic dorms, Y. kylin wall, Z. guest hall. Map by the author and Jamie Zhang.

frequent use are placed casually in front of each guardian. All of these clues, however impressionistic, alert even the irreverent or insensitive that one is entering a structure that resonates with age—this is not a shoe store, a pet store, a cell phone shop, or anything else—it can only be a temple, a shrine, or some other building of the (premodern) past. No linguistic clues are needed to reach this conclusion; it is communicated by the colors, the textures, the smells, the size and general appearance of the wooden and stone structure, and the statuary fronted by kneeling cushions.

Nonetheless, various linguistic clues lie in the Chinese characters. Two characters are visible in the approach to the door, read right to left—"Purple Cloud." Inside the gate are two pairs of inscribed couplets hung on the interior columns. The most prominent and celebrated is Hongyi's calligraphy of words attributed to Zhu Xi: "In olden days this place was called a Buddhist kingdom; its streets were full of sages." If those inscriptions are not enough to suggest the cultural value of the site, another sign in Chinese and English identifies the site as a National Protected Key Unit of Cultural Heritage. Such words and calligraphy evoke venerable antiquity and a sense of privilege to be in this place. Resident monks, employees, and locals with some connections are allowed to pass through the gate and enter the main courtyard. Other visitors, until 2015, were required to purchase an entry ticket (¥10/$1.60) at a small window inside the gate and pass through a turnstile.

A sense of good fortune, happiness, and expectation may seem to embrace entrance to the large stone courtyard flanked by towering banyan trees. The stretch of stone pavement lined with trees draws the eye straight ahead to the massive Buddha hall raised on a stone platform, which enhances the height of the already exceptionally large structure. Left and right, the stone pagodas rise above the trees in the distance but seem close enough to reach out and touch. These elements, trees, stone pavement, pagodas, and large hall collectively assert their presence. As embodied actors, material culture affects somatic experience in immediate and mediated ways. One's feet feel the stone pavement of the main courtyard; one's body feels the shade of the trees; one's eyes are filled with the spectacle of the main hall lying ahead; the scent of incense smoke invades one's nostrils; the relative quiet brings relief to one's ears. All of this seems held together by the humid air that evokes the nearby sea. On Tuesday and Friday afternoons, the sounds of Buddha recitation broadcast from the main hall arrest one's attention.

In sum, on entering the physical space of the monastery, one is somatically aware of being in an environment qualitatively different from the one just left. This difference is guaranteed by the collective presence of the monastery's material features and the absence of the noise of buses, cars, and motorcycles and the smell of their exhaust just outside the gates of the monastery. Beyond the simple fact of alterity, the material features of the space have concretized schemes of meaning and value or cultural memory that different visitors engage with in different ways, leading them on different paths depending on their interests, goals, and dominant dispositions. This perspective is supported by a growing body of scholarship in multiple fields from philosophy to neurophysiology arguing that mind-body dualism is misguided, that experience reveals conjunctive (causal efficacy) as well as disjunctive relations (separate particulars), and that embodied somatic experience generates conceptual schemes including self-other, part-whole, and space-time (Throop and Laughlin 2002; Damasio 1994, 1999; Lakoff and Johnson 1999; Brasovan 2014; Blum 2015). I take these insights to analyze the impact of material culture (the built environment, trees, devotional and ritual objects) on the experience of visitors in dynamic play with their dispositions to generate different social identities, starting with an overview of the important features of Kaiyuan that give rise to the dynamic conditions for the making of space or the environmental matrix.

A dimension of the monastery's material presence common to other Chinese sites, be they temples or even entire cities, is a south-facing arrangement of buildings situated along a north-south axis enclosed in a wall in accord with ancient Chinese cosmological principles.[13] In the typical Buddhist temple or monastery, gates and halls are arrayed along the north-south axis; at the southernmost point is the main gate or mountain gate (*shanmen*).[14] Before the main gate at Kaiyuan is a short wall known as a spirit screen traditionally used to prevent the entry of malevolent spirits. It is named after its three-character inscription, "Purple Cloud Screen" (*ziyun ping* 紫云屏), and dates to 1576.[15] The first gate at Kaiyuan is best referred to as a triple gate (*sanmen*) or mountain gate rather than the more common hall of heavenly kings (*tianwang dian*).[16] Rather than housing the four guardian kings and Maitreya, the gate enshrines two towering seated guardian kings known as the *heng* and *ha* heavenly generals (*heng-ha erjiang* 哼哈二将). Glossed as the snorter and the blower, they were legendary generals of the Zhou dynasty (ca. 1211 BCE) who could annihilate enemies by snorting and blowing.[17]

Farther along the central axis is the large stone courtyard, flanked by eight banyan trees from two hundred to eight hundred years old and filled with stone artifacts from the Tang to the Qing dynasties. The most important of these artifacts are two Indian-style stone stupas, known as treasure boxes (*baoqie* 宝箧), erected by Liu Sanniang and her husband Liang An in 1145, almost a hundred years before the completion of the east and west pagodas, and decorated with scenes from the previous lives of the Buddha. They stand just in front of the main hall.[18] In addition to these are eight smaller stupas, erected in the early Ming dynasty, known as five-wheel pagodas (*wulun ta* 五轮塔).[19] Three *dhāraṇī* pillars in the main courtyard date from 854, 946, and 1008, respectively.[20] Last, standing near the middle of the courtyard, is a tall stone structure known as the silk-burning furnace (*fenbo lu* 焚帛炉) said to date from the Song dynasty and previously used to burn silk offerings during special ceremonies.

The first building beyond the main gate is the main hall or Buddha hall, literally the Precious Hall of the Great Hero (*daxiong baodian*), enshrining five Buddhas. At Kaiyuan, it is referred to as the Purple Cloud Hall. Also known as the Hundred Column Hall, it is exceptionally large, befitting its imperially patronized past.[21] It was rebuilt in 1398 and repaired by Zheng Zhilong in 1637. At Kaiyuan, the array of Buddhas enshrined are five monumental golden Buddhas. The central one is Vairocana, originally donated by the Tang emperor Xuanzong. During the Five Dynasties period, between the Tang and Song, four other Buddha figures were added by Wang Shengui when he repaired the main hall. Aksobya 阿初佛 of the East Fragrant World; Ratnasambhava 宝生佛 of the South Joyous World; Amitabha 阿弥陀佛 of the Western Paradise; and Amoghasiddhi 成就佛 of the North Lotus World. Together they are the Buddhas of the five directions.[22] Their appearances are identical except for their hands, which are placed in different mudras (*shou yin* 手印), namely, teaching mudra (*shuofa* 说法), giving mudra (*shiyu* 施与), leading mudra (*jieying* 接引), meditation mudra (*chan ding* 禅定), and fearlessness mudra (*wuwei* 无畏). Several statues are set between and around the five Buddhas: Śakyamūnī's disciples Ānanda and Mahākāśyapa; the celestial bodhisattvas Mañjuśrī, Samantabhadra, Avalokiteśvara, and Mahāsthāma; and the guardian figures Wei Tuo 韦驮 and Guan Gong 关公.[23] These are all lacquered and gilded statues made of unfired clay around wooden frames. In 2009, the five Buddhas were replaced with new statues after termite damage was discovered when one of the heads fell off and crashed to the floor.

A unique feature of Kaiyuan's main hall is the use of corbelled arches that support structural beams carved into the form of angelic figures, or *kalaviṇkas* (*pinjie* 频伽), each having outstretched arms holding musical instruments or cultural items such as paper and brush. The twenty-four figures represent the twenty-four divisions of a Chinese solar year. At the back of the hall are gilded statues of the eighteen arhats with Holy Guanyin 圣观音 in the middle dating to 1711. This Guanyin wears a crown with a small Amitabha seated in the middle of the crown and her hands form a relaxed meditation mudra. All of the statues are gilded. The line of columns along the back porch include two stone columns moved from a Yuan dynasty Hindu temple during the Ming reconstruction.[24] At Buddhist monasteries, the Buddha hall should be located in the middle of this axis and, indeed, Kaiyuan's main hall is at the geographic center (north-south and east-west) of the complex.[25]

Outside the main hall is a courtyard between the main hall and the ordination platform with two large bodhi trees on either side and a large incense burner in the middle. On *nianfo* days, this area becomes especially

FIG. 5.2 Four of five gilded monumental Buddha statues inside the main hall in 2006. To the right is one of two pyramidal towers of Buddha lights, kept lit through sponsorship. Photo by the author.

crowded with worshippers and incense. At the top of a short flight of stairs is the hall of the ordination platform, which includes one of the three great ordination platforms, the others being at Zhaoqing Monastery in Hangzhou and Jietai Monastery outside Beijing. The ordination platform is named Sweet Dew, or *amṛīta* (*ganlu*), which is a metaphor for nirvana, indicating ordination as a gate to nirvana (C. Wang 2008, 117–118). The rectangular platform of five levels is made of stone and largely hidden beneath dozens of statues, lacquered stands, and tables. The interior of the hall is dimly lit, natural light falling in from doors and windows. The overall impression of the interior is a tangle of antique red, gold, and black.

The roof of the building is a complex octagonal style that comes to a central point. Similar to those in the main hall, the structural arches supporting the roofing beams are uniquely carved into the form of twenty-four heavenly angels, or *apsaras* (*feitian* 飞天), holding musical instruments of local Minnan tradition; these, however, do not have wings, flight is indicated by billowing hair and clothing. Outside the hall is a gilded statue of the popular guardian figure Weituo (Skanda). On the first level of the platform, flanking each of the four entry points at each of the cardinal directions, are two life-sized vajra guardians; these figures (*ba da jingang* 八大金刚) were replaced in 2006. At the front of the hall on the second level of the platform is a delicately crafted and gilded thousand-armed, thousand-eyed Guanyin statue standing one foot tall and made from a single piece of sandalwood in 1398; it is protected by a glass case and set on a lacquered table just behind a lower table for offerings. Just behind Guanyin on the third level is a brightly gilded standing Amitabha flanked by the legendary Tang dynasty monks Hanshan and Shide 拾得, each bearing characteristically playful expressions. Just behind these statues is a stone stupa said to contain seven Buddha relics brought from Fuzhou Gushan Temple (C. Wang 2008, 137). Behind this stupa is a gilded statue of Shakyamuni Buddha seated in meditation. On the highest level, on a pedestal, rising above all the other statues, is a gilded Vairocana wearing a crown seated on a magnificent base of a thousand red lotus petals, each depicting a golden Buddha emerging from a golden lotus in three-quarters relief. Back at the front of the hall to the right (eastern) side is the large bell and to the left (western) is the drum, both sounded daily in the morning and evening. At the back of this hall is a gilded statue of Chinese Maitreya (*mile fo* 弥勒佛) inside a glass case on top of a rectangular pedestal blocking the entrance to the Tang dynasty well.

Most guests do not venture beyond the ordination hall; those who do find the dharma hall and the sutra library above it. Other than the morning and evening services, little happens in the dharma hall and visitors are not allowed in the sutra library, which houses a valuable collection of Buddhist texts such as pages of a sutra written in gold from the interregnum sponsored by Wang Shenzhi and pages of the *Lotus Sutra* written in blood by Ruzhao (Yuan dynasty). Just behind the dharma hall is the hall of patriarchs, which enshrines the purported mummy of the Indian monk Zhiliang and a similarly sized statue of the founding abbot Kuanghu. In addition are photos of early twentieth-century abbots. The large ancient mulberry tree stands just behind the main hall to the left (see chapter 6). Thus ends the journey from south to north. The most iconic features of Kaiyuan are, however, the twin pagodas in the east and west.

The East and West Pagodas

The most distinctive architectural feature of a Buddhist monastery in East Asia is without question the pagoda. Eugene Wang, a historian of Asian art, notes that Buddhist monasteries aspired to be utopias and suggests that "To this end, certain distinctive architectural features and signposts—in particular, the heavenward aspiring pagoda—imbue the precinct with religious overtones to make the enclave nothing short of a monastery. There is hardly a Buddhist monastery without a pagoda" (2010, 65). Kaiyuan's pagodas are without question distinctively Buddhist and religious—their primary religious function is to identify the compound as Buddhist. They do not guarantee, however, the existence of a functioning monastery, which requires actuation through the dynamic social relations and manifest values and ideology.

FIG. 5.3 The west pagoda of Quanzhou Kaiyuan Monastery, completed in 1237, in 2006. Photo by the author.

Having been destroyed and rebuilt several times since their initial construction in 865 and 916, the current east and west pagodas were completed in 1250 and 1237, respectively, and rise to an impressive height of some 150 feet.[26] They are entirely local granite in a local style that mimicks monumental construction in wood.[27] A contemporary example in Japan is the Great South Gate (Nandaimon) of Nara's Todaiji.[28] Because of their similar height and appearance, Kaiyuan's east and west pagodas are often called the twin towers (*shuang ta* 双塔) or the Purple Cloud Twin Pagodas (*ziyun shuang ta* 紫云双塔).

Each five-story pagoda is decorated with eighty life-size sculptures in middle relief depicting figures from Buddhist history and lore such as arhats, patriarchs, bodhisattvas, eminent monks, and guardians. Among the more noteworthy are sculptures of the monkey king Sun Wukong 孙悟空, and the Guanyin (Avalokiteśvara) bodhisattva depicted as a male with a mustache on the west pagoda, and on the east pagoda a potbellied Xuanzang accompanied by a small monkey figure.[29] The greenstone reliefs along the base of the east pagoda are especially noteworthy for both their artistic beauty as well as the knowledge of Indian Buddhist scripture they disclose. Writing about these sculptures, the eminent Buddhologist Paul Demiéville practically gushed: "Such a vivid and comprehensive 'Bible de pierre' [Bible of stone] is hardly to be found elsewhere in the Far East" (Ecke and Demiéville 1935, 81).

The west pagoda received its name after an auspicious green and yellow light is said to have emanated from its top and turned into five colored lights that remained throughout the night of October 10, 1114. Local officials reported this event to Emperor Huizong 徽宗, who then renamed the pagoda Benevolence and Longevity (*renshou* 仁寿), as it is still known today (Yuanxian 1643, I.8b). This name is engraved in stone on the south face of the west pagoda; the name Pagoda That Stabilizes the Country (*zhenguo ta*) is engraved on the south face of the east pagoda. The twin pagodas stand today as solemn and graceful reminders of Kaiyuan's glorious past and of Quanzhou's golden age.

Surviving massive earthquakes that have leveled other buildings in Quanzhou, especially that of 1604, with an estimated magnitude of just over 8, the east and west pagodas of Kaiyuan have held their ground, dominating the skyline of central Quanzhou for more than 750 years.[30] After seeing scores of mutilated sculptures in China with missing heads, I marvel that the sculptures at the base of the east pagoda have survived complete with their heads, which is all the more remarkable given that their location is easily accessible and unprotected by any barrier or guards.

Their surviving a devastating earthquake is repeated in the survival of all of Kaiyuan's major buildings. Although the main hall is from the Ming and other structures are from the Qing or later, they remain structures attesting to the records of the monastery and a core of buildings that have been part of Kaiyuan from the beginning. As Flath notes about Kong Temple, part of its remaining allure is grounded in its connections to a glorious past through structures continually restored and rebuilt (2016). Kaiyuan's visitors are able to connect with the past through a full complement of historical structures. Building on this notion, I argue that monumental architecture, like the pagodas and main hall, should be seen in part as a way of overcoming the inevitable transience of time, memory, place, and space. This materialization of an imagined past in the present is a kind of permanence in the face of decay and mortality. It may be likened to the sentiment expressed in *huaigu* 怀古 laments, understood as romantic or melancholic yearnings for antiquity provoked by a ruined city or abandoned place, feeling both linked to the past and hopelessly removed from it (H. Wu 2012; Flath 2016, 88). The built environment that remains at Kaiyuan evokes a sentiment of connection to the past that is also and immediately a recognition of distance from it. We are required to construct a present experience and cultural memory in relation to the past and a desired future. Those with a religious disposition will construct a shared present with the sages and monks of the past. Those with a secular disposition construct a present with a new understanding or appreciation of the past, many marveling at the stonework, the artistry, or the construction. In short, the antiquity of the pagodas enables a connection with the past and their uniqueness offers a point of pride to locals and point of interest for outsiders, all of which is part of their affective appeal.

Kaiyuan's pagodas are the most common symbols of Quanzhou and appear on countless tourist publications, advertisements, and websites. Nothing in China is comparable to Kaiyuan's pair of pagodas in their age, artistry, and stateliness.[31] The role they possess as valuable cultural symbols for the people of Quanzhou has assisted the maintenance and protection necessary for their survival as well as that of Quanzhou Kaiyuan Monastery.[32]

They have assisted the maintenance and protection of Kaiyuan by creating an affective bond with the people of Quanzhou. Mayor Wang referred to this bond using the word *ganqing* (warm affection or sentiment). Yi-fu Tuan developed a notion of "topophilia" to describe "the affective bond between people and place or setting" (1974, 4). Tuan is an early, if not the first, attempt to bring to the attention of geographers the importance of human emotion and attachment in the significance of geographic environments and place, both natural and built environments. My research has found an affective bond of two varieties, one leading to civic pride and the other to reverence, which I examine after reviewing additional features of the built environment.

Despite variation among the number and type of halls from temple to temple, their rectilinear arrangement along a north-south axis, fronted with courtyards of various sizes, is followed at the vast majority of China's thousands of temples. It is this regularity that prompts exasperated visitors to say that all temples look alike. It is also this regularity that so clearly communicates, without linguistic markers, that one has entered a space of traditional culture, of history, of religion—all of which transcend everyday egoistic and consumeristic existence. The visceral experience of entering a space unlike the everyday world beyond the monastery walls is effected by the collective deployment of material features. These features concretize Buddhist values in their distinctive forms, especially skyward aspiring pagodas and their sculptures, the distinctively shaped stupas, and the golden buddhas and bodhisattvas inside the halls. This material culture must nonetheless be enlivened by the dynamic participation of viewers and users. It is here that the dispositions or habitus of individuals is critical in determining the meaning of the site, the nature of cultural memory. It is within each individual that the concretized values, ideas, traditions, and systems of production are interpreted. The material space itself remains one of distinctive alterity, but its value, whether sacred or secular, remains ambiguous until determined by a perceiving consciousness.

That Kaiyuan and other monasteries manifest a set of distinct material features is no accident. The act of entering the monastery, it has been suggested, is meant to be an act of leaving samsara (the round of suffering) for the Pure Land or nirvana (Walsh 2010). Dogen viewed the monastic compound as a material manifestation of the means for achieving awakening as well as a concretized expression of enlightenment. "In this way, the insentient materials of the monastery itself preach the dharma by their very nature" (Winfield 2017, 43). As Michael Walsh, who has "spent considerable periods of time visiting Buddhist monasteries and examining historical texts in an effort to better understand what makes Buddhist space a religious space," writes, monasteries "are soteriological by design," representing a journey from samsara to nirvana (2010, 8, 37). This seems viscerally communicated at Kaiyuan and similar sites on leaving behind the bright, bustling, and noisy street and entering a shaded courtyard dramatically quieter than the street. The crowded street, the tacky signs, the tables of goods, the hangers of clothes, the motorcycles and buses disappear to be replaced by an expansive courtyard, towering banyans, a Ming dynasty hall, stone stupas all in muted shades, some echoing distinctively Buddhist messages. The material culture of the monastery asserts its difference with the world just left behind. But what kinds of world has one entered? Is it enough to say it is a Pure Land? Doing so would be to fall into the habit of relying on scripturally based interpretations.

At this point, we must recognize the ambiguous nature of nonlinguistic material culture and the way in which its meanings not only depend on context, but also vary among observers. Monasteries may seek to communicate a soteriological message with their buildings, courtyards, walls, and Buddhas, but is this all they aim to convey? Writing about visual culture, Klemens Karlsson writes,

> There is no such thing as a fixed, predetermined or unified meaning in individual visual objects. Meaning is always context dependent and it resides in the mind of artists, sponsors, beholders, etc.—and the beholder's view may not always correspond to the artist's intention. (2006, 70)

The ambiguity of meaning in material culture is a result of the dynamism required to bring a space into being. Material culture, institutional supports, and ritual practices together concretize cultural memory encoded with values and identity formations, which must then be reconstructed in each new present. Although this cultural memory may be reconstructed in as many ways as there are viewers, interviews with and observations of clerics, lay Buddhists, worshippers, tourists, officials, and other members of the community revealed three salient frameworks for interpreting the dynamic production of social identity in relation to material culture. Subsequent observations confirmed their usefulness in capturing the behaviors exhibited at the site. The frameworks are Buddha-religion, culture-history, and park-leisure. I have met and interviewed multiple individuals who fit into each of these categories, giving me confidence in the strength of these typologies. I have extracted the key terms and phrases my informants used. The key terms are provided in Chinese for precision. Although some individuals fit into one framework or another, many participate in multiple frameworks at different times or simultaneously. The key value of these frameworks is in giving specificity to the multivalence of material culture at religious sites.

The Religious Value of Monastic Material Culture

Those bearing a religious habitus and attuned to the Buddhist or religious values of the monastery are predisposed to look for the religious character of the monastery or are at least sensitive to the religious significations of Kaiyuan's material culture. Generally speaking, these are the worshippers, laypersons, and clerics. These groups are most likely to respond to the Buddhist messaging of the buildings, statuary, inscriptions, and spatial arrangement that put Buddha literally and figuratively at the center. Images of Buddha in particular are understood within the tradition to serve as substitutes for the deceased Buddha and have thus been a way for Buddhists to connect with the body of the Buddha (Lancaster 1974). In recognition of this tradition, the laity and worshippers typically bring or acquire incense that they light and offer, bowing or prostrating (*shaoxiang baifo*), to the enshrined buddhas and bodhisattvas. The material culture encourages this recognition in specific ways. Apart from the presence of monumental gilded buddhas and bodhisattvas fronted with fruit, flowers, and lamps indicating the appropriateness of offerings, not only are there three large and one small incense burners in the highest traffic locations along the central axis, but smoke is also generally rising from them, signaling active use. If this were not enough, the candles in six sets of large candelabra burn expressly for the lighting of incense. These aspects of the material culture of the monastery enable individuals to embody a supplicatory identity in general and, for those so inclined, a Buddhist identity in particular by facilitating contact with the body of the Buddha, the anchor of the tradition. Clerics regularly conduct assemblies (*fahui*) in which they make offerings to buddhas, bodhisattvas, and patriarchs, represented by the iconographic statuary of the site. Clerics and laity both circumambulate the images in the halls. The dynamic interplay between the material features of the site and the clerics, laypersons, and worshippers in the act of worship or liturgical service bring to life the public religious character of the site. In this case, cultural memory is reconstructed as a religious social identity. Temples without monks or lay Buddhists or material support for liturgical or devotional ritual have no public religious life. Old temples that have not been restored to religious use are sometimes converted into parks, such as Randeng Pagoda 燃灯塔 in Tongzhou outside Beijing, or Ningbo's Tianfeng Pagoda 天封塔. Also in Ningbo is Baoguo Temple 报国寺, presented as a museum of ancient architecture 古建筑博物馆, several of its halls made into museum displays. These are popular sites, but people do not visit for religious observances because the buildings no longer have the appropriate material cues for worship (buddhas and bodhisattvas fronted with offerings tables and kneeling cushions and the like) that are on full display at Kaiyuan and other functioning temples.

Kaiyuan's religious supporters, while recognizing the historic value of the monastery, are generally more focused on devotional and ritual use of the space, which brings shrine halls and courtyards to life with incense, prostrations, chanting, recitation, and circumambulation. These visitors can be quite enthusiastic about the religious character of the site. I mentioned the woman praising the bodhisattvas feeding the people during lunar twenty-sixth. Every day are visitors like the worshipper who came to make an offering, "to bless and protect my business flourishing."[33] An older woman spoke of her wish to "bring blessing of peace to my family and bless my grandson's improvement in study."[34] An older lay Buddhist spoke of the importance of the site, declaring that it was "a sacred place" (*shendi*). When asked, monks and lay Buddhists alike confirm Kaiyuan and its statues as a place of spiritual efficacy (*ling*), as a place for the accumulation of merit (*gongde*) and the receipt of blessings (*fu* 福). It is a place where one may make a promise or request (*xuyuan* or *fayuan*) and fulfill or repay a promise or request (*huanyuan*) or request prayer recitations (*xuanshu* 宣疏). The language and activities of these supporters is imbued with unmistakably religious or sacred (*shensheng* 神圣) notions in dynamic response to the materialization of Buddhist messaging encoded within the material culture preserving and enabling cultural memory.

Religious supporters characteristically view cultural properties with an attitude of reverence manifestly distinct from the curiosity or interest of those secularly inclined. When Kaiyuan's cultural propcrtics arc approached with reverence, they are transformed into devotional objects. As devotional objects, they are most properly addressed by forms of obeisance or supplication, especially offerings of incense (*shaoxiang*) and prostrations (*baifo*). The uniquely religious property of devotional objects, in the view of many religiously motivated supporters, is spiritual power (*ling*), which is thought to be accessed by making offerings and simple gestures of obeisance.[35] These supporters participate in a traditional worldview in which certain objects, places, or persons are seen to be imbued with *ling*. Individuals with this paradigmatic dispositional attitude are less concerned about the historic value of the monastery's cultural properties than with their spiritual efficacy or their connection with the Buddha or dharma—it is for this that they are venerated. This concern with "using" the cultural properties rather than protecting them is perhaps most evident in the way that stone or wooden statues with the reputation of healing devotees by rubbing the corresponding part are sometimes rubbed away.[36]

Religiously sympathetic visitors typically offer incense to the Buddhas in the main hall. Many others offer incense to Guanyin at the back of the main hall, Weituo in front of the ordination platform, and various Buddhist figures on the ordination platform. The halls of worship and venerated statues are protected relics from the Qing and Ming dynasties. Although the pagodas do not have a censor to collect incense, religious visitors occasionally toss sticks of incense, coins, and even fruit through the gated doorways of the pagodas as offerings. These gestures of veneration or petition are examples of the capacity of material objects to elicit religious behavior when it is socially and politically permitted, when conditions have appropriately ripened. But even more important, such veneration demonstrates a disposition or habitus distinct from that of the cultural tourist.

Having been told by multiple sources of the spiritual efficacy associated with the site, I asked the monk in the ordination hall whether the bodhisattvas enshrined there are spiritually efficacious. "Of course," he responded. "How about the main hall?" I asked. "It's the same," he said. His more complete answer, however, revealed a twofold, scaffolded understanding. In response to further questions, he advanced a more studied understanding and spoke of the ten grounds of the path of the bodhisattva and the vow to relieve the suffering of all by staying in samsara. When I returned to the popular belief regarding spiritually efficacious statues, he said,

> Buddhism is a culture; it's not superstitious [*mixin*]. People praying to bodhisattvas is a secularization or vulgarization [*shisuhua*]. What is that? People think if they come and pray this Buddha and this Bodhisattva will bless and protect me [*baoyou*]. Is that possible? That's impossible. You have to do good. You do bad, you will suffer. You must be good. If you run into trouble and do something bad, the police will get you. You have to do good so that doesn't happen. We must benefit other people. China and other countries are the same, right?

This monk as well as others emphasized the need to perform meritorious deeds to receive merit, but recognized a popular belief among worshippers praying for blessings. Another monk considered such popular beliefs and practices as an entry-level form of belief that was a skillful means of opening the door to Buddhist teaching. The same monks who speak of popular worship of buddhas and bodhisattvas as provisional also affirm that they are "spiritually efficacious" and regularly make ritual offerings to them. Perhaps the best way of understanding this is through the logic of play as an interpretive lens for ritual (Sharf 2005). This also helps overcome the misplaced emphasis on belief. These monks are not interested in defending popular belief in spiritual efficacy, but they are perfectly willing to suspend disbelief and proceed as if the material icons of the monastery are responsive. As Robert Sharf notes, "One does not believe that the wafer is flesh, nor that the icon is buddha; belief has little to do with it. One simply proceeds as if it were the case. ... Through ritual we rediscover a world wherein a stick is a horse, a wafer is divine flesh, a stone image is a god" (2005, 257).[37]

The critical component of this ritual-play, which transcends belief and disbelief, is the material icon, in this case, statuary. As Sharf and other scholars point out, "Chan practice, like Mahayana monastic practice throughout Asia, was highly ritualized and involved the veneration and contemplation of sacred realia including consecrated icons" (2005, 260).[38] The centrality of material icons in institutional Buddhism is captured by an early name of Buddhism in China—*xiangjiao* 像教, or the religion of images (Sharf 2005, 258). This, though, was not a Chinese innovation of the tradition. Gregory Schopen points out how Buddhist communities in medieval India (from the fifth to fourteenth century) treated the Buddha as a permanent resident capable of receiving gifts represented by statues enshrined in monastic compounds as an institutional feature (1990). The innovation of Chinese Buddhism was the institutional effort of the Chan schools to replace these clay, wood, and metal statues of the Buddha with the living presence of the enlightened abbot or Chan master.[39] Perhaps this can be a method of determining an orthodox Chan monastery from an emergent one: one in which the abbot is widely respected as an authorized lineage holder from one in which no one has a clear claim to such authority. In the meantime, the tradition of material substitutes for the awakened one and a retinue of bodhisattvas remains alive and well. The statues function as efficacious icons activated through dynamic exchanges with worshippers, laity, and monks. At the same time, they are recognized as a form of *upāya,* a way of opening a dharma gate.

The thousands of worshippers who participate in monthly Buddha recitation services or the two hundred laypersons who recite the Buddha's name during biweekly services are not focused on questions of heritage but instead on questions of receiving blessings, eradicating bad luck, and earning merit to benefit themselves, their family, or their ancestors or to advance in their practice. Their participation in devotional activities support the actualization and maintenance of a religiously active environment and their social identities as worshippers (*xiangke*), but the material culture of the monastery has other values as well.

The Monastery as Cultural Heritage

Supporters who emphasize the historic and cultural value of the monastery and its material culture speak of culture (*wenhua*), history (*lishi*), and art (*yishu*). First and foremost they speak about the east and west pagodas (*dong-xi ta*), as they are commonly called. They come to tour (*lüyou*), examine (*kankan*), photograph (*paizhao*), admire (*xinshang*), contemplate (*xiangxiang*), and study (*xuexi*) the many material artifacts. These individuals are most characteristically represented by educators, scholars, tour guides, amateur historians, and officials who appreciate temples as sites of cultural heritage and tend to espouse a secularized narrative of culture; their interests are not simply secular; they are agents of secularization. The discourse of Mayor Wang exemplifies this secular motivation.

The mayor frames the issue as one of culture and explicitly distances his actions from any concern with religion (*zongjiao*). His actions, he asserts, were carried out in the name of cultural preservation. Although his response is in line with a form of new orthodoxy in China that values China's cultural heritage and seeks to preserve it and promote it for economic development in the form of tourism and sociopolitical solidarity in the form of nationalism, it also indicates the manifest importance of Kaiyuan's cultural properties in the successful protection of the monastery. Mayor Wang also speaks with visible pride about the cultural value of Kaiyuan Monastery to the city of Quanzhou. The historian Wang Hanfeng, who lived at Kaiyuan for decades as part of the Heritage Management Committee before being evicted by Daoyuan, expressed a similar view, emphasizing Kaiyuan's material culture as an "elegant cultural legacy" of value today for its "architectural art and engineering technology" (1982, 17).[40] He also wrote that the cultural legacy of Kaiyuan's buildings and art makes us proud (*zihao*) of the accomplishments of our ancestors. Recent signage at the monastery announces that it is the "pride of Fujian."[41]

The same signage directs attention to the monastery's artistic, cultural, and historic values: "the main hall and the hall of ordination and their contents are architectural and artistic treasures."[42] The new introduction posted at the entrances ends by inviting everyone to "tour and sightsee."[43] When Kaiyuan's cultural properties are approached with a secular disposition attuned to culture and history, they appear as cultural treasures of artistic, technical (*jishu*), or historical value that should be preserved and made available to the public. This disposition, most clearly manifest in pride (*zihao*), is exemplified in various actions that fall under the rubric of "tourism," which include not only sightseeing and photography but also study, discussion, and conservation. Unlike religiously oriented visitors, their culturally oriented counterparts do not offer incense to the east pagoda but examine the sign nearby explaining its architectural value as demonstrated by its surviving the great earthquake of 1604. I have heard guides extolling the architectural marvel of the pagodas but failing to speak of their Buddhist value. Tourists may nonetheless also enjoy the site of robed monks or lay Buddhists making their way across the monastery grounds. In this way, monks and lay Buddhists become part of material culture of the site and scenery for the tourist.

It is from an interest in cultural heritage that scholars, artists, amateur historians, and even musicians take an interest in and offer support for the monastery and its material culture. Groups of musicians and scholars who study the traditional Nanyin music of Quanzhou have visited Kaiyuan to view and study the apsaras and kalaviṅkas holding traditional instruments in the main hall and the ordination platform hall. Cultural enthusiasts regularly view and inquire into the Hindu sculptures at the front and back of the main hall. Arborists take an interest in Kaiyuan's magnificent banyans, grand bodhi trees, and ancient mulberry tree. Scholars from China and abroad have taken an interest in its art and architecture from the first investigations in the 1920s (Ecke and Demiéville 1935) to the more recent ones (H. Wang 2001b, 1992, 1982; H. Wang and Zeng 1986; C. Wang 2008; Lee 2012). In all of these cases, secular interests dominate and the pursuant actions vary from visiting and study to protection and preservation. The difference between this support and that portrayed in the *MS Vinaya* is that in the *Vinaya* the support, though inspired by material culture, was offered by laity to clerics. Here, monastic property inspires support, but not from laypersons or even individuals interested in supporting the clergy. In contemporary China, this is best understood as a strategy for gaining broad-based support from different interest groups, especially political support. An economic metaphor of diversification to attract greater market share may be helpful to understand what is at stake. Just as most businesses would do well to attract a diverse group of customers (young and old, upper and lower income, ethnically diverse, and so on) to sell more products, the same logic applies to religious institutions today. Churches in North America increasingly add services like cafes, libraries, and childcare, and rent spaces for religious and nonreligious events alike. Religious sites in China have begun to do similar things. Some have added shrine halls and other features to broaden appeal in order to be economically viable (Chan and Lang 2015). Kaiyuan, in addition to supporting lay Buddhists and worshippers with an active liturgical schedule, also offers an on-site tour guide service and supports tourism in various other ways, all of which broaden its base of support, both economic and political. These issues are examined in chapter 7. In regard to the varied meanings of Kaiyuan's material culture, a third interest group is drawn to the same site for still different sets of reasons.

The Monastery as a Site of Recreation

A third group of visitors, a subset of those secularly inclined, are locals and tourists who approach the monastery as a site of recreation or leisure. In a pioneering monograph, Justin McDaniel explores the way Buddhist sites serve as spaces of leisure (2017). Visitors in search of a green space for their dance or tai chi groups, or for a stroll alone, or a date are important stakeholders at Kaiyuan. The temple has always allowed ticket-free entry to locals who arrive early in the morning to exercise, practice tai chi (*taijiquan*), or dance in the large courtyards and open spaces of the monastery, just as one sees in parks and green spaces throughout China. These visitors arrive with the explicit intention of joining a morning group of exercisers, or folk dancers. They typically gather in groups of five, eight, or ten. Sometimes they have wooden swords or large fans as dancing props. For them, the monastic compound is little more than a green space, a publicly accessible space large enough to accommodate a group of people in synchronized or choreographed activity. Early in the morning, workers stretch out a net and play badminton. Others come to stretch their legs and chat with friends, or to sit and play cards at one of the tables in the eastern side of the complex. Stone tables and stools stand in a shaded area near the liberation of life pond where retirees from the surrounding neighborhood can be seen sitting together in groups of two, three, or four, talking, playing cards or mah-jongg (*da majiang* 打麻将). Monks, including the abbot, can occasionally be spotted stopping and looking over their shoulders to watch the competition. Grandparents bring children of all ages to Kaiyuan again just as they might do in a park or green space. Others are seen strolling the grounds as young couples or families with their children. Since the gate ticket was abolished, the number of such visitors has increased. Individuals and small groups always seem to be relaxing around the east pagoda, staring down at their phones, eating street food they have brought in with them; grandparents follow toddlers; elders just pass the time. When asked about their visits, such visitors have said that visiting Kaiyuan is fun (*haowan*), that it is pretty (*piaoliang*), or that it is just a quiet place (*anjing*). Those from the neighborhood using the space as a park were found to have little interest in or knowledge of the historic, cultural, or religious features of the site. These visitors spend their time mostly in the eastern sections of the temple where no devotional activity is taking place. In this way they can sit, smoke, chat, and pass time without being distracted by devotional activities taking place along the central corridor.

In an effort to get at the special features drawing visitors to Kaiyuan, I would ask whether they had visited other temples in Quanzhou or elsewhere and if so to explain the differences between, for example, Chengtian Temple and Kaiyuan. The answers were consistent: Kaiyuan is bigger; its architecture (*jianzhu*) is outstanding and pretty (*piaoliang*). Another visitor, interviewed on the eastern side of monastery, mentioned the "collection of Buddhist objects" as he gestured toward the museums. When asked about how they felt inside the monastery grounds relative to outside, the answers were also consistent. "The environment is pretty good," said one young man. He elaborated, "outside is the city, more cars, a heavy modern feel. Then you come inside, the environment, I feel a big difference, when inside my state of mind feels more open." Another visitor remarked, "I feel relaxed, very good. Far away from the

FIG. 5.4 A group of tai chi exercisers in the main courtyard; other groups of dancers and exercisers may be found in the courtyards almost every morning from 6:00 to 8:00 a.m., 2006. Photo by the author.

clamor of the city."[44] These statements also draw attention to improved air quality and lower noise inside the monastery grounds. One young visitor said he was meeting friends he had met online; Kaiyuan was considered an interesting place to have fun. An older neighborhood resident said that when he was a child he considered Kaiyuan a park because the neighborhood had no other public parks.

The shaded courtyards and landscaped grounds of the monastery support such uses and speak to the manifest multivalence of the material features of such a site. Naquin's study of Beijing temples notes that temples were spacious and open to the public as well as how "temples became the focus for community-building and identity-defining activities by providing space to assemble" (2008, xxxi). With respect to early Buddhist literature, Schopen isolates the motif of "pleasure garden" as model for descriptions of monasteries (2006). Martin Collcutt notes that even urban monasteries in premodern China conceived of themselves as a "mountain retreat" incorporating the word for "mountain" in their formal names (1981, 182). Historiographic and ethnographic research confirm that monasteries in China have served and continue to serve as sites of recreation tantamount to a "pleasure garden." Expanding on these aspects of a park or garden might be called karmic affiliation with the place, or *diyuan* 地缘. This was explained by a monk and includes climate, weather, and environment; he said that some monks, as well as visitors, come to Kaiyuan for this reason, a karmic affinity.

The third framework for understanding how material culture is activated at this site is park-leisure. This function is essentially a social one that brings little to no direct economic benefit to the monastery. It does, however, generate public support that in turn provides political influence, which, for example, led to the successful banning of private combustion engine vehicles along the street in front of the monastery. The street is now crowded with electric scooters and the air quality inside and just outside the temple has further improved, enhancing the environment of the site for all visitors, both human and nonhuman.

Iron Temple, Water Monks

In 2019, a monk asked about the dramatic reduction in the number of monks replied, "The temple is forged like iron, but the monks flow like water" (铁打的丛林, 流水的僧). He elaborated that some monks find that monastic life does not suit them and move on, but the monastery remains. The phrase seemed to match my own conclusions about the value of the material culture of the monastery. The historic artifacts and the monumental architecture offer a concretization of transcendent meaning and a materialization of cultural memory that is variably approached and interpreted by individuals and groups. With the continually restored suite of buildings is a relative durability, a transcendence of limits, to the monastery (forged in iron). Monks and visitors alike, on the other hand, come and go, with varying interpretations, like water.

The ambiguous nature of material culture requires a perceiving consciousness informed by intentions and inevitably oriented by dispositions to bring it to life and reconstruct cultural memory and social identity in a dynamic and dialectical way. This dynamic interplay is what gives rise to a living space from an inert collection of objects. The nature of this encounter with cultural memory means that when approached with different habitus, different systems of value and interests, it will be viewed and "used" in different ways. It will be different for each perceiver. This is what is meant by the polyvalence of material culture; it can serve distinct if related systems of value and interests. This chapter outlines three ways the material culture of Kaiyuan is approached, enlivened, and experienced with three distinct value systems and ends. The presence of material objects of cultural heritage and the physical deployment of buildings and space produce an experience that, depending on the individual's intentions and embodied disposition, may be interpreted religiously, secularly, or as a mix of the two. Whereas the first group finds a sacred place where one worships and practices devotion, the second experiences a place of history and culture that one tours and studies, and the third finds a park where one exercises, strolls, meets friends, or takes a date. These are some of the roles that monasteries in China have played, it turns out, for centuries (Brook 2005). I argue that the monastery's material culture is designed to communicate these three messages: buddha-religion, culture-history, and park-leisure. Monks are aware of them and skillfully promote different aspects to specific audiences. Administrative monks point out the cultural and historical value in meetings with officials and in publications intended for their eyes. They openly accommodate the recreational needs of the community by allowing locals free entry, maintaining open spaces for group activities, and installing benches, tables, and waste bins. As expected, monks also promote the religious value to laypersons and worshippers in publications referencing the spiritual power of the site and signage posted before liturgical celebrations detailing different ways to access religious merit and the blessing of buddhas and bodhisattvas.

The state formally recognizes the historic and cultural values of monasteries by designating them as sites of protected national heritage, a designation many monasteries in China have received. A related designation at monasteries with properties of national heritage or scenic vistas is formal recognition as a four- or five-star tourist site. Is it possible that multiple layers of meaning have always been encoded in Buddhist visual culture? That these sites of practice have always served multiple ends that are both traditionally religious and worldly? This is the suggestion of Vidya Dehejia, who argues that if Buddhist writers such as Aśvaghoṣa or Āryaśūra could intentionally use words with multiple meanings, then we can expect the Buddhist artists to also intend multiple layers of meaning in early Buddhist visual culture (1991, 45). I extend this notion to the material presence of the monastery as a whole. Certainly, in the contemporary period, administrative monks are generally aware of the monastery's different values (place of practice, tourist attraction, and park) and actively work to accommodate and represent each. Their motives may be construed in many ways, all of which have some measure of truth. They have an economic motive (money); they have a political motive (protection and stability); and they have a *dharmic* motive (promoting and spreading Buddhism). All of these motives can be subsumed under a concern with protecting, preserving, and promoting Buddhism. It is in this sense that they are understandable as actions of the sangha in line with the vocation of monastics.

As the influential monk Daoxuan wrote in the seventh century,

> Therefore a monastery and other living quarters were established [on earth] that were totally unlike ordinary human habitations, and images were created so strange as to stir the common heart to see the [Buddha truth]—so much that when ordinary folk were made to hear of it, they would be shaken into knowing the words

> and the paths of the faith; when they were made to see, they would understand the form [of the monastery] and discern the extraordinary path [of deliverance].[45]

Daoxuan indicates motivations that are salvic and compassionate; at the same time, it is only fair to expect that "stirring the human heart" and so forth would also lend itself to drawing support for the monastery, as suggested by the *MS Vinaya*. In addition to inspiring faith and arousing support, the material culture of monasteries can also elicit protection. Protection of the monastery, in addition to protection of the sangha, is also protection of the Buddha (symbolically represented by the material culture of monasteries), and the dharma (represented by collections of scripture and dharma assemblies). Thus protection of the monastery represents protection of the three treasures or refuges of Buddhism, which are the basic anchors of the tradition. In discussing the myriad functions and goals of the monastery, Michael Walsh sounds a similar note: "protecting the sangha was paramount, for without the sangha there could be no perpetuation of the Dharma. Promoting the stability and growth of a Buddhist monastery was tantamount to ensuring the survival of Buddhism" (2010, 7). Kaiyuan's physical survival through the Cultural Revolution and early revival in the post-Mao period is a testament to the effectiveness of having material features designated as cultural heritage and valued by secular powers.

The example of Kaiyuan demonstrates that having features that can be co-opted by larger sociocultural forces, especially nonreligious ones, can prove beneficial to survival and success. Just as the artwork of the Jetavana monastery in ancient India may have encouraged donations, the artistry of Kaiyuan's Song dynasty pagodas and other cultural properties in large measure enabled it to survive under the stresses that destroyed dozens of other temples in the immediate vicinity. Monasteries' abilities to appeal to a diverse group of religious and nonreligious patrons may be seen as a conscious strategy, one common to Buddhist monasteries in China and beyond. Susan Naquin writes,

> In fact, at Tanzhesi diversification seems to have been pursued as a strategy of survival, and even prized. ... For a place like Tanzhesi, to rely on a single integrated community, even had it been possible, might have been much less effective than promotion of many versions of the monastery and many patrons. (1998, 207)

In developing a general description of this phenomenon, I hope not only to shed light on the role played by material culture at this one field site, but also to provide models of interaction between material culture and individuals that may be used to analyze the multivalence of material culture at other religious sites and in other contexts. A monastery cannot be reduced to the schedules and activities of monks and visitors. Nor can it be reduced to a description of the physical plan, structures, and properties. Both of these dimensions, the people and their activities and the structures and their functions, are essential to the identity of a monastery; this chapter shows how they dynamically interact to reconstruct cultural memory and social identities in the production of space. Pagodas, buildings, stupas, statues, steles, courtyards, and trees not only provide the setting for the experience of visitors and the lives of monastics, but also frame, condition, and dynamically evoke both religious and secular experiences of visitors and clergy in addition to contributing to a monastery's economic success and longevity. Although material culture functions nonlinguistically in the production of space, the monastery also deploys linguistic signifiers. The values these signifiers promote are explored in the next chapter.

6

Founding Legends

Sanctifying and Branding Space

A CROWD OF SOME THIRTY TOURISTS GATHERED around the stone fence surrounding Kaiyuan's famous mulberry tree. Their gaze shifted from the tree to their tour guide. Some looked over at me, the foreigner (*laowai*), as their tour guide repeated the story she tells day after day, month after month, year after year:

> In the year 686 of the Tang Dynasty Huang Shougong dreamed of a monk beseeching him for his mulberry orchard to build a temple. Mr. Huang said if my orchard trees bloom lotus blossoms, it's yours. Sure enough, after two days the trees really bloomed white lotus blossoms. This is one of those trees that miraculously bloomed lotus blossoms more than 1000 years ago!

This tour guide informed the group that tea made with the leaves is used by locals for medicine and that they are free to take any that have fallen. Some of the tourists stooped down to collect leaves; others snapped photos.

The story of lotus-blooming mulberry trees along with the tale of the purple cloud covering the ground are part of every tour, every guidebook, every snippet one is likely to read about Quanzhou Kaiyuan. The mulberry and purple cloud are part of the packaging for this site. Using preternatural and auspicious events to promote a site for pilgrims or devotees is a common phenomenon or strategy around the world. As the bishop of Mostar, Pavao Zanic, speaking of Medjugorje, noted, "Wherever somebody says that Our

Lady appeared then people come as a fly to honey—you get the miracles first, the cars and buses next" (Reader 2014, 85). As Ian Reader explains in his study of marketing pilgrimage, "Legends redolent with miraculous promises of liberation in the afterlife and that link the pilgrimage to retired emperors and Buddhist guardians of the underworld are far more conducive to making the pilgrimage attractive than are mere historical narratives" (2).

The prominence of these legends in representing and promoting Kaiyuan led me to include them as one of the key dimensions of life at this site deserving a closer look. Recognizing the mutual imbrication of physical, social, and mental dimensions of space rather than the physical and social dimensions addressed in chapter 5, this chapter focuses on the "mental" dimension of space, which may include ideology, imagination, or cosmological referents (Knott 2010, 36). Simon Coleman and John Elsner point out that in addition to physical landscape and architecture, sites of pilgrimage also include myths and traditions associated with those features. Thus they write of "physical and mytho-historical landscapes" providing the "backdrop" for the journey of pilgrims who travel "through a terrain of culturally constructed symbols" (1995, 212).

The ideological, mythological, and cosmological backdrop of the space at Kaiyuan is fundamentally governed by the deployment of preternatural and auspicious signifiers. References to these legendary events recorded in gazetteers and epigraphy are concretized in the walls, structures, statuary, and signboards of the monastery. This chapter explores the role of miraculous and correlative events in the making of religious space before turning to the role of myths and legends at this site. In particular, it examines the founding legends and how they are preserved and promoted at the site to enhance both brand recognition and a kind of enchantment that may be considered sanctification or, to coin a term, *linghua* 灵化.

When Wu Hengchun 吴亨春 penned the Republican period preface to the *Monastic Gazetteer* in 1927, he lauded Quanzhou Kaiyuan as the best among a forest of Chan temples by referencing its eminent monks and auspicious events:

> The auspicious sign of the mulberry tree that bloomed lotus blossoms expresses delight at the magnificent spread of the dharma realm [*xi fajia yi hongkai* 喜法界以宏开]. Fragrantly flowing amrita celebrates the exalted religious ethos. Manjushri descended and wrote a sutra; arhats entered a dream. Venerable masters of the three teachings—meditation, doctrine and discipline—have arisen one after another, too many to count, they are truly capable of effecting changes in customs and traditions [*yifeng yisu* 移风易俗], helping the world and giving direction to people so that a seaside city of Confucius became a solemn land of Buddha. (Yuanxian 1643, 2.1a)

In celebrating Kaiyuan's excellence, Wu focuses on two features: the great masters of the past and auspicious events. Lotus-blooming mulberry, amrita, Manjushri, and the dream of arhats are all code words that point to Kaiyuan's auspicious past. The recollection of auspicious phenomena is a way of invoking the numinous past and remembering eminent monks who have passed through the monastery's halls, which is in turn a way of praising and promoting Kaiyuan's reputation and framing the monastery cosmologically as a numinous place. Guidebooks and other forms of contemporary literature also invoke auspicious events or reproduce lists of them.

Susan Naquin, examining documents from the eighteenth century related to Tanzhe Monastery, writes, "In all these works, information about the monastic community was usually excluded, and the temple cast as a site for history, for imperial and literati visits, for the individual but not the group, for the marvelous and poetic experience but not the devotional one" (1998, 202). James Robson points out that although elements of wonder, culture, and history are prominent in the representation of monasteries, they have not adequately entered our scholarly purview:

> One of the main elements found in those sources was a (sometimes quite detailed) treatment of the special qualities, or anomalous elements, of the natural setting, the connections with eminent monks who resided there, and accounts of miracles that were connected with the site and their sacred possessions. Those accounts could demonstrate that a monastery was an efficacious place for a monk or nun to pursue their calling and may have had profound effects on the future viability and economic success of monasteries, due to their ability to attract both pilgrims and patrons. As visible as these resolutely anti-modernist themes are in local monastic records, they have remained topics that have largely been occluded from the ken of those who have studied Chinese Buddhist monasteries. (2010b, 59)

Robson emphasizes three features prominent in the representation of monasteries in local sources: special qualities of the natural setting, eminent monks who lived at the site, and miracles associated with the site or its material culture. Because Kaiyuan is an urban monastery, the natural features are less important (Robson's materials deal with monasteries in mountain settings), but tales of eminent monks and auspicious or miraculous tales are well represented in the literature associated with the monastery.

Although Naquin and Robson are writing about the representation of Buddhist monasteries in pre-nineteenth-century documents, I have observed two of the features they mention—cultural properties and miraculous or marvelous events—as two of the most prominent features in not only historical documents but also contemporary presentations of Kaiyuan. My reading of archival materials and my conversations with monks, worshippers, enthusiasts, and officials have all pointed to the centrality of Kaiyuan's buildings and its legendary founding, making it a place deserving the interest, protection, and patronage of the public and worshippers alike. Such memorialization and related discourse contributes to religious life, I suggest, by sacralizing the grounds and shrines of the monastery and to the institutional (read economic) life through branding. Before turning to the case of Kaiyuan, I establish important context by examining the place of miracles in Buddhism and Chinese religion.

Numinous powers within the Buddhist tradition are an expected attainment (*siddhi*) as one advances in meditation but not a goal in themselves.[1] The vinaya ultimately forbid monks from making miraculous displays before the laity (Davis 1998, 13). Despite this canonical view, supernormal powers are an important part of the hagiographic literature of eminent monks. They are so prominent, in fact, that in his study of biographies of eminent monks in Chinese literature, John Kieschnick makes the thaumaturge one of three types of monks eulogized, the others being scholars and ascetics (1997, 67–111). Buddhist literature preserved accounts of the numinous powers of monks to promote the prestige of the monastic community and earn them the support of the state and the elite.[2] One of the more frequently depicted types of preternatural event associated with monks is the provocation of sympathetic or correlative responses in nature.

Extraordinary Correlative Responses

Since the Han dynasty, before Buddhism had penetrated the Chinese cultural sphere, the Chinese have believed that the presence of a sage evokes wondrous responses (*ganying*) from nature.[3] After Buddhism spread to China, extraordinary correlative responses in the natural world have been commonly used as evidence of a monk's eminence. In his study of biographies of eminent monks written from the sixth through the tenth centuries, Kieschnick observes that "when a sage appears, one can expect a spontaneous, correlative response from Nature, whether it be changes in the weather, new configurations of the stars, or the appearance of prodigious plants and animals" (1997, 98).[4] The biographer Huijiao recorded many of these types of events in his *Preliminary Collection of Biographies of Eminent Monks* (*Gaoseng zhuan chuji* 高僧传初集), which he categorized as divine wonders (*shenyi* 神异).[5] Daoxuan, in his *Continued Biographies of Eminent Monks* (*Xu gaoseng zhuan* 续高僧传), called the same type of phenomenon spiritual resonance (*gantong* 感通).[6]

The *Biographies of Purple Cloud Bodhisattvas* and the *Monastic Gazetteer* both include numerous accounts of preternatural responses in nature elicited by Kaiyuan's monks. These sources relate a full range of preternatural responses from nature, including animal, vegetable, mineral, liquid, celestial, sonic, and olfactory. Apart from lotus-blooming trees and purple clouds, examples from the *Monastic Gazetteer* include amrita that fell on the place where the ordination platform would be built as well as mysterious lights, music, and fragrances associated with such events as the births of masters or their chanting of scripture.[7] Among the more sensual examples, red lotuses are said to have turned white while the fragrance of cinnamon (cassia) flowers filled the air when the interregnum monk Xicen 栖岑 lectured on the *Xifang guan shangsheng Sutra* 西方观上生经, a sutra relating to rebirth in the Western Paradise of Amitabha (Yuanxian 1643, I.29b–30a). Responses in the animal world include doves listening to sutras. The most recent example of a correlative response in the natural world to the presence of eminent monks is said to be the phenomenon of "peach trees blooming red lotuses" when Yuanying, Zhuandao, and Zhuanwu entered Kaiyuan to initiate the Republican period revival in 1924.

This kind of miraculous display is structured in such a way that it does not violate the vinaya because the sympathetic resonance of the environment to the presence of a sage appears to be an involuntary relation. In other words, the monk does not will the purple cloud or other sights or sounds into existence; they are spontaneous responses to the presence of moral excellence. Just as the Buddhist notion of karma operates as a kind of natural law, so does the correlative response or spiritual resonance between virtue embodied on the micro level of the human body naturally relate to the larger cosmos on the macro level.[8] This occurs in Chinese thought given the unity between the human body and the larger world and the lack of dichotomy between matter and spirit.[9]

The examples of correlative responses to excellence in the *Monastic Gazetteer* and *Biographies of Purple Cloud Bodhisattvas* are different from the kinds of *gantong* in other collections such as the *Record of Manifestations [Resulting] from Recitation of Guanyin Sutras and Mantras* (*Guanshiyin jingzhou zhiyan ji*) compiled by layperson Zhou Kefu 周克復 in 1659. The stories in this collection and others were examined by Chün-fang Yü in her 2001 study of Guanyin and all reveal the response, not of an impersonal heaven or cosmic force, but of Guanyin Bodhisattva's intervention in the lives of the faithful.[10] Although informed by the idea of correlative response, it seems that such stories are more properly referred to as examples of the efficacious response (*lingying*) of the Bodhisattva to distinguish them from the more impersonal or naturalistic conceptions of correspondences. These two conceptions of the cosmos, anthropomorphic and naturalistic, have been evident in China from very early on.[11]

The Chinese conceptualization of what in a Western context would be called miracles merits a brief comparison with this Western notion and its conceptual framework to clarify the nature of the auspicious events under consideration. The word "miracle" is derived from the Latin *miraculum,* "to wonder." Noting this, Thomas Aquinas defined one saying, "A miracle is so called as being full of wonder, in other words, as having a cause absolutely hidden from all. This cause is God. Therefore those things which God does outside the causes which we know are called miracles."[12] This is a common notion in Western societies. To better understand how it contrasts with the Chinese notion, we must understand what is meant by God and compare this with Chinese thought.

The Christian God is a being of ontological transcendence, he is (wholly) Other. Just as a dichotomy is erected between matter and spirit, so is one erected between the human and the divine. Such dichotomous perceptions are foreign to Chinese thought. There are gods, ghosts, and spirits in China, and they are distinguishable from humans, but they are not ontologically transcendent; they are not of some wholly other substance or being. A line of continuity runs through humans, spirits, and gods. Although humans in traditional Chinese thought are believed to have souls, *hun* 魂 and *po* 魄, they are not immaterial. They are rarified forms of energy, a subtle form of matter.[13] This profound difference places the Chinese on a radically different religious and philosophical footing.[14] This difference, I argue, enables the Chinese to reinterpret their auspicious events in more scientific terms without them significantly losing their power.

Auspicious events of the correlative response variety, then, are responses within a bounded cosmos, within the organism of the world. Miracles in the Judeo-Christian context are intrusions from beyond the world, from a spiritual beyond, into the phenomenal world.[15] These ideas of wholly other transcendence are foreign to the Chinese view, where the world as heaven and earth is perceived as an organic whole.[16] Despite these ontological differences, correlative responses of the kind we are considering are accepted as signs of great attainment, they are also thought to imbue the place where they occur with their numinous presence.

Places that serve as the site of such wondrous displays are, through such association, rendered sacred (*shendi*). As sacred places, they are considered to possess numinous power or efficacy (*ling*). The amount of perceived spiritual efficacy is a crucial determinant in the success of a temple in folk and Daoist traditions. Adam Chau writes, "The believed in degree of efficacy or 'efficacious response' (*lingying*) is the most important determinant of a deity's ranking in the local world of spiritual power" (2006, 241). Efficacy also plays a crucial role in winning popular support for a Buddhist monastery.

During the imperial era, spiritual efficacy was also a key factor in determining the level of elite and state support. Just how numinous power was related to institutional support during the imperial period of China's history is revealed by Judith Boltz, who points out that Chinese historical literature is full of references to officials and their relationships to supernatural forces. In particular, many accounts attest to how officials in imperial China strove to suppress spirits (*shen*) that were considered threatening through ritual means or through the closing or destruction of shrines (Boltz 1993). The Song dynasty chronicler Hung Mai 洪迈/邁 (1123–1202) in his *Yijian zhi* 夷堅志 explained that the shrines that commanded respect were those that were spiritually efficacious (*ling*), numinously manifest (*ling xian* 灵显), or spiritually responsive (*ling xiang* 灵相).[17] During purges, the only shrines that had a hope of survival were those considered effectively numinous, spiritually powerful, or *ling*. An example from the eleventh century is that of the magistrate Jiang Jing (earned *jinshi* in 1079) of Yixing 宜兴 in Jiangsu, who ordered the destruction of three hundred shrines considered "excessive," sparing only the one temple considered the most powerful, a temple dedicated to a certain General Liu.[18]

The relationship between officials and what they perceived as the numinous realm provides an important window into factors contributing to the patronage of religious sites such as Kaiyuan over the centuries. Longevity, to a great extent, has often boiled down to being tolerated by the state, which has always seen the regulation of religious activity and institutions as part of its duty. The Chinese bureaucracy, educated in the Confucian tradition, has often been influenced by skeptical and cautionary tendencies in that tradition; it has, at points throughout the imperial era, held Buddhism, Taoism, and folk practices at arm's length and has participated in the regulation and suppression of religious forces deemed unhealthy or unorthodox.[19] Over the course of the twentieth century, Confucian ideology has been replaced by Marxist historical materialism, which considers religion an instrument of exploitation. As a consequence, the current generation of Chinese bureaucrats continues in a long tradition of officials who perceive religion as something that requires close regulation and restriction.[20] Other temples and monasteries have come and gone in Quanzhou, but Kaiyuan remains because political forces over the centuries have supported its continued existence. No one reason explains why, but Kaiyuan's reputation as a place of spiritual power, and, more recently, its possession of valuable cultural properties, have been critical factors.

Kaiyuan's perceived numinous power attracted the patronage responsible for the final imperial period restoration of Kaiyuan's buildings. The restoration was carried out by Commander General Bai Yude, who was not local to the area, in the early nineteenth century. Why was he moved to restore Kaiyuan's halls? Dispatched to fight pirates in the region, he went to Kaiyuan and prayed for rain to end a terrible drought in Quanzhou. When his prayer was answered, he committed to restoring Kaiyuan's halls.[21] Bai Yude, we must infer, turned to Kaiyuan because locals had informed him that it was a place of merit and spiritual power. Even if they did not, the commander perceived this to be the case himself and it was his experience with Kaiyuan's perceived spiritual efficacy that moved him to have the monastery restored. Such acts of patronage are a common feature of Chinese religion and either established or reinforced associations of spiritual efficacy.

How then, has Kaiyuan promoted an idea of spiritual efficacy? A common way for temples to set themselves apart has been their founding narratives. Some temples are founded by eminent monks and have no need to refer to preternatural signs, such as Xi'an's Ci'en Monastery built for the great Tang dynasty master and pilgrim Xuanzang. Others are founded around a sacred relic or image. Many such stories are related by Daoxuan in his *Ji shenzhou sanbao gantong lu* (T. 2106:52) about "miraculous images" that may be said to be associated with the founding or legitimization of monasteries.[22] Kaiyuan became established as a place of spiritual efficacy when the mulberry trees are said to have bloomed lotus blossoms, an indication of efficacy reiterated when an auspicious purple cloud descended as the main hall was being built.

Ever since the ninth century, when Huang Tao memorialized Kaiyuan's legendary founding, the monastery has continued to memorialize related auspicious events, which mark Kaiyuan as a place of numinous power.[23] Almost all subsequent treatments of the monastery, including records from the Song, Yuan, Ming, and Qing dynasties and recent guidebooks, relate the legends.[24] More than six hundred years ago, a list of auspicious events was inscribed on a wall bounding the main gate; the same events are recalled by tour guides today. Tales have been passed down in unbroken succession to the present; they have been integrated into the fabric of Kaiyuan's identity and distinguish it as an outstanding place of merit and spiritual power.

Kaiyuan, like other temples and sites in China, is full of inscriptions, steles, and plaques; these texts in stone and wood are not as dormant as they may seem. They actively contribute to the experience of visitors, whether literate or not. For the illiterate, their calligraphy, their age, or their sheer literary presence suggest a mysterious power. For those who can read, they impress with their literary allusions, their antiquity, and their artistry. To capture this active function of inscriptions at temples, Chau proposes the term "text act."[25] As text acts, inscriptions are endowed with the power to influence the perceptions of visitors, enhance the reputation of the monastery, and ward off those who may wish to harm the monastery. Although the reputation for spiritual power would have helped attract state support and protection during the imperial period, it does not in the modern period. Chapter 5 stresses the importance of cultural properties in winning state support in recent decades. Although spiritual power is no longer a field of discourse that speaks to the state, it continues to attract worshippers and tourists.

These events are said to have happened in the past but are widely thought to imbue the land, its buildings, trees, and statues with a residue of their charisma and spiritual power in the present. A lay Buddhist standing in the courtyard one day spoke about the mulberry tree that bloomed lotus blossoms. With a big smile on his face and visible pride, he said, "This is holy ground" (*shendi*). Another said of the auspicious stories associated with Kaiyuan and their influence on the monastery, "they inspire people, monks as well as visitors." He explained that a type of aura had been detected over temples in China, a phenomenon he associated with their sacred power.

The notion of auras over temples may neither be widespread nor well documented, but the notion that temples have a sacred power that visitors can access is. If a temple can document a record of auspicious phenomena associated with it, its monks, or properties, then it can promote its reputation as a site of spiritual power and increase the number of devotees eager to contribute to the temple in hopes of receiving its blessings and protection. In addition, if properties exist associated with such preternatural events, whether mineral, vegetable, or animal, they attract not only believers, whether pious or opportunistic, but also curiosity-seekers with no particular religious pretensions. As with material culture, their meanings are multivalent.

Eight Auspicious Phenomena

Whereas Kaiyuan has long recalled the two auspicious events associated with its founding, it was in the fourteenth century that Dagui (aka Mengguan) in the *Biographies of Purple Cloud Bodhisattvas* recorded dozens associated with Kaiyuan's eminent monks. It was also at this time that lists of eight auspicious phenomena and six unique sites were inscribed on walls outside the main gate.[26] These lists have been passed down since that time and were reproduced in 2005 in a promotional book published by Kaiyuan Monastery. The book features many color photos of Kaiyuan's cultural properties and includes the Yuan dynasty lists of eight auspicious phenomena and six unique sites presented in four character phrases. The eight auspicious phenomena are purple clouds covering the land (*ziyun gaidi* 紫云盖地), mulberry trees blooming lotus blossoms (*sangshu bailian* 桑树白莲), the courtyard in which weeds do not grow (*fancao busheng* 凡草不生), white doves listening to a sutra (*baige tingjing* 白鸽听经), dream of the arhats (*yingmeng luohan* 应梦罗汉), eminent monks of branch cloisters (*zhiyuan gaoseng* 支院高僧), manjushri's handwriting (*wenshu moji* 文殊墨迹), and the mummy of the bare-shouldered monk (*tanbo zhenshen* 袒膊真身).

The first two items relate to the founding of the monastery. The third is the large stone courtyard said to have been auspiciously free of weeds—an auspicious event for anyone who has had to weed a large courtyard. The

Table 2 The Eight Auspicious Phenomena of Quanzhou Kaiyuan Temple

Name	Memorialized or Present	Notes
1. Purple clouds covering the land	yes	front gate name board, spirit screen, statue of Kuanghu
2. Lotus-blooming mulberry trees	yes	the tree, wall inscription, main hall name board, Kuanghu, Huang Shougong, donor's hall
3. The weed-free courtyard	yes	the front courtyard itself
4. White doves listening to a sutra	yes	small dove sculptures on roof of main hall
5. Dream of the arhats	no	NA
6. Eminent monks of branch cloisters	yes	couplet inside main gate
7. Manjushri's handwriting	no	NA
8. The mummy of Zhiliang	yes	inside the patriarch's hall

Monastic Gazetteer notes, however, that it was invaded by weeds as early as the Yuan dynasty (Yuanxian 1643, I.30b–31a). The monastery nonetheless makes an effort to keep the courtyard weeded and it remains mostly free of grasses. Although no sources or informants have given this event any symbolic meaning, it is possible, if not likely, meant to represent moral uprightness.[27]

The fourth auspicious phenomenon is the dove that listened to sutras. This is a reference to one of the more unique stories about Kaiyuan's eminent monks; it concerns Chan master Jiehuan 戒环, whose story begins at Kaiyuan in his previous incarnation as a dove. This particular dove is said to have visited Kaiyuan's Thousand Buddha Cloister (*qianfo yuan* 千佛院) daily to listen to the head monk chanting the *Lotus Sutra*. One day, the dove did not appear. That night, the head monk dreamed someone told him, "I am the dove and through the power of your chanting I have been reincarnated as a human." The person in the dream described where he was born and asked the head monk to find him, indicating that he could be positively identified by a white feather under his arm. The head monk followed the directions and found a baby boy with a white feather under his arm. His parents agreed to let him become a monk and after he grew up he became the head monk's disciple and was given the name Jiehuan (Yuanxian 1643, I.40a, I.17a). The story of the dove reborn as the monk Jiehuan is symbolically represented at the monastery today in the small wooden sculptures of white doves on the roof of the main hall. Given so many impressive sights to compete for their attention, most visitors fail to look up and notice them, and few guides mention them for the same reason. Yet they remain as subtle reminders of a dove reincarnated as a Chan master for those initiated into the lore of the monastery with the leisure to seek out all of its charms.

The sixth auspicious phenomenon is a reference to the many great masters who lived at the monastery during the Song dynasty, when it expanded to include more than a hundred cloisters. Hongyi's calligraphy about the Buddha kingdom full of sages may be considered an indirect reference to this. It hangs just inside the main gate as a text act contributing to the experience of visitors. Guides and guidebooks regularly mention the history of Kaiyuan's 120 branch cloisters. Although no effort is made to elaborate on the diversity of doctrine and practice those cloisters represent, that they are mentioned as relevant suggests that traces of the charisma of the fecund times have somehow become sedimented in the grounds of the site.

The eighth auspicious phenomenon is the mummy of Zhiliang. Zhiliang was a monk thought to be from India because he wore his robe with one of his shoulders bared and because he begged for food (an ascetic practice from Indian Buddhism that the Chinese never embraced). He is reputed to have had the ability to bring sun or rain as requested and to have had wild tigers at his side when he lived at Mount Daiyun (Yuanxian 1643, I.22a–b). In regard to his mummy, the *Monastic Gazetteer* states that "His disciples encased his corpse in mud and placed it in a hall where it became a source of prosperity (*fu*) for the people of Quanzhou" (Yuanxian 1643, I.22a–b).

Today a small lacquered figure in the patriarch's hall is said to contain the full body relic (*quanshen sheli* 全身舍利) of Zhiliang.[28] Mummies have been effective in attracting patronage in Chinese Buddhism since as early as the Sui dynasty, when the mummy of master Zhiyi 智顗 (538–579) attracted the attention of the imperial court (Ritzinger and Bingenheimer 2006, 62–69).[29] By the time of Zhiliang, mummies had become a relatively common strategy to bring a monastery fame and patronage. That a lacquer figure said to be Zhiliang's mummy has been preserved for so many centuries and recorded in Kaiyuan's list of auspicious phenomena speaks to the value the monastery historically placed on it. Buddhist mummies at other monasteries have been said to have protected their monasteries from the raids by military marauders.[30] As a property of spiritual value, Zhiliang's mummy may have played a similarly protective role over the centuries, but such a role has not been documented. Traditionally, it would have been both a spiritual and economic asset, but today the figure receives little attention by either monks or the public. Furthermore, although the pious believe it to be authentic, skeptics hold that the figure is too small and light to contain a complete mummy.[31] No effort is made to draw attention to it today, but the monks do pay obeisance to the images in the hall of patriarchs, including the figure of Zhiliang, every fortnight. For the many who are aware of its presence, the mummy adds a distinct layer of curiosity, if not spiritual significance.

Kaiyuan's auspicious past is made alive by clues throughout the monastic grounds, symbolic and verbal clues, as well as by properties said to date from the time of those auspicious events such as the mummy and the mulberry tree. As Stanley Tambiah argues in his study of Buddhist amulets in Thailand (2007), the surviving artifacts and the grounds of the monastery should be seen as having the charisma of associated monks and events within them and as having a kind of power the faithful believe they might access. Beyond charisma, these objects should also be understood to concretize cultural memory more broadly, which dialectically enables individuals to participate in and construct a shared identity. Although objects associated with the source events, the founding in particular, may be thought to have charismatic power within them, memorializations of events serve to direct attention toward the auspicious or miraculous legends. In addition to these in situ clues are references in publications and in the discourse of tour guides.

Among the most significant forms of memorialization are the two large walls constructed by Daoyuan to flank the main gate inscribed with references to two auspicious events, one from the monastery's founding, the other from the Republican period. The main gate, then, is effectively surrounded on four sides by literary references to three auspicious events serving as text acts influencing the experience of visitors. Behind the main gate is the large spirit screen with the sixteenth-century inscription that reads "Purple Cloud Screen." Hanging above the entrance is a simple board bearing two characters that have been a nickname of the monastery since the Tang Dynasty, "Purple Cloud." To the right and left of the gate are the large walls erected by Daoyuan in 2002 with four large characters on each side. The one on the right proclaims "Dharma World of the Lotus-Blooming Mulberry Tree." The one on the left stretches toward the west pagoda: "Lotus-Blooming Peach Tree Manifests the Auspicious" (*taolian yingrui* 桃莲映瑞), invoking the Republican period restoration. The two numinous events span thirteen centuries of the monastery's history and suggest to visitors that they are entering a sacred site whose spiritual efficacy has been verified for more than a millennium. These large characters cannot be missed and demonstrate the current leadership's use of auspicious events to represent and promote Kaiyuan as a place of legendary spiritual power. All visitors are thus exposed to the extraordinary reputation of the site and asked to see it through a cosmology that affirms the possibility of correlative responses to Buddhist virtue.

The words "Dharma World of the Lotus-Blooming Mulberry" found outside the temple are found again inside the grounds, inscribed on a huge

FIG. 6.1 The main gate of Quanzhou Kaiyuan Monastery in 2006. The bounding wall to the right reads "Dharma World of the Lotus-Blooming Mulberry." The areas in front are filled with vendors during the monthly *nianfo* days and throughout the year on festival days. Photo by the author.

horizontal wooden plaque that hangs above the central doors of the main hall. These words as text act are positioned so that they make their way willy-nilly into every photo of the main hall taken from the large open courtyard. Similarly, any photo taken of the main gate from outside the monastery will include the name board reading "Purple Cloud" and likely one of the inscriptions on the bounding walls. In this way, and in the relating of the story of Kaiyuan's founding by every tour guide and guidebook, the story of the lotus-blooming mulberry trees and the purple cloud are repeated visually and orally and have become identifying features that orient thinking about Kaiyuan. In addition to the memorials is the ancient tree said to be one of the originals left from Huang's original land grant.

This mulberry tree, said to have bloomed white lotus blossoms more than 1,300 years ago, is, after the stone pagodas, Kaiyuan's most well-known attraction. The mulberry is the only area at Kaiyuan protected by a barrier and kept under lock and key. Arguably the most sacred in the monastery, it is closed to the public. It is also a preferred location for distinguished guests to take pictures with the abbot; several such photos are displayed in the abbot's audience hall. Permission to enter the gated mulberry tree area feels like a rare privilege, to pay respects to the tree rather than, say, to inspect or photograph it. The tree is large and unwieldy, however, and not especially suited to being photographed at close range. It sprawls over the corridor between it and the main hall, stretching east and south toward the dragons and doves on the roof of the main hall. The tree also extends toward the ordination platform in the north and toward the west pagoda in the west, thus stretching out in three directions. Locals like to say the tree itself now resembles a lotus flower. Its leaves are surprisingly vibrant and healthy in appearance; its bark, which it seems to be shedding, like a snake, is dark and crumbling. Tea made with its leaves is reputed to have special healing properties. Older locals are sometimes seen picking them up from the stone pavement between the main hall and the hall of the ordination platform.

The story of Huang's mulberry trees is manifest at Kaiyuan not only by the lone surviving tree and the inscriptions inside and outside the monastery but also by the figures of the event's two protagonists, the landowner Elder Huang and the monk Kuanghu. Kuanghu is enshrined with a small statue in the Patriarch's Hall.[32] Elder Huang has his own complex of three rooms in the donor's ancestral hall (*tanyue ci*), which runs along the east side of the ordination platform. In one room hangs a portrait of Huang, in another a small statue of him. Both Elder Huang, who gave his orchard, and the monk Kuanghu, who received it, are thus formally enshrined and receive offerings on a regular basis. Elder Huang, in particular is regularly honored with offerings from the "Purple Cloud Huang" family, which annually gathers to pay their respects at this shrine.[33] Kaiyuan has survived many changes and transformations, including expansions, contractions, and changes of name, but the events and figures associated with its founding narrative are not forgotten. They are a remembrance that has helped the monastery to distinguish itself and attract patronage, including important patronage from the (extended) Huang family from the Ming dynasty onward.

Monks at other temples in Quanzhou say that auspicious stories are associated with their temples, but none I have heard are as central to the temple's identity as those at Kaiyuan. Kaiyuan has been more successful than other monasteries in the region in memorializing its auspicious past, especially its founding. This is true in the present as well as in the historical record.[34] I like to understand the story of the mulberry trees as a metaphor for the blossoming of Buddhism in South China, where lotus blossoms represent the dharma and mulberry trees, which are used to cultivate silkworms, represent South China, home to the most famous centers of silk production. Confirming that such was the conscious intention is not of course possible, but the story remains nevertheless a reading that adds a layer of possible meaning.

A further layer of reference relates to the founding of the Jetavana, used by the Buddha and his disciples. According to the *Dharmaguptaka Vinaya,* when Anāthapiṇḍada found the park of Prince Jeta and determined to purchase it for the sangha, the owner, Prince Jeta, was reluctant and said that the land's price was the amount of gold required to cover the park in its entirety. Anāthapiṇḍada began to do just this and had nearly finished. Prince Jeta was duly impressed, stopped him, and covered the remaining area with his own gold. It was thus that Anāthapiṇḍada acquired the land that was given to the Buddha and the early sangha.

Structural parallels between this story and that of Huang Shougong's donation of the mulberry orchard immediately come to mind. Like Prince Jeta, Huang was reluctant to give up his land but, rather than simply refusing, made what he considered to be prohibitive conditions. In both cases, however, the conditions were met (the land was to be covered in gold and the mulberry trees were covered with lotus blossoms), the landowners were impressed, and the land was transferred to the sangha.

A further addendum to the Huang donation story, most likely added during the Ming dynasty, claims that when Huang asked the monk Kuanghu how much land he needed, the monk said only as much land as covered by his robe's shadow. Huang, perhaps relieved, agreed, at which point Kuanghu removed his robe and tossed it high into the sky so that it blocked out the sun and created a shadow that covered Huang's entire orchard. The robe, however, had a hole in it, which let the sun shine on a small patch of the orchard; it was at this spot, according to the legend, where a shrine was built to honor the donor, Elder Huang. This story, likely invented by members of the Huang family during the Ming or Qing dynasty, nevertheless offers a further parallel with the donation of the Jetavana.[35] Recall that a small piece of land was not covered with Anāthapiṇḍada's gold but instead with Prince Jeta's. Thus in both cases the donor retained a symbolic measure of interest in the land defined by a parcel that had been left "uncovered" by the one requesting the land.

Further examination of these structural parallels is beyond the scope of this book, but the parallels are worth noting for the archetypal overtones they give the founding narrative of Kaiyuan, iconic overtones that may have contributed to its success.

Although many if not most people do not literally believe that mulberry trees bloomed lotus blossoms, they still venerate the surviving mulberry as a very old tree and believe something happened that gave rise to the donation of the land to Kuanghu. Not wishing to abandon the story as baseless, they have searched for more scientific explanations. The most popular comes from an edition of the "Huang Surname Genealogical Records," which claims that in the year 686 southern Fujian had rain for forty-nine consecutive days. It has been suggested that under these unusually warm and humid conditions Huang's mulberry trees could have grown white wood ear fungus 银耳, which from a distance could have looked like lotus blossoms (Zhang 2003, 23). This explanation has been given by both monks and laypersons and is circulated by some tour guides as well. I contribute its popularity to the influence of the historical materialist ideology and anti-superstition campaigns that have created a fashion for finding natural explanations for supernatural phenomena.[36]

A similar development has taken place to render the Republican period miracle more consonant with scientific understanding. A monk at Kaiyuan who takes an interest in such stories informed me that peach trees grew at Kaiyuan at the time and bloomed large blossoms, so large that people, taking some artistic license, referred to them as lotuses. When people circulate such explanations, they are not, it seems, dramatically diminishing the overall force of the stories and their ability to sacralize the grounds. Those who proffer such explanations still maintain that something unusual happened. This "something unusual" is the hallmark of spiritual power. The nature of the unusual has been reined in considerably in these retellings but remains anomalous, remarkable, and most certainly auspicious. As discussed earlier, no radically other agent is involved in these auspicious manifestations. Thus one can lower the drama element (mushrooms not lotuses) without eliminating the source of power—conditions came together under the influence of a sage and produced a marvelous sign. The fundamental structure and elements of the event have not changed; Chinese cosmology provides a means of making such a readjustment without sacrificing the logic of correlative response. Furthermore, the desire to make these adjustments suggests a desire not to abandon, but to preserve for posterity these auspicious stories by articulating them in an idiom appropriate to the present generation. As William James notes, "The philosophic climate of our time inevitably forces its own clothing on us" (1961, 338).

It is one of the virtues of Chinese cosmography that such a redescription is possible without unhinging an element of mystery—a mainstay of religion. Robert Campany, in his groundbreaking survey of strange tales (*zhiguai* 志怪) compiled in medieval China over several centuries (the Six Dynasties, the Sui, and the Tang), argues against the thesis that these stories of anomalies are a form of early fiction writing (1996).[37] Instead, he suggests, they constitute a genre concerned with cosmography that sees itself as historiographic. Many of the tales are concerned with magical responses, such as Kaiyuan's mulberry. The effort to explain Kaiyuan's auspicious events in more scientific language suggests, like Campany's view of medieval *zhiguai* accounts, that they are not perceived as fiction but instead as a form of historiography that requires glossing. If they were simply fictions, there would be no reason to find an explanation for them apart from debunking them as fictitious. One monk who thinks that white mushrooms grew on the trees instead of lotuses has said that the authors of the early records used artistic license to describe the unusual phenomenon. In other words, something unusual happened and, to draw attention to it, a more colorful description was used; that is, an auspicious, anomalous event was not invented.

Regardless of what actually happened or what adjustments are made, the monastery's founding story is told in guidebooks and by tour guides every day and the events are memorialized in inscriptions and shrines throughout the monastic grounds so that most visitors are aware of them. These auspicious events, especially the story of the lotus-blooming mulberry trees and the purple cloud, condition the mental dimension of the space by asserting its spiritual pedigree within a cosmology of correlative events. This framing and branding influences the experience of visitors and the reputation of the monastery. How this influence plays out differs according to the disposition or habitus of the one learning the stories. This is where the dialectical exchange between perceiving consciousness and material artifact or conceptual representation takes place in the making of space. These stories, drawing on the three social identities or groups identified in chapter 5, enhance the monastery's reputation of spiritual efficacy for the religionist, mark Kaiyuan as a unique place of historical interest for the tourist, and are only so much white noise for those seeking recreation. A visitor meeting friends at Kaiyuan to "have fun," for example, said he saw "Purple Cloud" but thought it was strange and didn't know what it meant. What is most interesting here is the intentional way that monks in particular deploy references to auspicious and miraculous events. They demonstrate two primary approaches captured by the notions of branding and sanctification, or *linghua*.

Branding

Branding is a phenomenon fundamentally tied to product marketing. Its application has been broadened in recent years in literature dealing with the branding of place and the branding of cities in the interest of harnessing the economic potentials of tourism.[38] The branding of cities has become an important part of tapping into potential tourism markets and investment for Chinese cities (Chan and Lang 2015, 52). David Geary explores various schemes of branding in relation to the site of Śākyamuni's enlightenment at Bodhgaya in northern India (2017). Although Kaiyuan Monastery has not hired or considered hiring a marketing agent, it has followed a long tradition of promoting its special features to set itself apart and attract patrons. The special features that have been promoted from the very beginning are the founding legends. Chan and Lang have explored attempts by officials and investors to create cultural brands for temples in Guangdong using television media and holding festivals (2015, 50–56). The efforts at Kaiyuan are much more organic, and no effort has been made to invent new associations, at least in regard to Kaiyuan's legendary past.

The surviving mulberry tree and Kaiyuan's memorials to auspicious events distinguish the monastery from other Buddhist monasteries, particularly those that may have old buildings or pagodas, or share the name Kaiyuan.[39] Visitors who take little or no religious interest in Kaiyuan but who are attracted to its historic and cultural properties will nonetheless learn of its associations with auspicious purple clouds and the legend of the lotus-blooming mulberry. For them, the stories may not mark Kaiyuan as a sacred place but do mark it as a unique site, distinguishing it from countless other Buddhist temples in China and throughout Asia. As announced by a monumental stone screen in the western garden of the monastery, it is "The Best Among 10,000 Monasteries" (*wan shan diyi* 万山第一).

One of the administrative monks at Kaiyuan explained the use of these references: "Brand logos are very important in modern society. 'Dharma World of the Lotus-Blooming Mulberry' 桑连法界 is just like a registered trademark."[40] It is used by one of the administrative monks as his social media username on WeChat (*weixin*). Both the cloud and the mulberry are thus deployed much like trademarks that participate in the promotion of Kaiyuan as a tourist attraction by giving it distinctive and attractive nicknames. By 2019, the monastery had adopted this logo and begun using it as a genuine trademark consisting of five buddhas on a lotus with the words "Dharma World of the Lotus Mulberry" above their heads. Below the image, "Quanzhou Kaiyuan Temple" is written in Chinese and English. It is placed on visitor signage at the monastery and in monastery publications.

Tourists in China inevitably find themselves visiting Buddhist temples. A popular description of sightseeing in China is "see temples during the day, sleep at night," which is much catchier in Chinese—*baitian kanmiao, wanshang shuijiao* 白天看庙晚上睡觉—because it is balanced and rhymes. All but the most intrepid historians or pious Buddhists are likely to tire of visiting temples that have many similar features. Thus when the guide on the bus announces to the group that they will tour Kaiyuan Temple, the group will not be nearly as enthusiastic as one told they will visit the "Purple Cloud, home of an ancient mulberry tree that bloomed white lotus blossoms during the Tang dynasty!" Kaiyuan has actively promoted these colorful and imagistic tags for centuries; their deployment has enhanced Quanzhou Kaiyuan's brand and contributed to its success as a tourist site as well as a place of worship and pilgrimage.

Other temples and monasteries also develop their brand. The famous Baima or White Horse Monastery in Luoyang seized on the image of the white horse to do so. Baima Monastery is promoted as the first Buddhist monastery established in China and shares with Quanzhou Kaiyuan a founding story associated with an auspicious dream. In Baima's case, the dream was by the Han emperor Ming 汉明帝 (r. 58–75 CE) who dreamed of a flying golden figure. His advisors informed him that his dream referred to the Buddha, a sage in the West. The emperor sent envoys who returned after several years with two Indian monks, the *Sutra in Forty-two Sections,* and a white horse. The emperor is said to have had White Horse Monastery built for the monks.[41] Today, a statue of a stone horse stands outside the monastery as a symbol of the monastery and its legendary past. Baima deployed the image of the white horse much as Kaiyuan promoted Purple Cloud, both are memorable imagistic names. The monastery also promotes a list of six sites (*liu jing* 六景) traced to a Qing dynasty monk who carved them on the wall; the inscription can be seen today.[42] Its properties of cultural heritage include a Jin dynasty pagoda, stone statues from the Song, a gate from the Ming and statues from the Yuan. It also boasts, akin to Kaiyuan's famous dragon eye fruits, a famous large pomegranate known as the "Baima sweet pomegranate" (*baima tianliu*). Baima's array of cultural properties and effectively memorialized founding story are points it has in common with Kaiyuan, points that have contributed to each of their success.[43]

Sanctification

Kaiyuan's association with auspicious events and eminent monks not only brands it as unique, but also reinforces its reputation as a place of spiritual power. Kaiyuan's events are also, and more fundamentally, sacred markers, indicating a place distinguished not only from other temples but also from the rest of the mundane world. It is an assertion of spatial heterogeneity or premodern enchantment. Before the monastery was established, the land it stands on was part of the mundane world—a mulberry orchard. As an orchard, it had two distinguishing features, land and trees. Both were marked by auspicious appearances that effectively signaled the blossoming of a place to practice Buddhism in China: the trees bloomed lotuses and land was covered by a purple cloud. It was as if the land and the trees themselves spoke up and said, yes, this is where a monastery should be built. Such is the import of these two legends—the monastery's location is not arbitrary, it was mandated by the appearance of auspicious signs, marvelous correlative responses in nature. Since that time, it has been the location of a Buddhist monastery. This point is made by the pair of inscriptions bounding the main gate that reference the earliest and the most recent auspicious events.

Yuanxian, in writing the *Monastic Gazetteer,* suggests that Kaiyuan's auspicious heritage is a condition for the cultivation of monastic excellence. It existed in the past and today (in the seventeenth century):

> After writing these biographies of bodhisattvas, I am amazed at the great number of worthies the Purple Cloud has had. How could this be so, if it is not an auspicious place of singular merit (*jixiang shusheng* 吉祥殊胜)? It has almost been a thousand years since the appearing of the auspicious sign of the lotus-blooming mulberry tree. So it was in ancient times, so it remains today. (Yuanxian 1643, I.45b–46a)

The memorialization of Kaiyuan's legendary founding marks the monastery as an auspicious place of singular merit, as a place manifestly numinous. The space of the monastery has numinous messaging baked into the walls, doorways, and halls, even into the grounds with the presence of the mulberry tree. This messaging promotes a traditional cosmology of cosmic resonances and spiritual efficaciousness. In the absence of inscriptions, signboards, guidebooks, and tour guides, the legendary cosmic resonance of Kaiyuan would be mute to all but a handful of experts in local history and lore. This is to emphasize the dialectical dynamism of space and the need for artifacts, symbols, and lore as well as people with the proper disposition to see and hear the numinous messaging. As Henry David Thoreau wrote, "It takes two to speak the truth; one to speak, another to hear" ([1849] 1998, 215). Not that numinous cosmology is *the* truth, but it is the "truth" embodied in the legends and it is hidden without the kind of promotion and memorialization accessed by throngs of visitors. Also relevant to this issue is a point Alessandro Portelli makes about form and meaning in oral history (1991). Portelli found that his informants made errors with regard to facts, but that these errors were meaningful, they pointed to what was important to those speaking; "errors, inventions, and myths lead us through and beyond facts to their meanings" (1991, 2). Similarly, for the anthropologist it does not matter whether mulberry trees bloomed lotuses; what is important is how the persistence of these legends continues to inspire others and bolster the traditional/emic notion of cosmic resonance. From an outsider/etic interpretative position, we may see a resilience of spatial heterogeneity that is either a possible place of resistance to or disruption of projects of modernity and/or revelatory of a failure of the totalizing discourse of secular modernity.[44]

Kuanghu's legendary founding charisma drifts through the ages and is awakened by the words "purple cloud" and "lotus-blooming mulberry" and is manifest in the survival of a small, awkward statue that now sits behind glass in the hall of patriarchs. The hall of patriarchs is situated on the highest elevation of the monastery and the statue of Kuanghu and the portraits of Republican period monks gaze south toward the central axis of Kaiyuan, overlooking the whole monastery. In short, Kuanghu and the Republican period monks occupy a place of honor physically and spiritually.

Having a reputation for being spiritually efficacious remains a critical factor in the production of ideological frameworks based on mythology promoting traditional forms of cosmology marked by sympathetic resonance. In the context of the traditional role of officials as patrons or oppressors of religious sites and the custom of allowing at least the most spiritually powerful to survive, Kaiyuan Monastery has effectively promoted an identity as the most spiritually powerful site in Quanzhou, as the king of *ling*—as Yuanxian suggests, "No one eats the great fruit." Although the perception of spiritual efficacy was important for state support only in the past, it remains important only in attracting popular support in the present.

Kaiyuan's promotion of its founding legends mark the site as unique (branding) and spiritually efficacious (sanctification), two key ideological frames with broad appeal in the making of space. These frameworks promote a traditional cosmology of sympathetic resonance that continues to be updated with explanations consistent with more scientific narratives. This chapter argues that Chinese traditional thought marked by a lack of hard duality between humans and nature and spirit and matter facilitates such updating of preternatural events in ways that preserve the integrity of the legends and contributes to the resiliency of traditional cosmology.

The founding legends have promoted the site as unique and sacred, but other narratives and ideological frames compete for recognition, if not dominance. The most important is the more secular framework of cultural heritage. Chapter 7 examines this final layer of life at the monastery, the cooperation and struggle between curators of cultural heritage and religious revivalists.

7

Curators and the Revivalists

Negotiating Spatial Dynamics

ON A DECEMBER MORNING IN 2002, KAIYUAN'S abbot, Daoyuan, returned to his monastery after attending a meeting of the Municipal People's Congress. On arriving at the main gate, Daoyuan, a small man then in his sixties, met a security guard with whom he had had disagreements in the past. Another argument broke out between them. The abbot repaired to the monks' living quarters and summoned the monks to attack the security guard. Some twenty or more monks, armed with knives and blunt objects, did just that. Two coworkers of the guard came to his aid and were also assaulted. From here, the main gate, or hall of heavenly kings, the monks advanced to the office of the administrative commission, which employed the security guards, and proceeded to vandalize it. No one was seriously wounded in the fray, but the guard was hospitalized for treatment and released. The monks involved were temporarily suspended from the monastery.

This event, witnessed by tourists and worshippers alike, had been preceded by months of tension between the monks and the Temple Administrative Commission (*Siyuan guanli weiyuanhui* 寺院管理委员会). Disputes between the abbot and members of this group had become more frequent at least since the previous winter, when the abbot had monks attack the vice director of the commission after an argument related to New Year's decorations. In August of 2002, relations with the security crew reached a critical point. One of the guards had parked his car in the front gate hall and refused to move it when the abbot asked him to do so. The abbot then called together more than ten monks, who threatened to damage the car if it were not promptly removed. At that point, the monks and the abbot vowed to have the Temple Administrative Commission and its employees removed from the temple within two years.

This chapter examines two interested parties I designate as curators and revivalists. Each has a different vision of what temples should be in contemporary China and is involved in negotiating the identities of monasteries like Kaiyuan all over China. In short, the curators are interested in protecting cultural relics and charging the public a fee to visit temples and view their cultural properties, whereas the revivalists want to reestablish temples as places devoted to religious practice. The term "curator" functions, somewhat incidentally, as an euphemism for specific organs of the state that have varying degrees of jurisdiction over Buddhist temples in China. These organs are present in various configurations and differ from temple to temple. When a temple becomes designated an Important National Cultural Heritage Protected Site (全国重点文物保护单位) or a AAAA National Tourist Attraction (国家等级旅游区), for example, certain government entities, in addition to what was the Religious Affairs Bureau and is now the State Administration of Religious Affairs, become associated with the temple in various capacities of oversight, management, and exploitation. These include bureaus and committees that deal with tourism (*lüyou ju* 旅游局), culture (*wenhua ju* 文化局), heritage (*wenwu ju* 文物局), and temple management (*guanli weiyuan hui* 管理委员会). These entities tend to function as curators whose efforts to frame religion as an artifact of the past rather than a living phenomenon with a future, are in line with the Communist Party's ultimate view on religion. The revivalists, on the other hand, are the monastics, lay Buddhists, and worshippers, all eager to recover monastic and temple spaces and restore them to religious use.

A dominant theme in the study of religion in contemporary China has been the issue of relations between state and religion.[1] Many studies, especially earlier ones, have portrayed revival, in varying degrees, as a popular struggle against a monolithic state.[2] Yoshiko Ashiwa and David Wank (2009) as well as Adam Chau (2006) recognize the inadequacy of portraying the revival of religion as a battle between a monolithic and hegemonic state and religion or society. They propose, instead, a more nuanced analysis of what Chau calls the "the state-society interface" (8). Chau argues that

> Too much emphasis on communal resistance diverts attention from other important aspects of popular religious revivals such as the actions of the local state and the power claims of local elites, and the frequent mutual accommodation, negotiation, and collusion between local state agents and local elites. In the local world, state and society are completely imbricated.

In addition to the conflict between curators and revivalists at Kaiyuan is cooperation and collusion. Furthermore, curators are not synonymous with the state. They are instead low-level officials and state employees working for a state that is much larger than they. Some are sympathetic to religious revival; some may identify as Buddhists; others are comfortable with state-promoted scientific materialism and atheism and are highly suspicious of religious revival. To contextualize their relation to the central state, recall Zhao Puchu, who effectively represented both Buddhists and the state against such lesser entities (Ashiwa and Wank 2006, 350–351). So although at times in the analysis to follow it may seem that the curators are standing in for the state, I caution against such an oversimplification. The state is not monolithic and although generally it seeks to regulate religion, on a local level it often accommodates and promotes religious revival.[3] It also captures religious elites on some level through their participation in state-linked religious associations such as the Buddhist Association of China. The agencies referred to as curators in this chapter are minor bureaucrats and state employees and represent individuals like them all over China whose duties bring them into contact and into conflict with religious entities such as clerics or organizers of popular religious festivities.[4] Although these two parties, the curators and revivalists, are distinct, as Susan McCarthy argues in her study of the revival of Dai Buddhist culture and tourist development in Xishuangbanna (2010), their goals are not antithetical. It is true that curators, strictly speaking, support the cause of tourism over religious revival, yet, as discussed in chapter 5, Buddhist monasteries have long hosted those in pursuit of leisure, culture, beauty, and history as well as those in search of religion.[5]

Tourism and Buddhist Monasteries

Often located in beautiful mountain settings, Chinese Buddhist monasteries have attracted tourists and pilgrims for centuries. The association between natural settings and monasteries is revealed in such terms as "Chan forest" (*chanlin* 禅林) to designate a Chan monastery or, more generally, the phrase "mountain gate" (*shanmen* 山门) to indicate the main gate of a monastery, even one in a flat, or relatively flat, urban area such as Kaiyuan. Visiting monasteries in China, even those in urban areas, is analogous to climbing a mountain with the front gate at the lowest elevation and the back hall at the highest.

The sixth-century *Record of Buddhist Monasteries in Luoyang*, an important historical document and work of literature, contains much information about early monasteries in China. Its descriptions of monasteries and pagodas in particular are remarkable, however, for their praise of aesthetic features rather than for any religious significance or power. The Yongning

Pagoda of 516, for example, is described as having nine roofs hung with a total of 120 golden bells with doors painted vermillion and accented with gold nails (H. Yang 1984, 16).[6] The tradition of pagodas as the pride of monasteries and cities alike, as sights to behold, as marvels that enthrall the eye—what we today call tourist sites—appears to stretch back to the sixth and seventh centuries, when they began to dot the Chinese landscape (Kieschnick 2003, 39).

In the seventeenth century, Yuanxian promoted Kaiyuan's reputation by noting that people nostalgic for old things can be satisfied by visiting it. Evidence of self-promotion along these lines occurred at Kaiyuan as early as the Yuan dynasty. Accommodation, and even the encouragement of sightseers, is evidenced by the fourteenth-century walls erected at Kaiyuan's front gate bearing characters announcing the presence of "eight auspicious phenomena" and "six unique sites." Groups of visitors were certainly visiting Kaiyuan Monastery for its scenic appeal during this period, however, as demonstrated by an inscription that amounts to a kind of graffiti on the central column of the East Pagoda, left by a group of visitors in 1349; it describes the pleasant weather and magnificent view from the pagoda but makes no references to Buddhism nor the monastery:

> Today the sun is in the south, the weather is pleasantly warm, ominous clouds are breaking up while the mountains and the city are exceptionally magnificent. It makes us feel that time is passing so quickly and because getting together is so difficult we engrave this stone to remember this trip.[7]

Timothy Brook (1993) examines the patronage of Buddhist monasteries by the late-Ming gentry and finds that they retreated to Buddhist monasteries to escape the hustle and bustle of the world and enjoy cultural pursuits. A Fujian gazetteer describes monasteries as places where gentry retreat "to enjoy the view, drink wine, compose poetry, and cleanse themselves thoroughly of the dust of this world."[8] Such motivations were so common in Nanjing at the end of the sixteenth century that Feng Mengzhen 冯梦镇 (1546–1605) complained, "The gentry come just for the sights and no longer understand anything about Buddhist doctrine."[9] A growing consensus among scholars is that such uses of monasteries can be traced back to their earliest manifestations. John Kieschnick observes, "In addition to serving as a dwelling for monks and nuns—the definition of a monastery—modern monasteries also serve as tourist sites and as devotional, economic, and social centers. None of this is new. ... from the beginning, monasteries served as sites of lay as well as monastic devotion, for secular entertainment as well as Buddhist ritual" (2003, 186–187).

The Economic and Political Roles of Temples

Although the connection between temples and what we call tourism can be traced back as far as the Tang dynasty and the cultural properties of temples were targeted for preservation in the 1950s and early 1960s, the notion that temples and monasteries may play a key role in planned economic development has come to prominence only in the past thirty years, under such mottoes as "Culture sets the stage and the economy performs" (*wenhua datai, jingji changxi* 文化搭台 经济唱戏) (Ji 2004).[10] Local elites see their support of temples not as a source of blessings or merit as they once did, but instead as part of the community's economic development scheme. A popular temple, whether it boasts historical artifacts, spiritual power, or both, can attract tourists or pilgrims from outside the community who contribute to the local economy.[11] Temples also stimulate consumption among locals during festivals or special occasions.[12]

A somewhat ironic consequence of this notion is that historical artifacts and sites of historical importance are recognized as valuable commodities in the modernization of towns and cities.[13] In the summer of 2009, I visited a coastal city north of Shanghai slated to be developed into a thriving international port. We visited the brand-new, multistory, state-of-the-art exhibition hall displaying the development plans for the otherwise underwhelming city of Lianyungang 连云港. The hall sits at one end of a large plaza just across from the city hall; its multimedia displays, which introduce potential investors to the city and its development plans, include several exhibits on the ancient history of the area and its significant cultural and historical features. On the other end of the plaza is a new museum displaying a modest collection of historical artifacts from the area as well as local crafts.

What was clear from the exhibits and the language city officials used was that the promotion of the culture and history of Lianyungang was an essential ingredient in the plan to develop this city into a modern city and transportation hub. Taiwan's Foguang Shan had secured permission to rebuild a Buddhist monastery in the region; this was no easy task and required no small amount of political maneuvering. Their success must be attributed in part to the economic development plans of the city officials. The presence of functioning Buddhist monasteries is a reassurance to foreign investors that China has become a more open society that guarantees, in its words, freedom to believe in religion (*xinyang zongjiao ziyou* 信仰宗教自由). The guarantee of this freedom and the presence of open and vibrant temples tended by monastics is especially reassuring to overseas Chinese investors, who have long been the major source of foreign investment in China, especially investors from Hong Kong, Singapore, and Taiwan (Lei and Yao 2009, 91).[14] Buddhist monasteries fit into plans to attract investment on the one hand and domestic tourists on the other; as the saying goes, "Culture sets the stage and the economy performs." Buddhist monasteries and their restoration have long been part of Communist China's regional strategy of diplomatic relations but only recently found a niche in China's program of economic development.[15]

China's reform-era obsession with economic development wedded to the notion that culture sets the stage for such development has been a boon, in some sense, to monasteries with or without cultural artifacts; it has been the principal strategy used to secure the support of local officials for restoration projects.[16] Party officials and monks alike regularly talk about the economic benefits that accrue to a community that restores a temple. When asked how temples benefit the economy, the answer from officials and others is always tourism. The phrase an official in Quanzhou's Bureau of Cultural Heritage (*Wenwu ju*) used to describe temples such as Kaiyuan is colorful, yet forbidding: he described such sites as "smokeless factories" (*wuyan gongchang* 无烟工厂).[17] He was expressing a view repeated by government employees all over China, that restoring places of historic or cultural interest is an integral part of economic development (*jingji fazhan* 经济发展), that restored temples promote economic development (*cujin jingjifazhan* 促进经济发展). The connections between economic development, cultural preservation, and cultural revival on the one hand, and the central place of religion in Chinese culture on the other, has generated a great deal of cooperation between curators and revivalists in the restoration of temples in China since the 1980s.[18]

In addition, historic restoration and cultural revival hold particular appeal to overseas Chinese (*huaqiao*) investors. Quanzhou's foreign investors are drawn primarily from the overseas Chinese who have immigrated to Taiwan or Southeast Asia and who trace their roots to the Quanzhou region. When these investors return to their hometowns, apart from visiting any family that may remain, they typically wish to visit the temples where their family once worshipped; if these temples no longer exist, they are typically eager to assist in their rebuilding or restoration.[19] As the largest and most central monastery in Quanzhou, Kaiyuan tops the lists of temples that many overseas Chinese (and would-be investors) wish to visit on their trips to Quanzhou.[20] The state, by supporting the restoration of religious structures that are important to returning overseas Chinese, is making an investment in economic development.

The role of cultural properties in economic development and overseas investment is somewhat straightforward, but what about nationalism? Nationalism requires the identification of a national ethnic history replete with heroes and cultural achievements. It is in the name of protecting national heritage that sites of historic and cultural value are protected. In Benedict Anderson's terms, they are needed to created the "imagined communities" of nation states (1991). Kaiyuan's cultural properties, in particular the pagodas, represent the skill and ingenuity of the Chinese people and therefore deserve protection at the national level as properties of value to the nation. The current regime naturally emphasizes the technical and artistic value of cultural properties rather than their religious value. One might say then, that Kaiyuan and its cultural properties, like other temples throughout China, have been integrated into a secularized national heritage that accords with the disenchanted worldview of the Communist Party. Rather than being obliterated, as was attempted during the Cultural Revolution, these cultural properties are now incorporated into a desacralized narrative of national heritage. As part of the national heritage, they fit into the construction of national identity and into a related project of developing nationalism as a guard against foreign threats and influence.

Museumification

Although large famous temples like Kaiyuan have had an easier time with physical restoration and financial support for the sangha, their position as places of historic and cultural value typically ensures that they will attract tourists. Tourists may bring in income but destroy the tranquility that is most appropriate for regular, sustained religious practice. Beyond the influence of megaphone-bearing tour guides and their crowds is the danger of "museumification," the process by which a temple becomes directed toward display, spectacle, and secular education and, by degrees, away from worship and religious cultivation.[21] It is in evidence when shrine halls have been transformed from places of worship into display rooms for cultural and historic exhibits or souvenir shops. Such places are staffed not by monks but by workers, often young ladies in matching uniforms, who introduce visitors to the products for sale.

A range of configurations can be found at Buddhist temples in mainland China: from those not inhabited by monastics and managed by the local bureau of tourism or bureau of cultural heritage, such as Beijing's White Pagoda Temple (Baita si 白塔寺) or Yangzhou's Tianning Temple 扬州天宁寺 (aka the Yangzhou Buddhist Culture Museum 扬州佛教文化博物馆); to Ningbo's Baoguo Temple, presented as a museum of ancient architecture (古建筑博物馆) set in a scenic area (*fenjing chu* 风景区); to those that host more than a hundred monks and enjoy a high degree of autonomy, such as Mount Taimu's Pingxing Monastery in Fujian, which has no historic or cultural relics. Those directly managed by bureaus of culture, tourism, or cultural heritage inevitably have valuable cultural properties, historic value, or a parklike setting. Monasteries of exceptional historic or cultural value have an easier time attracting the support of officials and Buddhist patrons so necessary for restoration and upkeep. At the same time, they are more likely to attract tourists and the interest of the government bureaus already mentioned. Once one of these bureaus or commissions has the upper hand on management decisions, the temple will exhibit varying degrees of museumification. Museumification is at its most vulgar when a temple falls under the management of a government bureau to the exclusion of monastic leadership.

Museumification became a strategy for incorporating important religious sites into the nation-building projects of the early Maoist period. In the post-Mao period, with the reopening to "normal religion," curatorial efforts often benefit the tourist without enhancing the experience of would-be worshippers.[22] This phenomenon is more prevalent nearer to Beijing, the political center, and perhaps provincial capitals (which serve as satellites of Beijing). In 2009, three temples in particular exhibited high degrees of occupation by secular forces: Hongluo Temple 红螺寺 and Yunju Temple 云居寺, both on the outskirts of Beijing, and Longxing Temple 隆兴寺 in Hebei Province, just south of Beijing.[23]

Hongluo Temple is part temple and part park and is situated in the mountains near the Mutianyu 慕田峪 section of the Great Wall. It had at the time no resident monks, was directly managed by the local government bureau of tourism, and was staffed by a team of young ladies in white shirts. Although it is more than a thousand years old, it has no cultural relics and is almost entirely reconstructed.[24] The tourism bureau, having no cultural properties to promote, has turned instead to the piety and leisure market. Buddhist hymns are played over loudspeakers throughout the temple, incense and other religious paraphernalia are sold throughout the grounds, and a steady stream of worshippers offer incense to statues of Buddhas, bodhisattvas, and patriarchs as they tour the extensive grounds that rise to hilltops, which afford panoramic views of the surrounding mountains and the smog of Beijing. Although no monastics lived at the temple, monks or other employees with shaved heads and dressed in robes reported to work in the morning, tended some of the halls, and returned home at five.

Beijing's Yunju Temple, which boasts the world's largest collection of stone-inscribed scriptures, is managed by the Temple Administrative Commission rather than the sangha. In addition to the more than ten thousand stone sutras, it has Tang dynasty stupas and an attractive natural setting. Most of the halls of this monastery have been converted into museum-like display halls presenting interpretive exhibits of cultural relics found at the temple, such as ceramics and sutras written in blood. Employees in light-blue knit shirts tend the halls and sell items throughout the grounds; the products they sell are primarily religious in nature. When I entered the main hall, a young lady who was a member of the staff accosted me, quickly introduced the figures enshrined and immediately suggested I purchase what appeared to be a small plastic temple credit card. The cards entitled the bearer to the benefits of monks chanting in the hall for a full year. They were available in three grades, ¥50, ¥100, and ¥200; the ¥100 ($14) card would include a banner in the hall and a ritual service; the ¥200 card would include a scroll of calligraphy, an alms bowl in a tote bag, and two services. The cards and the benefits of each are also explained on large posters in multiple shrine rooms; at the bottom of these posters is the name of the entity in charge: the Yunju Monastery Temple Administrative Commission (*Yunju si siguanhui*). This is commercialization atop museumification, two related but different processes. Yunju Temple, however, unlike Hongluo, has a community of eleven monks. One who had been there for three months said simply that Yunju was not a Buddhist temple but a tourist site. Not enough monks lived there, he explained. A Buddhist temple, in other words, must be tended by the sangha. At this temple, management was instead in the hands of the Temple Administrative Commission.[25]

Hebei's Longxing Temple, also known as Big Buddha Temple (*dafo si* 大佛寺), is about a three-hour drive from Beijing in the city of Zhengding 正定. Longxing is an urban temple that functions primarily as a museum, showcasing a fabulous collection of cultural properties from the tenth century onward, including paintings, statues, buildings, and the inevitable oversized Qianlong and Kangxi steles. The abbot of the nearby Linji Temple 临济寺 explained that the sangha was working to reestablish itself there. What is likely to happen, however, is analogous to the situation at Xi'an's famous Famen Temple, which is divided into two halves, one controlled by the bureau of tourism, the other by the monks.

These three temples near Beijing, despite their unique characteristics, present one end of the spectrum of Buddhism in China today, one that would have dominated impressions of visitors throughout most of the Communist period, when only a handful of showcase monasteries were preserved to show foreign visitors. As Sarah and John Strong reported nearly fifty years ago, "Today, more than ever, Buddhist monasteries are becoming sites of historical interest, and the Chinese people who visit them see them in the way they were presented to us—as pieces of the past. ... We saw 10 of these monasteries or ex-monasteries"; some still had monks but "others are kept only as museums or historical sites" (1973, 323–324). Most of the sites they visited have been taken over by monastic management but a wide range of others remain. At one end are sites preserved as historic properties that are exclusively museums, two of which being Yangzhou's Tianning Temple and Ningbo's Baoguo Temple. Further along the spectrum are the three discussed sites of cultural heritage managed by nonclerics that continue to welcome worshippers.

Quanzhou Kaiyuan's Quest for Greater Autonomy

Kaiyuan, which is far from Beijing, not in a provincial capital, and in Fujian, a province known for widespread religious participation, presents a different model of how a famous temple full of cultural treasures negotiates with the secular powers that be. Kaiyuan provides an example of how such a monastery may negotiate a degree of autonomy from such curatorial pressures. We have already seen how the abbot has handled the administrative commission and its security guards on select occasions. The narrative of Kaiyuan's post-Mao revival under the leadership of the current abbot, Daoyuan, is a path of restoration that led to blows.

As narrated in chapter 2, Kaiyuan's recovery began soon after the death of Mao and under the small nucleus of monks who had stayed at the temple throughout the Cultural Revolution. Funding assistance came from compatriots in Singapore. Statues were uncovered and regilded and worshippers bearing incense began to return, but throughout the 1980s the halls remained under the jurisdiction of the Cultural Heritage Management Committee and the Temple Administrative Commission. The Heritage Committee had been established in the 1950s to protect and maintain the temple properties; it went underground during the Cultural Revolution, and, like the monks, reemerged after the death of Mao to assert its jurisdiction over Kaiyuan's cultural properties.[26] Tables staffed by committee employees were set up in all the halls that housed historic properties. The committee also operated a research center and a souvenir shop in one of the shrine halls, precisely the kind of shop that many lay Buddhists consider inappropriate.

The Heritage Management Committee, however, was not the only government entity with jurisdiction over Kaiyuan. As a tourist attraction and the home of dozens of monastics holding morning and evening devotions, Kaiyuan was seen fit, in the eyes of the government and the State Administration for Religious Affairs, to have a Temple Administrative Commission. The commission is a product of 1980s reform and opening policy that loosened restrictions against religion and, at the same time, established a strategy of oversight and control of the legally recognized religious groups. At Kaiyuan, the Temple Administrative Commission operated entry and exit gates, saw that the grounds were secure, and offered tour guide services; it was self-funded by the sale of entrance tickets and tour services. Entrance tickets began at 5¢/¥ in the late 1970s and slowly moved up in price to ¥10 by the mid 2000s. Members of this commission also operated two small kiosks. One of them sold photo supplies and drinks; by 2012 this vendor had begun selling small souvenirs of Quanzhou and incense. The other kiosk was staffed by a man who writes poems using the characters of one's name—a common form of art found at tourist sites.

The combined effect of these two curatorial forces was to give Kaiyuan the kind of touristy and contested feel that Gareth Fisher describes of temples in Beijing (2011). Secular employees working as curators rather than religionists sold tickets, monitored the gates, the grounds, and the halls, and sold souvenir items, which generally had nothing to do with religion, inside the donor ancestral hall. Although a similar situation prevailed at Yunju, Hongluo, and Longxing Temples, as well as many others in the mid-2000s, such as Beijing's famous Tanzhe 潭柘寺 and Jietai Temples 戒台寺 or Shanghai's Jade Buddha 玉佛寺, the situation at Kaiyuan began to change in the late 1990s.

Cultural Heritage and Temple Management

The situation progressed under the leadership of the abbot Daoyuan who, as described in chapter 2, was successful in removing dozens of individuals employed by as many as a dozen entities occupying monastic space. He also engaged in many building and renovation projects, such as replacing eight vajra guardians on the ordination platform and building the Anyang Cloister and the Hall of the Buddha's Life. What his actions suggest is his concern, as a revivalist, for restoration, even if that means rebuilding or replacing, over and above any concern for preservation, which is the organizing concern for the curators. Despite his many successes, the abbot still had to share authority with two government committees, the Cultural Heritage Committee and the Temple Administrative Commission.

In 1982, the Heritage Management Committee funded the opening of a stele rubbing and souvenir shop in the donor's ancestral hall. Rubbings were made of the various stone steles that had been collected at Kaiyuan during the curatorial turn of the Maoist period and sold to visitors.[27] This shop was a visible and prominent contributor to museumification and commercialization at Kaiyuan; it was a classic case of a shrine hall being converted to commercial uses and managed by nonmonastics, members of the curatorial forces. It was a sore point settled by Daoyuan in 2004.

Daoyuan was able to deal with the Cultural Heritage Committee in much the same way that he dealt with the other groups occupying space on temple property: he successfully argued to municipal authorities that the property belonged to the monastery and was therefore illegally occupied and he offered adequate financial compensation to the affected parties. The financial settlement for the Quanzhou Heritage Stele Rubbings shop (*Quanzhou shi wenwu beituo shangdian* 泉州市文武碑拓商店) was calculated by the relevant municipal authorities, including the Bureaus of Finance and Labor and Social Security, at ¥106,020 ($15,000). Daoyuan negotiated that Kaiyuan would pay ¥70,000 ($10,000), and that the remaining ¥36,020 ($5,000) would be paid by the Bureau of Finance. The arguments offered for the recovery of this property under monastic control were that the donor's ancestral hall was an important part of Kaiyuan Monastery and an important institution to many overseas Chinese who are Huang family descendants. The city of

Quanzhou was then applying to UNESCO for world heritage status as the starting point of the maritime silk route; the return and restoration of the donor's ancestral hall was seen as contributing to Quanzhou's application. The Heritage Management Committee vacated the hall and the remaining rubbings were sent to the city museum; the steles are said to have been distributed to various museums in the area. The donor's ancestral hall was cleaned up and returned to its state as an ancestral shrine to Elder Huang. In this way, the hall that had been used as a souvenir shop was restored to monastic control and now functions solely as a shrine. It was officially reopened in exceptionally grand style in September 2009. The three-day memorial celebration marked the 1,380th anniversary of Huang Shougong's birth and the 1,323rd anniversary of the founding of Kaiyuan; it was attended by thousands of members of the Purple Cloud Huang family from as far away as Shanghai, Singapore, and Malaysia.[28]

In addition, the other divisions of the Cultural Heritage Committee, such as the research center, have been removed from Kaiyuan's property and placed into a newly formed bureau of cultural heritage located in an office far from Kaiyuan. The transfer from curator to revivalist in the case of the Cultural Heritage Committee and their shrine hall souvenir shop has been complete and thorough—a true victory for the revivalists.

The situation with the post-Mao entity known as the Temple Administrative Commission, however, has not been so thoroughly resolved. An ad hoc decision or buyout has not been possible because, unlike all the others, the commission is part of reform-era national policy as promulgated by the State Administration of Religious Affairs.[29] Large, important temples designated as national tourist attractions or important national cultural heritage protected sites will typically have a temple administrative commission on site charged with monitoring activities to make sure that the temple acts in accordance with the law. This system of oversight is a nationally recognized system of religious management sometimes referred to as a two-track management system (*shuanggui guanli moshi* 双轨管理模式). The two tracks are management by the government and management by members of the religious order. This dual system of management creates a bifurcated institutional structure that has effectively formalized the three roles of the monastery: religious practice, cultural sightseeing, and leisure. The abbot and the monastic bureaucracy oversee matters pertaining to religious pursuits and the Administrative Commission oversees tourist pursuits. Although the monks never collected entry tickets or provided tourist services, they (especially the guest prefect) are sometimes called on to accompany high-profile visitors on their tours of the monastery. The Administrative Commission staffed entrance and exit gates, sold tickets, staffed a small office, ran a small tour office, and operated two small kiosks on the property of Kaiyuan. In these activities—selling and collecting entry tickets, offering tour guide service from the grounds of Kaiyuan, and operating tourist-oriented kiosks—the Temple Administrative Commission was responsible for institutionalizing tourism as a feature of the monastery.

After the strong-arm tactics of 2002, the abbot has managed to win concessions and clearly gain the upper hand without, however, completely dislodging the Administrative Commission. The first concession was that security guards are no longer stationed in the gates and no one is allowed to park in front of the main gate, including tour buses.[30] Another early victory was to remove commission employees from all the temple buildings except the ticket booths in the gates and two small offices; monks were henceforth responsible for monitoring all of the halls. The monks also began to take on the task of watching the gates, especially in the evening. From the late 1990s to 2009, the number of employees of the Administrative Commission had been reduced by half, from sixty to fewer than forty. The temple was also able to negotiate to receive 50 percent of the sales from entrance tickets, whereas previously they had received none. According to one estimate. this change brought in ¥4 million to the temple per year. The abbot maintained, however, that he would not sell tickets if he were able to abolish the Administrative Commission.[31] By the end of the 2000s, the abbot had effectively been able to force the commission to recognize him as an authority and win back a significant level of autonomy on behalf of the sangha.

Until 2014, the Temple Administrative Commission maintained a visible presence on the grounds at Kaiyuan in charge of selling entrance tickets, offering tours, and operating two kiosks. In February 2014, however, the abbot was successful in finally abolishing the entrance ticket, which required negotiating with the Administrative Commission. The arrangement involved the retiring of most of the Administrative Commission staff (more than thirty employees) and permitting the few remaining to continue to receive the same salary. These changes made a significant difference to visitors; the site became free for everyone all the time. Entry ticket signs are gone and visitors are able to pass through without being pressured to purchase a ticket. The main courtyard no longer houses the kiosk selling drinks and souvenirs. The Administrative Commission remains primarily in name; the abbot has succeeded in removing its visible presence and any meaningful influence. In short, the abbot has effectively ended the internal institutionalization of tourism. This has been a victory for greater autonomy. Kaiyuan has become a monastery that attracts tourists rather than a tourist site where a few monks live.

This last point is quite important because we may be inclined to place all temples that serve as tourist attractions together in the same category, a category that tends to devalue such places as tourist temples. The reality is more nuanced. Temples and monasteries in China lie along a spectrum: at one end is the temple converted into a museum, such as Tianning; at the other is Pingxing, which has practically no tourists and is dedicated to religious cultivation. Between these extremes are many others, such as the three temples surveyed near Beijing, all managed by nonmonastics who present them more as museums and less as sites of religious cultivation. Kaiyuan offers a contrast with the museumified temples as well as those managed by nonclerics; the key difference is that Kaiyuan is managed by revivalists, by its monastic leadership, who have invested the monastery with a distinctly religious atmosphere and revived liturgical calendar, as discussed in chapter 3.

Tourism remains an important feature of Kaiyuan and the monastic leadership has no interest in reducing tourist numbers. The monks accept such interest as an inevitable fact of life for such an historically rich site. Their focus is now on improving the religious atmosphere (*daofeng* 道风) of the site despite the flow of tourists; it is a focus promoted by the Quanzhou Buddhist Association, based at Kaiyuan and staffed by Kaiyuan monks now located in the offices formerly occupied by the Temple Administrative Commission.[32] The site has been thoroughly reclaimed by the monastic leadership, a victory for the revivalists, and a victory for the strong-willed abbot.

Conclusion

> People tend to revere the past and despise the present. Its fame has distracted our attention and effort away from reaching the substance of matters [in the present].
>
> *Cao Pi,* Thesis on Classic Literature

THE ENCOUNTER WITH QUANZHOU KAIYUAN MONASTERY IS an encounter with ritual, monks, material culture, mythic referents, and negotiated space. This book examines these five dimensions by elaborating their present manifestations in the context of Buddhist and Chinese history in an attempt to understand their role in the making of a Buddhist monastery. The results are an institution that is recognizable to a student of lived Buddhist history as revealed in scholarship, but strange to anyone still holding on to an idealized view of monks as renouncers cut off from society.[1] Kaiyuan has been successful in attracting legions of worshippers and a regular group of lay Buddhists whose embodiment of liturgical rites has reanimated the space with religious and salvic meaning. Busloads of tourists enjoy it as an historic and cultural treasure. For the monastic community, a basic level of tradition (robes, dharma instruments, recitation, circumambulation) has been restored. In addition, three salient features of the daily, weekly, and monthly regimen have been highlighted: *dhāraṇī* recitation, *nianfo*, and ancestor veneration. This book captures a snapshot of this site at a particular moment in time, but my efforts to connect current practices to Buddhist tradition as well as Chinese culture and history demonstrate that the five dimensions examined have historical and doctrinal precedents. The history of the site also suggests that it will continue to evolve, that its evolution will depend on socioeconomic conditions, political conditions, leadership, and—as always—dumb luck or karmic destiny. Before turning to possible futures, I explore two questions. What can we learn about Chinese Buddhist monasticism from this study? What does this study suggest about the relationship between religious and secular in Chinese religion? The first enables us to bridge the findings of this site specific study to enhance our understanding of Chinese Buddhism. The second is an important issue in the study of Chinese religion and has yet to be thoroughly investigated through the lens of Buddhist traditions. The first is addressed from an institutional point of view and as a community of practice.

The Nature of the Institution

Holmes Welch presents a model of Buddhist monasticism that he recognizes as a kind of "utopia" (1967, 3). In his conclusion, he wonders how he and other scholars could make such dramatically different assessments of Chinese monasticism: "When modern Buddhism is discussed in almost any Western book about China, we find vivid descriptions of the commercialism, illiteracy, and vice, but seldom a word about the piety, scholarship, or discipline" (408). The monastery of this study exhibits a mixture of virtue and vice, of piety and instrumentalism, of discipline and license. The monk Chen-hua wrote, "Within the Buddhist religion there are many people who claim to be engaged in spiritual exercises, but those who can truly lay aside selfish considerations, and root out all entangling affinities and treat spiritual work as a matter of life and death are *fewer than few*" (1992, 117, emphasis added). At most 5 to 10 percent of monks in a monastery have likely ever been exemplars of the tradition, psychologically and somatically focused on pursuing awakening on a basis of virtue. Similarly, at most 5 to 10 percent of monasteries have ever been widely recognized as exceptional in their adherence to the demanding requirements of traditional monastic rules (vinaya), Baizhang or other.[2] In the context of globally recognized exemplary universities and exemplary students, the percentages are even smaller.[3]

What does this say about the vast majority of monks and monasteries? Some lay Buddhists in China offer harsh critiques that the commercialism of monasteries and the worship of Buddhas and Bodhisattvas as beneficent deities are corruptions of original Buddhism.[4] One lay Buddhist also mentioned Jingkong as a genuine Buddhist who, for that reason, has been run out of China; he suggested that China was not a place suitable for genuine Buddhism to flourish.[5] Such critiques go too far. The challenges monasteries face today are not insurmountable. Room and potential for growth as centers of scholarship as well as practice are considerable. Before getting to that, though, it is important to address the critiques that have come from both monks and lay Buddhists. The most common critiques fall into two categories: on the one hand is the commercialism and commodification, on the other is the poor adherence to monastic precepts. The first can be examined more systematically and understood by looking at the institutional dimensions that are necessary aspects of any monastery.[6] The perennial issue of vice seems best understood, as with other issues, through the lens of history and what we know about past monks.

It has been known at least since Gernet's 1956 study of the economic dimensions of Chinese Buddhism that monasteries are more than sites of contemplative practice (1995). As James Robson notes, "Monasteries were, in other words, precisely where the linkage between the religious and the commercial was concretely realized" (2010b, 44). As institutions desiring self-perpetuation, monasteries have always needed to accumulate economic as well as political capital. In the past, monasteries sought patronage from elites who donated land and supported the maintenance and restoration of buildings. Today, monasteries do what they can to attract the broadest spectrum of patrons. Patterns of financing have of coursed shifted from the imperial period to the present.

A traditional source of such patronage for Kaiyuan has been the cultivation of ties with the Huang ancestral clan.[7] Members of the Purple Cloud Huang family have supported the restoration of the temple during the Ming, Qing, and Republican periods. In the fall of 2009, the Huang family (from Shanghai to the Philippines) gathered by the thousands at the official reopening of the donor's ancestral shrine, which enshrines images and spirit tablets for Elder Huang, evincing a vibrant tradition of clan-based patronage. How common and how important has such clan-based patronage been in southern Fujian? In other parts of China? These are questions for further research.

Related to the patronage required to keep a monastic community viable is the overall economic health of the community. Kaiyuan's fortunes rose with those of the city of Quanzhou from the tenth century through the thirteenth. When prosperity left Quanzhou at the end of the Yuan dynasty, it left Kaiyuan Monastery as well. Although Kaiyuan continued to attract patronage during the Ming and Qing dynasties, it never returned to the size, scope, and vitality that it had enjoyed before the Ming. Other factors are surely relevant, but a connection remains between the prosperity of the city and the prosperity of the monastery that is evinced by their imbricated histories. A link between the economic health of the community and the economic health of the monastery has also been demonstrated over the current period of restoration. During the earliest phase of revival, Kaiyuan relied on funding from overseas Chinese in Southeast Asia. As the local economy improved after

Fujian became one of two special economic zones, the donations from locals to Kaiyuan steadily increased in tandem with Quanzhou and southern Fujian's growing prosperity.

An obvious point, but one worth considering, is that money is required to support a large monastery such as Kaiyuan, which previously maintained almost one hundred monks and more than two dozen buildings on nineteen acres. Such a monastery needs to generate significant income to meet operating expenses. To do so, a healthy economy is important, but even more so is the ability of the institution to attract donors. Kaiyuan has done so by promoting its reputation as a place that is both spiritually efficacious (founding legends) and culturally valuable (material culture). This has enabled Kaiyuan to generate support from both secularly motivated tourists and officials on the one hand and religiously motivated worshippers and laity on the other. The former perceive Kaiyuan's monastic signifiers (devotional practice, material culture, founding legends) as signs of a tourist attraction (traditional culture, cultural heritage, curiosity), the latter as religious signs (religious cultivation, place of worship, site of spiritual efficacy). Kaiyuan's leadership understands this process and takes advantage of it. Rather than cynicism, this approach is in line with serving the institutional goals of the monastery, which have the greater goal of perpetuating Buddhism in sight.

Another important source of patronage operating during the imperial period as well as today is that of political elites. Several imperial courts had relations with Quanzhou Kaiyuan, conferring names on it, bestowing its monks with honors such as the purple robe, and sending it gifts. Similarly, local prefects were responsible for supporting Kaiyuan's expansions during its golden age. Although China no longer has an imperial court, a political hierarchy remains and visits by high-ranking officials (such as Jiang Zemin and Zhao Puchu) have been an important part of Kaiyuan's restoration; they function as political capital that legitimizes the current revival. The relationship between political elites and Buddhist monasteries past and present is an area for further research building on Stanley Tambiah's groundbreaking work on Buddhism and kingship (2007) and Timothy Brook's work on gentry patronage in China (1993).

Fawen brought up an additional historical defense for current economic practices, pointing out the government support for monasteries during the Tang dynasty that provided monasteries with land and resources as well as support for scholarly projects such as translations. Such monks were able to write, translate, and teach without worrying about how to support themselves and their monasteries. It is true that during the imperial period large monasteries such as Kaiyuan were supported by large landholdings that produced a stream of revenue. When these sources of funding were lost along with government support, monks were forced to find other ways of supporting themselves and their monasteries. This is the reason for greater focus on income-generating rituals, including mortuary ones.

This perspective brings up an issue of sociopolitical change beyond the issues raised by our tracing of "monastic cycles." It brings up the question of how bodies dedicated to self-realization, moral cultivation, scholarship, and cultural production maintain functionality, not to mention integrity, despite a loss of public funding. Universities around the world are struggling with this issue. It behooves the public to realize that if they value such institutions and wish them to function at their optimum levels they need to realize the role of nonprivate financial support.[8] It raises the question of what happens to institutions that are not traditional providers of goods and services, but instead for facilitating moral, intellectual, spiritual, or even medical and psychological improvement when they are not publicly funded. Without broadening the net too far, what happens to prisons or hospitals when they are not publicly funded? Chinese monasteries are another example of an institution in a very different cultural context that is facing the challenge of a competitive market. Monasteries and temples may be thought of as religious service providers, but surely something will be lost if that is all they are.

Regardless of the nature of support, religious institutions must pay the bills. More research on such mundane concerns will help bring our perceptions of monasteries in line with reality so that we are less likely to think in terms of the authentic-corrupt binary when it comes to gauging matters of monks, monasteries, and money.[9] The reality is that monasteries have always needed to generate funds; fundraising methods have been forced to adapt to the loss of landholdings and monasteries are today experimenting with various methods. Rather than automatically assuming all forms of commercial exchange as corruptions, researchers should make an effort to understand the culture of temples and religious sites on a case-by-case basis. This study, for example, indicates an important distinction between sites that are managed by the sangha for the sangha and those managed by state agencies or private investors. Future accounts of the current revival should distinguish between sites run by secular authorities, commercialized sites run by the sangha or private investors, sites dedicated to practice with few tourists, and sites such as Kaiyuan that strike a balance in accommodating the demands of tourism with the goals of providing liturgical and devotional activities and services.

A Community of Practice

This is the first study of Chinese monastic Buddhism of its kind. Presentations of Buddhism are most often focused on ethical principles, doctrinal features and debates, and personal cultivation or transformation, emphases that parallel the classic exposition of the Buddhist path as a threefold training in ethics, wisdom, and meditation (*śīla, prajñā, samādhi*). The Buddhism at this site has been found to not particularly emphasize any of these three, at least not in any way anticipated by most studies of Buddhism. This site is focused on monastic practice centered around the five assemblies, lay Buddhist recitation (*nianfo*), liturgical traditions, and ritual assemblies to generate and distribute blessings, and ritual care of ancestors.

The five assemblies are the only form of communal cultivation for the monastics, one that does not privilege or feature seated meditation, strict ethical discipline, or scholarly inquiry, the forms one familiar with Buddhism would most expect. Monks attending daily services can cultivate the kind of mental tranquility and focus essential for success in Buddhist meditation but it is no substitute for formal meditation (*dazuo* 打坐). The most salient feature of the daily services apart from the critical role played by dharma instruments and the institutionalization of Pure Land Buddhism is the prominence of *dhāraṇī*, an important, but unappreciated, feature of Chinese monastic Buddhism.

The most visible beneficiaries of the traditions revived at the site are local lay Buddhists who are afforded the opportunity to *nianfo* with monks twice a week and on the lunar twenty-sixth. Although it may not be the ideal form of cultivation in the Buddhist *imaginaire*, it helps us understand what is meant by the often repeated fact that Pure Land Buddhism is the most popular form of Buddhism.[10] My participation in *nianfo* services enabled me to better understand how the serpentine recitation element in particular could function as a form of meditation, with the potential to lead to *samādhi*, as tradition claims (Stevenson 1995). Methodologically, I emphasize the importance of recognizing the somatic dimension of sensing and knowing that can provide valuable insights such as the way serpentine recitation affects body, speech, and mind. At this site, *nianfo* is the primary form of cultivation, institutionalized in daily, weekly, and monthly services that include it. This is why one monk accurately described Great Kaiyuan Chan Monastery as "Chan on the outside, Pure Land on the inside."

The third feature, the prominence of liturgical services and ritual assemblies to generate blessings and eliminate disasters, is a form of religion focused on more immediate practical goals, which is an important mode of Chinese religious practice in Adam Chau's fivefold scheme of "doing religion" (2011). Along very similar lines, Thomas Dubois, in his study of religion in a North China village, identified the two purposes of temples as community protection and individual supplication or devotion (2005, 33, 49). Such forms of religious behavior are prominent among worshippers and lay Buddhists seeking blessing and protection. This type of religiosity regularly takes form with rituals enacted to eliminate disasters and bring benefits, performed at regular intervals throughout the year and on demand. Monks have a scaffolded view of this instrumental form of religiosity. On the one hand, it is a dharma gate that leads to deeper engagement with the tradition; on the other, it is worldly and not suitable for one seeking liberation. They consider seeking blessings to be a form of religiosity associated with popular or vernacular religion.[11] Its prominence at an established institution alerts us to the danger of assuming that institutional religion matches clerical ideals; as Leonard Primiano advises, even so-called elites practice or make room for vernacular forms of religion (1995).

This study also draws attention to ways in which the material culture of temples and monasteries enables basic forms of devotion and supplication as well as larger ritual services. Material culture and founding legends are deployed together to promote the site as a place of spiritual efficacy. The claims of spiritual power—along with daily and annual schedules marking heterogeneous time, material culture, and preternatural legends generating heterogeneous space—demonstrate the resilience of traditional cosmology. This suggests that religious sites in China and perhaps elsewhere may serve as places of resistance to or sites disruptive of projects of modernity. The persistence of symbols representing the cosmology of sympathetic response present another failure of the totalizing discourse of secular modernity.

Another feature is the prominence of rituals to care for ancestors at interment, at anniversaries of death, and at certain points during the year. These practices are represented by the underground columbarium, the hall of merit full of spirit tablets and long-life tablets, ritual offerings of paper houses and other offerings, along with the regular burning of spirit money and gold paper. All of these functions and services have become a principal source of income for the monastery and are an important feature of the site. Such features have come to dominate impressions of Buddhism in Japan, which has been denigrated as "funeral Buddhism" (Rowe 2011, 7–8). At the end of the nineteenth century, J. J. M. de Groot estimated that making sacrifices to departed ancestors made up at least three-quarters of the religious practice of the people in Xiamen (1884, 22). Ritualized ancestor veneration is certainly the most common form of practice among worshippers at Kaiyuan Monastery. Its prominence is attested by the robust use of the furnace to make offerings, such that it had to be enlarged and fitted with a filter. Large offerings of paper houses as part of funerary rituals were conducted an average of one hundred times per year in 2006. Like the seeking of blessings, the veneration of ancestors is another form of vernacular religion that invites us to reassess the nature of the Buddhist tradition in China.

The monastery, then, does not emphasize the "three trainings" in anticipated ways, but what about the three treasures, the three refuges: Buddha, Dharma, and Sangha? The presence of the Buddha, as mentioned in chapter 5, is traditionally understood to be through enshrined statues or stupas. Given the five monumental Buddhas in the central hall and Vairocana,

Amitabha, and Maitreya in or outside the ordination hall, that the site is Buddhist is unmistakable. The Buddha is present in grand style.

How about Dharma? At first it might seem that given a lack of organized scripture study or dharma talks that the dharma is missing. But according to the emic view the Dharma, like the Buddha, is built into the structures of the monastery and its schedules. Chapter 3 opens with the soundscape of the morning bell and drum leading to the block and bell leading to morning assembly. The instruments are collectively known as dharma instruments. Life at the monastery is organized and framed by dharma instruments. As the abbot of Nanputuo says, "dharma instruments can bring the faithful to the dharma."[12] The assemblies of monks are known as dharma assemblies (*fahui* 法会). Senior monks are known by the laity as dharma masters (*fashi* 法师). The counsel they provide is, broadly speaking, Dharma. So, although from an outsider perspective little Dharma is taught, from an insider view Dharma is unavoidable. It may be helpful to recall the trope of 84,000 dharma gates. Dharma is everywhere and even more so at a Buddhist monastery.

The third treasure is Sangha and the monastery, with dozens of robed monks and hundreds of robed laity, is a vibrant home of a sangha. Once again, it may not be the sangha we might imagine, with complex lines of support, commitment, and dedication, but it is most certainly a sangha, especially for the hundreds of lay women who fill the main hall week after week. So, although this monastery presented several unanticipated forms of practice, it clearly remains a lively representation of the Buddha and Sangha, the Dharma being available in liturgical form and through informal individual initiative.

Building the Sangha with a Lack of Qualified Dharma Leaders

Chapter 4 reveals the fundamentally private and diverse nature of advanced religious cultivation, represented by the trope 84,000 dharma gates. Laity using this phrase is one thing, but monks are supposed to have leaders, elders, to help point the way. The turmoil sketched at the end of chapter 1 and the nature of recovery in chapter 2 (focused on recovery of property and institution building) explain why so few monasteries have qualified spiritual leaders, leaders capable of training monks in one or more of the three monastic specialties—ethical discipline, scholarship, or meditation. Chapter 1 ends with the closing of Kaiyuan and occupation of its grounds by the community during the Cultural Revolution. Chapter 2 describes the restoration of religious practice focused on recovering properties, renovating and rebuilding structures, and reestablishing traditions of worship. The few monks with more knowledge and experience were consumed with rebuilding traditions from the ground up. An emphasis on rebuilding traditions of teaching and learning at this site is yet to be established. In addition to leaders, a cohort is also important to provide support, encouragement, and motivation. These aspects of recovery have come more quickly to some monasteries than others. It is reasonable to assume that such leaders and cohorts have never been common, much less ubiquitous.

Critiques of the immorality of Buddhist monks is practically a literary genre in China, though Confucian critiques are largely formulaic and generally increase in tandem with the growing power of Buddhist monks (Brose 2014, 76–77). Of greater credibility are the critiques of monks themselves, such as those embedded in Zongshou's popular thirteenth-century book of rules for young monks, *Daily Life in the Assembly* (*Ruzhong riyong*).[13] Writing of his motivation, Zongshou begins by lamenting that monks who have no one to criticize and correct them will both be difficult to reform and bring ruin to monasteries. Adding, "I frequently see such transgressions and evils, which are commonplace before my very eyes," he thus feels compelled to lay out these detailed rules of behavior and decorum. Zongshou admonishes would-be monks, "From morning to night, to avoid every particular offense, one must straightaway obey every single provision." These short prefatory remarks likely tell us more about actual daily life in the assembly than the rest of the text. It is no easy task to discipline body and mind moment to moment day in and day out. Small wonder that transgressions are common in the absence of discipline, critique, and guidance. This is the situation at Kaiyuan and many other sites. Monks are left to their own devices and inclinations. It is a formula sure to lead to mixed results, including, predictably, monks who fail to maintain the precepts. The key element is the leadership and authority concentrated in the person of the abbot. As a case in point, it was the abbot who finally purged the married monks. It will also be the abbot who puts an end to drinking alcohol, eating meat, and having sexual relations. For now, though, the emphasis with respect to monastic discipline has been on showing up for events and organizing, participating, and enacting the ritual and liturgical program. This includes keeping one's head shaved and robes clean and thus keeping up appearances for the public. As long as monks tend to these liturgical duties, rituals, and ceremonies, they may remain in the good graces of the abbot. It seems to be for this reason that most of the monks at this site are said to consider being a monk a job rather than a vocation.

This situation makes it difficult for the few monks who seek to cultivate a path leading to insight. When ninety monks were at the monastery, five to seven were in this category; now that the total is fewer than fifty, the number is between three and five. These well-intentioned monks are left to work things out without guidance. This was made clear in a conversation held in 2019 between me, the head monk, and a monk striving to practice.

We were having a wide-ranging conversation about various topics including charity and the social influence of Kaiyuan. I asked about the kind of dharma gate Kaiyuan offers, adding that the making of offerings (*gongyang*) seemed more like folk religion. I asked whether Kaiyuan also provided higher forms of education. The head monk, whom I call Dawen, defended these beginner-level beliefs (*chuji de xinyang*) in which people make offerings in exchange for blessing and protection (*baoyou*) as a form of *upāya* (*fangbian*) or "kind gate" (*shanmen*) that brings people in. "They first have to come in," he said, "then they can learn something." At this point, Deyi, an earnest monk who had been listening, joined the conversation. He asked about the training available for monks, "Higher-level spiritual training, that is suitable for monks but not the laity. Does Kaiyuan provide any chances to advance?" He answered himself, "No." Dawen says he cannot say that there is none, but that it takes time. It takes decades of study.

Deyi clarified that monks have the opportunity to practice on their own (*geren*), but what is missing is group (*jiti*) practice. He said plainly that such higher-level spiritual training is not available at Kaiyuan. Dawen agreed, but explained that group practice is not possible because everyone is different, the good and bad are intermingled (*liangyou buqi*). According to Dawen, some are advanced, some are beginners, some are fast, some are slow; they cannot practice together. In the end, he made two points. First, there is no way to know the influence of seeds that are planted. In other words, the devotional and liturgical atmosphere and practices have an influence and self-effort and struggle have an influence; it is impossible to measure the final impact of such small seeds. Second, it is important to have a teacher or master (*shifu*) to advance.

To demonstrate the first point, he related the story of a visitor who had never drunk tea until he came to Kaiyuan. He visited Dawen a few times and drank tea then went into the tea business at Mt. Wuyi. Who would have imagined such an impact from brief visits? The second point was illustrated with a reference to practicing calligraphy. Dawen spoke of his lack of progress from working on his own, and of the rapid progress possible with a good teacher. Alas, he said, it is very difficult to improve without a teacher.

Tying it all together, Dawen spoke of 84,000 dharma gates; given how many paths there are to take, there is a path for everyone. Deyi expressed his wish that some day advanced spiritual practice would be available at Kaiyuan. In the end, he acquiesced to the lonely struggle of self-cultivation, noting that it was imperative to choose a method and a path. One could study broadly, but for serious practice it was necessary to choose a path and stick to it. This bit of guidance was general but also critical. In the end, the conversation reinforced previous ones about the lack of qualified leaders to rebuild traditions of communal cultivation.

An analogy for Buddhist monasteries in post-Mao China might be Chinese restaurants in the United States. Certainly authentic food can be found in big cities with large Chinatowns, but the typical Chinese restaurant, found by the thousands across the country, is generally opened by individuals with no special knowledge or training of restaurant quality, much less high Chinese cuisine. What they produce, though, is passable as Chinese food in America. Most Americans never know that the food in these restaurants is but a shadow of what is available at the average restaurant in China. Similarly, monasteries in the first phases of restoration have been managed and staffed by elderly or underqualified monks producing passable results but lacking expert dharma masters to satisfy the most demanding or knowing critics.

Buddhist monasteries have been rebuilt and restored by the thousands in China, producing results that look, smell, and sound like Buddhist temples. Most worshippers and uncritical laity can get what they are searching for from these restored sites of liturgical and devotional practice; no doubt the situation is worlds better than it was fifty years ago, when places of religious practice were closed altogether. Most monks are also satisfied with the state of their temples; it is only the minority, generously 5 to 10 percent of the monastic population, who are looking for more advanced training. These monks are joined by scholars and serious laity in their less than glowing assessment of the state of Buddhist monasticism. It is up to these monks, laity, and scholars to work to improve systems of discipline, practice, and scholarship.

Religious and Secular in the Revival of Religion in China

In chapter 6, the Chinese nondichotomous view of spirit and matter and human and divine is noted as part of the examination of preternatural events. Preceding from these presuppositions, Chinese notions of religious and secular do not neatly map onto Euro-American understandings. Kristopher Schipper writes, "In everyday life, religious activity had no particular name or status, since—as the French sinologist Marcel Granet was fond of pointing out—in China, religion was formerly not distinguished from social activity in general" (1993, 3). John Lagerwey begins his presentation of the culmination of three decades of ethnographic research into Chinese religion with the following words: "China is a religious state and Chinese society is a religious society" (2010, 1). He then elaborates, "China is a space and all space in China is conceived of as sacred, that is, inhabited by divine energies which, because they sustain us, must receive in return our sacrificial recognition" (17). Richard Madsen writes, "Religion was secular. The secular was religious" (2014, 16). He continues. "when the institutions [temples] are being used for this-worldly, 'secular' purposes, they still point beyond the immediate, the instrumental and pragmatic" (23). Raoul Birnbaum observes that "the Chinese Buddhist world has never been separate from Chinese society" (2003a, 113). Scholars of Buddhism, Daoism, Confucianism, and folk traditions have all noted the inseparability between the religious and the secular in Chinese traditions.[14] From within Chinese Buddhist tradition, we have countless expressions of nondualism, of collapsing the modern Euro-American categories of religious and secular. As a monk from Kaiyuan put it, "noumena and phenomena are nondual."[15] One of the strongest statements appears in the *Platform Sutra* of Huineng: "Buddha dharma is in the world, we awaken without leaving the world; leaving the world to find *bodhi* [wisdom], is like seeking the horns of a rabbit."[16]

A nondichotomous view does not entail the obliteration of difference. From the Buddhist point of view, nonduality (不二) is not monism; the two sides remain distinct yet their nonduality remains. This approach is represented by the "two truths," that of worldly convention and the ultimate (the empty nature of all phenomena). What is relevant to this study is the way that religious practice and religious pursuits connected to a nexus of texts and traditions that may also be identified as religious are very much a part of the world, but also directed beyond it, beyond immediate, instrumental concerns. For this book, religion is defined as words, thought, and actions deploying or informed by symbols of ultimate value (such as buddha or nirvana) tethered to cosmological conceptions (karma, rebirth). Based on this understanding, repeatedly chanting the Buddha's name is an explicitly religious activity. It is in some sense simultaneously an action, speech, and thought involving reference to a symbol of ultimate value, namely, Amitabha Buddha, which is supported by a tradition and body of texts and teaching (Pure Land sutras) detailing a cosmology of soteriological significance (rebirth in the Pure Land). The special (that is, religious) nature of this practice is revealed by the problematic nature of it in the modern period and the anxiety practitioners feel about it's being potentially perceived as superstitious (*mixin*) (X. Yu 2009, 14). The solution to the *nianfo* problem advised by the modern monk Juzan (1908–1984) was to express the devotion through laboring with peasants as a replacement to *nianfo*, once again collapsing this explicitly religious action into an indisputable worldly or secular activity. Rather than think that a modern reformer monk like Juzan is simply out of step with mainstream Chinese Buddhist tradition, consider instead the traditional emphasis on labor as a form of practice in Chan as represented by the tropes "chop wood, carry water" and "when hungry eat, when tired sleep." So, yes, despite a collapsing of difference, activities, speech, and thought recognizable as explicitly religious remain and, though manifest within the world, are directed and informed by ideals that point beyond the world.

Even if the Chinese did not traditionally think in terms of a distinct separation of religious and secular spheres, the modern government thinks in terms of the freedom to believe or not believe in religion, religious sites that must be registered, religious activities that must be in accord with the law, and so on, thus delineating a sphere for religion separate from nonreligion. It is within this new political paradigm that I speak of curators as agents of secularization, seeking to disaggregate religious meanings from religious objects, for example, and revivalists, seeking to reinvest objects and spaces with religious meaning and activity. This book has sought to demonstrate how it is possible for curatorial forces to gain control of a former temple and rebrand it as a museum of culture or architecture, how clerical and nonclerical managers negotiate hybrid identities, or how clerics gain control and dictate the terms of revival.

Throughout part 3 of this book, I argue that values that could be glossed as "secular" and "religious" have worked in tandem to broaden the appeal and base of support for Kaiyuan. Strategically leveraging its secular and religious values, Kaiyuan has attracted the support of secular elites as well as popular support among the religious. The dual promotion of the monastery as a nationally protected site of cultural relics and place of spiritual efficacy smoothly integrates with the three social identities described in chapter 5, demonstrating the practical value of this integrated approach. Although the abbot has focused on recovering and clearing properties, and building and renovating, he has also focused on continuing the revival of traditions such as lunar twenty-sixth and buddha recitation. It is not the only path for a Buddhist monastery in China, but it has worked well given the community and political support available for an early and robust revival of liturgical Buddhism in post-Mao China.

Ian Reader's *Pilgrimage in the Marketplace* seeks to show "how pilgrimages are embedded in a context of markets, consumer activity, publicity and promotion, and how they operate not just in the marketplace but through it" and "challenge the tendency in pilgrimage studies to portray the dynamics of the marketplace as disjunctions from pilgrimage's 'true' and sacred nature" (2014, 8, 14). He starts out by emphasizing how the worldly and the religious, and the spiritual and commercial, are "crucially bound together" (16). As he goes on, he takes exceptionally strong reductionistic positions that appear to leave no difference between plastic trinkets sold outside a shrine complex and blessed amulets inside it. He takes Michael Stausberg to task for positing a *continuum* between souvenirs and relics, related to the continuum between tourists and pilgrims (Stausberg 2011, 209). Reader writes, "the very idea of a continuum implies some form of *differentiation*. ... This is where I part company with him [Stausberg]" (2014, 149, emphasis added). I am interested in considering what may be lost in such an analysis. I am also interested in how the regnant neoliberal paradigm may be providing hermeneutic logic or operating in the background without critical reflection. What Reader is suggesting is the homogenization of a rich and variegated cultural phenomenon. His reductionistic view, although it helpfully highlights the role of market economics in contemporary pilgrimage, runs the risk of distorting the revelatory potential of pilgrimage and emergent noninstrumentalist possibilities that may result from the encounter. Those potentials and possibilities remain part of the worldview of monks and laity at Kaiyuan and Buddhist monasteries throughout China and elsewhere. In the language of one Kaiyuan monk, common concerns of peace, health, wealth, and avoidance of calamities is secular (*shisi de* 世俗的) and a monk should be concerned with leaving the three realms of samsara, which is explicitly *not* worldly or secular. It remains important to distinguish religious and secular motivations, if only because clergy do.

But are there reasons from a scholarly etic point of view to maintain these distinctions? Are there reasons of relevance to monks, laity, and nonbelievers alike? I propose that there are. Secularism as part of modernity is understood as leading to the disenchantment of reality in order to provide "direct access" without the mediation of "myth, magic, and the sacred" (Asad 2003, 13–14). Throughout his study, Reader relates ways in which pilgrimage in Japan and elsewhere has been commercialized and sanitized of miraculous tales without recognizing this as a "project of modernity" being instituted by people with power. He summarizes his observations: "Pilgrimage is thus made ever more into a commodity coterminous with modern convenience and consumerism while being 'liberated' from awkward questions of faith, belief and troublesome locals that might put off prospective visitors" (Reader 2014, 188). Here he speaks of pilgrimage being "liberated" from questions of faith, belief, and troublesome locals; elsewhere he speaks of this process as "sanitisation and transformation" (186). He seems to accept sanitization as a fact rather than as an ideological project carried out by priests, business people, scholars, politicians, and others. Who benefits from this transformation and what is lost? What is at stake?

At stake is maintaining conceptions, activities, motivations, and intentions that point beyond mundane concerns and are disconnected from instrumental reason. Such conceptions, intentions, and so on remain a vital resource for responding to the excesses and dangers of consumerism, industrialization, and free-market economics that otherwise dovetail in a bond of unquestionable authority under the logic of neoliberalism. Religious traditions exist in a material world under practical economic, social, and political arrangements and constraints, but they also function as a wedge against being fully consumed by the logic of instrumental reason, the drive to consume, or, even, biologic impulses. For me, this is related to the need to safeguard public access to art, music, education, and nature as goods that awaken and enliven our heart-mind-body. Neoliberal logic seeks to eliminate the sphere of public goods and services reducing them to sectors of a universal free market, free to be bought and sold, which leads to (artificial) scarcity, hoarding, and loss of access. Religious traditions, especially Chinese and Indigenous, are important resources for resisting consumerism and repairing a severed connection with the earth and other sentient beings and living more gently within limits.[17] Scholars who seek to reduce phenomena to commercial logic and market forces, collapsing religious and secular distinctions, run the risk of hampering imaginations to create alternatives to regnant destructive paradigms. In our current geohistorical moment, ethnography and other scholarship that examine society and culture, in my view, is called not only to deepen understanding of human culture and society but also to provide openings for their future flourishing.

The Future of the Current "Revival"

> Recent years have seen the restoration of the ordination platform and the dharma hall. Fortunately, the main hall has also been renovated. It seems like a time of renewal. We should respond to this opportunity at our best even though we do not know whether this recovery will be partial or complete. If we are concerned only about old property not being returned rather than practicing virtue, then, even if all the buildings and property were recovered, what would be the point? If we can diligently practice virtue, then even in shabby buildings and old rooms we can still sit cross-legged (that is, meditate). A person can live like a snail in its shell, in a grass hut that can just accommodate the length of seven feet (that is, a human body). Moreover, all people have Buddha nature, everyone can shine. Who knows whether another elder Huang may reappear today. "It all depends on the self-exertion of you gentlemen!" (Yuanxian 1643, I.19b-20a)

These words, written by Yuanxian at the end of the Ming dynasty during a period of renewal could with a few changes be applied to the Kaiyuan of today. Again, Kaiyuan, along with the mainland Chinese sangha as a whole, is enjoying a period of restoration and renewal. Again it is not known whether the recovery will be partial, piecemeal, and compromised or complete, comprehensive, and stable. What is known is that as long as the monks are focused on generating income, recovering lost property, renovating, and rebuilding, they will neither have the time nor likely the mood, to diligently practice. Diligent practice requires only the crudest accommodations and such practice itself is traditionally the root of patronage. Yuanxian invokes Kaiyuan's founding patron, Elder Huang, as a representative of all those who sponsor the recovery and maintenance of the sangha and suggests that if the monks will do their best they may attract such patronage. Patronage, in other words, material support, was an abiding concern during the late Ming dynasty restoration and remains an abiding concern of monasteries being restored throughout China today (Jing 2006).

Recovering property, rebuilding halls, and materially maintaining the sangha have been the focus of Daoyuan and most others during the current period of revival in China from Xi'an to Shanghai and Beijing to Yunnan. Some speak of the current emphasis as a phase in which the focus is on "hardware" (building and maintaining the physical plant) and they look, with optimism and hope, to a future where they can emphasize and develop the "software" (the education and training of monks, nuns, and laypersons).

The Quanzhou Kaiyuan Monastery will more than likely remain an important center of popular devotional practices as well as an important tourist destination for the foreseeable future. It will thus maintain a dual identity along the lines described. The only chance for greater development of the monastic software would seem to be in a change of leadership with a different vision of how to develop the talent of the sangha. Examples like Bailin Monastery in Hebei, Pingxing Monastery in Fujian, Gaomin Monastery in Jiangsu, Guangdong Yunmen Monastery, and Puhua on Mt. Wutai indicate that in post-Mao mainland China monastic leadership actively cultivating future dharma masters does exist. All of these monasteries have leadership that have reestablished traditions of Buddhist practice, study, and discipline and are widely respected in China. Whether such examples are multiplied or not, history will remember this period as one of a massive restoration of religion in China. It will be attested to by thousands of stele commemorating the building of shrine halls bearing the dates of the early years of the twenty-first century.

It may have been tourist brochures and the promise of cultural treasures that brought a given visitor to Kaiyuan, but once inside the gate, bereft of tacky tourist stalls, presented with monks quietly tending halls or leading laypersons in chanting, as individuals offer incense and prostrations inside venerable halls under the shade of ancient trees, they are overcome with a feeling beyond the instrumental wish to snap a photo of the pagodas and check Kaiyuan off their list of sites to see. This feeling drives them to make an offering of incense, make a donation, or say a prayer, or just take it all in. In these acts they may have another feeling, one of the promise of a transcendent power capable of granting one's wishes, of lightening one's burdens, or of simply being part of something larger. They may feel immediately (and temporarily) relieved of some burden and leave more content than when they arrived. In short, their heart-mind has been temporarily set at ease. Some accept the traditional cosmology suggesting that this location has a special spiritual power that in turn may grant blessings; others have simply temporarily left the mundane details of life behind. By coming to Kaiyuan and witnessing its ties to an ancient tradition, such guests are awakened to the possibility of ancient traditions remaining present and efficacious.

Notes

INTRODUCTION

1 Personal communication, Quanzhou, November 2006.

2 From 2006 to 2009, about ninety monks permanently resided at Kaiyuan; including visiting monks pushes the number to one hundred. By 2019, that number had dropped to less than fifty. In October 2007, Fuzhou's illustrious Yongquan Monastery on Gushan maintained approximately the same monastic population. Smaller temples in China may have only a handful of resident monks; Nanputuo Monastery in Xiamen, which includes an Institute of Buddhist Studies (*foxue yuan*), on the other hand, houses some six hundred (Ashiwa and Wank 2006, 337).

3 These properties detailed in subsequent chapters include a Tang *dhāraṇī* pillar (ninth century), early Song dynasty *stupas* (twelfth century), monumental pagodas from the late Song (thirteenth century), sculptures from the Yuan (fourteenth century), a main hall and statues from the Ming dynasty (seventeenth century), and the ordination hall, sculptures, and bells from the Qing (nineteenth century).

4 Another recent study is Berthe Jansen's (2018) analysis of Tibetan Buddhist monastery rules in the context of Buddhist doctrine. She focuses on the textual tradition after her plan to study a single Tibetan monastery ethnographically did not work out because of access issues in eastern Tibet. The book is an important contribution to Tibetan monastic studies.

5 Welch focuses on *model* monasteries, namely, the meditation hall at Jinshan 金山寺, the most illustrious of its day, the innovative Buddha recitation (*nianfo* 念佛) hall led by the most renowned Pure Land master at the time Yinguang 印光 (1861–1940) at Suzhou's Lingyan Temple 灵岩寺, and the code of rule for the well-run Gaomin Temple 高旻寺 (1967). I have critiqued this along with an assessment of Welch's study elsewhere (Nichols 2017, 259).

6 This famous monastery in many respects is not ordinary, but it is average in terms of its status as a site under pressure to revive traditions while accommodating tourists and worshippers led by an abbot not known for developing innovative interpretations, practices, or institutional features that mark other monasteries. Monasteries not ordinary in this sense include remarkable efforts in research (Fagu shan) or mobilization of lay Buddhists for charitable work (Ciji), or Buddhist education (Foguang shan), or summer camps (Bailin), or a seminary (Nanputuo), or home of the national Buddhist Association of China and the publication *Voice of Dharma* (Guangji si).

7 Steven Covell's study of Temple Buddhism similarly examines sites that serve as the "public face" of Buddhism in Japan (2005).

8 The terms Lefebvre uses are "representations of space," "spaces of representation," and "spatial practice."

9 See also Knott 2005, 23–24.

10 The scholarship on religion in post-Mao China seems to be growing every year. Three books on Tibetan Buddhism in post-Mao China are Charlene Makley (2007), Melvyn Goldstein and Matthew Kapstein (1998), and Ester Bianchi (2001). Books on popular forms of religion include Adam Chau (2006), Jing Jun (1996), Erik Mueggler (2001), Ole Brun (2003), Thomas Dubois (2005), and Guo Yuhua (2000). Kenneth Dean (1993, 1998) has written on Daoism. Studies of Catholicism include Richard Madsen (1998) and Eriberto Lozada (2001). Dru Gladney (1996) has written on Islam. Among the edited volumes on different religions that include discussion of Buddhism are Yoshiko Ashiwa and David Wank (2009), Mayfair Mei-Hui Yang (2008), Daniel Overmyer (2003), Julia Pas (1989), and Adam Chau (2010). Other works include a monograph on Han Buddhism by Gareth Fisher (2014); two books on Dai Buddhism in Southwest China, one by Thomas Borchert (2017) and another by Sara Davis (2006); and the groundbreaking edited volume *Buddhism after Mao,* edited by Ji Zhe, Gareth Fisher, and André Laliberté (2019).

11 In 1979, four special economic zones were established on an experimental basis: Shenzhen 深圳, Zhuhai 珠海, and Shantou 汕头 in Guangzhou Province and Xiamen in Fujian Province. The experimental nature of the zones quickly faded as they met with rapid success; the model was eventually expanded across China's east and southeast coasts.

12 The germ of China's current policy on religion can be traced to 1945, when Mao called for the protection of the freedom of religious belief and disbelief (Welch 1972, 2). Within two years of founding of the People's Republic of China in 1949, Mao's notion of freedom of religious belief was articulated in Article 5 of the Chinese People's Political Consultative Conference, which guaranteed the freedom to believe or not to believe religious ideas. The justification in the eyes of communist ideology was that people were still backward and in a low stage of development and would leave religious beliefs behind as they advanced in understanding (class consciousness) and technology (means of production) (Welch 1972, 3–4). It was pointed out that after thirty years of socialism in the Soviet Union remnants of the old religion remained; it was therefore unreasonable to attempt to wipe them out by force (Welch 1972, 5). Although this policy of tolerance (in a more restrictive sense than found in modern liberal democracies) abruptly ended with the onset of the Cultural Revolution in 1966, it was revived under the leadership of Deng Xiaoping in 1979.

13 In 1980, Michel Strickmann recognized the religious importance of Fujian and suggested that it holds the most promise for understanding lived Chinese religion. He wrote, "Sophisticated studies of the Fukinese cultural area may well have a stimulating effect on sinology in general. They will certainly help clarify the role of religion at the local level, and this in turn should aid us in understanding the function of religion in Chinese history. ... Perhaps it is the too frequent abstraction of sinology from living realities that in part accounts for our backwardness in coming to grips with Chinese religion. In the perspective of local society, religion has been the vital cohesive force rather than an academic enigma" (1980, 248). By the Fukinese cultural area, Strickmann had in mind Taiwan, Malaysia, and Indonesia, which are home to significant numbers of immigrants from Fujian. Foster Stockwell, who published the first survey of religion in post-Mao China, is even more specific: "The starting point for any survey of religion in China, ancient or modern, should be Quanzhou" (1993, 5). His reasoning is the great diversity of religion historically found in Quanzhou, certainly among the most diverse in the world, including all the Chinese traditions as well as Hinduism, Islam, Manichaeism, and Nestorian Christianity.

14 The programs were Woodenfish in China programs organized by Yifa in 2009 and 2012 and the University of British Columbia program in China organized by Chen Jinhua in 2009.

15 By 2009, I had reached what in sociological research is known as "data saturation" or "theoretical saturation." Follow-up research verified this and added more exempla.

16 But see Rethmann 2007. For more on the aesthetics of religious scholarship and balancing analytical and logical argument with imaginative interpretation in religious scholarship, see Gold 2003. I agree with Gold that any "imaginative" interpretation *must* be balanced by rational analysis and reason.

17 The earliest known collection is the Qianlong edition of 1765, which was updated in 1830 (Daoguang period of the Qing) and printed, according to Ecke and Demiéville, in 1866. The edition now available, which I have consulted, is a modern printed book in two volumes (1,870 pages) published in 1989.

CHAPTER ONE: THE MONASTIC CYCLE

1 The primary source used in this compilation of Kaiyuan's history is Yuanxian's seventeenth-century *Gazetter of Quanzhou Kaiyuan Monastery* (*Wenling kaiyuansi zhi*). I have also cross-checked this source with Mengguan Shi's (aka Dagui) fourteenth-century *Biographies of Purple Cloud Bodhisattvas,* one of the primary sources Yuanxian used in his composition of the *Kaiyuansi zhi* (Dagui 1929). These sources were supplemented by municipal, prefectural, and provincial gazetteers and inscriptions. Among the gazetteers consulted were the eighteenth-century [Daoguang] *Jinjiang County Gazetteer* (*Jinjiang xianzhi*), the eighteenth-century *Quanzhou Prefectural Gazetteer* (*Quanzhou fuzhi*), and the twelfth-century *Gazetteer of Fuzhou* (*Sanshan zhi*). Epigraphical sources include steles from the Tang, Ming, and Qing dynasties and in situ inscriptions from the Song, Yuan, and Qing dynasties. Some material on the late Qing and most of the information on the Maoist period come from oral interviews with antiquarians and amateur historians in Quanzhou. Information from interviews was cross-checked with inscriptions or other archival materials to the extent possible; anything uncorroborated is indicated in the main text as such.

2 Yuanxian 1643, I.1a-b. References to the *Quanzhou kaiyuansi zhi* within the body of this text are abbreviated in the text as *Monastic Gazetteer* or *Kaiyuan Gazetteer* and cited in the notes as Yuanxian 1643. For a modern printed edition of the *Kaiyuan Gazetteer,* scc S. Zhou 1999.

3 At this time during the Tang dynasty, peasant families were assigned on average about thirteen and a half acres per couple and more land allotted for children. This was done so as to provide a fair basis for the per capita tax system. "Only one-fifth of the allotment could be held permanently, *usually as a mulberry orchard for silk culture*; the remainder of the land had to be returned to the government in case of death, or the cultivator's exceeding the given age limit" (Morton and Lewis 2005, 95, emphasis added). This leads me to suspect that Huang may have been a rather average landowner in his day, a point that has not been suggested in other literature. Dates for Elder Huang are from *The History of the Purple Cloud Huang Clan of Xiangtang* [Putian] (Quan Guo Dang Hui 1984, 280; personal copy of Huang Yushan).

4 Historical records (gazetteers, inscriptions, and so on) agree on the timing (686) and the name (Huang Shougong) of the donor, for example, *Quanzhou fuzhi,* book 16, 18a-b; *Jinjiang xianzhi* 69,1650; *Bamin tongzhi,* 1160; Huang 1967, 279. The earliest source, an 897 inscription by Huang Tao, however, suggests a date of one year later. Huang Tao's 897 *Quanzhou Kaiyuansi fodian beiji* 泉州开元寺佛殿碑记 (Stele record of the Quanzhou Kaiyuan Monastery Buddha Hall) suggests the year 687 (the third year of Chuigong). Huang Tao was a poet and official who composed many inscriptions glorifying the works of Wang Shenzhi.

This inscription, preserved in the *Quan tang wen* 全唐文 (Collected Works of Tang Literature), includes exaggerations and other suspect information mentioned in the discussion of the five buddhas in the main hall so it is not clear that it reflects a more accurate date despite its greater antiquity. See Dean and Zheng 2003, 4–6, inscription #4. The *Bamin tongzhi* agrees that the founding year is 686, but rather than designating this as the second year of Chuigong, records the date as the third year of *sisheng* 嗣聖 of Tang Emperor Zhongzong 唐中宗; although Sisheng's reign began in 684, it lasted less than a year, because he was deposed by his mother, the later Empress Wu, in favor of his younger brother Ruizong. See also C. Wang 2008, 11n21.

5 The emperor's decree forbid princes, dukes, and other landowners from presenting petitions in their own names for the transference of their own lands to be used as monasteries or monastic estates. See Gernet 1995, 122.

6 I translate *zunsheng* 尊胜 as "venerated site" because the cloister was built in the place where lotus are said to have miraculously bloomed in mulberry trees. It could also be translated as "great" or "honorable" "victory" given that the phrase is used to translate the Sanskrit term *vijayā*.

7 According to Chou Yi-liang, the Empress Wu had ordered that temples be established in each prefecture and capital named Great Cloud (Dayun 大云) in 690 and it was these that were changed to Kaiyuan in 738 (Chou 1945, 293n47). This may be true, but no record of Quanzhou Kaiyuan's having been named Great Cloud exists.

8 Services were to be held on the fifteenth day of the first, seventh, and tenth months of the lunar year and memorial services for deceased emperors. In prefectures that maintained a Longxing monastery, the ceremony for deceased emperors would be held there rather than at the Kaiyuan (Ch'en 1964, 223).

9 The date of this inscription is not known but I believe it to be from the Yuan dynasty because that is when a list of six unique sites is recorded as being articulated, one of which is the "imperially bestowed Buddha image." Furthermore, it is in a different style than other Ming dynasty sculptures at the main hall. It appears to have been saved from an early building and incorporated into the Ming building. It was present when a survey of antiquities was conducted in the early years of the People's Republic but was not listed; Wang Hanfeng 王寒枫 notes that its origin is unknown (2001a, 5).

10 Imperial recognition through such means as name boards was a way to survive political suppressions of Buddhism (Schlütter 2008, loc. 1161).

11 In 884, Wang Chao entered Quanzhou, laid siege, ultimately gained control of Quanzhou, and served as prefect. In 944 and 945, the Empire of Min collapsed and most of the Wang family was eradicated. Thus my years for Wang rule in Fujian are from 884 to 945. For more on this period in Fujian history, see Schafer 1954; Clark 2006, 1991; So 2000; Sima Guang's *Zizhi tongzhi*; *Jinjiang xianzhi*; *Wuguo gushi*; *Bamin tongzhi*.

12 *Wuguo Gushi* 2:10a.

13 Huileng was a principle disciple of the important Chan Patriarch Xuefeng Yicun 雪峰义存 (J. Seppo Gisōn 822–908).

14 *Wudeng quanshu* 五燈全書 X81, no. 1571.15. For a translation of four koans associated with Yanbin, see Ferguson 2000, 304–305.

15 此地古称佛国, 满街都是圣人.

16 Pearson et al. 2002, 34. Two detailed studies of the pagodas examine their artistry and architecture: Ecke and Demiéville's *Pagodas of Zayton* (1935) and Wang Hanfeng's *Quanzhou's East West Pagodas* (1992).

17 The construction of Kaiyuan's first ordination platform was initiated in response to Emperor Shenzong's (1067–1085) call for universal tonsure and ordination (*pudu* 普度) (Yuanxian 1643, I.3a-b). *Pudu* would appear to refer to a *pudu*

sengni 普度僧尼, which was a periodic call for "universal tonsure and ordination" that the government might use for celebratory reasons in which restrictions on ordinations were lifted for a time. The *pudu* was a policy governing religious ceremonies (personal communications, Jianying 2007, Dazhuo 2007).

18 A well was in fact discovered under the platform during the Qing dynasty. The entrance to it lies to the back of the current ordination platform but has been sealed off.

19 The five-story Stone Lake pagoda appears to have been used as a model for Zizheng's pagoda.

20 Greenstone is a type of diorite, an intrusive igneous rock.

21 Gustav Ecke and Paul Demiéville provide an excellent account of the narratives depicted in these carvings which demonstrate a broad knowledge of Buddhist traditions and Indian Buddhist literature (1935, 80–81, 92, 42–65).

22 The *Kaiyuan Gazetteer* refers to Tianxi, not by name, but as a "preaching monk from Tianzhu 天竺." His being so described has led some to speculate that he was an Indian monk because Tianzhu Guo 天竺国 means India. Li Yukun 李玉昆 notes this was the view presented in *The Port of Quanzhou and Ancient Maritime Communications* (*Quanzhou gang yu gudai haiwai jiaotong* 泉州港与古代海外交通) (1988, 31). This unsupported notion is also part of an oral tradition in Quanzhou. The identity of this monk, however, can rather securely be identified with Tianxi 天锡 (aka Chuzhuo 樗拙, 1209–1263) from Kaiyuan's own Tianzhu cloister (Tianzhu *yuan* 天竺院) who is named in three local records as the builder of the top story of the east pagoda. These records are the *Jinjiang xianzhi* 69, 1652; *Quanzhou fuzhi* XVI, 20a; and the biographical section of the *Gazetteer of Xuefeng Temple* (*Xuefengsi zhi* 雪峰寺志). See also Li Yukun 1988, 31. Demiéville suggested that *Tianzhu* might refer to Tianzhu temple near Hangzhou. Demiéville also noticed the name of Tianxi 天锡 in the *Gazetteer of Quanzhou Prefecture,* but thought that Tianxi 天锡 was most likely a misprint of Tianzhu 天竺 (Ecke and Demiéville 1935, 92). The evidence from these three sources above for the existence of a Tianzhu cloister at Kaiyuan leads me to favor the interpretation that the monk is Tianxi from Kaiyuan's Tianzhu cloister.

23 Yuanxian 1643, I.35b-36b. The Langzhong 郎中 of Qiao Langzhong 乔郎中 is a title that indicates the director of a bureau or section of a ministry. Thus it seems that Qiao held a higher position before becoming prefect of Qizhou 蕲州 and thus had the power to influence affairs at Quanzhou Kaiyuan.

24 For the most complete study of Song dynasty Chan monasticism and the development of transmission lineages, as well as different approaches to Chan meditation, see Schlütter 2008.

25 For more information on Kaiyuan's cloisters, see the first chapter of the *Kaiyuan Gazetteer*.

26 The three cloisters that remained after 1285 were the Venerated Site Cloister, the East Pagoda Cloister, and the Cloister of Bliss.

27 Hearing of his reputation, the emperor bestowed on him the title Foguo Hongjue 佛果弘觉 (Buddha Fruit Great Awakening). Yuanxian 1643, I.43a-b, biography #43.

28 For an account of the eight auspicious sites, see chapter 6.

29 Kenneth Dean points out that, although Quanzhou's trade declined, the broader southern Fujian region maintained and developed trade contacts with Southeast Asia. Many scholars have not appreciated how harbors shifted and the trading port moved from Quanzhou, eventually to Xiamen (2010, 236–239).

30 Nanjing Tianjie Monastery was then the principal monastery in the Ming capital of Nanjing; it was also the location of the Buddhist Worthies Department (Shanshi yuan) established by Taizu in 1368 as the central coordinating office of Buddhist affairs; this department later became the Central Buddhist Registration (Senglusi) and was known as such by the time Zhengying was sent from there to

Quanzhou Kaiyuan. For more on the Buddhist Worthies Department during the Ming dynasty, see C. Yu 1981, 166–170.

31 Yongle was a disciple of the "Lamaist" monk Halima 哈立麻 (De-bshin-gsegs-pa), but is most famous for his building of Beijing as the Ming capital and his association with the maritime voyages of Zheng He 郑和. The Yongle emperor moved the capital from Nanjing to Beijing and set to work on a new imperial palace, the Forbidden City. Zheng He is recorded to have stopped at Quanzhou to pray in one the mosques, but otherwise had no strong connections with the city whose once busy international port was no longer in operation. Two books about Zheng He suggest that Emperor Jianwen 建文帝 temporarily and secretly took refuge at Kaiyuan in 1403 before taking a boat to Southeast Asia. See *Jiechu hanghaijia Zheng He* 杰出航海家郑和 by the Taiwanese writer Chen Shuiyua 陈水源 and *Zheng He xia xiyang* 郑和下西洋 by the Japanese scholar Chitoshi Uesugi 上杉千年.

32 Lay societies that practiced vegetarianism and the "release of life" (freeing of animals being sold for food) were popular throughout the Ming dynasty and often raised money to build such ponds as a place to release fish, ducks, and turtles. For background on these societies, see C. Yu 1981, 75–81.

33 Lamley 1990, 263–265. For more on mid- and late Ming disorder in Fujian, see Ng Chin-keong 1972, 1971. T'ien Ju-K'ang discusses the depredations of Fujian monasteries during this period (1990, 92–95).

34 Yuanxian 1643, II.35a-37b. Jinjiang was left with eleven *qing* six *mu* eight *fen*; Nan'an was left with nine *qing* one *mu*; Huian was left with nine *qing* eighty-five *mu* six *fen*; Tong'an lost none, leaving forty-four *mu* four *li* one *hao*; Anxi was left with none; Yongchun was left with two *qing* fifty-two *mu*; Xianyou was left with four *qing* twenty-seven *mu* four *fen* three *li*; in Putian, Longxi, and Changtai all holdings were sold.

35 C. Yu 1981, 154. Ascending the throne at the tender age of nine, Shenzong was first guided by his able minister Zhang Juzheng 張居正 (1525–1582).

36 At other temples, this structure is referred to as a spirit wall (*ying bi* 影壁). See Prip-Møller 1937, 7.

37 *Xianfu* 宪副, that is, *fu du yushi* 副都御史.

38 Huang Wenbin's inscription records that Huang Shougong had four sons and they moved to the "four Ans," thus establishing the Huang clan throughout southern Fujian. The four Ans are Anxi 安溪, Huian 惠安, Nanan 南安, Tongan 同安. See Zhou 1999, 4.37.

39 For a discussion of the Huang lineage's relationship to Kaiyuan's Donor Ancestral Hall, see C. Wang 2008, 195–208.

40 This earlier monastic record is no longer extant but was derided by Yuanxian in his 1643 preface to the *Kaiyuan Gazetteer* as being poorly researched (2a).

41 Zheng Zhilong was a pirate, merchant, naval commander for Ming and later for the Qing. Born in Fujian, he was baptized a Catholic in Macau. He married a Japanese woman named Tagawa Matsu and lived in Japan, Taiwan, and China. He is famous now as the father of Zheng Chenggong 鄭成功 (1624–1662), who as a Ming loyalist attacked Nanjing from 1658 to 1659 after it had been taken by the Qing and in retreat took Taiwan from the Dutch in 1662, where his successors remained until it was captured by the Qing in 1683 and made part of Fujian. The Dutch had been in Taiwan since 1624, when they founded a naval and trading post.

42 A Tamil language inscription indicates the presence of a temple dedicated to Shiva; it is not known whether these sculptures would have been from the same temple, but it is a distinct possibility (Guy 2010).

43 For more on these and other Yuan dynasty artifacts in Quanzhou, see Guy 2010.

44 Zheng Zhilong's iron incense burner is alluded to in the poem "Ode to Quanzhou" *Yong Quanzhou* 咏泉州 by the famous twentieth-century poet Guo Moruo 郭沫若 (1892–1978). It is now located in Kaiyuan's Buddhist Museum.

45 Some of its large stone columns may date from the Tang or Northern Song dynasty; these columns exhibit entasis (swelling) such as in Greek architecture. Columns with tapering at the top and base are known in Chinese architecture as shuttle (*suo* 梭) columns and are known to be from Tang times. I am not aware of how rare such columns exhibiting entasis are in East Asia. Tracy Miller has identified such columns dating from the eleventh century at the Sage Mother Hall 聖母殿 of the Jin Memorial Shrines (Jinci 晋祠) in Shanxi (2007, 110–111). Such columns may also be found at the eighth-century main hall or *kondo* of Japan's Toshodaiji Buddhist Monastery 唐招提寺 in Nara. This monastery was founded by the Chinese monk Jianzhen (J. Ganjin) 鑒真 or 鑑真 (688–763) in the eighth century who traveled to Japan to construct an ordination platform and establish a valid ordination lineage. My working hypothesis would be that this artistic technology traveled with Buddhism from Greek communities in what is now North Afghanistan, linking the ancient Mediterranean to the medieval far east.

46 On Zhang Dai, see Brook 1993. All of this was built on the growing integration of literati culture and Buddhism in the late Ming (Brook 1993; J. Wu 2008).

47 Jiang Wu sketches the literati turn to Buddhism from the mid/late Ming to the early Qing (2008, 100–105). See also Brook 1993, 121–126.

48 For more on the Obaku school, the third sect of Zen in Japan, see Baroni 2000; J. Wu 2015.

49 Ruhuan 如幻 1664.

50 This *dhāraṇī* is still recited during morning and evening services at Chinese Buddhist monasteries.

51 Iconographically, this incarnation of Guanyin typically has eighteen arms and three eyes; philosophically, it is one who saves humans. The three eyes represent saving (*jiu* 救) humans from three principal obstacles, delusion, karma, and suffering (*huo* 惑, *ye* 业, *ku* 苦), aka Dorje Tsundi. The temple was located in the northeast corner of Kaiyuan Monastery and formally named the Cundī Chan Forest 准提禅林 (Ruhuan 如幻, 1664). It is likely that the replica of the ordination hall that was part of the Cundī Chan Forest served as a model for the rebuilding of the actual ordination hall two years later.

52 Nian Bensheng 粘本盛, 1666, *Chongjie ganlu jietan beiji* 重建甘露戒坛碑记 (Stele Record of the Reconstruction of the *Ganlu jietan*), in the hall of the ordination platform, in Dean and Zheng 2003, 214–215, inscription #216. Weilin also compiled the 泉州开元寺话录 *Quanzhou Kaiyuansi hualu* (A Record of Utterances of Quanzhou Kaiyuan Monastery).

53 For the most detailed study of Yingyuan, founder of the Obaku, school, see J. Wu 2008. For more on the Obaku school, see Baroni 2000; Foulk 1988; Collcutt 1981, 215.

54 Biographical information on Muan, see Shen Yushui 1990.

55 These poems are preserved in Shen Yushui 1990, 73–75. The groupings of Kaiyuan's eight phenomena and six sites are at least as old as the Yuan dynasty.

56 Yinyuan had first traveled to Nagasaki, where he founded monasteries before being asked to establish the head monastery outside Kyoto on imperially bestowed land.

57 Shen Yushui 1990, 3. For an excellent study on Yinyuan, the founder of the Obaku school, and the early days of the school, see J. Wu 2015. For more on the art of these early patriarchs of the Obaku school, see Weidner and Berger 1994, 80–82.

58 In 1701, six chains at the top of the west pagoda were replaced each weighing 170 *jin*. Lin Zhaochang 林肇昌, 1701, *Kaiyuansi xita tike* 开元寺西塔题刻 (Inscription on the West Pagoda of Kaiyuan Monastery). The inscription is found on the central column of the west pagoda (see also Dean and Zheng 2003, 227, inscription #231). In 1719, twenty-one Buddha statues in the east and west pagodas

were remade by the military envoy Ya Huiqi 雅讳奇 by an unnamed monk. Anon. 1719, *Kaiyuansi xita tike* 开元寺西塔题刻 (Inscription on the West Pagoda of Kaiyuan Monastery). The inscription is located on the center column of the west pagoda. See also Dean and Zheng 2003, 237, inscription #243.

59 Huang Zigong Yi 黄子公议, 1729, *Kaiyuansi huangshi citang beiji* 开元寺黄氏祠堂碑记 (Stele Record of the Huang Surname Ancestral Hall within Kaiyuan Monastery) located in Kaiyuan's Tanyueci. See also Dean and Zheng 2003, 242–243, inscription #250.

60 *Chongjian Kaiyuansi beiji* 重建开元寺碑记 (Stele Record of the Reconstruction of Kaiyuan Monastery). *Jinjiang xianzhi* 69, 1651–1652. See also Dean and Zheng 2003, 314–315, inscription #324.

61 Cai 2017. In support of oral testimony from different sources.

62 Dates for Miaoxiang are from Huang Yushan (personal communication 2009). Other information was confirmed by the in situ inscription above the entrance of the ordination hall (Cai 2017; Daoxing, personal communication, 2008).

63 The seizure of monasteries for education uses was proposed by the Qing intellectual Huang Zongxi as early as 1662 (Welch 1968, 10–11). For good summaries of the temple destruction and anti-superstition campaigns, see Goossaert and Palmer 2011, 44–63; Nedostup 2009, 11–16. For the most thorough treatment with case studies, see Katz 2014, 17–67.

64 Daoxing, interview, 2009.

65 From the 1927 preface by Wu Hengchun 吴亨春 (Yuanxian 1643, 2.2b).

66 See also Ch'en 1964, 448.

67 此处生莲垂拱二年, 支令勿坏以全其天.

68 Yuanying fashi jinian kan bianzuan weiyuanhui 1954, 12. Yuanying invited Zhuandao and Zhuanwu to Ningbo to study the orphanage and school that had been established there.

69 C. Wang 2008, 254. Zhuandao served as abbot of Kaiyuan, Yuanying served as the provost (*dujian* 都监), and Zhuanwu served as the general manager (*jianyuan*). Zhuandao, it seems, quickly returned to Singapore in an effort to raise funds.

70 Yuanxian 1643, second preface, 2a.

71 I read Yu as saying that ordination ceremonies were held twice in each year at both locations (他曾兩度在泉州開元寺和承天寺開壇傳戒). Johannes Prip-Møller wrote a detailed account of a three-platform ordination ceremony held during this period at Jiangsu's Longchang Temple 隆昌寺 (1937, 298–339). The account includes descriptions of the ceremonies taken from the diary of a participant, an account of the ritual procedures and the three types of precepts (novice, monk or *bhikkhu*, and bodhisattva); also included are images of the ceremony as well as reproductions of ordination certificates.

72 Much has been published in Chinese on Hongyi. In English, Raul Birnbaum offers a study of Hongyi's autobiographical writing (2003b).

73 For more on the content of Hongyi's lectures at Kaiyuan, see Chen and Su 2015.

74 Hongyi's notions of correct standards for monks centered on observance of the Vinaya and criticized monks performing rituals for fees (Kiely 2016, 223).

75 This Miaolian is not to be confused with another famous Miaolian abbot of Fuzhou's Gushan and the earliest monk known to travel from China to Southeast Asia in modern times.

76 余予未命终前, 临命终时, 既命终后, 皆托妙莲师一人负责, 他人无论何人, 皆不能干预. Sealed with Hongyi's chop, dated October 7, lunar August 28 (Miaolian et al. 1986).

77 The first relic pagoda was built where Hongyi passed away in Xiaoshan congzhu 小山丛竹 (formerly the site of one of Neo-Confucian master Zhuxi's schools) in 1943; it was lost during the Cultural Revolution. A second relic pagoda was built

for him at Quanzhou's Mount Qingyuan in 1952 and rebuilt in 1962 (S. Luo 2001, 67–68).

78 One of the undetonated missiles used to be kept at Kaiyuan but was moved at some unspecified time (oral interviews). I told the monks that they could put it on display as evidence of a kind of miracle similar to a missile I had seen at the Cathedral of San Lorenzo in Genoa, Italy but they saw no sense in displaying artillery at a monastery.

79 Xue Yu documents the Chinese Buddhist involvement in the war with Japan (2005).

80 Guangjing's remains are marked by a stone stupa behind the Patriarch's Hall at Kaiyuan and his photo is enshrined in the hall of patriarchs.

81 Daoxing, interview, 2009.

82 For more on the founding and early directives of the Religious Affairs Bureau, see Welch 1972, 30–35.

83 For more details on the formation and duties of the BAC, see Welch 1961, 5–9.

84 Daoxing, interview, 2009.

85 For more details on Communist policies and their effects on the Sangha during this period, see Welch 1972, 42–81; see also Kiely 2016; Xue Yu 2009.

86 At the same time, monks were allotted the same amount of land as peasants but were required to cultivate it themselves, not manage it as landlords as they had in the past. For this reason many monks simply returned to lay life. A case study of Suzhou Buddhism in the 1950s details the destruction of Buddhism in that city (Kiely 2016).

87 A former student and resident of Kaiyuan's school said that monks remained at Kaiyuan throughout the 1950s and early 1960s. He was too young then to have a clear memory of that time, but suggested about thirty monks being there during that period. I also received other information that suggests this to be quite plausible.

88 Interview with former student, 2009.

89 Daoyuan and Chuanmin 2004, 3.

90 This figure is also maintained by David Yu (1971, 54).

91 Figures on restoration and preservation work were collected by Welch from Chinese and Japanese reports of the day (1972, 147–149).

92 Welch also notes that as material historical artifacts Chinese Marxists thought they should be analyzed to understand the stage of history to which they belong (1972, 145).

93 A stele was erected near the east pagoda commemorating the history and repair of the pagodas in the summer of 1952, a project that was supervised by the Quanzhou Municipal Construction Department (泉州市建设局).

94 Holmes Welch noted the Communist period trend toward preservation. See Welch 1972, 145–168; see also Bush 1970, 326–329.

95 Fujiansheng wenguan hui gongzuo zu 1962, 2–3.

96 Fujiansheng wenguan hui gongzuo zu 1962, 2.

97 Smaller and more valuable artifacts were stored in the sutra library (second floor) and larger items such as bronze or iron bells and stone statuary in the dharma hall, on the first floor (Daoxing, interview, 2009). A prominent Qing dynasty artifact in the main courtyard of the monastery today is a stele inscribed with a poem in the Kangxi emperor's calligraphy. This was recently moved from behind the dharma hall where it was located in the 1950s to the front of Kaiyuan's courtyard. It provides no historical information, is simply a copy of a poem by Mi Fu 米芾 of the Northern Song written in 1702. The stele makes no mention of Kaiyuan and appears to be one of the artifacts moved to the monastery in the 1950s. A stone statue of Guanyin bodhisattva dating to 909 was found during a construction project and moved to Kaiyuan in 1964. Today this statue remains

inside the hall of the land and water temple (*shuilü si*) behind the new guest hall. Information on dates are taken from a small sign posted above the statue.

98 For more on Longxing Temple, see X. Zhang 2000.

99 Daoyuan and Chuanmin 2004, 3.

100 Some have said the trees were from Xiamen's Nanputuo Monastery, but I have not been able to confirm this.

101 They are already many times larger than their mother tree so it is possible that they are being fed by the "amrita well" beneath the ordination platform (Z. Zhang 2003, 20–21).

102 Puti 2000, 21. The article includes a biography of Yuanzhuo and an overview of his accomplishments.

103 Putian is a neighboring city and the destruction of its most important religious sites during the Cultural Revolution was considerable (Dean 2010, 244).

104 Local legend has it that Mayor Wang did telephone Zhou Enlai, but Wang said that he did not need to do so, he only needed to offer to do so if they did not take his word for it.

105 Wang Jinsheng, interview, October 25, 2006, Quanzhou. For more on Mayor Wang's revolutionary background see Z. Lin, Ceng, and J. Lin 2006.

106 "Release of life" is a common Buddhist practice in which captive animals such as birds, turtles, or fish are purchased and released.

107 "Vegetarian auntie" is a local tradition of women who become dedicated Buddhist practitioners and most notably maintain a vegetarian diet, but do not shave their heads. It began at the end of the Qing dynasty and remains an important component of the local Buddhist community. Another term is "pure auntie" (*qinggu* 清姑). Master Hongyi respected this tradition and gave them teachings. For more on this tradition in the Quanzhou region, see Ashiwa and Wank 2019.

108 Interview, Quanzhou, 2007.

109 Interview, Quanzhou, 2006. Xue Yu has written about monks being forced to marry but remaining at temples during the early years of the Maoist period (2009, 233).

110 In the *Guang'an zhanglao yongsi jinianji* (2003), Chuanxi wrote of a group of thirteen living at Kaiyuan during the Cultural Revolution. Given that Chuanxi was living there at the time, his published recall needs to be taken as the most accurate available.

111 I am indebted to Daoxing for the names and dates for these monks (personal interview, 2009).

112 Daoxing, interview, 2009. Daoxing spoke of the monks as using the interest (*lixi*) earned by this deposit, but Huang Yushan said that the money was kept in the sutra library and deposited in a local bank in the 1980s and that little was left.

113 According to a report in the Guang'an memorial booklet, Guang'an also lived in the sutra library (Daoyuan and Chuanmin 2004, 35).

114 Welch 1972, 418–424. It would now be possible to corroborate some of these numbers in fieldwork, as I did in Quanzhou.

115 This was also the case at Tibet's largest monastery of Drepung, where monks continued to live (discreetly) throughout the Cultural Revolution (Goldstein 1998, 25). Other anecdotal evidence indicates that monasteries in other parts of China continued to house monks throughout the Cultural Revolution; a more comprehensive account requires further research. According to a small book I was shown during fieldwork in Quanzhou, Pingxing Monastery in the mountains north of Fuzhou had ten monks continuing to live devotional lives during the Cultural Revolution.

116 A catch-all category of the four bad elements (*silei fenzi* 四类分子); the others are landlords, antirevolutionaries, and wealthy peasants.

117 Huang Yushan, interview, 2009; Daoyuan and Chuanmin 2004.

118 The Qilin has the head of a dragon, scales of a fish, hooves of an ox, and tail of a lion (S. Huang 2005, 34–35).

119 Sometime during the post-Mao period, they were moved to the main location of the Maritime Museum.

120 I have seen this stone and the plum blossom image. Oral history from neighborhood resident Huang Yushan. In 2007 or 2008, the stone was returned to its original location at Chengtian Monastery.

121 Chuanxi 2004; Huang Yushan, interview, 2006.

122 See, for example, Birnbaum 2003a; Mitchell 2008, 234; Hahn 1989; Thompson 1996, 134–143; Robinson, Johnson, and Bhikkhu 2005, 215–218; MacInnis 1989. For relatively balanced accounts of Buddhism under communism from the 1950s to the Cultural Revolution, leaving the future open to question, see Welch 1972; Bush 1970, 297–347. The only exception I am aware of that provides a continuous narrative of continuous monastic presence from the Republican period, throughout the Cultural Revolution and into the current revival is the study of the Tiexiang Nunnery in Chengdu by Esther Bianchi (2001).

123 Huang Zhongzhao 2006, 75–79.

124 Yang Fenggang provides a sketch of degrees of state restriction of religion from extremes of eradication and monopoly to free market and oligopoly (2006, 95–96).

125 Morton Schlütter has documented how the Song government sought to supervise and regulate monastic Buddhism (2005).

126 The most complete study of gentry patronage of Buddhism in China is Timothy Brook's *Praying for Power* (1993).

CHAPTER TWO: THE POST-MAO REVIVAL

1 Ashiwa and Wank focus on clerics associated with Nanputuo, but do not look at Quanzhou (Ashiwa 2000; Ashiwa and Wank 2005).

2 The Gang of Four was blamed for inciting the worst excesses of the Cultural Revolution. The leader was Mao Zedong's last wife, Jiang Qing 江青; her associates were Zhang Chunqiao 张春桥, Yao Wenyuan 姚文元, and Wang Hongwen 王洪文.

3 In 1984, he shaved his head and went to Nanshan Monastery to live for three years.

4 Daoxing is currently abbot of both Ci'en Temple 慈恩寺 and Amitabha Temple 弥陀寺 on Mount Qingyuan in Quanzhou. He and Chuanjian both left Kaiyuan when Daoyuan became abbot to avoid a conflict in seniority that would have been natural between them. Within the monastic order, seniority is determined by years as a monk. Both Daoxing and Chuanjian were ordained before Daoyuan, making them his seniors. It would not have been proper for them to serve under Daoyuan as abbot; so, after what has been vaguely described as a struggle (*douzheng* 斗争), both left Kaiyuan ahead of Daoyuan's succession as abbot in 2000. Daoxing first went to Chengtian Monastery, where he served as the general manager (*jianyuan*), and then in 1999 or so to Mount Qingyuan, where he began to recover the properties associated with the two temples. Chuanjian is from Xiamen. He became a monk at Xiamen's Nanputuo Monastery in 1984; he went to Zhangzhou Nanshan Monastery where he met Daoxing.

5 Huang Yushan, interview, Kaiyuan, 2009.

6 In 1983, the same status was bestowed on Xiamen's Nanputuo, Fuzhou's Gushan and Zhangzhou's Nanshan Temples.

7 Wu Songbai, interview, 2009.

8 For a biography and study of Zhao Puchu's contributions to Chinese Buddhism, see Ji 2017; for an account of his humanistic Buddhism, see Ji 2013.

9 Wu Sonbgai, interview, 2009.

10 Daoxing, interview, 2009.

11 Daoxing, interview, 2009. A different source (nonmonastic) claimed that between ten and twenty monks were resident in 1995.

12 The main hall of Xuefeng Monastery had been preserved during the Cultural Revolution because images of chairman Mao had been hung on its walls.

13 Chengtian Monastery was restored from 1984 to 1990 with ¥10,000,000 in funds collected by venerable Hongchuan from Singapore (Wu Songbai, interview, 2009).

14 The statue is no longer in the hall of patriarchs and its location was unknown at the time of my research.

15 Benzhi, interview, 2006.

16 Yoshiko Ashiwa explores the relations that several of these monks have with Xiamen's Nanputuo Temple, where Zhaunfeng had served as abbot (Ashiwa 2000). Ashiwa connects the revival of Xiamen Nanputuo Monastery to its overseas connections with Southeast Asia as well. Those networks are very similar to those of Quanzhou Kaiyuan because Zhuanfeng was associated with both monasteries (Ashiwa 2009, 60–62).

17 According to Wu Songbai, Kaiyuan was renovated during this period with most funds coming from domestic sources, ¥4,600,000 (interview, 2009). This, however, was not mentioned in the 1993 stele inscription, which named the Singapore temples and monks as contributors. This stele was damaged by a falling banyan tree in the 2010s and apparently discarded.

18 Chuanjian, interview, 2009.

19 The funeral was conducted by Venerable Benxing 本性, a vice president and secretary general of the Fujian Buddhism Association. Benxing now serves as the abbot of Fuzhou Kaiyuan Monastery. Venerable Xuecheng 学诚 was then the vice secretary general of the Chinese Buddhist Association as well as the president of the Fujian Buddhism Association and the director of the Committee for Venerable Miaolian's Funeral. Chen Tianshuang 陈田爽, vice director of the Fujian United Front Work Department and Yu Xianfeng 余险峰, then vice director (*fu juzhang*) of the Fujian Bureau of Religious Affairs served as vice directors for the funeral committee. Miaolian's remains were cremated at Xuefeng Temple at Mount Yangmei 杨梅山 in Nan'an on November 12.

20 It is possible that changing his official residence (*hukou*) from the village of Qingniu to the city of Quanzhou may have been among his motivations in becoming a monk. He mentions that he was able to do this by becoming a monk.

21 Chuanjing was respected by local lay Buddhists and had many disciples. I was present for his eighty-ninth birthday celebration in 2006. He was then hard of hearing and did not speak much, but a layperson said that he was highly respected and could once attract a crowd to listen to him teach. Chuanjing became a monk during the war with Japan in 1937 in Hui'an Keshan Temple 科山寺. He first lived at Kaiyuan in 1942, then returned to his home temple to become abbot in 1949. He returned to Kaiyuan in 1979 and lived there until his death in 2017.

22 Daoyuan was visited by the then vice president of the Fujian Bureau of Religion, Yu Tingzhang; both of them speak fondly of their time together in Brazil. Having good relations with high-ranking officials who have jurisdiction over religion in Fujian is part of Daoyuan's skill set.

23 Ashiwa recounts how, in the early 1990s Xiamen's Bialudong Temple compensated the army with ¥485,000 to recover property it had lost (Ashiwa 2009, 25).

24 They relocated to another part of the city and are now a successful landscape and gardening business.

25 Amounts given in dollars are approximate and the exchange rate used to calculate varies from the late 1990s (¥8 to $1) to 2009 (less than ¥7 to $1).

26 The book was first published by Kaiming Books in 1929. For more on Feng Zikai, see Tarocco 2008.

27 Sometime between 2017 and 2019, the artifacts from the Buddhist Museum were moved into the Bensheng Yuan and the former buildings of the Buddhist museum became used as part of the Hongyi Memorial Museum.

28 Debating the necessity of replacing statuary pertained especially to replacing the eight vajra protectors (interviews, Quanzhou, 2006, 2009).

29 This group independently meets without the participation of monks; they previously met in a building behind the abbot's quarters and were moved to this space in 2007 or 2008.

30 Although the Republican period orphanage has been a prominent part of Kaiyuan's recent history, it seems that an attempt is being made to dissociate it from Kaiyuan's past. An article was published in 2000 in the national Buddhist periodical *Fayin* to mark the completion of renovations by Daoyuan. It provided a sketch of Kaiyuan's history, mentioning details of the Republican period restoration under Yuanying, Zhuandao, and Zhuanwu (dharma hall, pagodas, and so on) but omitting any mention of the orphanage and school (Wen 2000).

31 Personal communication, 2006: 信念和毅力应对所有的挑战.

32 Personal communication, 2006: 坚定的信仰调伏自心.

33 Personal communication, 2006: 弘法为家务, 利生是事业.

34 Personal communication, 2006: 方丈的作用就是做一些人事的协调工作.

35 Personal communication, 2006.

36 Yoshiko Ashiwa and Davis Wank have written the most detailed studies of the revival of Nanputuo (see Ashiwa and Wank 2006, 2009; Ashiwa 2009).

37 Gareth Fisher notes a similar situation with Beijing Guangji Temple, which also had a Republican period school and orphanage that closed in the post-Mao period even as the temple donated money to build a school far away in Sichuan (2016). Fisher argues that this could be understood as moving from serving local society to a more translocal and utopic-universal charity. In the case of Daoyuan, he has donated money both within and beyond the home province of Fujian.

38 On Buddhist charities in post-Mao China, see McCarthy 2019. For its Buddhist value, see McCarthy 2013; for more on the relationship between charity and party-state goals and initiatives, see McCarthy 2019.

39 "Branch" temple is used informally to refer to temples established by monks resident at or associated with Quanzhou Kaiyuan, not temples with a formal relationship. These branches do not have formal obligations or relations with Kaiyuan.

40 The Republican period phenomenon referred to is building temples in the local region, not temples overseas that became sources of financial support. In other words, the small temples built around town are not formally associated as subtemples of Kaiyuan. They are functionally independent. Naturally, if cooperation is needed for a large ceremony at Kaiyuan, for example, monks can be expected to help as needed.

41 Gareth Fisher writes about the phenomenon of monks raising funds to build temples and establish themselves as their leaders in post-Mao China (2008).

42 In 2009, I was told that seven or eight monks lived there and that Chuanjian was the head monk.

43 Wu Songbai, interview, 2009.

CHAPTER THREE: COMMUNAL RELIGIOUS LIFE

1 Similarly, Pi-Yen Chen describes Chinese Buddhist liturgical chants as "the most pervasive traditional elements in religious life" (2010, ix).

2 Over the course of my fieldwork, the schedule changed in various ways. By 2019, the morning service began at 5:10 a.m.

3 The morning service may have begun at 4 a.m. in previous years. I was also told that in the winter it is moved to 5:00 a.m. I attended *zaoke* in December of 2006 that began at 5:20 a.m.

4 In 2006, the evening service was moved back to 5:30 p.m. in an effort to enable more monks to attend the evening service after finishing duties such as watching halls.

5 In winter, he begins half an hour later, at 4 a.m.

6 I was able to detect this by carefully reviewing my continuous video recordings. Pi-Yen Chen also notes it (1999, 119).

7 Major defilements or *kleśa*s include greed, delusion, pride, jealousy, and so on.

8 A similar tradition seems to be followed in Japan. Griffith Foulk describes Zen monasteries in Japan during the 1980s as having three sessions of sutra chanting per day (1988, 170).

9 Personal communication, Nanputuo Temple, April 2019.

10 The evening service had been held after dinner around 5:30, but the time was changed to allow more monks to attend. Too many of them did not attend after dinner.

11 Pi-Yen Chen also notes that although much of Chinese Buddhism is not unified, the daily service "has been largely standardized throughout Chinese-speaking areas for centuries" (2010, 8).

12 For a detailed account of the components of the daily service, see P. Chen 2010, 31–41.

13 For an in-depth examination of the musical aspects of the morning and evening service, see P. Chen 2010, 1999.

14 Theoretically, a scholarly monk with knowledge of Sanskrit could derive meaning from a *dhāraṇī,* but the possibility remains theoretic until someone proves otherwise.

15 Fasicle 45 of Xuanzang's translation of the *Yogācārabhūmi* attributes *dhāraṇī* as enabling bodhisattvas to memorize and understand sutras as well as achieve *samādhi* (T 30,542C). *Dhāraṇīs* are similarly praised in *prajñā-pāramitā* sutras. See Abé 1999, 164–167.

16 See also P. Chen 1999, 122.

17 The five *kleśas* are greed, anger, ignorance, pride, and doubt. The three poisons are greed, anger, and ignorance.

18 The five contemplations in Chinese are: 计功多少, 量彼来处; 忖己德行, 全缺应供; 防心离过, 贪等为宗; 正事良药, 为疗形枯; and 为成道业, 应受此食.

19 Presiding over meals is traditionally one of the duties of the abbot. I have seen the abbot of Bailin Monastery eating with the monks (see also Welch 1967, 148).

20 Eggs were not served during my stay in 2006. Eggs are traditionally not part of a monastic diet in East Asia.

21 It is my understanding that they receive compensation for their service; in other words, they are not unpaid volunteers, unlike the cooks, for free-noodle day on lunar twenty-sixth.

22 For more on *nianfo* and the goal of the evening service, see P. Chen 2010, 6, 37; Xingci 1989, 10.

23 Early Buddhist sources spoke of ages of decline and disappearance of the dharma. In particular, Buddhism speaks of three ages of dharma of progressive degeneration: true dharma, the image of dharma, and the latter or degenerate dharma. These teachings appear in Chinese texts in the third or fourth century CE (Nattier 1995). The degenerate age was thought to have begun in China in 550 CE and produced much anxiety among Buddhist monks in China (Ch'en 1964, 338–350).

24 *Zhunian* or "stopping thoughts" using *nianfo* can bring about *nianfo sanmei* (Qin 2000, 360–361; see also Stevenson 1995).

25 The Sutra on the Buddha of Infinite Light aka The Larger Sutra on Amitāyus or *Sukhāvatīvyūha Sūtra* (T 12:360) (cited in Hisao and Stewart 2003, 30–31).

26 Talal Asad shows how power is deployed and coercion and violence carried out to protect our modern regimes and their projects. He suggests that a way of overcoming the hegemony of modernity is to reject the ideal of simple space and homogenous time and accept the more realistic complexity of space marked by intersecting identities, mixed loyalties and so on, and heterogeneity of time (2003, 178–179).

27 They are the largest regular gathering of laypersons in the immediate region, which is a stronghold of devotional Buddhism.

28 For *nianfo* as a form of meditation, see also Stevenson 1995.

29 Tim Olaveson details the functional equivalence of Durkheim's collective effervescence and Turner's *communitas* (2001).

30 I have been told by one monk that many Chinese monasteries hold twice-weekly recitations of the *prātimokṣa* during the three-month rainy season retreat, but not in Quanzhou.

31 Laypersons identify as Buddhists or have formally taken refuge or worship intentionally and exclusively at Buddhist sites. Worshippers do not identify as Buddhists and worship at both Buddhist and non-Buddhist temples; I argue that they should be distinguished from lay Buddhists and prefer the term worshipper because this is their identifying behavior (Nichols 2015). The term "devotee" is sometimes used for lay devotee to emphasis their commitment to the site by coming regularly to the biweekly *nianfo* sessions.

32 C. S. Wong also notes the tradition of lay visitors for lunar first and fifteenth at Chinese temples (1963, 16).

33 Still others have vaguely claimed that the practice began during the Qing dynasty; but I have been unable to find any records to corroborate this earlier tradition.

34 This type of concern about foreign "reporters" looking to show a bad side of China has been encountered by others (see, for example, Hessler 2001, 380–385).

35 The difference between *fayuan* (vow) and *xuyuan* (request) is personal cultivation goal versus a wish or request for supernatural aid. Both, however, are to be closed or repaid with *huanyuan*.

36 The hall of patriarchs enshrines only monks associated with the temple. It has no Bodhidharma or Huineng, as one often finds; this may be one reason for its lack of appeal. Another reason, or perhaps cause, is the lack of upkeep to this hall; the shrine case is very dusty and there is no active upkeep or care taken in its presentation. When I visited in 2019, it was kept closed except for the first and fifteenth of the lunar month.

37 For more on the significance of *dāna* in contemporary Buddhist society, see Gutschow 2004, 87–89.

38 Jean DeBernardi documents and analyzes the phenomenon of purchasing exorbitantly priced rights to offer first, second, and third incense during the double ninth festival at Mt. Wudang (2008). Incense is not commodified in this way at Kaiyuan, but the culture of wanting to be first on New Year's day is in strong evidence.

39 Figure from interviews conducted in 2006 and 2009; income generated was certainly much less in the 1980s and 1990s and likely increasing in step with the increasing wealth of China.

40 Personal communication, Kaiyuan, February 2009.

41 For temples as enterprises, see Chan and Lang 2015, 2011.

42 For rituals organized by nonmonastics at temples near Beijing, see Nichols 2019b.

43 I was told that the rite calls for 108 mudras when done properly. For the Tang origin of the *fang yankou* ritual, see Orzech 1989; for a detailed description of the rite according to canonical sources, see Orzech 2002, 221–225.

44 Patrons pay to light two pyramidal shaped towers of dozens of Buddha lights for a year. This is a common service at Mahayana temples everywhere.

45 For discussions of the history of the ghost festival, see Teiser 1988.

46 But see also Borup 2008, 115.

CHAPTER FOUR: MONKS

Some portions of this chapter overlap with material in my chapter in *Chinese Buddhism: Past, Present, and Future,* edited by Xie Da-ning (Nichols 2015), in which I develop a typology of people associated with Buddhist monasteries.

1 Yao and Badham's study was based on a survey of 3,196 Han Chinese (drawn evenly from ten provinces or municipalities, excluding Xinjiang and Tibet) consisting of structured interviews (using fifty-one-page questionnaires) averaging 47.3 minutes and conducted by 110 Chinese assistants in 2005. Three types of information were collected: personal and demographic data; reports on religious experience; and religious conceptions, beliefs, and practices.

2 I have heard the nominal use of belief (*xinyang*) used by monks to discuss the low level of belief in general among both monks and laity.

3 See Lewis 1986, 20–21.

4 Hackmann 1910, 241; Welch 1967, 482n5.

5 This behavior is associated with the *ldab ldob* (working monks) in Tibetan Buddhism who engage in menial forms of labor, not the scholarly or meditative monks (Cabezón 1993, 93).

6 For a typology of religious actors at Buddhist sites in China, see Nichols 2015. For more on the temple management commission, see Nichols 2019a. In short, lay Buddhists (*jushi*) are those who have formally taken refuge or who self-identify as such; worshippers (*xiangke*) are those whose primary identifying rubric is to visit the temple as a guest to worship Buddhas and burn incense (*baifo shaoxiang*) much the same way they visit other (non-Buddhist) temples and worship non-Buddhist deities.

7 The term *nigu* is a Buddhist technical term used for female monastics; in other vernacular contexts it could be used derogatively. Similarly, Buddhists will use the term (*lao*) *heshang* 老和尚 as a technical term for male monks as well as a kind of honorific term, but outside Buddhist contexts it can be used derogatively.

8 For more on Daoan, see Yifa 2002, 8–25; Che'en 1964, 94–100.

9 See Yu Linggo 2005, 353B; Yifa 2002, 8–16; Poceski 2003, 47–48.

10 The code was important and influential in medieval China and even spread to Japan where Dogen adapted it for use in Japan. For more on the *Chanyuan qinggui,* see Yifa's excellent study and annotated translation (2002).

11 Monastic offices are based on those at this site. Dujian was written 都监, but may also be written 督监.

12 Some (conservative) monks consider Bailin and Gaomin to be less suitable for serious practice because they welcome both male and female practitioners. Bailin also offers a popular summer camp which includes meditation (C. Sun 2002). For an interview with Bailin's abbot Jinghui, see Wu, Liu, and Yuan 2002.

13 QQ, an instant messaging service, has since been replaced by the ubiquitous phone-based social media app WeChat/*weixin*.

14 Interview, 2006. 生下来就有, 不用学. 和吃饭一样, 人一生下来就知道要找东西吃. 到一定年龄就会有. 好像再大街上看到漂亮女孩子就想多看几眼. 每个人都会, 所以是人性自然就有的. 去除情欲是违抗人性的, 所以成佛太难.

15 For a profile of Jingkong, see Sun 2017.

16 This is not to say that he was also the most knowledgeable. Likely two other monks are more knowledgeable, but that situation could certainly change.

17 Dreyfus provides no details about the life of most monks. He trained as a scholar-monk and that is what he describes in detail (2003, 65).
18 For a detailed study of such rites conducted by incense and flower monks in contemporary Guangdong, see Tam 2012.
19 For a study of lay Buddhism in contemporary China, examining some critical and noncritical lay Buddhists, see Fisher 2014.
20 Elsewhere (Nichols 2015), I argue for the need to consider the management of such quotidian features a form of religious doing and therefore a need to expand the useful typology of religious doing proposed by Adam Chau (2006).
21 For Guangdong, see Tam 2012.

CHAPTER FIVE: MATERIAL CULTURE

Epigraphs. Yang Xuanzhi 楊衒之, *Luoyang qielan* 洛阳伽蓝记, translated by Wang Yi-T'ung 王伊同, in *A Record of Buddhist Monasteries in Lo-Yang* (H. Yang 1984, 16). The second epigraph is my translation of an excerpt from a famous poem attributed to Hanshan, a famous, possibly legendary, Tang dynasty monk (for a bilingual Chinese-English record of the poem, see Porter 2000, 52–53). For the third epigraph, see Yuanxian 1643, I.8a.

1 For discussion of Chinese critiques of monastic wealth, see Kieschnick 2003, 12–14.
2 For a discussion of a Protestant bias against material objects in the study of religion, see Kieschnick 2003, 19–23.
3 Within the field of Buddhist studies the shift in focus to material culture is evidenced by not only Gregory Schopen's pioneering work but also numerous others (Schopen 1997, 2004; Sharf and Sharf 2001; Kieschnick 2003; Germano and Trainor 2004; Rambelli 2007; Gerhart 2009; Tarocco 2008, 2011; Winfield and Heine 2017).
4 For similar understandings of space, see Zito 1997.
5 The iconic nature of the Jetavana in China is evidenced by large numbers of inscriptions associated with the building or repair of monasteries that reference Anāthapiṇḍada's gift of the Jetavana (Kieschnick 2003, 191).
6 Puay-Peng Ho examines how the eminent Tang monk Daoxuan used the Jetavana monastery to create a template of the ideal Buddhist monastery (1995). His article also examines some of the doctrinal significances of the monastery buildings and their layout as conceived by Daoxuan.
7 Although the *Mūlasarvāstivāda vinaya* was likely redacted some centuries after the Buddha, it has been dated to at least the time of Kaniska (fl. 130 CE) and may be a century or more earlier. It records, then, rules for how monasteries were to be administered in India before and during the time that Buddhism began to penetrate the Chinese cultural sphere (Schopen 2004, 20–22).
8 Lessons of impermanence are tied to this will to beautify as well. A dramatic example is the destruction by Tibetan monks of sand mandalas they had just meticulously constructed. Less dramatic is the constant maintenance required to keep a Japanese garden tended; the weeding, the pruning, the sweeping, the raking of pebbles, and so on require continual attention that simultaneously cultivates insight into impermanence.
9 The *MS Vinaya* was translated into Chinese around the year 700 by the Buddhist pilgrim Yijing 义净 (635–713); it was the fifth complete vinaya to be translated into Chinese but was never to receive as much attention as the *Four-Part Vinaya* (*sifen lu*) of the Dharmaguptaka (Yifa 2002, 6–7).
10 Wang Jinsheng, interview, Quanzhou 2006.
11 Kim Knott, following Lily Kong, speaks of two broad approaches in spatial studies of religion as the poetics of space and the politics of space (Knott 2010; Kong 2001).

The poetics is associated with the phenomenology of sacred places and the politics examines the constructed nature of space and how it is imbued with power. My approach is fundamentally concerned with the way the space is constructed through social, economic, political, and religious actions, conceptions, and pressures. My use of "phenomenology" in this chapter is not the substantialist variety made famous by Mircea Eliade (Blum 2012), but the technical use of phenomenology as a method of description, incorporating embodied sensation (bracketing conceptual or religious frameworks).

12 Support for this approach comes from a growing number of scholars, including Jeffrey Maitland, who emphasizes the need to recognize embodied psychospatial orientation to the world as our fundamental way of being and knowing (1995), and Allan Wallace who emphasizes the value of meditation to scientific exploration of consciousness (2009).

13 For the cosmological layout of cities, see Wheatley 1971. For the cosmological ideas applied to Buddhist monasteries in China, see Meyer 1992. For more on the history of the application of these cosmological paradigm, see Ledderhose 2000, 113–117.

14 Johannes Prip-Møller's study remains the most complete account of the general layout of Chinese Buddhist monasteries (1937). Monasteries are traditionally thought of as metaphorical mountains, which has been used as an alternative name for monasteries, as in the "five mountains" grouping of famous monasteries in China and Japan: "Wherever the monastery was built, however, it was conceived of as a mountain retreat" (Collcutt 1981, 182).

15 The inscription is in *li* style calligraphy by Chen Yuwang.

16 Maps and guides to Kaiyuan often refer, imprecisely, to the front gate as a Hall of Heavenly Kings (*tianwang dian*).

17 C. S. Wong describes the snort as being bell-like and emitting white shafts of light that would annihilate enemies, while the blower blew deadly yellow gas (1963, 45). Wang Hanfeng suggests alternative identifications (2001, 3–4): Miji Jin'gang 密迹金刚 and Brahma (*fanwang* 梵王), but the open and closed mouths on the figures, representing the Sanskrit syllables *hum* and *ah,* strongly suggest the *Heng-Ha* generals.

18 A similar stupa is found on the Luoyang Bridge 洛阳桥 just outside the city of Quanzhou.

19 For more on the meaning of these, see C. Wang 2008, 31–32.

20 Ecke and Demiéville 1935, 88. The earliest of these was moved to Kaiyuan in 1953. The next earliest was erected by Wang Jixun in 946 and is said to have been originally located inside one of the stone stupas built by Liu Sanniang and her husband in 1145. It was discovered along with a gilt silver statue of Guanyin when a typhoon damaged the left stupa in 1982 (C. Wang 2008, 33). Both *dhāraṇī* pillars bear the text of the *Uṣṇīṣavijayādhāraṇī;* the first of these was erected in 1008 by Yuanshao 元绍. The text on the pillar is from the translation by Amoghavajra and the calligraphy is that of Lin Xun 林篔. This pillar contains a notice written by the monk Zongmei 宗美 and was originally located at the Water and Land Temple. The second Song dynasty *dhāraṇī* pillar was erected in 1031 (Ecke and Demiéville 1935, 88). For additional information on Kaiyuan's *dhāraṇī* pillars, see C. Wang 2008, 34–40. The third pillar is thought to have been moved to Kaiyuan at the end of the Ming or the early Qing dynasty.

21 The hall's plan calls for one hundred columns but fourteen were removed to make room for the statues and to make space for worshippers, leaving eighty-six.

22 The four Buddhas added by Wang Shengui also form an independent set of four meditation or *dhyāni* Buddhas.

23 Mahāsthāma is the bodhisattva said to represent the Buddha wisdom of Amitabha. A common figure in Chinese iconography, he forms part of the three holy

ones of the Western regions with Avalokiteshvara and Amitabha (Soothill and Hodous 1937, 85).

24 Each of these finely chiseled sixteen-sided columns has twelve carvings that include Śiva, Brahma, and figures from Hindu mythology.

25 Walsh points out the ideal configuration of Buddhist monasteries calls for the Buddha hall to be centrally located (2007, 48). Martin Collcutt also notes that the Buddha hall has served as the devotional center of monasteries since medieval times (1981, 191).

26 For dates of construction for the pagodas, see Yuanxian 1643, I.6b-9a.

27 For more on the pagodas, see Ecke and Demiéville 1935; H. Wang 1992.

28 See Ecke and Demiéville 1935, 9; for Chinese, see H. Wang 1992.

29 The suggestion, quite naturally, is that the artisans responsible for building the east and west pagodas in the thirteenth century were familiar with an oral version of the extraordinarily popular Chinese epic *Journey to the West* (*Xiyouji* 西游记), which features the monkey king, Sun Wukong, and the Buddhist pilgrim Xuanzang and was not written down until the Ming dynasty several centuries later. Sun Wukong is modeled after the monkey king of the important Hindu epic the *Ramayana*. Quanzhou was most certainly a place where this legend would have entered China (the port of Guangzhou would be another) and was likely narrated by members of Quanzhou's Indian community. Another researcher may wish to look into the history of wooden puppet-making in Quanzhou, which is a celebrated local craft, to see whether it is possible to determine how early puppets were made of the monkey king in Quanzhou. As for Guanyin, she is most commonly depicted in Chinese art as a woman but appears as male twice at Kaiyuan, in a Tang dynasty stone sculpture in the round and in the relief on the west pagoda. Again, this suggests the influence of India where Guanyin was a prince (Avalokiteśvara).

30 "A Seismic History of the Twin Pagodas of Quanzhou"—stone inscription on site at Kaiyuan Monastery.

31 The closest comparable pagoda is a single one similar in design that served as a lighthouse on the coast of Quanzhou during the Song and Yuan dynasties. Known as Shihu Pagoda 石湖塔 (Stone Lake Pagoda), it welcomed ships to the first and southernmost port of Quanzhou at the mouth of the Jinjiang River as early as the Northern Song dynasty. It was built around 1113, thus predating Kaiyuan's twin pagodas by over a century. Quanzhou's second port is located in Houzhu Bay 后渚 at the mouth of the Luoyang River.

32 Pagodas traditionally represent the Buddha by marking the enshrinement of relics of the Buddha or his disciples. When the east pagoda was first built in the ninth century, Buddha relics were installed. No records indicate what might have been installed below the west pagoda, but relics and other items are presumed to exist. Even though Kaiyuan's pagodas thus have these Buddhist significances, these concerns did not emerge as important factors in interviews. For this reason, this traditional doctrinal significance is not included in this discussion.

33 保佑生意兴隆.

34 保佑全家平安, 保佑孙子读书读好一点.

35 On the importance of *ling* in the veneration of visual icons in Sino-Japanese Buddhism, see Faure 1996.

36 Examples of culturally valuable statuary being damaged by the faithful are easy to come by. Some examples that come to mind are the Binzuru (Pindola) statue sitting outside Todaiji in Nara, which has been withered by the hands of those seeking healing, and the toes of the right foot of the ancient bronze statue of St. Peter, which have been rubbed away by the faithful visiting the Vatican.

37 For a fulsome exploration of the value of such as-if rituals, see Puett and Gross-Loh 2016.

38 See also Foulk 1993; Faure 1994.

39 For a good description of the ritualization of the enlightened Chan abbot, see Sharf 2005, 261–266.
40 精美文化遗产，建筑艺术，工程技术.
41 福建的骄傲.
42 建筑艺术的瑰宝.
43 旅游观光.
44 在外面现代城市气息比较重 ... 进来以后心境比较开阔. ... 远离城市的喧嚣.
45 Daoxuan's *Zhong tianzhu sheweiguo qihuansi tujing* 中天竺舍衛國祇洹寺圖經 (Illustrated Scripture of Jetavana Vihara of Sravati in Central India) T.45.890, a28–b2, in Ho 1995, 18; see also Robson 2010a, 15.

CHAPTER SIX: FOUNDING LEGENDS

1 Canonical literature lists six kinds of powers, including magical powers (*ruyi*) (Kieschnick 1997, 70).
2 One way support was earned was successfully prognosticating future events of concern to leaders (Kieschnick 1997, 71–76).
3 The Han dynasty belief is articulated in the *Huainanzi* (see Le Blanc 1985; Kieschnick 1997, 98; Campany 1996, 367–368).
4 For more on such miraculous occurrences during the Han, see Loewe 1982, 80–90. David Chappell also notes the early non-Buddhist presence of this notion in Chinese thought: "In the tradition of correlative thinking from the Han dynasty, the formless ultimate was seen as responsive to human morality; exceptional spiritual achievement would naturally manifest itself in external natural wonders" (2005, 61).
5 Also known as the *Liang Biographies of Eminent Monks* (*Liang Gaoseng zhuan* 梁高僧傳). See Kieschnick 1997, 99.
6 *Daoxuan lushi gantong lu,* T 2106, v. 52; *Luxiang gantong zhuan,* T. 1898, v. 45. I follow Kieschnick, following Birnbaum, in translating *gantong* as "spiritual resonance" (see Kieschnick 1997, 98–101). For *Xu gaoseng zhuan* 续高僧传, see Kieschnick 1997, 88–89.
7 Benguan's 本观 mother (d. 1100), for example, dreamed a golden figure who gave her a white lotus before she discovered she was with child and when he was born a purple aura surrounded his head and strange light is said to have filled the room (Yuanxian 1643, I.34b). Daozhao 道昭, who lived during the interregnum, was also born with a purple aura around his head (Yuanxian 1643, I.24b). The monk Benyuan 本源 while traveling in Zhangpu 漳浦 sat on a rock beside the path and every night thereafter the rock is said to have glowed (Yuanxian 1643, I.45a).
8 This was how early Buddhists in China adapted the idea of karma to Chinese thought; the only major difference was the idea of rebirth (Campany 1996, 369).
9 The Chinese nondualism, as I understand it, is thorough and accounts for salient characteristics of Chinese religion. It contrasts with the traditional perception in the Western world of a dichotomy between matter and spirit and body and mind.
10 Chün-fang Yü examines many such miracle tales (2000, 158–19).
11 Robert Sharf notes this and literati efforts to combat more personalist or anthropomorphic versions of cosmic forces (2002, 95). It seems to me that a more naturalistic approach reflects a preference in the Zhou dynasty to speak about Heaven (*tian*) rather than Shangdi (Lord on High) as cosmic arbiter. For a good overview of the many ways that *ganying* cosmology applies to important traditions of Chinese thought and practice, including folk, Confucian, Daoist, and Buddhist, see Sharf 2002, 77–133.
12 Aquinas, *Summa Contra Gentiles* (Pegis 1945, 980; briefly discussed in Davis 1998, 5).

13 See Schipper 1993, 41. Another difference is the notion of miracle as an intentional act by God. The naturalistic notion (not the anthropomorphic) of sympathetic response entails no intention; it is a natural or spontaneous response to stimuli. Anthropomorphic agents of response are, however, also common. It is not possible to claim that lack of intention is a common feature to all phenomena associated with *ganying*.

14 "Transcendence" in the Chinese context means more along the lines of "rarification" rather than what it means in a Judeo-Christian context.

15 It is also contact with the wholly other God, beyond this world, that makes something holy according to the Bible (Japhet 1998, 57–58). Sara Japhet points out that it is only contact with or connection to God that makes something holy in the Bible. Association with saints, holy people, or their relics does not make something sacred according to the Bible.

16 On the Chinese universe as an organism, see Needham 1951.

17 *Yijian zhi;* Boltz 1993, 247. For more on the *Yijian zhi*, its author, themes, and social context see Inglis 2006. Edward Davis has used the *Yijian zhi* and other texts in his *Society and the Supernatural in Song China* (2001).

18 *Yijian zhi jia*,1.2; Boltz 1993, 247.

19 For Ming attitudes about regulating Buddhism and Daoism, see Brook 2005b.

20 See A. Yu 2005; Brook 2009, 40; Potter 2003.

21 *Chongjian Kaiyuansi beiji* 重建开元寺碑记 (Stele Record of the Reconstruction of Kaiyuan Monastery) in situ at Kaiyuan.

22 *Ji shenzhou sanbao gantong lu* (T. 2106:52.404–435), in Shinohara 1998.

23 Huang Tao's 897 *Quanzhou Kaiyuansi fodian beiji* 泉州开元寺佛殿碑记 (Stele Record of the Quanzhou Kaiyuan Monastery Buddha Hall) collected in the *Quan Tang wen* 全唐文 (Collected Works of Tang Literature) and in Dean and Zheng 2003, 1: 4–6, inscription #4.

24 See H. Wang 1986.

25 See Chau 2006, 95–98.

26 They were erected in 1327. Chan master Muan wrote poems for the six and the eight in the seventeenth century (for the poems, see Shen 1990, 73–75).

27 Flath suggests that literary reference to weeds in the courtyard may refer to moral failings (2016, 6).

28 The technique of covering mummies with lacquer developed in China as early as the seventh century. Daoxuan in his *Xu gaoseng zhuan* describes the mummy of Daoxiu 道修 as being covered with a cloth soaked in lacquer (Ritzinger and Bingenheimer 2006, 66–67). As the Tang dynasty wore on the use of lacquer to cover mummies became more the rule than the exception; it was protective and lightweight and made the mummies more easily transportable (70–71).

29 For more on the tradition of mummies, perhaps better distinguished as "whole body relics," see Ritzinger and Bingenheimer 2006. This article provides an overview of research on the subject as well as an excellent historical sketch of the practice in China. See also Faure 1994, 148–178; Sharf 1992.

30 Stories of this kind are associated with Chan master Chu'nan 楚南 (813–888) (T50, 2061: 817 c28-a01), Faqin 法钦 (714–792) (T50, 2061: 765a08–10), and Wuzhuo Wenxi 無著文喜 (821–900) (X80, 1565, 193c2–6). Cited in Ritzinger and Bingenheimer 2006, 79.

31 I have not made verifying the authenticity of this mummy my task; it awaits future investigators.

32 A small figure is seated just in front of the figure of Kuanghu; it is said to contain the mummified remains of the Tang dynasty bare-shouldered monk Zhiliang. In addition to these two statues, the hall features images of Republican period masters Yuanying, Zhuandao, Zhuanwu, and, from the post-Mao period, Guangjing.

33 Several members of the family are buried locally. Dozens of tombstones in the large cemetery on the side of Mt. Qingyuan read "Purple Cloud Huang" (*ziyun huang* 紫云黄).

34 A survey of sections on temples in Fuzhou and Quanzhou in the early Ming gazetteer of Fujian (*Bamin tongzhi* 75–77:1089–1129, 1160–1173) found no other Buddhist temple among the 1,907 listed with as colorful a founding legend.

35 A parallel story is associated with Mount Wolf 狼山 Temple in Jiangsu (Jiangsu Provincial Tourism Bureau 2001, 227–228).

36 Hiking with a guide in the Wuyi mountains of Fujian in 2006, I noted striking discrepancies between the oral account of the mountains provided by the guide and the written accounts posted on signs along the trail: the former were mythological tales of deities full of love and betrayal, the latter were full of details of geologic stratification and shifts that would bore anyone but a geologist. The signs suggested the presence of the state and an attempt at deenchantment, secularization, and reeducation.

37 The thesis that they were a kind of fiction writing developed under the famous author Lu Xun (1881–1936) and was supported by some scholars (see DeWoskin 1977). Alister Inglis has carried forward Campany's thesis in his study of Hong Mai's *Yijian zhi* (2006).

38 For place branding as it related to tourist sites, see Morgan, Pritchard, and Pride 2004; for study of the branded city in Asia (especially Hong Kong and Shanghai), see Donald and Gammack 2007; for a "guide" to place branding, see Olins 2004.

39 Recall that every prefecture was to have a Kaiyuan temple during the Kaiyuan period of the Tang dynasty and many of these Kaiyuans still survive in one form or another. Within Fujian, for example, Fuzhou Kaiyuan still exists; it is significantly smaller than Quanzhou Kaiyuan, however, and houses only a handful of monks and receives a relatively few tourists.

40 Personal communication, 2009. 现代社会品牌商标非常重要. 桑莲法界 就像开元寺的注册商标一样.

41 This story is considered legend by modern scholars (see Chen 1972, 30–33; Zürcher 1972, 31–32).

42 The six sites at Baima Temple are the Pure and Cool platform (*qingliang tai*) rebuilt in the Ming, burning sutra platform (*fenjing tai*) now in ruins, midnight bell (*yeban zhong*), tenglan tombs (*tenglan mu*) from the Han, rise into the clouds pagoda (*qiyun ta*), and the broken words stele (*duanwen bei*). The bell tower and bell have been rebuilt along with the drum tower. All seem to be present today, if in a ruined state (such as the burning sutra platform).

43 Shaolin Monastery has effectively promoted its brand by focusing on its reputation as the home of Kungfu; it is also the site of a cave where Bodhidharma is said to have meditated and a forest of pagodas.

44 Along such lines, John Lagerwey proclaims China a "religious state" (2010). Rebecca Nedostup more systematically exposes the superstition and religion at the heart of China's modern nation-building (2009).

CHAPTER SEVEN: CURATORS AND THE REVIVALISTS

This chapter is a significantly revised and updated version of "Tourist Temples and Places of Practice: Charting Multiple Paths in the Revival of Monastic Buddhism" in *Buddhism after Mao,* edited by Ji Zhe, André Laliberte, and Gareth Fisher, 97–119 (Honolulu: University of Hawai'i Press, 2019).

1 F. Yang 2006; Ashiwa and Wank 2009; M. Yang 2009; Jun Jing 1996; Flower and Leonard 1997; Gladney 1991; Madsen 1993; Eng and Lin 2002.

2 See Anagost 1994; Feuchtwang 2000; Jun Jing 1996; M. Yang 2004a; Wang Mingming 1996, 70, 76; Overmyer 2003; Potter 2003.

3 On state support of Hebei Bailin Monastery, see, for example, Yang and Wei 2005.

4 For relations between authorities and popular religious festivities, see Dean 1993; Chau 2006. For more on conflicts between monks and agencies interested in tourist development, see Nichols 2019b.

5 For more on religious tourism at Buddhist monasteries, see Nichols 2020.

6 See also Kieschnick 2003, 39–40.

7 Inscription on the central column of the east pagoda (1349, in situ at Kaiyuan), author's name not legible. The rest of the inscription reads, "Third day of lunar November [*zhongdong* 仲冬] of 1349 (ninth year of Zhizheng) in the Yuan dynasty. I accompanied Secretariat Drafter Zhang Bao Bo'ang [*Zhongshu zhisheng sheren* 中书直省舍人章宝伯昂] and Prefectural Supervisor [*Jianjun* 监郡] Xie Yuli Shiyu 偰玉立世玉 came to climb the East Pagoda. Today the sun is in the south ... we engrave this stone to remember this trip." The names of more than fifteen others are listed as present, not including the two previously named. Three of the visitors were from Gaochang 高昌 in today's Xinjiang 新疆 (to the west of China proper); they are surnamed Xie 偰, which is not a Han surname, suggesting that they are natives of the country to the west of China now dominated by Uighur Muslims.

8 *Shouning xianzhi* 1686, 7:21b, in Brook 1993, 108.

9 *Jinshan zhilüe* 1681, I, *Tiandi jiue*, 4a, in Brook 1993, 110.

10 The term "temple" is used to refer to sites that do not serve as training grounds for monastics; the term "monastery" is used for sites known to house monastics.

11 See Lang, Chan, and Ragvald 2005; Borchert 2005.

12 Several studies have mentioned the economic motivations of local officials when supporting the construction or reconstruction of temples. See for example, Ashiwa and Wank 2006, 348; Eng and Lin 2002, 1271–1773; Fisher 2008, 152; Feuchtwang 2001, 246; Lai 2003, 112; Yang and Wei 2005, 74–77; McCarthy 2010.

13 This is similar to the promotion and selling of the traditional ("backward") culture of ethnic minorities to develop the economy and enjoy a higher (more modern) standard of living. See Borchert 2005, 93; Kang 2009, 229. For religion, modernity, and identity in Han communities, see Jing 1996; Flower 2004.

14 See also Michie and Smith 1998, 38–39.

15 Buddhist temples from early on in the Communist era have been used as a bridge to build relations with countries that share a Buddhist heritage such as Japan and Burma (Welch 1961, 11). More recently, Buddhism has been used to build relations with not only countries sympathetic to Buddhism but also the world community to improve China's image in the eyes of those who critique China for human rights violations. The most recent and dramatic example has been the hosting of world Buddhist forums by China every three years since 2006. For a survey of temples in Guangdong, see Lang, Chan, and Ragvald 2005. Thomas Borchert notes the economic motives behind religious revival in the Dai-lue region of Yunnan (2005).

16 "Culture" certainly includes Daoism and certain folk deities (such as Tianhou or Mazu) and they too benefit from the notion that cultural revival promotes economic growth. A group of Daoist and folk temples, for example, have been restored in downtown Suzhou as part of its economic and tourist development scheme. See also Lang, Chan, and Ragvald 2005.

17 Personal communication, Bureau of Cultural Heritage, Quanzhou, 2009.

18 See McCarthy 2010; Flower and Leonard 1998; Flower 2004; Eng and Lin 2002, 1271–1773; Fisher 2008, 152; Ashiwa and Wank 2006. The cooperation between

curators and revivalists has, however, at times turned to competition and rivalry (see Kang 2009).

19 Khun Eng Kuah-Pearce has researched the phenomenon of Singaporeans returning to rebuild their ancestral homes in Anxi, a mountainous region that neighbors Quanzhou in southern Fujian (2011).

20 Other important temples in Quanzhou are the non-Buddhist temples of Guandi and Tianhou (Mazu).

21 Benedict Anderson's second edition of *Imagined Communities* includes the chapter "Census, Map, Museum," which includes the term "museumized" to describe colonial secular states' archeological projects of restored monuments like Borobudur, restored not as functioning religious sites, but as museums focused on tourism (1991, 181–182). This is similar to my use, but the formally atheist Chinese Communist Party makes my use of the "museumification" more pointed and ultimately more intentional than the museum impulse inherited by postcolonial states. See also M. Yang 2004b, 734–738.

22 What I have in mind here are such amenities that were rare in the past, such as multilingual signs pointing out directions and introducing buildings as well as benches, new restrooms, and manicured landscaping.

23 Tanzhe and Jietai Temples, each lying just outside Beijing, as well as Baita (white stupa) Temple within the city of Beijing also fall into the category of museumification at work. I had not yet identified the key role of the Temple Administrative Commission when I visited them, however, and therefore did not ask the appropriate questions or make the appropriate observations to determine how they fit into the museumification scheme presented here.

24 Hongluo Temple was founded in the fourth century.

25 For a more aggressive approach to nonclerical management and commercialization, see Marina Svensson's discussion of a Daoist temple run by a "tourist company" in Wuzhen, Zhejiang accused by locals of pressuring and tricking individuals into buying incense and amulets and clerics being described as "fake monks" (2010).

26 Many entities and practices that were open to attack by Red Guards went underground during the Cultural Revolution and then reemerged after the death of Mao. These entities and practices include all things having to do with religion, not to mention all things perceived to be contrary to the progress of the revolution, which included most literature, art, and everyday items such as small tea cups—so many things that have become ubiquitous over the past twenty years it bears recalling how they once were not.

27 Ink rubbings on rice paper of historic steles is a relatively common souvenir item, for which steles have been collected, such as the forest of steles in Xi'an.

28 The platform before the main hall served as a kind of stage where speeches were made by Daoyuan and other distinguished guests in front of members of the Huang family, whether from the Quanzhou region, the Philippines, Malaysia, Singapore, Shanghai, or beyond, who were arrayed by point of origin in folding chairs set up throughout Kaiyuan's expansive courtyard. Bands played, a small parade was held and dozens of young ladies in uniform were on hand as greeters and tea servers. The culmination, perhaps, was the grand sacrifice offered to the ancestral tablets of Huang Shougong in the donor's ancestral hall. The Huang family expected to make meat sacrifices, but Kaiyuan insisted the offering be vegetarian; a characteristically Chinese compromise was reached by having animal forms made from vegetarian materials and offered.

29 Yoshiko Ashiwa and David Wank recorded a similar conflict between the monastic leadership and the administrative commission at Xiamen's Nanputuo Temple. Unlike Kaiyuan, Nanputuo's commission profited from an array of tourist related business it operated near the temple entrance. Zhao Puchu helped reduce

the power of the commission by having it redesignated a business post (*shiwu suo*) rather than a commission with administrative duties (Ashiwa and Wank 2006, 41–42).

30 James Flath records a similar incident from 1820 involving the front gate of the Confucian temple in Qufu, in which the chief of temple security severely beat the driver of a cart that had crashed into a horse-dismounting stele; afterward he banned carts from the area (2016, 96–97). The effect of this change at Kaiyuan has been so dramatic that businesses outside the main gate complain that they have lost considerable income since the change and some restaurants have had to close.

31 Personal communication, 2006.

32 This most recent focus on religious atmosphere (*daofeng*) may be seen as part of a broader campaign by Xi Jinping to decouple commercialized tourist development from religious sites. Although this book traces developments up to 2019, it is fundamentally a study of Buddhism after Mao and before Xi.

CONCLUSION

Epigraph. Cao Pi 曹丕 (187–226), *Thesis on Classic Literature* 典论论文.

1 See Bodiford 2010; Naquin 2000, 1998; Robson 2010b; Schopen 1997, 2004. Monks and monasteries, in popular treatments and, until recently, scholarly treatments alike, tend to be idealized as renunciates cut off from society and living in relative or absolute poverty or at least as pursuing a vocation and striving to lead a life of devotion (see, for example, D'Avila-Latourrette 2000; Duckett 2000; Norris 2014).

2 These percentages are not based on hard data. They are a studied estimate intended to give a general idea of an ethnographically based perspective backed up by studies of living monastic populations (Dreyfus 2003; Buswell 1992; Welch 1967).

3 This analogy is not perfect. Plenty of good teaching, study, and research go on at the nonexemplary universities. The key point is that the world-class, brand recognition of the exemplary universities is rare. Analogously, Buddhist monasteries broadly recognized as exemplary places to practice by Chinese Buddhists are also very few in number.

4 A local lay Buddhist in Quanzhou included Kaiyuan in his damning critique.

5 For a general introduction to Jingkong, see Yanfei Sun 2017.

6 For a monk's critique of commercialization of monasteries, see Jing Jun 2006.

7 Such ties have been common in China. The apocryphal *Xiangfa jueyi jing* 像法決疑經 (Sūtra of Resolving Doubts during the Age of the Semblance Dharma), for example, warns of the slight merit accruing to individuals who only contribute to building Buddhist edifices connected to one's family or serving as one's family sanctuary, which was a common practice in medieval China (*Xiangfa jue yi jing* 1336a). See Gernet 1995, 283.

8 Objections could be made that I am idealizing the function or purpose of monasteries and universities and that both could be thought of as fulfilling different social functions. For example, monasteries might be seen as offering a place for devotees to connect with the tradition and universities functioning as points of access into different social and occupational groups. The point of highlighting the ideals behind each of these institutions is to recognize their continuing value. That they may be under threat or eroding is all the more reason to raise questions about these ideals, to better appreciate what may be at stake in their loss.

9 Gregory Schopen suggests scholars need to rethink the history of Buddhist monasticism when it comes to understanding monks and money. His study of

the *Mūlasarvāstivāda Vinaya* finds an openness to monks owning and inheriting wealth (2000).

10 The "Buddhist imaginaire" is represented by the catalogues of publishers such as Wisdom Publications, Snow Lion, and Shambala. It is also represented by learned lay and monastic Buddhists in my fieldwork and outside my formal fieldwork.

11 Leonard Primiano advises use of the term "vernacular" as a way of getting beyond the binary elite or popular (1995).

12 Personal interview, 2019.

13 Excerpts from Foulk 1995, 462.

14 Barrett 1990; Paper 1995, 36; Mote 1977, 203; Tu 2001. Rebecca Nedostup approaches the issue from modern Chinese political history and reaches corresponding conclusions about the ever-presence of religion within secular nationalism (2009).

15 理事不二 . Personal interview, 2019.

16 Author's translation of 佛法在世间，不离世间觉；离世觅菩提，恰如求兔角 T.2008.1.

17 For more on Chinese religions as a resource to counter consumerism and the unlimited growth paradigm, see Kaza 2019; Loy 2019; Miller 2020; Tu 2001.

References

Modern Scholarship

Abé, Ryūichi. 1999. *The Weaving of Mantra: Kūkai and the Construction of Esoteric Buddhist Discourse*. New York: Columbia University Press.

Anagnost, Ann S. 1994. "The Politics of Ritual Displacement." In *Asian Visions of Authority: Religion and the Modern States of East and Southeast Asia*, edited by Charles F. Keyes, Laurel Kendall, and Helen Hardacre. Honolulu: University of Hawai'i Press.

Anderson, Benedict R. 1991. *Imagined Communities: Reflections on the Origin and Spread of Nationalism*, rev. ed. London: Verso.

Arora, Vishal. 2013. "Bhutan Makes Condoms Available to Buddhist Monks to Stop Spread of STDs." *Huffington Post*, April 29. Accessed November 19, 2021. http://www.huffingtonpost.com/2013/03/29/bhutas-makes-condoms-available-to-monks-to-stop-spread-of-stds_n_2976401.html.

Asad, Talal. 2003. *Formations of the Secular: Christianity, Islam, Modernity*. Stanford, CA: Stanford University Press.

Ashiwa, Yoshiko. 2000. "Dynamics of the Buddhist Revival Movement in South China: State, Society, and Transnationalism." *Hitotsubashi Journal of Social Studies* 32(1): 15–31.

——. 2009. "Positioning Religion in Modernity: State and Buddhism in China." In *Making Religion, Making the State: The Politics of Religion in Modern China*, edited by Yoshiko Ashiwa and David Wank, 43–73. Stanford, CA: Stanford University Press.

Ashiwa, Yoshiko, and David Wank. 2005. "The Globalization of Chinese Buddhism: Clergy and Devotee Networks in the 20th Century." *International Journal of Asian Studies* 2(2): 217–237.

——. 2006. "The Politics of a Reviving Buddhist Temple in Contemporary China: State, Association and Religion in Southeast China." *Journal of Asian Studies* 65(2): 337–360.

——, eds. 2009. *Making Religion, Making the State: The Politics of Religion in Modern China*. Stanford, CA: Stanford University Press.

——. 2019. "A Study of Laynuns in Minnan, 1920–2010s." In *Buddhism after Mao: Negotiations, Continuities, and Reinventions*, edited by Ji Zhe, Gareth Fisher, and André Laliberté, 210–248. Honolulu: University of Hawai'i Press.

Assman, Jan. 1995. "Collective Memory and Cultural Identity." *New German Critique* 65:125-133.

Baroni, Helen Josephine. 2000. *Obaku Zen: The Emergence of the Third Sect of Zen in Tokugawa, Japan*. Honolulu: University of Hawai'i Press.

Barrett, T. H. 1990. "Religious Traditions in Chinese Civilization: Buddhism and Taoism." In *Heritage of China: Contemporary Perspectives on Chinese*

Civilization, edited by Paul S. Ropp, 138–163. Berkeley: University of California Press.

Bianchi, Esther. 2001. *The Iron Statue Monastery [Tiexiangsi]: A Buddhist Nunnery of Tibetan Tradition in Contemporary China*. Florence: Instituto Venezia E L'Oriente.

Birnbaum, Raoul. 2003a. "Buddhist China at the Century's Turn." *China Quarterly* 174:428–450.

——. 2003b. "Master Hongyi Looks Back: A 'Modern Man' Becomes a Monk in Twentieth-Century China." In *Buddhism in the Modern World*, edited by Steven Heine and Charles Prebish, 75–124. New York: Oxford University Press.

Blum, Jason N. 2012. "Retrieving Phenomenology of Religion as a Method for Religious Studies." *Journal of the American Academy of Religion* 80(4): 1025–1048.

——. 2015. "William James on How to Study Experience: Integrating Phenomenology of Religion and Radical Empiricism." *Method & Theory in the Study of Religion* 27(4/5): 423–446.

Bodiford, William. 2010. "The Monastic Institution in Medieval Japan." In *Buddhist Monasticism in East Asia*, edited by James A. Benn, Lori Meeks, and James Robson, 1–17. New York: Routledge.

Boivin, Nicole. 2009. "Grasping the Elusive and Unknowable: Material Culture in Ritual Practice." *Material Religion: The Journal of Objects, Art and Belief* 5(3): 266–287.

Boltz, Judith Magee. 1993. "Not by the Seal of Office Alone." In *Religion and Society in T'ang and Sung China*, edited by Patricia Ebrey and Peter Gregory, 241–305. Honolulu: University of Hawai'i Press.

Borchert, Thomas. 2005. "Of Temples and Tourists: The Effects of the Tourist Economy on a Minority Buddhist Community in Southwest China." In *State, Market, and Religions in Chinese Societies*, edited by Yang Fenggang, 87–111. Leiden: Brill.

Borup, Jørn. 2008. *Japanese Rinzai Zen Buddhism: Myōshinji, a Living Religion*. Leiden: Brill.

Brasovan, Nicholas S. 2014. "Conjunctions and/or Disjunctions: Radical Empiricism in the History of Philosophy." *Frontiers of Philosophy in China* 9(1): 130–148.

Brook, Timothy. 1993. *Praying for Power: Buddhism and the Formation of Gentry Society in Late-Ming China*. Cambridge, MA: Harvard University Press.

——. 2005a. "Institution." In *Critical Terms for the Study of Buddhism*, edited by Donald Lopez, 144–161. Chicago: University of Chicago Press.

——. 2005b. *The Chinese State in Ming Society*. London: Routledge Curzon.

Brose, Benjamin. 2014. "Credulous Kings and Immoral Monks: Critiques of Buddhists during the Five Dynasties and Ten Kingdoms." *Asia Major* 27(1): 73–98.

Bush, Richard C. 1970. *Religion in Communist China*. New York: Abingdon Press.

Buswell, Robert E. 1992. *The Zen Monastic Experience: Buddhist Practice in Contemporary Korea*. Princeton, NJ: Princeton University Press.

Cabezón, José I. 1993. *Buddhism, Sexuality, and Gender*. Albany: State University of New York Press.

Cai Zimin 蔡紫旻. 2017. *Kaiyuansi li mendao duo hai ceng you nu zhuchi ting huang shougong hou ren jiang gushi* 开元寺里'门道'多 还曾有女住持 听黄守恭后人讲故事 [There Are Many Doors at Kaiyuan Monastery, There Was Once Even a Female Abbot: Hear the Stories of Huang Shougong's Descendant]. 海丝泉州频道, May 16. Accessed June 2, 2020. http://hsqz.china.com.cn/chinanet/index.php/home/index/readcontent/contentid/1030.

Campany, Robert Ford. 1996. *Strange Writing: Anomaly Accounts in Early Medieval China*. Albany: State University of New York Press.

Campbell, Patricia Q. 2011. *Knowing Body, Moving Mind: Ritualizing and Learning at Two Buddhist Centers*. New York: Oxford University Press.

Carrithers, Michael. 1983. *The Forest Monks of Sri Lanka*. New Delhi: Oxford University Press.

Chan, Selina Ching, and Graeme Lang. 2011. "Temples as Enterprises." In *Religion in Contemporary China: Revitalization and Innovation*, edited by Adam Yuet Chau, 133–153. London: Routledge.

——. 2015. *Building Temples in China: Memories, Tourism and Identities*. London: Routledge.

Chappell, David. 2005. "The *Precious Scroll of the Liang Emperor:* Buddhist and Daoist Repentance to Save the Dead." In *Going Forth: Visions of Buddhist Vinaya*, edited by William Bodiford, 41–64. Honolulu: University of Hawai'i Press.

Chau, Adam Yuet. 2006. *Miraculous Response: Doing Popular Religion in Contemporary China*. Stanford, CA: Stanford University Press.

——. 2010. "Modalities of Doing Religion." In *Chinese Religious Life*, edited by David A. Palmer, Glenn Shive, and Philip L. Wickerie, 67–84. New York: Oxford University Press.

Chen Dubin 陈笃彬, and Su Liming 苏黎明. 2015. *Hongyi dashi zai Quanzhou* 弘一大师在泉州 [Master Hongyi in Quanzhou]. Jinan 晋南: Qilu shushe 齐鲁书社.

Chen-hua. 1992. *In Search of the Dharma: Memoirs of a Modern Chinese Buddhist Pilgrim*. Edited by Chün-fang Yü. Translated by Denis C. Mair. Albany: State University of New York.

Ch'en, Kenneth. 1973. *Buddhism in China: A Historical Survey*. Princeton, NJ: Princeton University Press.

Chen, Pi-Yen. 1999. "Morning and Evening Service: The Practice of Ritual, Music, and Doctrine in the Buddhist Monastic Community." PhD diss., University of Chicago.

——. 2010. *Fan Bai: Chinese Buddhist Monastic Chants*. Middleton, WI: A-R Editions.

Chen, Shuiyua 陈水源. 2000. *Jiechu hanghaijia Zheng He* 杰出航海家郑和 [Extraordinary Seafarer Zheng He]. Taichong City: Chenxing Publishing House.

Chitoshi, Uesugi 上杉千年. 2004. *Zheng He xia xiyang: 1421 zhongguo faxian shijie* 郑和下西洋: 1421中国发现世界 [Zheng's Journey to the Western Seas: 1421 China Discovers the World]. Shanghai: Shanghai Academy of Social Sciences Publishing House.

Chou Yi-liang. 1945. "Tantrism in China." *Harvard Journal of Asiatic Studies* 8(3/4): 235–332.

Clark, Hugh R. 1982. "Quanzhou (Fujian) During the Tang-Song Interregnum, 879–978." *T'oung-pao* 68(1–3): 132–149.

——. 1991. *Community, Trade, and Networks: Southern Fujian Province from the Third to the Thirteenth Century*. Cambridge: Cambridge University Press.

——. 2006. "The Religious Culture of Fujian 750–1450: Preliminary Reflections on Contacts across a Maritime Frontier." *Asia Major, Third Series* 19(1/2): 211–240.

——. 2007. *Portrait of a Community: Society, Culture, and the Structures of Kinship in the Mulan River Valley (Fujian) from the Late Tang through the Song*. Hong Kong: Chinese University Press.

Cleary, J. C. 1989. *Zibo: The Last Great Zen Master of China*. Freemont, CA: Jain Publishing.

Coleman, Simon, and John Elsner. 1995. *Pilgrimage: Past & Present in the World Religions*. Collingdale, PA: Diane Publishing.

Collcutt, Martin. 1981. *Five Mountains: The Rinzai Zen Monastic Institution in Medieval Japan*. Cambridge, MA: Harvard University Press.

Covell, Stephen G. 2005. *Japanese Temple Buddhism: Worldliness in a Religion of Renunciation*. Topics in Contemporary Buddhism. Honolulu: University of Hawai'i Press.

Damasio, Antonio R. 1994. *Descartes' Error: Emotion, Reason and the Human Brain*. New York: Avon Books.

——. 1999. *The Feeling of What Happens: Body and Emotion in the Making of Consciousness*. New York: Harcourt Brace.

Daoyuan et al. 2005. 泉州开元, *The Kaiyuan Temple in Quanzhou*. Beijing: Religion and Culture Press 宗教文化出版社.

D'Avila-Latourrette, Victor-Antoine. 2000. *A Monastic Year: Reflections from a Monastery*. Ann Arbor, MI: Charis Books.

Davis, Edward L. 2001. *Society and the Supernatural in Song China*. Honolulu: University of Hawai'i Press.

Davis, Richard H. 1998. "Introduction: Miracles as Social Acts." In *Images, Miracles, and Authority in Asian Religious Traditions*, edited by Richard Davis, 1–22. Boulder, CO: Westview.

Davis, Sara L. M. 2006. *Song and Silence: Ethnic Revival on China's Southwest Borders*. Chiang Mai, TH: Silk Worm Books.

Dean, Kenneth. 1988. "Funerals in Fujian." *Cahiers d'Extreme-asie* 4:19–78.

——. 1993. *Taoist Ritual and Popular Cults of Southeast China*. Princeton, NJ: Princeton University Press.

——. 1998. *Lord of the Three in One: The Spread of a Cult in Southeast China*. Princeton, NJ: Princeton University Press.

——. 2010. "The Return Visits of Overseas Chinese to Ancestral Villages in Putian." In *Faiths on Display: Religion, Tourism, and the Chinese State*, edited by Tim Oakes and Donald S. Sutton, 235–263. Lanham, MD: Rowman & Littlefield.

DeBernardi, Jean. 2008. "Commodifying Blessings: Celebrating the Double-Yang Festival in Penang, Malaysia and Wudang Mountain, China." In *Religious Commodifications in Asia: Marketing Gods*, edited by Pattana Kitiarsa, 49–67. New York: Routledge.

de Certeau, Michel. 1988. *The Practice of Everyday Life*. Translated by Steven Rendall. Reprint edition. Berkeley: University of California Press.

de Groot, J. J. M. 1884. *Buddhist Masses for the Dead at Amoy*. Leiden: Brill.

Dehijia, Dehejia. 1991. "Aniconism and the Multivalence of Emblems." *Ars Orientali* 21:45–66.

DeWoskin, Kenneth J. 1977. "The Six Dynasties and the Birth of Fiction." In *Chinese Narrative: Critical and Theoretical Essays*, edited by Andrew H. Plaks, 21–52. Princeton, NJ: Princeton University Press.

Dilthey, Wilhelm. 1962. *Pattern and Meaning in History: Thoughts on History and Society*. New York: Harper & Row.

Donald, Stephanie, and John G. Gammack. 2007. *Tourism and the Branded City: Film and Identity on the Pacific Rim*. New Directions in Tourism Analysis. Aldershot, UK: Ashgate.

Dreyfus, Georges B. J. 2003. *The Sound of Two Hands Clapping: The Education of a Tibetan Buddhist Monk*. Berkeley: University of California Press.

DuBois, Thomas David. 2005. *The Sacred Village: Social Change and Religious Life in Rural North China*. Honolulu: University of Hawai'i Press.

Duckett, Eleanor Shipley. 2000. *The Gateway to the Middle Ages: Monasticism*. Ann Arbor: University of Michigan Press.

Eck, Diana L. 2000. "Dialogue and Method: Reconstructing the Study of Religion." In *A Magic Still Dwells: Comparative Religion in the Postmodern Age*, edited by Kimberly Patton and Benjamin Ray, 131–149. Berkeley: University of California Press.

Ecke, Gustav, and Paul Demiéville. 1935. *The Twin Pagodas of Zayton*. Cambridge, MA: Harvard University Press.

Eng, Irene, and Lin Yi-Min. 2002. "Religious Festivities, Communal Rivalry, and Restructuring of Authority Relations in Rural Chaozhou, Southeast China." *Journal of Asian Studies* 61(4): 1259–1285.

Faure, Bernard. 1994. *The Rhetoric of Immediacy: A Cultural Critique of Chan/Zen Buddhism*. Princeton, NJ: Princeton University Press.

——. 1996. *Visions of Power: Imagining Medieval Japanese Buddhism*. Princeton, NJ: Princeton University Press.

——. 1998. "The Buddhist Icon and the Modern Gaze." *Critical Inquiry* 24(3): 768–813.

Ferguson, Andrew. 2000. *Zen's Chinese Heritage: The Masters and Their Teachings*. Somerville, MA: Wisdom Publications.

Feuchtwang, Stephan. 2000. "Religion as Resistance." In *Chinese Society: Change, Conflict, and Resistance*, edited by Elizabeth J. Perry and Mark Selden, 161–177. London: Routledge.

——. 2001. *Popular Religion in China: The Imperial Metaphor*. Richmond, UK: Curzon Press.

Fisher, Gareth. 2008. "The Spiritual Land Rush: Merit and Morality in New Chinese Buddhist Temple Construction." *Journal of Asian Studies* 67(1): 143–170.

——. 2011. "In the Footsteps of the Tourists: Buddhist Revival at Museum-Temple Sites in Beijing." *Social Compass* 58(4): 511–524.

——. 2014. *From Comrades to Bodhisattvas: Moral Dimensions of Lay Buddhist Practice in Contemporary China*. Honolulu: University of Hawai'i Press.

——. 2016. "Losing the Neighborhood Temple (Or Finding the Temple and Losing the Neighborhood): Transformations of Temple Space in Modern Beijing." In *Place/No-Place in Urban Asian Religiosity*, edited by Joanne P. Waghorne, 109–129. Singapore: Springer.

Flath, James A. 2016. *Traces of the Sage. Monument, Materiality, and the First Temple of Confucius*. Honolulu: University of Hawai'i Press.

Flower, John. 2004. "A Road is Made: Roads, Temples, and Historical Memory in Ya'an County, Sichuan." *Journal of Asian Studies* 63(3): 649–685.

Flower, John, and Pamela Leonard. 1998. "Defining Cultural Life in the Chinese Countryside: The Case of Chuan Zhu Temple." In *Cooperative and Collective in China's Rural Development*, edited by Eduard B. Vermeer, Frank N. Pieke, and Woei Lien Chong, 273–291. Armonk, NY: M. E. Sharpe.

Foot, John. 2007. "Micro-History of a House: Memory and Place in a Milanese Neighborhood, 1890–2000." *Urban History* 34(3): 431–452.

Foulk, T. Griffith. 1988. "The Zen Institution in Modern Japan." In *Zen: Tradition and Transition*, edited by Kenneth Kraft, 157–177. New York: Grove Press.

——. 1993. "Myth, Riutal, and Monastic Practice in Sung Ch'an Buddhism." In *Religion and Society in T'ang and Sung China*, edited by Patricia Buckley Ebrey and Peter N. Gregory, 147–194. Honolulu: University of Hawai'i Press.

——. 1995. "Daily Life in the Assembly." In *Buddhism in Practice*, edited by Donald S. Lopez, 359–379. Princeton, NJ: Princeton University Press.

Fujiansheng wenguan hui gongzuo zu 福建省文管会工作组 [Fujian Province Cultural Management Association Work Group]. 1962. 福建泉州开元寺 [Fujian's Quanzhou Kaiyuan Temple]. Quanzhou: Jinjiang Zhuanshu Wenhua Ju 晋江专署文化局 and Quanzhou Shi Wenwu Guanli Weiyuan Hui 文物管理委员会.

Geary, David. 2017. *The Rebirth of Bodh Gaya: Buddhism and the Making of a World Heritage Site*. Seattle: University of Washington Press.

Geertz, Clifford. 1973. *The Interpretation of Cultures*. New York: Basic Books.

Gerhart, Karen M. 2009. *The Material Culture of Death in Medieval Japan*. Honolulu: University of Hawai'i Press.

Germano, David, and Kevin Trainor. 2004. *Embodying the Dharma Buddhist Relic Veneration in Asia*. Albany: State University of New York Press.

Gernet, Jacques. 1995. *Buddhism in Chinese Society: An Economic History from the Fifth to the Tenth Centuries*. Translated by Franciscus Verellen. New York: Columbia University Press.

Gildow, Douglas M. 2014. "The Chinese Ritual Field: Common Public Rituals in PRC Monasteries Today." *Journal of Chinese Buddhist Studies* 27:59–127.

Ginzburg, Carlo. 2012. *Threads and Traces: True False Fictive*. Berkeley: University of California Press.

Gladney, Dru C. 1991. *Muslim Chinese: Ethnic Nationalism in the People's Republic*. Cambridge, MA: Harvard University Press.

Gold, Daniel. 2003. *Aesthetics and Analysis in Writing on Religion: Modern Fascinations*. Berkeley: University of California Press.

Goldstein, Melvyn C. 1998. "The Revival of Monastic Life in Drepung Monastery." In *Buddhism in Contemporary Tibet*, edited by Melvyn C. Goldstein and Matthew T. Kapstein, 15–52. Berkeley: University of California Press.

Goldstein, Melvyn C., and Matthew T. Kapstein, eds. 1998. *Buddhism in Contemporary Tibet*. Berkeley: University of California Press.

Gombrich, Richard F. 1988. *Theravada Buddhism: A Social History from Ancient Benares to Modern Colombo*. London: Routledge and Kegan Paul.

Gutschow, Kim. 2004. *Being a Buddhist Nun: The Struggle for Enlightenment in the Himalayas*. Cambridge, MA: Harvard University Press.

Guy, John. 2010. "Quanzhou: Cosmopolitan City of Faiths." In *The World of Khubilai Khan: Chinese Art in the Yuan Dynasty*, edited by James C. Y. Watt, 159–178. New York: Metropolitan Museum of Art.

Hackmann, Heinrich Friedrich. 1910. *Buddhism as a Religion: Its Historical Development and Its Present Conditions*. London: Probsthain & Co.

Hahn, Thomas H. 1989. "New Developments Concerning Buddhist and Taoist Monasteries." In *The Turning of the Tide: Religion in China Today*, edited by Julian F. Pas, 79–101. New York: Oxford University Press.

Hayles, N. Katherine. 2017. *Unthought: The Power of the Cognitive Nonconscious*. Chicago: University of Chicago Press.

He Mianshan 何绵山. 2000. "Jindai sida gaoseng yu fujian fojiao" 近代四大高僧与福建佛教 [Four Contemporary Eminent Monks of Fujian Buddhism]. *Fayin* 法音 [Voice of Dharma] 1:10–20.

——. 2005. "Hongyi Dashi zai Fujian 弘一大师在福建" [Master Hongyi in Fujian]. In *Hongyi Dashi Jinian Wenji* 弘一大师纪念文集 [Master Hongyi Memorial Collection], edited by Chen Zhenzhen 陈珍珍 and Chen Xiangyue 陈祥耀, 372–383. Quanzhou: Haifeng Publishing House 海风出版社.

Heine, Steven. 2012. *Sacred High City, Sacred Low City: A Tale of Religious Sites in Two Tokyo Neighborhoods*. New York: Oxford University Press.

Heise, Ingmar. 2012. "For Buddhas, Families, and Ghosts: The Transformation of the Ghost Festival into a Dharma Assembly in Southeast China." In *Buddhist Funeral Cultures of Southeast Asia and China*, edited by Paul Williams and Patrice Ladwig, 217–237. Cambridge: Cambridge University Press.

Hessler, Peter. 2001. *River Town: Two Years on the Yangtze*. New York: Harper Collins.

Hisao Inagaki, and Harold Stewart. 2003. *The Three Pure Land Sutras*. Berkeley, CA: Numata Center for Buddhist Translation and Research.

Ho Puay-Peng. 1995. "The Ideal Monastery: Daoxuan's Description of the Central Indian Jetavana Vihara." *East Asian History* 10:1–18.

Huang Shuikan 黄水看. 2005. 泉州文化古跡 [The Culture and Historic Sites of Quanzhou]. Beijing: Zhong Guo Wenlian Publishing House 中国文联出版社.

Humphrey, Caroline, and Hürelbaatar Ujeed. 2014. *A Monastery in Time: The Making of Mongolian Buddhism*. Chicago: University of Chicago Press.

Inglis, Alister David. 2006. *Hong Mai's Record of the Listener and its Song Dynasty Context*. Albany: State University of New York Press.

Jaffe, Richard M. 2011. *Neither Monk Nor Layman: Clerical Marriage in Modern Japanese Buddhism*. Honolulu: University of Hawaiʻi Press.

James, William. 1961. *The Varieties of Religious Experience*. New York: Macmillan. First published 1902 by Random House (New York).

Jansen, Berthe. 2018. *The Monastery Rules: Buddhist Monastic Organization in Pre-Modern Tibet*. Oakland: University of California Press.
Japhet, Sara. 1998. "Some Biblical Concepts of Sacred Space." In *Sacred Space: Shrine, City, Land*, edited by Benjamin Z. Kedar and R. J. Zwi Werblowsky, 55–72. Washington Square: New York University Press.
Ji Zhe. 2004. "Buddhism and the State: A New Relationship." *China Perspectives* 55(2): 2–10. Accessed November 22, 2021. http://www.cefc.com.hk/article/buddhism-and-the-state-a-new-relationship-increasing-numbers-of-believers-bring-great-changes-to-the-monastic-economy-in-china.
———. 2013. "Zhao Puchu and His Renjian Buddhism." *Eastern Buddhist*, New Series 44(2): 35–58.
———. 2017. "Comrade Zhao Puchu: Bodhisattva Under the Red Flag." In *Making Saints in Modern China*, edited by David Ownby, Vincent Goossaert, and Ji Zhe, 312–348. New York: Oxford University Press.
Jiangsu Provincial Tourism Bureau. 2001. *Travel Round Jiangsu*. Beijing: China Forestry Publishing House.
Jing Jun. 1996. *The Temple of Memories: History, Power, and Morality in a Chinese Village*. Stanford, CA: Stanford University Press.
———. 2006. "Buddhism and Economic Reform in Mainland China." In *Chinese Religions in Contemporary Societies*, edited by James Miller, 85–100. Santa Barbara, CA: ABC-CLIO.
Kang Xiaofei. 2009. "Two Temples, Three Religions, and a Tourist Attraction: Contesting Sacred Space on China's Ethnic Frontier." *Modern China* 35(3): 227–255.
Karlsson, Klemens. 2006. "The Formation of Early Buddhist Visual Culture." *Material Religion: The Journal of Objects, Art and Belief* 2(1): 68–95.
Kaza, Stephanie. 2019. *Green Buddhism: Practice and Compassionate Action in Uncertain Times*. Boulder, CO: Shambhala Publications.
Kiely, Jan. 2016. "The Communist Dismantling of Temple and Monastic Buddhism in Suzhou." In *Recovering Buddhism in Modern China*, edited by Jan Kiely and J. Brooks Jessup, 216–253. New York: Columbia University Press.
Kieschnick, John. 1997. *The Eminent Monk: Buddhist Ideals in Medieval Chinese Hagiography*. Honolulu: University of Hawai'i Press.
———. 2003. *The Impact of Buddhism on Chinese Material Culture*. Princeton, NJ: Princeton University Press.
Knott, Kim. 2005. *The Location of Religion: A Spatial Analysis*. New York: Routledge.
———. 2010. "Religion, Space, and Place: The Spatial Turn in Research on Religion." *Religion and Society: Advances in Research I* 1(1): 29–43.
Kong, Lily. 2001. "Mapping 'New' Geographies of Religion: Politics and Poetics in Modernity." *Progress in Human Geography* 25(2): 211–33.
Kuah-Pearce, Khun Eng. 2011. *Rebuilding the Ancestral Village: Singaporeans in China*. Hong Kong: Hong Kong University Press.
———. 2010. *China: A Religious State*. Hong Kong: Hong Kong University Press.
Lai Chi-Tim. 2003. "Daoism in China Today, 1980–2002." *China Quarterly* 174: 413–27.
Laliberté, André, and Stefania Trafagnin. 2019. "Epistemic Communities of Buddhist Scholarship in Modern China: Narratives and Paradigms." In *Concepts and Methods for the Study of Chinese Religions I: State of the Field and Disciplinary Approaches*, edited by André Laliberté and Stefania Trafagnin, 115–138. Berlin: DeGruyter.
Lamley, Harry J. 1990. "Lineage and Surname Feuds in Southern Fukien and Eastern Kwantung under the Ch'ing." In *Orthodoxy in Late Imperial China*, edited by Kwang-Ching Liu, 254–278. Berkeley: University of California Press.
Lancaster, Lewis. 1974. "An Early Mahayana Sermon about the Body of the Buddha and the Making of Images." *Artibus Asiae* 36(4): 287–291.

Lakoff, George, and Mark Johnson. 1999. *Philosophy in the Flesh: The Embodied Mind and Its Challenge to Western Thought*. New York: Basic Books.

Lang, Graeme, Selina Chan, and Lars Ragvald. 2005. "Temples and the Religious Economy." In *State, Market, and Religions in Chinese Societies*, edited by Fenggang Yang and Joseph B. Tamney, 149–180. Leiden: Brill.

Ledderose, Lothar. 2000. *Ten Thousand Things: Module and Mass Production in Chinese Art*. Princeton, NJ: Princeton University Press.

Lee, Risha. 2012. "Constructing Community: Tamil Merchant Temples in India and China, 850–1281." PhD diss., Columbia University.

Lefebvre, Henri. 2009. *The Production of Space*. Translated by Donald Nicholson-Smith. Malden, MA: Blackwell.

Lei, Chun Kwok, and Shujie Yao. 2009. *Economic Convergence in Greater China: Mainland China, Hong Kong, Macau and Taiwan*. London: Routledge.

Le Blanc, Charles. 1985. *Hui Nan Tzu: Philosophical Synthesis in Early Han Thought*. Hong Kong: Hong Kong University Press.

Lewis, Ioan M. 1986. *Religion in Context: Cults and Charisma*. Cambridge: Cambridge University Press.

Li Yukun 李玉昆. 1988. "Quanzhou gang yu gudai haiwai jiaotong" 泉州港与古代海外交通 [The Port of Quanzhou and Ancient Maritime Communications]. *Fayin* 法音 [Voice of Dharma] 1:30–32.

Lin Zhao 林钊. 1959. "Quanzhou Kaiyuansi dadian" 泉州开元寺大殿 [The Main Hall of Quanzhou Kaiyuan Temple]. *Wenwu* 文物 [Cultural Heritage] 2: 42–43, 45.

Lin Zhijue 林志觉, Ceng Conghong 曾聪虹, and Lin Jinfeng 林劲峰. 2006. "市领导慰问革命老同志" [City Leader Expresses Regards for his Revolutionary Comrade]. 泉州晚报 [Quanzhou Evening Paper], October 21.

Loewe, Michael. 1982. *Chinese Ideas of Life and Death: Faith, Myth and Reason in the Han Period (202 BC–AD 220)*. London: Allen & Unwin.

Lopez, Donald S., ed. 1995. *Buddhism in Practice*. Princeton, NJ: Princeton University Press.

Loy, David. 2019. *Ecodharma: Buddhist Teachings for the Ecological Crisis*. Somerville, MA: Wisdom Publications.

Luo Shazhou 骆沙舟 2001. "*Quanzhou de sanzuo hongyi daishi zhita*" 泉州的三座弘一大师之塔 [Quanzhou's Three Pagodas for Great Master Hongyi]. *Fujian fojiao* 福建佛教 1:67–68.

Lynn, Richard John. 1994. *The Classic of Changes: A New Translation of the I Ching as Interpreted by Wang Bi*. New York: Columbia University Press.

MacInnis, Donald E. 1989. *Religion in China Today: Policy and Practice*. Maryknoll, NY: Orbis Books.

Madsen, Richard. 1993. "The Public Sphere, Civil Society and Moral Community: A Research Agenda for Contemporary Chinese Studies." *Modern China* 19(2): 183–198.

——. 1998. *China's Catholics: Tragedy and Hope in an Emerging Civil Society*. Berkeley: University of California Press.

——. 2014. "Secular Belief, Religious Belonging in China." *Review of Religion and Chinese Society* 1:13–28.

Maitland, Jeffrey. 1995. *Spacious Body: Explorations in Somatic Ontology*. Berkeley, CA: North Atlantic Books.

Makley, Charlene E. 2007. *The Violence of Liberation: Gender and Tibetan Buddhist Revival in Post-Mao China*. Berkeley: University of California Press.

McBride, Richard D. 2005. "Dharani and Spells in Medieval Sinitic Buddhism." *Journal of the International Association of Buddhist Studies* 28(1): 85–114.

McCarthy, Susan K. 2010. "Economic Development and the Buddhist-Industrial Complex of Xishuangbanna." In *Faiths on Display: Religion, Tourism, and the*

Chinese State, edited by Tim Oakes and Donald S. Sutton, 157–181. Lanham, MD: Rowman & Littlefield.
——. 2013. "Serving Society, Repurposing the State: Religious Charity and Resistance in China." *China Journal* 70(1): 48–72.
——. 2019. "Spiritual Technologies and the Politics of Buddhist Charity." In *Buddhism after Mao*, edited by Ji Zhe, Gareth Fisher, and André Laliberte, 77–96. Honolulu: University of Hawai'i Press.
McDaniel, Justin. 2017. *Architects of Buddhist Leisure: Socially Disengaged Buddhism in Asia's Museums, Monuments, and Amusement Parks*. Honolulu: University of Hawai'i Press.
Menakem, Resmaa. 2017. *My Grandmother's Hands: Racialized Trauma and the Pathway to Mending Our Hearts and Bodies*. Las Vegas, NV: Central Recovery Press.
Merleau-Ponty, Maurice. 2012. *Phenomenology of Perception*. Translated by Donald A. Landes. New York: Routledge.
Meyer, Jeffrey. 1992. "Chinese Buddhist Monastic Temples as Cosmograms." In *Sacred Architecture in the Traditions of India, China, Judaism, and Islam*, edited by Emily B. Lyle, 71–92. Edinburgh: Edinburgh University Press.
Miaolian 妙莲 et al., eds. 1986. *Quanzhou Kaiyuansi* 泉州开元寺 [Quanzhou Kaiyuan Monastery]. Pt. 1, vol. 3, *Zhongguo fojiao mingsi gucha* 中国佛教名寺古刹. Quanzhou: Kaiyuan Monastery.
Michie, Jonathan, and John Grieve Smith. 1998. *Globalization, Growth, and Governance: Creating an Innovative Economy*. Oxford: Oxford University Press.
Miller, James. 2020. *China's Green Religion: Daoism and the Quest for a Sustainable Future*. New York: Columbia University Press.
Miller, Tracy. 2007. *The Divine Nature of Power: Chinese Ritual Architecture at the Sacred Site of Jinci*. Cambridge, MA: Harvard University Asia Center for the Harvard-Yenching Institute.
Mitchell, Donald W. 2008. *Buddhism: Introducing the Buddhist Experience*. New York: Oxford University Press.
Morgan, Nigel, Annette Pritchard, and Roger Pride, eds. 2004. *Destination Branding: Creating the Unique Destination Proposition*. Oxford: Elsevier Butterworth-Heinemann.
Morton, W. Scott, and Charlton M. Lewis. 2005. *China: Its History and Culture*. New York: McGraw-Hill.
Mote, Frank. 1977. "Yuan and Ming." In *Food in Chinese Culture*, edited by Kwang-chih Chang, 193–257. New Haven, CT: Yale University Press.
Naquin, Susan. 1998. "Sites, Saints and Sights at the Tanzhe Monastery." *Cahiers d'Extrême-Asia* 10:183–211.
——. 2000. *Peking: Temples and City Life, 1400–1900*. Berkeley: University of California Press.
Nattier, Jan. 1995. "A Prophecy of the Death of the Dharma." In *Buddhism in Practice*, edited by Donald S. Lopez, 249–256. Princeton, NJ: Princeton University Press.
Nedostup, Rebecca. 2009. *Superstitious Regimes: Religion and the Politics of Chinese Modernity*. Cambridge, MA: Harvard University Asia Center.
Needham, Joseph. 1951. "Human Laws and Laws of Nature in China and the West." *Journal of the History of Ideas* 12(1): 3–30; 12(2): 194–230.
Ng Chin-keong. 1971. "The Fukienese Martime Trade in the Second Half of the Ming Period: Government Policy and Elite Groups' Attitudes." *Nanyang University Journal* 5:81–100.
——. 1972. "A Study of the Peasant Society of South Fukien, 1506–1644." *Nanyang University Journal* 6:189–212.
Ng, Zhiru. 2007. *The Making of a Savior Bodhisattva: Dizang in Medieval China*. Honolulu: University of Hawai'i Press.

Nichols, Brian J. 2015. "Typologizing Religious Practice at Buddhist Monasteries in Contemporary China." In *Chinese Buddhism: Past, Present, and Future*, edited by Xie Da-ning 謝大檸, 411–436. Yilan, TW: Fo Guang University Center for Buddhist Studies.

——. 2016. "Farong: A Modernist Buddhist Monk with Chinese Characteristics." In *Buddhist Figures of Modernity*, edited by Jeffrey Samuels, Justin T. McDaniel, and Mark Rowe, 110–112. Honolulu: University of Hawaiʻi Press.

——. 2017. "Taking Welch and The Practice of Chinese Buddhism into the 21st Century." *Studies in Chinese Religions* 3(3): 258–280.

——. 2019a. "Advancing the Ethnography of Buddhism in China." In *Concepts and Methods for the Study of Chinese Religions I: State of the Field and Disciplinary Approaches*, edited by André Laliberté and Stefania Travagnin, 139–162. Berlin: DeGruyter.

——. 2019b. "Tourist Temples and Places of Practice: Charting Multiple Paths in the Revival of Monastic Buddhism." In *Buddhism after Mao*, edited by Ji Zhe, Gareth Fisher, and André Laliberté, 97–119. Honolulu: University of Hawaiʻi Press.

——. 2020. "Interrogating Religious Tourism at Buddhist Monasteries in China." In *Buddhist Tourism in Asia: Imagining, Secularizing, and Commodifying the Sacred*, edited by Courtney Bruntz and Brooke Schedneck. Honolulu: University of Hawaiʻi Press.

Norris, Kathleen. 2014. *The Cloister Walk*. New York: Riverhead Books.

Olaveson, Tim. 2001. "Collective Effervescence and Communitas: Processual Models of Ritual and Society in Emile Durkheim and Victor Turner." *Dialectical Anthropology* 26(2): 89–124.

Olins, W. 2004. *On Br®and*. London: Thames and Hudson.

Orzech, Charles D. 1989. "Seeing Chen-Yen Buddhism: Traditional Scholarship and the Vajrayana in China." *History of Religions* 29:87–114.

——. 1995. "Saving the Burning-Mouth Hungry Ghost." In *Religions of China in Practice*, edited by Donald S. Lopez, 278–283. Princeton, NJ: Princeton University Press.

——. 2002. "Fang Yankou and Pudu: Translation, Metaphor, and Religious Identity." In *Daoist Identity: History, Lineage, and Ritual*, edited by Livia Kohn and Harold D. Roth, 213–234. Honolulu: University of Hawaiʻi Press.

Overmyer, Daniel L., ed. 2003. *Religion in China Today*. The China Quarterly Special Issues, New Series no. 3. Cambridge: Cambridge University Press.

Paper, Jordan. 1995. *The Spirits Are Drunk: Comparative Approaches to Chinese Religion*. Albany: State University of New York Press.

Pas, Julian F., ed. 1989. *The Turning of the Tide: Religion in China Today*. New York: Oxford University Press.

Pegis, Anton C., ed. 1945. *The Basic Writings of Saint Thomas Aquinas*. New York: Random House.

Poceski, Mario. 2003. "Xuefeng's Code and the Chan School's Participation in the Development of Monastic Regulations." *Asia Major* 16(2): 33–56.

Portelli, Alessandro. 1991. *The Death of Luigi Trastulli, and Other Stories: Form and Meaning in Oral History*. Albany: State University of New York Press.

Porter, Bill (Red Pine). 2000. *The Collected Songs of Cold Mountain*. Port Townsend, WA: Copper Canyon Press.

Potter, Pitman B. 2003. "Belief in Control: Regulation of Religion in China." *China Quarterly* 174(June): 317–337.

Primiano, Leonard N. 1995. "Vernacular Religion and the Search for Method in Religious Folklife." *Western Folklore* 54(1): 37–56.

Prip-Møller, Johannes. 1937. *Chinese Buddhist Monasteries: Their Plan and Its Function as a Setting for Buddhist Monastic Life*. London: Oxford University Press.

Puett, Michael, and Christine Gross-Loh. 2016. *The Path: What Chinese Philosophers Can Teach Us about the Good Life*. New York: Simon & Schuster.

Puti 菩提. 2000. "*Yidai gaoseng, Yuanzhuo lao fashi*" 一代高僧圆拙老法师 [Old Master Yuanzhuo, an Eminent Monk of Our Generation]. *Fayin* 法音 [Voice of Dharma] 1:21–23.

Qin, Wen-jie. 2000. "The Buddhist Revival in Post-Mao China: Women Reconstruct Buddhism on Mt. Emei." PhD diss., Harvard University.

Quan Guo Dang Hui 泉国档会. 1984. *Ziyun xiangtang huangshi zupu* 紫云象塘黄氏族谱 [The History of the Purple Cloud Huang Clan of Xiangtang (Putian)]. 国家档案局文件 (personal copy of Huang Yushan 黄玉山).

Rambelli, Fabio. 2007. *Buddhist Materiality: A Cultural History of Objects in Japanese Buddhism*. Stanford, CA: Stanford University Press.

Rappaport, Roy A. 1999. *Ritual and Religion in the Making of Humanity*. Cambridge: Cambridge University Press.

Reader, Ian. 2014. *Pilgrimage in the Marketplace*. New York: Routledge.

Rethmann, Petra. 2007. "On Presence." In *Extraordinary Anthropology*, edited by Jean-Guy A. Goulet and Bruce Granville Miller, 36–52. Lincoln: University of Nebraska Press.

Ritzinger, Justin, and Marcus Bingenheimer. 2006. "Whole-Body Relics in Chinese Buddhism." *Indian International Journal of Buddhist Studies* 7:37–94.

Roberts, John M., Chien Chiao, and Triloki N. Pandey. 1975. "Meaningful God Sets from a Chinese Personal Pantheon and a Hindu Personal Pantheon." *Ethnology* 14(2): 121–148.

Roberts, John M., Saburo Morita, and L. Keith Brown. 1986. "Personal Categories of Japanese Sacred Places and Gods: Views Elicited from a Conjugal Pair." *American Anthropologist* 88(4): 807–824.

Robinson, Richard H., Willard L. Johnson, and Thānissaro Bhikkhu. 2005. *Buddhist Religions: A Historical Introduction*. Belmont, CA: Wadsworth.

Robson, James. 2010a. "'Neither Too Far, Nor Too Near': The Historical and Cultural Contexts of Buddhist Monasteries in Medieval China and Japan." In *Buddhist Monasticism in East Asia*, edited by James A. Benn, Lori Meeks, and James Robson, 1–17. New York: Routledge.

——. 2010b. "Monastic Spaces and Sacred Traces: Facets of Chinese Buddhist Monastic Records." In *Buddhist Monasticism in East Asia*, edited by James A. Benn, Lori Meeks, and James Robson, 43–64. New York: Routledge.

Rowe, Mark M. 2011. *Bonds of the Dead: Temples, Burial, and the Transformation of Contemporary Japanese Buddhism*. Chicago: University of Chicago Press.

Sangren, Paul Steven. 2000. *Chinese Sociologics: An Anthropological Account of Alienation and Social Reproduction*. London: Athlone.

Schafer, Edward. 1954. *The Empire of the Min*. Reprint. Rutland, VT: Tuttle, 2006.

Schipper, Kristofer Marinus. 1993. *The Taoist Body*. Berkeley: University of California Press.

Schlütter, Morton. 2005. "Vinaya Monasteries, Public Abbacies, and State Control of Buddhism under the Song (960–1279)." In *Going Forth*, edited by William Bodiford, 136–160. Honolulu: University of Hawai'i Press.

——. 2008. *How Zen Became Zen: The Dispute over Enlightenment and the Formation of Chan Buddhism in Song-Dynasty China*. Kindle Edition. Honolulu: University of Hawai'i Press.

Schopen, Gregory. 1990. "The Buddha as an Owner of Property and Permanent Resident in Medieval Indian Monasteries." *Journal of Indian Philosophy* 18(3): 181–217.

——. 1997. *Bones, Stones, and Buddhist Monks: Collected Papers on the Archaeology, Epigraphy, and Texts of Monastic Buddhism in India*. Honolulu: University of Hawai'i Press.

——. 2000. "The Good Monk and his Money in a Buddhist Monasticism of the 'Mahāyāna Period.'" *The Eastern Buddhist, New Series* 32(1): 85–105.

——. 2004. *Buddhist Monks and Business Matters: Still More Papers on Monastic Buddhism in India*. Honolulu: University of Hawai'i Press.

——. 2006. "'The Buddhist Monastery' and the Indian Garden: Aesthetics, Assimilations, and the Siting of Monastic Establishments." *Journal of the American Oriental Society* 126(4): 487–505.

Sharf, Robert H. 1992. "The Idolization of Enlightenment: On Mummification of Ch'an Masters in Medieval China." *History of Religions* 32(1): 1–31.

——. 2002. *Coming to Terms with Chinese Buddhism: A Reading of the Treasure Store Treatise*. Honolulu: University of Hawai'i Press.

——. 2005. "Ritual." In *Critical Terms for the Study of Buddhism*, edited by Donald Lopez, 144–161. Chicago: University of Chicago Press.

Sharf, Robert H., and Elizabeth Horton Sharf. 2001. *Living Images: Japanese Buddhist Icons in Context*. Stanford, CA: Stanford University Press.

Shayne, Clarke. 2009. "Monks Who Have Sex: 'Parajika' Penance in Indian Buddhist Monasticisms." *Journal of Indian Philosophy* 37(1): 1–43.

Shen Yushui 沈玉水. 1990. *Muan chanshi xingji xinian* 木庵禅师行迹系年 [Year-by-Year Account of Chan Master Muan's Activities]. Quanzhou: Quanzhou shi Kaiyuan Wanshou Chansi Bianyin.

Shinohara, Koichi. 1998. "Changing Roles for Miraculous Images in Medieval Chinese Buddhism: A Study of the Miracle Image Section in Daoxuan's 'Collected Records'." In *Images, Miracles and Authority in Asian Religious Traditions*, edited by Richard H. David, 141–188. Boulder, CO: Westview Press.

Soothill, William Edward, and Lewis Hodous. 1977. *A Dictionary of Chinese Buddhist Terms: With Sanskrit and English Equivalents and a Sanskrit-Pali Index*. New York: Routledge.

Southwold, Martin. 1983. *Buddhism in Life: The Anthropological Study of Religion and the Sinhalese Practice of Buddhism*. Manchester, UK: Manchester University Press.

Spiro, Milford. 1982. *Buddhism and Society: A Great Tradition and its Burmese Vicissitudes*, 2nd ed. Berkeley: University of California Press.

Stausberg, Michael. 2011. *Religion and Tourism: Crossroads, Destinations, and Encounters*. New York: Routledge.

Stevenson, Daniel. 1995. "Pure Land Buddhist Worship and Meditation in China." In *Buddhism in Practice*, edited by Donald S. Lopez, 359–379. Princeton, NJ: Princeton University Press.

Stockwell, Foster. 1993. *Religion in China Today*. Beijing: New World Press.

Strickmann, Michel. 1980. "Review: History, Anthropology, and Chinese Religion." *Harvard Journal of Asiatic Studies* 40(1): 201–248.

So, Billy K. L. 2000. *Prosperity, Region, and Institutions in Maritime China: The South Fukien Pattern, 946–1368*. Harvard East Asian monographs, 195. Cambridge, MA: Harvard University Asia Center.

Sun Chong. 2002. "Shenghuo ru ge, chan zuo xian: Bailin chansi 'Shenghuo chan xialingying' Shi Zhounian Ceji" 生活如歌禅做弦: 柏林禅寺生活禅夏令营十周年侧记 [Life Is Like a Song, Meditation Is Like the Strings that Strum It: Remarks on the Tenth Anniversary of the Bailin Zen Monastery's 'Living Zen Summer Camp']. *Zhongguo Zongjiao* [Chinese Religion] 5:21–23.

Sun, Yanfei. 2017. "Jingkong: From Universal Saint to Sectarian Saint." In *Making Saints in Modern China*, edited by David Ownby, Vincent Goossaert, and Ji Zhe, 394–418. New York: Oxford University Press.

Svensson, Marina. 2010. "Tourist Itineraries, Spatial Management, and Hidden Temples: The Revival of Religious Sites in a Water Town." In *Faiths on Display: Religion, Tourism, and the Chinese State*, edited by Tim Oakes and Donald S. Sutton, 211–233. Lanham, MD: Rowman & Littlefield.

Tam, Yik Fai. 2012. "Xianghua Foshi 香花佛事 (Incense and Flower Buddhist Rites): A Local Buddhist Funeral Ritual Tradition in Southeastern China." In *Buddhist Funeral Cultures of Southeast Asia and China*, edited by Paul Williams and Patrice Ladwig, 238–260. Cambridge: Cambridge University Press.

Tambiah, Stanley Jeyaraja. 2007. *The Buddhist Saints of the Forest and the Cult of Amulets: A Study in Charisma, Hagiography, Sectarianism, and Millennial Buddhism*. Cambridge: Cambridge University Press.

Tarocco, Francesca. 2008. *The Cultural Practices of Modern Chinese Buddhism: Attuning the Dharma*. London: Routledge.

——. 2011. "On the Market: Consumption and Material Culture in Modern Chinese Buddhism." *Religion* 41(4): 627–644.

Teiser, Stephen F. 1988. *The Ghost Festival in Medieval China*. Princeton, NJ: Princeton University Press.

Thøgersen, Stig. 2006. "Beyond Official Chinese: Language Codes and Strategies." In *Doing Fieldwork in China*, edited by Maria Heimer and Stig Thøgersen, 110–126. Honolulu: University of Hawai'i Press.

Thompson, Laurence G. 1996. *Chinese Religion: An Introduction*. Belmont, CA: Wadsworth.

Thoreau, Henry David. (1849) 1998. *A Week on the Concord and Merrimack Rivers*. Reprint, with introduction and notes by H. Daniel Peck. New York: Penguin Books.

Throop, C. Jason, and Charles D. Laughlin. 2002. "Ritual, Collective Effervescence and the Categories: Toward a Neo-Durkheimian Model of the Nature of Human Consciousness, Feeling and Understanding." *Journal of Ritual Studies* 16(1): 40–63.

T'ien Ju-K'ang. 1990. "The Decadence of Buddhist Temples in Fu-chien in Late Ming and Early Ch'ing." In *Development and Decline of Fukien Province in the 17th and 18th Centuries*, edited by Eduard B. Vermeer, 83–100. Leiden: Brill.

Tu, Wei-ming. 2001. "The Ecological Turn in New Confucian Humanism: Implications for China and the World." *Deadalus* 130(4): 243–264.

Tuan, Yifu. 1974. *Topophilia*. Englewood Cliffs, NJ: Prentice-Hall.

Varela, Francisco J., Evan Thompson, and Eleanor Rosch. 1991. *The Embodied Mind: Cognitive Science and Human Experience*. Cambridge, MA: MIT Press.

Wakeman, Frederic, Jr. 1966. *Strangers at the Gate: Social Disorder in South China, 1829–1861*. Berkeley: University of California Press.

Wallace, B. Allan. 2009. *Mind in the Balance: Meditation in Science, Buddhism, and Christianity*. New York: Columbia University Press.

Walsh, Michael J. 2007. "The Economics of Salvation: Toward a Theory of Exchange in Chinese Buddhism." *Journal of the American Academy of Religion* 75(2): 353–382.

——. 2010. *Sacred Economies: Buddhist Monasticism & Territoriality in Medieval China*. New York: Columbia University Press.

Wang, Chen-shan (Ellen). 2008. "Quanzhou Kaiyuan Monastery: Architecture, Iconography and Social Contexts." PhD diss., University of Pennsylvania.

Wang, Eugene. 2010. "Pictorial Program in the Making of Monastic Space." In *Buddhist Monasticism in East Asia*, edited by James A. Benn, Lori Meeks, and James Robson, 65–106. New York: Routledge.

Wang Hanfeng 王寒枫. 1982. "*Quanzhou kaiyuansi xingshuai chutan*" 泉州开元寺兴衰初探 [Quanzhou Kaiyuan Monastery Rising and Falling, Initial Thoughts]. Paper presented at the Quanzhou City Historical Research Association 1982 Symposium, Quanzhou, September 29.

——. 1992. *Quanzhou dongxi ta* 泉州东西塔 [Quanzhou's East and West Pagodas]. Fuzhou: Fujian People's Publishing House 福建人民出版社.

——. 2001a. "*Sanzong rongguan yi lu weizhong*" 三宗融贯以律为重 [Three Schools Harmonize with Vinaya Central] *Fujian fojiao* 福建佛教 [Fujian Buddhism] 1:19–21.

——. 2001b. "*Quanzhou kaiyuansi mizong guizhi de tantao*" 泉州开元寺密宗轨制的探讨 [A Discussion of the Mizong Elements at Quanzhou Kaiyuan Temple]. Paper written for the First Annual Huayen Academic conference [华严学术论文研讨会] held by the Taiwan Huayan Institution [Taiwan Huayan Xuehui 台湾华严学会] and Huayan Academic Research Center [Huayan Xueshu Yanjiu Zhongxin 华严学术研究中心].

Wang Hanfeng 王寒枫 and Zeng Xiuchuan 曾秀川. 1986. *Quanzhou Kaiyuansi qiguan* 泉州开元寺奇观, A *Brief Introduction to Kaiyuan Temple of Quanzhou*. Fuzhou: Fujian People's Publishing House 福建人民出版社.

Weidner, Marsha Smith. 2010. "Fit for Monks' Quarters: Monasteries as Centers of Aesthetic Activity in the Later Fourteenth Century." *Ars Orientalis* 37:49–77.

Weidner, Marsha Smith, and Patricia Ann Berger. 1994. *Latter Days of the Law: Images of Chinese Buddhism, 850–1850*. Honolulu: University of Hawai'i Press.

Welch, Holmes. 1961. "Buddhism under the Communists." *China Quarterly* 6 (April–June): 1–14.

——. 1967. *The Practice of Chinese Buddhism, 1900–1950*. Cambridge, MA: Harvard University Press.

——. 1968. *The Buddhist Revival in China*. Cambridge, MA: Harvard University Press.

——. 1969. "Buddhism since the Cultural Revolution." *China Quarterly* 40:127–136.

——. 1972. *Buddhism under Mao*. Cambridge, MA: Harvard University Press.

Wen Lan 文澜. 2000. *Foguo ming chuanjiu sanglian du shansheng: Ji quanzhou kaiyuansi* 佛国名传久桑莲独擅声: 记泉州开元寺 [An Introduction to Quanzhou Kaiyuan Monastery]. *Fayin* 法音 [Voice of Dharma] 1:50–51.

Wheatley, Paul. 1971. *The Pivot of the Four Quarters: A Preliminary Enquiry into the Origins and Character of the Ancient Chinese City*. Chicago: Aldine Publishing.

Winfield, Pamela. 2017. "Materializing the Zen Monastery." In *Zen and Material Culture*, edited by Pamela Winfield and Steven Heine, 37–69. New York: Oxford University Press.

Winfield, Pamela, and Steven Heine, eds. 2017. *Zen and Material Culture*. New York: Oxford University Press.

Wong, C. S. 1963. *Kek Lok Si: Temple of Paradise*. Singapore: Malaysian Sociological Research Institute.

Wright, Arthur F. 1959. *Buddhism in Chinese History*. Stanford, CA: Stanford University Press.

Wu, Hung. 2012. *A Story of Ruins: Presence and Absence in Chinese Art and Visual Culture*. London: Reaktion Books.

Wu, Jiang. 2008. *Enlightenment in Dispute: The Reinvention of Chan Buddhism in Seventeenth-Century China*. New York: Oxford University Press.

——. 2015. *Leaving for the Rising Sun: Chinese Zen Master Yinyuan & the Authenticity Crisis in Early Modern East Asia*. New York: Oxford University Press.

Wu Zhanjiang, Liu Huiwen, and Yuan Shuping. 2002. "*Qieji qieli de shenghuo chan: fang bailinsi fangzhang jinghui fashi*" 契机契理的生活禅—访柏林寺方丈净慧法师 [Novel and Traditional Living Zen: An Interview with the Abbot of the Bailin Monastery, Master Jinghui]. *Shijie Zongjiao Wenhua* [Religious Cultures of the World] (March 29): 15–17.

Yang, Fenggang. 2004. "Between Secularist Ideology and Desecularizing Reality: The Birth and Growth of Religious Research in Communist China." *Sociology of Religion* 65(2): 101–119.

——. 2006. "The Red, Black, and Gray Markets of Religion in China." *Sociological Quarterly* 47:93–122.

Yang, Fenggang, and Wei Dedong. 2005. "The Bailin Buddhist Temple: Thriving under Communism." In *State, Market, and Religions in Chinese Societies*, edited by Yang Fenggang, 63–86. Leiden: Brill.

Yang, Hsüan-chih. 1984. *A Record of Buddhist Monasteries in Lo-yang*, translated by Yi-t'ung Wang. Princeton, NJ: Princeton University Press.

Yang, Mayfair M. H. 2004a. "Goddess across the Taiwan Strait: Matrifocal Ritual Space, Nation-State and Satellite Television Footprints." *Public Culture* 16(2): 209–238.

——. 2004b. "Spatial Struggles: Post-Colonial Complex, State Disenchantment, and Popular Reappropriation of Space in Rural Southeast China." *Journal of Asian Studies* 63(3): 719–756.

——, ed. 2009. *Chinese Religiosities: Afflictions of Modernity and State Formation*. Berkeley: University of California Press.

Yao, Xinzhong, and Paul Badham. 2007. *Religious Experience in Contemporary China*. Cardiff: University of Wales Press.

Yifa, Ven. 2002. *The Origins of Buddhist Monastic Codes in China: An Annotated Translation and Study of the Chanyuan qinggui*. Honolulu: University of Hawai'i Press.

Yu, Anthony C. 2005. *State and Religion in China: Historical and Textual Perspectives*. Chicago: Open Court.

Yü, Chün-fang. 1981. *The Renewal of Buddhism in China: Chu-Hung and the Late Ming Synthesis*. New York: Columbia University Press.

——. 2000. *Kuan-yin: The Chinese Transformation of Avalokiteśvara*. New York: Columbia University Press.

Yu, David C. 1971. "Buddhism in Communist China: Demise or Co-Existence?" *Journal of the American Academy of Religion* 39(1): 48–61.

Yu Lingbo 于凌波. 1997. *Zhongguo fojiao haiwai hongfa renwu zhi* 中國佛教海外弘法人物誌 [A Record of Persons Who Have Propagated Chinese Buddhism Overseas]. Taipei: Huiju Publishing House 慧炬出版社.

——. 2005. *Minguo gaoseng zhuan* 民国高僧传 [A Record of Eminent Monks of the Republican Period]. Foxue congshu, 013–014. Taipei: Zhi Shufang Publishing House.

Yu, Xue. 2005. *Buddhism, War, and Nationalism: Chinese Monks in the Struggle against Japanese Aggressions, 1931–1945*. New York: Routledge.

——. 2009. "Buddhist Contribution to the Socialist Transformation of Buddhism in China: Activities of Ven. Juzan during 1949–1953." *Journal of Global Buddhism* 10:217–253.

Yuanying fashi jinian kan bianzuan weiyuanhui 圓瑛法師紀念刊編纂委員會 [Master Yuanying Memorial Booklet Compilation Committee]. 1954. *Yuanying fashi jinian kan* 圓瑛法師紀念刊 [Master Yuanying Memorial Booklet]. Singapore: Yuantong Temple 圆通寺.

Zhang Xiusheng 張秀生. 2000. Zhengding Longxing si 正定隆興寺. Beijing: Wenwu chubanshe文物出版社: Xinhua shudian jingxia 新華書店經銷.

Zhang Zhenhao 张真好. 2003. *Quannan foguo san da conglin lansheng* 泉南佛国三大丛林揽胜 [The Three Great Scenic Monasteries of the Buddhist Country of Southern Quanzhou]. Quanzhou: Quanzhou News Publishing Bureau 泉州市新闻出版局.

Zhou Shurong 周书荣. 1999. *Miaolian fashi yuanji* 妙莲法师圆寂 [Notice of Master Miaolian's Passing]. Fayin 法音 [Voice of Dharma] December: 43.

Zito, Angela. 1997. *Of Body & Brush: Grand Sacrifice as Text/Performance in Eighteenth-Century China*. Chicago: University of Chicago Press.

Zürcher, Erik. 1972. *The Buddhist Conquest of China: the Spread and Adaptation of Buddhism in Early Medieval China*. Leiden: Brill.

Primary Sources

Anon. (Tang Dynasty). 1983. *Quan Tang Wen* 全唐文 [Collected Works of Tang Literature]. Beijing: Zhonghua Book Company.

Anon. (Song Dynasty). 2003. *Wuguo gushi* 五國故事 [Tales of the Five Dynasties]. In *Quan song biji* 全宋筆記 [Complete Notes of the Song Dynasty], edited by Zhu Yian 朱易安 et al., vol. 1, 233–256. Zhengzhou: Daxiang Publishing House.

Bodhi. 2003. *The Connected Discourses of the Buddha: A Translation of the Saṃyutta Nikāya*. Somerville, MA: Wisdom Publications.

Chuanxi 传锡. 2004. "Wenge qijian de guang'an shi" 文革期间的广安师. In 广安长老永恩纪念集, edited by Daoyuan 释道元 and Chuanmin 传敏, 3. Quanzhou: Quanzhou Kaiyuan Monastery and Nan'an Xuefeng Monastery.

Dagui 大圭. (1348) 1929. *Ziyun kaishi zhuan* 紫雲開士傳 [Biographies of Purple Cloud Bodhisattvas].

Daoxuan 道宣 (596–667). 645. *Xu gaoseng zhuan* 續高僧傳 [Biographies of Eminent Monks, Continued]. CBETA T 50-2060.

——. ca. 660. *Daoxuan lushi gantong lu* 道宣律師感通録 [Record of Miraculous Responses by Vinaya Master Daoxuan]. CBETA T 52-2107.

——. ca. 660. *Luxiang gantong zhuan* 律相感通傳 [Characteristics of Stories of Spiritual Resonance]. CBETA T 45-1898.

Daoyuan 释道元 and Chuanmin 传敏, eds. 2004. *Guang'an zhanglao yongsu jinian ji* 廣安長老永思紀念集 [The Everlasting Grace of Master Guang'an Memorial Book]. Quanzhou: Quanzhou Kaiyuan Monastery and Nan'an Xuefeng Monastery.

Dean, Kenneth, and Zheng Zhenman 郑振满. 2003. *Fujian zongjiao beiming huibian: Quanzhou fu fence* 福建宗教碑铭汇编: 泉州府分册 [Epigraphical Materials on the History of Religion in Fujian: Quanzhou Region], 3 vols. Fuzhou: Fujian Renmin Publishing House.

Foshuo foming jing 佛说佛名经 [*Sutra of Buddha Names*]. CBETA T 440-14.

Huang Tao 黄滔. (*Jinshi* 895) 1967. *Puyang huang yushi ji* 莆陽黄御史集 [Collected Works of Censor Huang of Puyang]. Taipei: Yiwen yinshu guan 藝文印書館.

——. (897). 2003. *Quanzhou Kaiyuansi fodian beiji* 泉州開元寺佛殿碑記 [Stele Record of the Quanzhou Kaiyuan Monastery Buddha Hall]. In Dean and Zheng 2003, 1: 4–6.

Huang Zhongzhao 黄仲昭 (1435–1508). 2006. *Bamin tongzhi* 八闽通志 [Gazetteer of Fujian (*bamin*)]. Fujian difangzhi congkan 福建地方志丛刊. Fuzhou: Fujian People's Publishing House.

Huang Zigong Yi 黄子公议. 1729. *Kaiyuansi huangshi citang beiji* 开元寺黄氏祠堂碑记 [Stele Record of the Huang Surname Ancestral Hall within Kaiyuan Monastery]. Stone stele in situ at Quanzhou Kaiyuan's Tanyue ci.

Lin Hanzong 林汉宗. 2004. *Shenchu nijing yiyou chan* 身处逆境亦有禅 [In a Bad Situation Still Thinking of Chan]. In 广安长老永恩纪念集, edited by Daoyuan 释道元 and Chuanmin 传敏, 35. Quanzhou: Quanzhou Kaiyuan Monastery and Nan'an Xuefeng Monastery.

Nian Bensheng 粘本盛. 1666. *Chongjie ganlu jietan beiji* 重建甘露戒坛碑记 [Stele Record of the Reconstruction of the Amrita Ordination Platform]. In Dean and Zheng 2003, 1: 214-215, inscription #216.

Ruhuan 如幻. 1664. *Kaiyuansi Duqin'an yuanqi guiyue ji* 开元寺度亲庵缘起规约记 [Record of How Kaiyuan's Duqin Hermitage Was Founded and Its Rules]. In Dean and Zheng 2003, 1: 239–240, inscription #247.

Sima Guang 司馬光 (1019–1086). 1956. *Zizhi tongjian* 資治通鑑 [A Mirror for the Wise Ruler]. Beijing: Zhonghua Book Company.

Walshe, Maurice O'C. 2012. *The Long Discourses of the Buddha: A Translation of the Dīgha Nikāya*. Somerville, MA: Wisdom Publications.

Wang E. 王锷, Huang Wenzhao 黄文炤, and Wu Liangmo 吴良谟, eds. (1763) 1870–1927?. *Quanzhou fuzhi* 泉州府志 [Gazetteer of Quanzhou Prefecture].

Wudeng quanshu 五燈全書 [Five Lamps Complete Book]. CBETA X 81:1571.15.1-33.

Xingci. 1989. *Chongding erke hejie* [Revised Exegesis of the Two Lessons]. Taipei: Sheng Guo Press.

Yuanxian 元賢. 1643 (1927 edition). *Quanzhou Kaiyuansi zhi* 泉州開元寺志 [Quanzhou Kaiyuan Monastery Gazetteer].

Zhou Shurong 周書榮. 1999. "*Wenling Kaiyuansi zhi*" 温陵开元寺志 [Quanzhou Kaiyuan Monastery Gazetteer]. *Fujian Fojiao*, vols. 2–4. Fuzhou: Fujian Fojiao Xiehui 福建佛教协会 [Fujian Buddhist Association].

Zhou Xuezeng 周學, Hu Zhiwu 胡之鋘, et al. eds. (1830) 1990. [Daoguang] *Jinjiang xianzhi* [道光] 晉江縣志 [(Daoguang) Gazetteer of Jinjiang County]. Fuzhou: Fujian People's Publishing House 福建人民出版社.

——. 2008. *Xue feng zhi* 雪峰志 [Gazetteer of Xuefeng Temple]. Fuzhou: Fujian Xuefeng Monastery Publication.

Zhuanfa 转发. 2004. "*Guang'an zhanglao zhuanlue*" 广安长老传略 [Master Guang'an's Simple Biography]. In 广安长老永恩纪念集, edited by Daoyuan 释道元 and Chuanmin 传敏, 5. Quanzhou: Quanzhou Kaiyuan Monastery and Nan'an Xuefeng Monastery.

Index

Page numbers in **boldface** type refer to illustrations

About the Author

Brian J. Nichols is associate professor of religious studies at Mount Royal University, Calgary. His interests include Buddhism in contemporary China, material and spatial studies of religion, and the emerging fields of ecodharma and contemplative studies.